SOVIET POLITICS AND EDUCATION

Frank M. Sorrentino
Frances R. Curcio

UNIVERSITY
PRESS OF
AMERICA

LANHAM • NEW YORK • LONDON

Copyright © 1986 by

University Press of America,® Inc.

4720 Boston Way
Lanham, MD 20706

Library of Congress Cataloging in Publication Data

Sorrentino, Frank M., 1949-
  Soviet politics and education.
  Bibliography: p.
    1. Education—Soviet Union—Aims and objectives—
Addresses, essays, lectures.   2. Politics and education—
Soviet Union—Addresses, essays, lectures.   3. Education
and state—Soviet Union—Addresses, essays, lectures.
4. Soviet Union—Politics and government—20th century—
Addresses, essays, lectures.   5. Education—Soviet
Union—Curricula—Addresses, essays, lectures.
I. Curcio, Frances R.   II. Title.
LA832.S67   1985   370'.947   85-26600
ISBN 0-8191-5123-8 (alk. paper)
ISBN 0-8191-5124-6 (pbk. :   alk. paper)

Preface

The idea to compile a book of readings on Soviet politics and education occurred to us as we planned to conduct a teachers´ study-tour to the Soviet Union during the Spring 1985. Our goal was to provide the participants with literature which would prepare them for what they would experience. Many of the articles were selected and recommended for reading prior to the study-tour. After carefully reviewing and selecting the articles included, we realized that such an anthology would be a useful tool for students pursuing the study of Soviet politics and education.

We decided that a model for explaining the interrelationship of Soviet politics and education was needed. As a result, we undertook the task of attempting to explain the interrelationship of politics and education in general and then present the reader with specific articles on Soviet politics and education. We believe that the Soviet Union offers the analyst a unique laboratory to investigate the pervasive effects of politics on the educational system in light of the avowed goal of establishing a New Soviet Man. This New Soviet Man is patriotic, hardworking and selfless. No political system has ever attempted to metamorphosize man through its educational system.

We have assembled, in our judgment, some of the best literature on Soviet politics and education. The book includes articles by political theorists, government officials, journalists, political scientists and educators. We have taken great care that each article is presented in a most accurate manner.

We sincerely hope that this text provides the reader with insight, understanding, and appreciation of the Soviet culture. The work that was involved in preparing the manuscript proved to be quite valuable and rewarding for us.

We would like to acknowledge the support given to this project by St. Francis College which provided grant money for the preparation of the manuscript. We also wish to acknowledge James Lyons, Helen Hudson and the full staff of University Press of America for their assistance in the publication of this text. We as compilers, editors, and authors, however, take full responsibility for any errors that might appear in the manuscript.

Frank M. Sorrentino, Ph.D.
Frances R. Curcio, Ph.D.
September, 1985

SOVIET POLITICS AND EDUCATION
Table of Contents

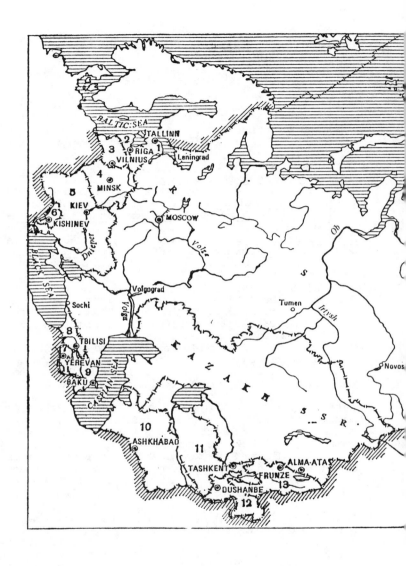

BALTIC SEA

TALLINN
2 RIGA 1
3 VILNIUS Leningrad
4
MINSK
5 KIEV
6 KISHINEV MOSCOW
Dnieper Volga
Ob
Volgograd
BLACK SEA Volga Tumen Irtysh
Sochi
8 TBILISI
7 KAZAKH
YEREVAN
9
BAKU S S R
CASPIAN SEA
Novos
10
ASHKHABAD
11
ALMA-ATA
TASHKENT FRUNZE
DUSHANBE 13
12

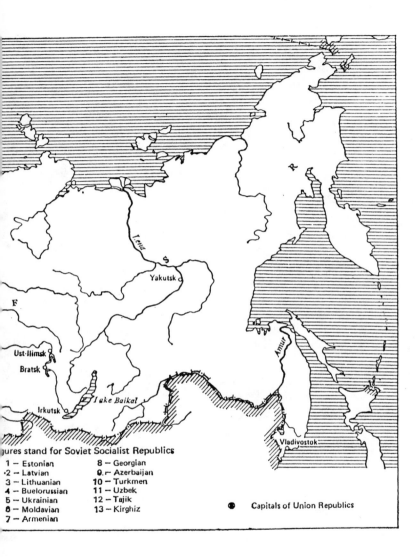

R

S

F

Lena

Yakutsk ○

Ust-Ilimsk ○
Bratsk ○

Lake Baikal

Irkutsk ○

Amur

Vladivostok

jures stand for Soviet Socialist Republics

1 — Estonian	8 — Georgian
·2 — Latvian	9. — Azerbaijan
3 — Lithuanian	10 — Turkmen
4 — Buelorussian	11 — Uzbek
5 — Ukrainian	12 — Tajik
6 — Moldavian	13 — Kirghiz
7 — Armenian	

●   Capitals of Union Republics

POLITICS AND EDUCATION

Frank M. Sorrentino and
Frances R. Curcio

General Overview

Politics and education are symbiotic variables in all
societies. Each is interwoven with the other and each is
influenced by the other. This complex, symbiotic relationship
is viewed as being interdependent. Usually the interaction
between these two variables results in cooperative efforts to
achieve the goals and needs of the society. However, sometimes
the interaction causes tension, as each institution, for one
reason or another, competes with the other. In this opening
essay, we wish to explore the relationship between these two
variables with particular reference to the Soviet Union.

Before drifting too far, it becomes imperative to define
what we mean by the concepts, politics and education. Both
have many different meanings ranging from broad, generic,
universal descriptions to specific, technical, rigorous
definitions.

Politics is one of the most misunderstood concepts. It is
alternately seen as the force of malevolence or petty nonsense
and favoritism which is all too common in our everyday
experiences. Politics, however, is much more. According to
political scientist David Easton, politics may be defined as
"the authoritative allocation of values." In other words,
politics is the struggle for the values which will be enforced
by the society through its government. Therefore, any
institution of the society that by its very nature involves the
basic values or attitudes of the society, will have a political
dimension. Thus, the media, the family, religious
institutions, the schools, etc., are involved in the political
process.

Some definitions of education include "learning,"
"changing behavior," and "the imparting or acquisition of
knowledge, skills, and attitudes." Education in its broadest
sense, is not limited to what happens in a formal system of
education. We are constantly in the process of being educated
by our parents, our friends, the churches, and the media.
However, we are more concerned here with the formal
institutions (e.g., the schools) and non-formal instructional
programs (e.g., Pioneer and Komsomol organizations in Soviet
society) established by society to perform systematically the
function of educating its youth.

1

The philosophy of education (i.e., the what, how, and why of teaching, and, the target population of instruction), is determined by the needs, values and goals of society. The schools, in turn, must determine the methods, techniques, materials, and content of instruction, which include the general and specific objectives of the curricula, literature to be read, the interpretation of history and philosophy, etc. This is how the philosophy of education is reflected in the schools. The decisions that schools make in these areas and in others, may have a direct or subtle influence on how young people perceive the world in which they live, their parents, the culture, the heroes to be idolized, the villans to be vilified, and the role of government and its relationship to other individuals. Education, thus, is inextricably involved in the value clarifications and value development aspects of society. It can therefore be seen that education and politics cannot be viewed as separate, independent entities.

It would be inaccurate to say that politics and education are equal in scope in fulfilling societal functions. Politics plays a more expansive role in that it deals with a whole host of other activities such as communications, health, natural resources, defense, transportation, etc. Politics itself is a part of a larger social system which deals with all the relationships among people in a society. Education, on the other hand, can be seen partially as a subsystem of politics. While the breadth of its activities are narrower it requires greater depth to accomplish its goals.

We would like to discuss more specifically the ways in which politics influences education, and how education in turn influences politics.

Political Influence on Education

Political influence on education is directly related to the philosophy of education as well as the concern over the attitudes and behaviors of those responsible for teaching children and supervising instruction. Political interest groups manage to exert influence over these aspects of formal education by controlling the "purse strings," entry and maintenance qualifications of school personnel and their compensation, and, the quality of the curriculum, that is, the content and methods of instruction. These three means of influence are discussed in this section.

Control of the "Purse Strings"
It is through the process of politics that the overall budget for school systems is developed. Money is one of the most indepensable ingredients to operate a formal system of education. The resources will determine how many students can

be educated and for how long. It will determine the size of classes and the amount of attention that can be given to individual students. The budget also determines whether schools be able to deal with children with learning difficulties or with the gifted child. The amount to be allotted to primary, secondary, and higher education is an important consideration, depending upon societal needs. Science education, which tends to be more expensive due to the cost of laboratories and equipment, is significantly affected by resources. In addition, whether to include subjects such as art, music, and physical education is dependent upon the money allotted to the education budget, reflecting the values of society. Also, how the money is distributed throughout the nation is a vital influence. Do certain geographical regions receive priority? Do certain urban areas get favored over rural areas? And finally, are certain ethnic or religious groups allocated more educational resources than others?

Control of Entry, Maintenance and Compensation of School Personnel

Secondly, the political system determines the qualifications, certification, and compensation of its teachers. Qualifications can range from educational prerequisites to moral character determinations. In addition, qualifications may be viewed from an ideological or partisan perspective. Does the political system accept recruits into the teaching profession from a broad range of political ideologies or does it insist on a rather specific adherence to orthodoxy? Does the political system hire only those who have demonstrated allegiance to a political party by being a member or at least approved by the party? What are the criteria for maintenance within the system and for promotion? Is innovation encouraged? Is student achievement measured solely by the results of standardized tests which may encourage rote memorization or emphasize only certain subjects? Is student behavior part of the criteria for maintenance and promotion? Does the percentage of students exhibiting anti-social or anti-state (ideological) attitudes and behavior affect the future well-being of the teacher in charge?

Compensation is also determined by the political system. Compensation must be understood in a broader context. It must include not only salaries, but also other material and non-material benefits. Among the material, it may include such fringe benefits as housing, opportunity for travel, leisure and special privileges. The non-material may include status, a sense of fulfillment and an appreciation by the society. While the political system cannot fully control the non-material benefits, it has a great influence. High compensation, including recognition and status could encourage the most talented members of society to enter the profession otherwise

3

some of the least talented might be recruited.

Control of the Curriculum
Thirdly, the political system strongly influences the curriculum. What courses are to be taught, what topics are to be included and which are to be excluded. In addition, what pedagogical techniques should be employed and which are to be avoided at all costs. Courses in the humanities or the social sciences can be taught in ways that challenge the values of the society or parrot them. Is critical thinking encouraged in these areas, or is rote memorization demanded? Do the teachers encourage individualization or a collective approach? For example, do students receive status by showing their unique views and positions or by cooperating and blending in with the others? With respect to the textbooks, are they prepared in a manner that presents various subjects according to viewpoints of the authors or do the texts have to be approved for philosophical and ideological correctness?

Politics has an enormous influence over the way formal education is conducted in any society. The amount of discretion offered the educational institutions varies extensively from society to society, depending upon what are the needs, values and goals of the political system at any given time.

This section focused on the influence that politics has on education. We would now like to turn to the forces of influence that education has on politics.

Educational Influence on Politics

Schools are bureaucratic institutions and while they nominally must adhere to the desires of the "political superiors," they have two very powerful political weapons, namely the power of expertise and the power of implementation. The educational bureaucracy will use its political weapons and its status to influence the politics of the society in four separate ways, namely: legitimation of the regime, socialization, admission and promotion of students, and in economic development.

The Power of Expertise and Implementation
Educators, because of their special training and years of experience are in a unique position to advise their political superiors on what is desirable and what is do-able. Also, they are relied upon to interpret the results of the effectiveness of the system. Furthermore, the teachers implement the policies. There is always a great deal of discretion given to any bureaucracy to use its judgment and to fill in the details of policy. Therefore, teachers as our bureaucrats are not

4

totally helpless even in an authoritarian state. In addition,
teachers, because of their education and resulting status,
become a significant interest group in which any state will
attempt to satisfy its demands to at least a certain extent.

Legitimation of the Regime. Educational institutions
perform the vital function of legitimation of the regime and
its leaders. Children are taught to accept the state as being
the lawful governors of the society and that the state is in
accordance with the established rules, principles and standards
of society. In addition, they are taught that the current
leaders rule authoritatively. They are duly constituted office
holders whose power is derived from the laws of the state.
Children who have these values and beliefs inculcated in them
learn virtually to accept both the state and its leaders as
given truths. This function is almost indispensable to any
government to function effectively because its citizens accept
them as a result of their own values and this provides a
reservoir of support even when the government does not act in
individual citizens´ interest.

Socialization. Secondly, the educational institutions
engage in the process of socialization. This is the process by
which the young and newly-arrived are inculcated with the
ideology, culture, mores, and folkways of the society that are
endorsed by the state. Legitimation of the state is part of
the socialization process, however, the process is much broader
and in some societies like the Soviet Union, it includes other
values such as collectivization, atheism, work ethic, etc.
Socialization, therefore, establishes the value preferences of
the state and its leaders as being far superior to any of the
alternatives. While education is only one of several
institutions engaged in socialization (the others include the
family, the churches, and the media), it can significantly
assist the state in accomplishing its goals. It must be noted
that socialization is never completed; it is a lifelong
process.

Socialization through education is accomplished by
pedagogical techniques employed, and the curriculum and its
selective use of facts and information. The young are
particularly susceptible to this type of training. Educational
institutions perform a critical role at a critical time in
child development. The successful achievement of this task is
essential for the maintenance of the state. Therefore,
educational institutions have an important leverage instrument
in their dealings with the state.

Admission and Promotion of Students. In advanced
technological societies, education plays an important role as
gatekeeper for social and economic mobility. Education

establishes the foundations upon which individuals can later claim a right to important positions. The admission and promotion policies for universities down to nursery school provide educational institutions with opportunities for rewarding their supporters and punishing their enemies. If the schools provide opportunities for the children of the political and economic elite, they in turn receive certain benefits. In addition, educational institutions may afford the political elite an opportunity to provide a system of gratifications and deprivations for following, or not following the current set of policies. In other words, the desire for upward mobility on the part of the population may be used as a trade-off for them accepting, or at least tolerating the government. The educational institutions thus, have a significant tool to offer the state in its quest for "power" and "freedom." It can further be deduced that these admission and promotion policies can be developed in such a manner as to promote some ethnic groups over others, some religious groups over others, and some geographic regions over others.

Economic Development. Lastly, educational institutions significantly affect the economic development of the society. Since the lack of economic development provides fewer opportunties and fewer material goods, political elites are very apprehensive of the potential degree of malcontentment which may lead to a lack of support for the regime. In addition, economic development supplies the government with the opportunity to provide for the defense against its enemies both foreign and domestic. Educational institutions, with their power of expertise and implementation, have a critical role to play in a society's economic development and are totally aware of its political implications.

Soviet Politics and Education

We have attempted to establish the important symbiotic relationship between politics and education. We see this relationship as one of the significant underpinnings of any society. We believe that to understand fully the politics or the educational system of any society, these two variables must be discussed at least partially in conjunction with each other.

In this book we propose to study the relationship between politics and education in the Soviet Union. The Soviet Union, as one of the two superpowers in the world, along with the United States, has a significant impact that affects everyone on this planet. They have launched a campaign to develop a "New Soviet Man" who will be selfless, hard working, and cooperative. But, never in the history of civilization has the will, the resources and the technical means been brought together to accomplish such radical goals. In addition, they

6

have as their mission to bring this New Soviet Man to all people on the globe. While Soviets do not seem in a rush to accomplish this mission, it is of tremendous importance that these are its goals.

Communist ideology (Marxism-Leninism), with its belief that its adherents have a superior understanding of history which allows them to impose their will on others, presents the greatest opportunity to investigate the interrelationship of politics and education. It is also significant that the Soviets have announced a new series of reforms which will have a profound impact on how these two institutions perform.

We believe that Soviet Politics and Education is a most significant topic at this epoch in history. As a result, we have undertaken the task of compiling this book of readings as a means to enhance not only the understanding of the relationship between Soviet politics and education but also the appreciation of Soviet culture. We have divided the book into four sections, namely, Soviet Ideology, Soviet Politics and Culture, Soviet Educational Philosophy and Current Practice, and, Curricular Emphases in Soviet Schools.

In the "Soviet Ideology" section, we examine the major writings of Communist ideology in the Soviet Union. These include the works of Karl Marx and Frederick Engels, V. I. Lenin, Joseph Stalin, and Nikita Khrushchev. The ideological foundations of Soviet society provides one with the prism upon which history and the events of the day are understood. Furthermore, it provides the values, beliefs, and attitudes that the political leaders hope to promote and upon whom they justify their legitimate use of power. While Communist ideology is not always clear and has many ambiguities and contradictions, it provides us with the clearist blueprint of Soviet intentions. An understanding of Soviet ideology would not tell us all we need to know but the absence of understanding Soviet ideology would lead us hopelessly in the dark. It is a necessary but not sufficient body of knowledge to understand Soviet politics and education.

In the second section entitled, "Soviet Politics and Culture," there is an explication of the Soviet political system which includes an explanation of the Soviet government machinery and the Party organization and role. This allows one to understand the governmental and political restraints in which Soviet politics operates. In addition, there is an analysis of Soviet political culture which serves as an environment in which Soviet ideology, government, and politics operate. Finally, there is a critical analysis of the role of education within the context of Soviet politics and culture. We believe that one must understand these confining conditions upon which politics and education operate in order to understand even partially the Soviet Union.

Articles about Soviet educational philosophy with respect to goals, curricula, and current practices, and the new school reforms are included in the third section entitled, "Soviet Educational Philosophy and Current Practice." The "why" and "whom" of education (i.e., the purposes and the target audience, respectively) are discussed.

The educational philosophy reflects the values, needs and goals of the Soviet society. The emphasis is placed on the creation of a "New Soviet Man" with a Communist world view, and the need for competent, skilled workers. Intense moral and political education are recurring themes that are expected to shape and mold the behavior and attitudes of Soviet youth in their attempts to reach the stated goals. To accomplish this, children are treated as very special members of the society and given the Soviet "best" in their upbringing.

Since philosophy cannot be totally separated from practice, the inherent problems of implementation create distortions on this idealic view. As a result, we can observe some deficiencies within the system. In particular, all children are exposed to the exact same curricula, and rote memorization is the acceptable method for teaching and learning. How a standardized, national curriculum can reach all children is questioned. Recognizing the inadequacies of the system, the new reforms were initiated to bring the schools into closer compliance with the ideological, sociological, economical, and political processes. The articles in this section were selected because they highlight the relationship among Soviet ideology, educational philosophy, and current practice.

The last section is entitled, "Curricular Emphases in Soviet Schools." The articles in this section emphasize the "what" and the "how" of accomplishing the goals of the Soviet educational system (i.e., the content of the curriculum, the subjects that are stressed, and the methods of teaching).

Beginning in the fourth grade, the greatest proportion of time is spent on the study of science, mathematics, and physical education. Science and mathematics are emphasized to prepare more sophisticated, competent workers. The methods of teaching these subjects stress rote memorization, although there is some movement towards developing creativity and independence.

Physical education is emphasized for moral development,

that is, fostering the values of a Communist world view. The
execution of physical skills is dependent upon a
"learning-by-doing" approach. Children are actively involved.
The values of comraderie, discipline, and a collective attitude
are inculcated.

Vocational education is implicit as well as explicit
throughout the formal system of education. In the earliest
grades, the objectives are related to the formation of proper
attitudes toward work and workers; regardless of the task, all
work is respected. As one progresses through the grades, the
focus is more on knowledge and skill development related to
specific tasks. The appreciation and understanding of the
Communist work ethic reflects Marxist principles.

The content of the curriculum, the subjects that are
stressed, and the methods of teaching are all influenced by the
dictates of the Party. How successful the educational system
is, is determined by the degree to which the needs, values, and
goals of society are met. It seems as though the system,
although it has brought literacy and educational opportunity to
millions of people in the past sixty years, is presently
inadequate in meeting the demands of the new, highly
technological society. It will be interesting to observe how
the Soviets meet the challenge of this problem in the next few
years.

Final Remarks

The exploration of the relationship between Politics and
Education in the Soviet Union remains in an embryonic stage.
We, however, believe that these readings contribute at least a
partial foundation which will serve as a vehicle to further
explore the vast universe of Soviet society.

SOVIET IDEOLOGY

Introduction

The ideological foundations of a society reveal important
dimensions of its past and of its future. Communism as an
ideology is often seen as a continuation of the Russian Empire
under the czars. Communism provides the prophetic messianic
message, the end of exploitation and the total equality, much
like the Russian Empire's goal of spreading the Orthodox
religion and bringing civilization to other national groups.
Communism provides for the dictatorship of the proletariat
through one party rule as the means of achieving its ends while
the czars required dictatorship on the basis of religion and
survival. It can be said that the Russian people have only
known an authoritarian state with expansionist or imperialistic
designs. Therefore, Communist Russia simply replaces Czarist
Russia. While this logic has great appeal, the reality is far
more complex. The very essence of the messages are very
different and the nature of the state under these regimes is
substantially different. In addition, the evolutionary
development of Communism in the Soviet Union has its own
history with major implications. Finally, the ever-changing
social, economic, political, and technical environment of world
civilization in general and Russian civilization in particular,
have affected how Communist ideology defined itself over time.
It, therefore, becomes imperative to investigate the
ideological underpinnings of Soviet society. This is best done
by analyzing the leading theoreticians and their major works.

Karl Marx (1818-1883)

The most influential writer in the development of modern
communism is Karl Marx who was born in the Rhineland. He
attended the University of Berlin for several years where he
studied history and philosophy. He became emersed in political
activities and in 1842 joined the staff of the Rheinsche
Zeitung, a radical newspaper, in Cologne. When the Prussian
Government suppressed the paper, Marx fled to Paris where he
met Friedrick Engels (1820-1895), a fellow Rhinelander who was
to become his friend, financial supporter and close
collaborator. Engels was the son of a German industrialist
with business interests in Germany and England.

In 1845, when King Louis Philippe feared that Marx's
criticism of bourgeois society might incite a rebellion against
his business-backed regimes, Marx left for Brussels after being

expelled. In Brussels, Marx with Engels wrote The Communist Manifesto (1848), his most influential work and among the most influential writings in history. Marx continued his political activities by participating in the 1848 revolutions in France and Germany. He was expelled from Germany in 1849 and forbidden to return to his homeland. He went to London where he stayed until his death in 1883. While in London, he researched his most profound work on the analysis of capitalism entitled, Das Kapital. The first volume was published in 1867, the second and third volumes were published posthumously and were edited by Engels.

Concepts of Marxist Theory

To understand the Marxist interpretation of history, it is important to analyze the major conceptual components of his philosophy. The major components, historical materialism, the dialectic, and surplus value, are discussed.

Historical Materialism. Marx believed that the physical realm was the only true reality. The world of ideas are mere reflections of where an individual stands in the physical world. And in this reality, the economic forces are the structures of society; that is, the main driving force while, laws, religion, and government are the superstructures of society that are dependent on which economic system is being practiced in this epoch of history. All previous and current economic systems are an exploitation of a lower class by an upper class.

The Dialectic. This is a form of logic first introduced by Aristotle and later developed by Hegel. Hegel believed that history was a series of conflicts in which the old idea (thesis), is disrupted by the emergence of a new idea (antithesis) which ultimately resolves itself into a new idea (synthesis). Hegel believed that history was the progressive unfolding of reason.

Marx is said to have stood Hegel on its head by replacing ideas with materialisms, more specifically with economic systems. Thus for Marx, history begins with Primitive Communism (thesis) which is disrupted by the emergence of Feudalism (antithesis). This conflict resolves itself in the development of Capitalism (synthesis). Capitalism then becomes the new thesis which is disrupted by the emergence of socialism (antithesis) which resolves itself into Communisim (the final synthesis). Unlike Hegel, the dialectic stops for Marx. Communism is a classless society; therefore, no exploitation exists and thus no state is needed.

Surplus Value. The concept of surplus value was originally developed by John Locke in a different context. According to Marx, the worker creates the total value of a particular item but receives in wages only a fraction of the price for which an item is sold. This difference between the individual worker's wages and the sale price is defined by Marx as surplus value. It is, according to Marx, something that is created by labor but is appropriated arbitrarily by employers. Marx did not see a role played by management or in supply and demand in determining the worth of an item.

The Communist Manifesto (1848)

The Manifesto begins with "The history of all hitherto existing society is the history of class struggles." Marx and Engels explain how change through revolution occurs. The methods of production over time become less effective in terms of producing wealth; thus, industry will replace agriculture yet the owners of land (the feudal lords) refuse to yield power to the new urban capitalist whom they have helped to create. In turn, the capitalist once in power refuses to yield that power to the collectivist system of production.

The owners of the means of production sincerely believe that their system is the most productive and equitable and therefore needs to be defended at all costs. In each case, the owners of the means of production will utilize all the tools at their disposal including government, law, religion, and ideology that stymie those forces who advocate the next progressive economic system.

Capitalism will destroy itself as did feudalism before it. This will not occur by some subversive conspiracy but by the social laws of history. The bourgeoise class exists for the accumulation of capital. The condition for capital is wage-labor which rests exclusively on competition between laborers. As technology advances, encourged by the bourgeoise in their thirst for capital, the isolation of laborers is replaced by the assembly of laborers. This assembly of laborers encourages them to understand their economic interest as a class vis-a-vis the bourgeois class. This combined with the gradual elimination of the petty bourgeoise whose small businesses are taken over by the bourgeoise throwing them into a wage-labor or proletariat class. Thus the bourgeoise have created their own gravediggers (the proletariat) who now represent, according to Marx, more than 90% of the population and are in a revolutionary consciousness with regard to their interests. However, since no leading class has ever voluntarily abdicated its power, Marx urges that Communists "openly declare that their ends can be only the forcible overthrow of all existing social conditions."

13

The workers' (Communist) party is the vanguard of the proletariat capable of leading the whole people to socialism. The dictatorship of the proletariat is necessary for the entire historic period separating Capitalism from Communism. This dictatorship is fundamentally different in that it is a majority dictating a minority (the bourgeoise) and it is non-exploiting since property is owned collectively. The state will ultimately wither away once all enemies are eliminated and a new consciousness arises. However, in the period of Socialism, even though some inequities will continue to exist, one must build Communism.

Marx was a towering figure of his time. As a prophet, he claimed for his writings a universal truth and validity to which many would not or could not concede. In effect, Marx's philosophy became a substitute for religion as opposed to a series of works by an individual scholar attempting to graple with the truth. In addition, his concept of historical materialism over-exaggerates the importance of economic factors in the minds of many, including Engels. The implication that man is so maleable to these forces reduces the significance of man as an entity deserving the things due to him, according to Marx.

Furthermore, the Hegelian Dialectic has not been established as a truth, that there is an inevitable progress from one level to the next, and that it would stop after a few stages is a direct contradiction of Hegel himself.

Marx underestimated the ability of the bourgeois state to reform itself and for labor unions to make and achieve significant gains. He did not foresee workers developing middle class attitudes or for that matter work becoming more varied and less uniform.

Finally, Marx did not foresee the effects of power on people in authority regardless of economic class. It has been observed that political leaders in Communist nations have been as exploitative as any leaders as Milovan Djilas (the Yugoslavian Vice President) observed in 1957 in his book entitled, The New Class.

Nikolai Lenin (Vladimir Ilich Ulganov)(1870-1924)

Lenin, as he later called himself, was the principal founder of the Soviet Union--the man who brought Marxism to the Soviet Union. Lenin was born and received his early education in Simbursk (now Ulganovsk) on the banks of the Volga. He studied law at Kazan University and was admitted to the bar in 1891, though he never practiced law. Lenin came from a middle class family; both his parents were teachers with socialist views. Their five surviving children became revolutionaries with Lenin's eldest brother, Alexander, being hung at the age of nineteen for complicity in an abortive plot against Czar Alexander III.

After law school, he moved to Petrograd (now Leningrad) and became a professional revolutionary which led to his exile in Siberia from 1895 to 1900. In exile, he guided a revolutionary organization and found time to author many works, including The Development of Capitalism in Russia. In 1898, he married Nadezhda Krupskaya, a fellow revolutionary in Siberian exile. While in exile, he changed his name to "Lenin," derived from the river Lena, which flowed through the region of his exile in Siberia.

Upon his release, he spent the next seventeen years in Europe, organizing and directing the revolutionary movement in Russia. After the Czarist regime toppled in 1917, he returned again to form a government but failed because he was suspected of having German ties and he fled to Finland where he wrote his most influential work, State and Revolution. He returned later in the year to lead the Bolshevik Revolution. After the successful revolution he became the head of the Soviet Government.

State and Revolution
    In the Communist literature, State and Revolution is of enormous importance. Where Marx and Engels neglected the factors of political power, Lenin was the master strategist being the leader of one of the "great" revolutions. This pamphlet quotes Marx and Engels extensively while it outlines the role of the party in the dictatorship of the proletariat and the political transition from the bourgeois state to Communist society.

The bourgeois state is the product of the irreconcilability of class antagonism. This state is an organ of the bourgeoise to exploit the proletariat, therefore there can be no reconciliation.

Lenin clarifies what Engels meant by the withering away of the state by suggesting that it is the withering away of the bourgeois state and not the proletariat state. This new state is necessary to carry out the will of the dictatorship of the proletariat to crush exploiters, to guide the masses - the petty bourgeoise, the semi-proletarians and the peasantry - in organizing a socialist economy. The workers' (Communist) party is the vanguard of the proletariat capable of leading the whole people to socialism.

The dictatorship of the proletariat is necessary to defeat

15

all of the old vestiges of capitalism, particularly the army and the bureaucracy. While the proletariat state will also disappear there will be a lengthy process in between which will be called socialism. The dictatorship of the proletariat under socialism produces democracy for the vast majority of people but suppression by force of the Capitalists. The people can surpress the exploiters by simple organization of armed masses.

While unjust differences in wealth will still exist under Socialism the exploitation of man by man will be impossible because the injustice of the private ownership of the means of production will be destroyed. Socialism, however, is not truly capable of immediately destroying the injustice of distribution according to work rather than need.

The withering away of the proletariat state to Communism will come when the people have learned to observe the rules of social life and their labor will be so productive that they will work voluntarily according to their ability. Until this is achieved, the society and state must strictly control the quantity and consumption of labor.

To evaluate Lenin, it is important to separate his deeds from his thoughts. As a revolutionary strategist, he was unsurpassed. His writings served the purpose of organizing and inspiring those in the revolution. However, as a philosopher, Lenin shared many of the problems of Marx. He denied that the vision of a society without a machinery of force and power (the state) was utopian. He presented the proposition that the army and the bureaucracy are the sole products of the bourgeois state. The Soviet Union is an example that these are functions of a highly complex industrial society. Lenin could not see the brutal exploitation that can take place in a Socialist society. Finally, he saw the perfection of man to a new order by the changing environment. There is no evidence that such a significant transformation can take place which will eliminate conflict.

Lenin's writings differ from Marx on the primacy of politics over economics as opposed to the reverse. In addition, Lenin pointed out the peculiar attractiveness of Communism to developing countries in general and Russia in particular.

Joseph Stalin (Iosif Vissarionovich Dzhugashoili)(1878-1953)

Joseph Stalin was the Secretary General of the Communist Party and Premier of the Soviet Union for almost thirty years. Stalin was born in Gori, Georgia, where he attended parochial schools, and at the age of fifteen, moved to Tiflis (Tbilisi)

16

to enter the seminary. He was expelled from the seminary in
1898 when he joined the Russian Socialist Party. He became a
professional revolutionary which led to his spending almost
sixteen years in and out of exile in Siberia. In 1903, he
became a member of the Boleshevik wing of the Party. He was
promoted to the Central Committee of the Party and in 1917, he
helped Lenin in the revolution and the formation of the party.
He was appointed by Lenin to Secretary General of the Party in
1922 which enabled him to succeed his arch rival, Leon Trotsky,
upon the death of Lenin in 1924. He later banished Trotsky and
eliminated many others who disagreed with him in a series of
purges. The most famous of these purges was the Moscow Trials
of 1936 and 1938 in which many top leaders in the Party,
Government, and Military were executed. Stalin developed the
concept of Communism under constant seige which justified the
elimination of anyone who disagreed with him on the basis of
being an enemy of the revolution and the party. During the
1930s, Stalin consciously raised himself to a god-like figure
in which public adulation and adherence were mandatory. During
World War II he became generalissimo of the army which further
enhanced concepts of adulation and discipline. He was credited
with the development of the machinery of the Soviet State and
Party. His writings, particularly the Foundations of Leninism
in 1924, served as a future justification of his methods of
implementation by his establishing that he was the ultimate
interpreter of the writings of Lenin.

Stalin was also well-known for the formation of the
Five-Year Plans, the first of which began in 1928 and called
for heavy industrialization and farm collectivization. Stalin
maintained his power and popularity among the Soviet people
until his death in 1953. However, his successors, most notably
Nikita Khruschev, led a movement against the "Cult of
Personality" of Stalin and his violent internal policies. This
led to the removal of his tomb next to Lenin´s from the
Mausoleum in Red Square.

Foundations of Leninism (1924)
     This was the major work of Stalin which began as a series
of lectures to justify the autocratic power of the party which
he controlled. Stalin used quotations from Lenin to justify
his positions.

     Stalin begins by defining "What is Leninism?" He states
that Leninism is Marxism for the era of imperialism and the
proletarian revolution, and thus, has a militant and
revolutionary character. He states that theory becomes aimless
if not connected with revolutionary practice, just as practice
gropes in the dark if not illuminated by revolutionary theory.
The "theory" of worshipping spontaneity in the labor movement
belittles the conscious elements and the leadership of the

Party in the movement, which is the basis of all opportunism. Spontaneity is neither desirable nor effective for it reduces the role of the Party. The Party is rightly regarded as the "rallying center of the finest elements in the working class." The Party is a Socialist seminary for training the leaders of the working class in Communist theory.

The revolutionary period requires a militant revolutionary party. The revolution is constantly under attack by the forces of the bourgeoise. The party is the vanguard of the working class. The party is the organized detachment of the working class and thus is the highest form of class organization of the proletariat. The Party is the sole instrument for achieving the dictatorship of the proletariat and for consolidating and expanding the dictatorship where it has been achieved. Stalin then deduces that achieving and maintaining the dictatorship of the proletariat is impossible without a Party of iron discipline. Iron discipline is incompatible with the existence of factions in the Party. Thus, it necessitates unity of will and action of all Party members, once a decision has been reached. Stalin finally concludes that the Party must purge itself of opportunist elements.

The contributions of Stalin to Communist theory were more practical or tactical than theoretical. He took Lenin´s concept of Party as the dictatorship of the proletariat to an extreme. His almost thirty-year reign has had a profound impact on the development of the Party and the State in the Soviet Union and throughout the Communist world. His practice, however, gives ample evidence that political power can be as abusive and exploitative as economic power.

Nikita Sergeyrvich Khrushchev (1894-1971)

First Secretary of the Communist Party and Premier of the Soviet Union, Khrushchev was born in Kalinovka in the Ukraine. He was a shepherd and a factory worker. He joined the Party after the Revolution. He was educated in Party-run schools. He became a director of the Party in Stlino and Kiev. He moved up quickly in the Party ranks becoming a member of the Central Committee in 1934. He became First Secretary of the Ukraine Party in 1938 and during the War, served as a lieutenant general. After the War, he became Premier of the Ukraine Government which led to the position of Soviet Minister of Agriculture, in 1950. As Minister, he was responsible for merging many small farms into collectives.

Khrushchev, in 1952, was also responsible for developing new Party statutes for the disciplining of Party members. Upon Stalin´s death in 1953, he became the First Secretary of the Communist Party. In 1958, he replaced Nikolai Bukharin as

Premier, and became the first person to hold the highest
positions in the Government and the Party.

He was replaced in 1964 by the Politburo Committee when
Leonid Brezhnev became First Secretary and Aleksei Kosygin
became Premier. He died in obscurity in 1971.

Khrushchev's major contribution was the liberalization of
the Soviet State. Under Stalin, the Communist State was
constantly under siege in the early stages. Thus, there was
support for his extreme methods. In addition, the goals of the
State were clear - heavy industrialization, collectivization,
and the defeat of Nazi Germany.

These early prime goals could have been accomplished with
edicts and the results could have been easily monitored.
However, as the issues became more complex and the society more
technological, it became imperative to utilize the knowledge
and talents of the intelligentsia and the Party members. These
groups would be reluctant to speak out under Stalin because of
fear of being labelled "an enemy of the people." Khrushchev
called for an end of the "cult of personality" and the "reign
of terror." He proposed economic incentives, varied industrial
organization, a more liberal program of free higher education
with study grants and allowances for students. He stated that
the war between Capitalism and Socialism was not inevitable and
that Socialism will become more and more varied.

Khrushchev's ideas were best represented by his Secret
Speech before the Twentieth Congress of the Communist Party of
the Soviet Union on February 25, 1956. The speech was never
published in the Soviet Union.

<u>Secret Speech on Stalin and the Cult of Personality</u> (1956)
Khrushchev begins by stating that it is against
Marxism-Leninism to transform one person into a Superman who is
infallible. Khrushchev cites Stalin's violations of Leninist
principles. Lenin was opposed to weakening the role of the
Party in the Soviet State. Lenin believed in collegiality of
leadership which was illustrated by the Party Central Committee
as an expression of collective leadership during his tenure.
Lenin never imposed by force his views upon his co-workers and
used extreme methods only against actual class enemies, and not
loyal Party members.

Khrushchev points out that Stalin directed a campaign for
his own adulation and infallibility. He reveals that Stalin
did not tolerate any differences of opinion and practiced
brutal violence towards anyone who opposed him. He further
states that in the period of 1935 to 1938, when Socialism was
already secure, Stalin developed the practice of mass

oppression through the government. Stalin abandoned the act
of persuasion. In the Secret Speech Khrushchev states that

> Stalin acted not through persuasion, explanation and
> patient cooperation with people, but by imposing his
> concepts and demanding absolute submission to this
> opinion. Whoever opposed this concept or tried to
> prove his viewpoint and correctness of his position,
> was doomed for removal from the leading collective and
> to subsequent moral and physical annihilation.

Khrushchev deduces that these tactics jeopardized
Socialism and the Soviet Union. In particular, it led to
Stalin ignoring the unmistakable signs of an imminent German
invasion in 1941, and for the subsequent military failures of
the Red Army. Khrushchev further states that Stalin's
arrogance against leaders such as Tito, jeopardized Socialist
unity. Finally, that the mass deportations during World War II
were monstrous acts which rudely violated Leninism. Khrushchev
concludes that the cult of the individual must be abolished
once and for all.

Khrushchev's contributions were unmistakable, he was
bringing Soviet tactics in line with the new realities of his
age. It should be clear that Khrushchev was not criticizing
Stalin's goals only his methods as being counterproductive.

Even though Khrushchev was toppled from power in October
1964, the Soviet State never returned to the Stalin-like State.
Brezhnev, his replacement, was more conservative in
experimenting with economic reforms and relied more on Party
supporters who were far less innovative.

Yuri Andropov who succeeded Brezhnev after his death in
1983, was more willing to experiment but was physically weak
through most of his tenure and died in 1984.

Konstantin U. Chernenko's brief tenure followed. His
principal qualification was his loyalty to Brezhnev. He was
perceived as that generation's last chance to maintain
themselves in power. His policies were imperceptibly different
from Brezhnev's.

Mikhail S. Gorbachev is the fourth Soviet leader in four
years. He was born after the Revolution and was not old enough
to serve in the Great Patriotic War (i.e., World War II). He
is the first of his generation to become the top leader in the
Soviet Union.

Gorbachev was the protégé of Yuri Andropov and is expected
to follow his policies of economic incentives and some

decentralization. He is young, healthy and telegenic. He has the opportunity and the challenge of making Soviet ideology relevant to the challenges of an ever-increasingly complex and changing system.

The ideology foundations of the Soviet Union, particularly those of Marx and Lenin, have given the set of priorities that are followed by the Soviet educational system. The degree of freedom and the imperatives of social, economic, and technological factors will further influence the public policies of Soviet education.

MANIFESTO OF THE COMMUNIST PARTY(1)

Karl Marx and Frederick Engels

A spectre is haunting Europe - the spectre of Communism.
All the Powers of old Europe have entered into a holy alliance
to exorcise this spectre: Pope and Czar, Metternich and
Guizot, French Radicals and German police-spies.

Where is the party in opposition that has not been decried
as Communistic by its opponents in power? Where the Opposition
that has not hurled back the branding reproach of Communism,
against the more advanced opposition parties, as well as
against its reactionary adversaries?

Two things result from this fact.
I. Communism is already acknowledged by all European Powers
to be itself a Power.
II. It is high time that Communists should openly, in the
face of the whole world, publish their views, their aims, their
tendencies, and meet this nursery tale of Spectre of Communism
with a Manifesto of the party itself.

To this end, Communists of various nationalities have
assembled in London, and sketched the following Manifesto, to
be published in the English, French, German, Italian, Flemish
and Danish languages.

I. Bourgeois and Proletarians(2)

The history of all hitherto existing society(3) is the
history of class struggles.

Freeman and slave, patrician and plebian, lord and serf,
guildmaster(4) and journeyman, in a word, oppressor and
oppressed, stood in constant opposition to one another, carried
on an uninteresting, now hidden, now open fight, a fight that
each time ended, either in a revolutionary re-construction of
society at large, or in the common ruin of the contending
classes.

In the earlier epochs of history, we find almost
everywhere a complicated arrangement of society into various
orders, a manifold gradation of social rank. In ancient Rome

From: Marx and Engels - Selected Works in One Volume. 1977
Progress Publishers, Moscow.

we have patricians, knights, plebians, slaves; in the Middle
Ages, feudal lords, vassals, guildmasters, journeymen,
apprentices, serfs; in almost all of these classes, again,
subordinate gradations.

The modern bourgeois society that has sprouted from the
ruins of feudal society has not done away with class
antagonisms. It has but established new classes, new
conditions of oppression, new forms of struggle in place of the
old ones.

Our epoch, the epoch of the bourgeoisie, possesses,
however, this distinctive feature: it has simplified the class
antagonisms. Society as a whole is more and more splitting up
into two great hostile camps, into two great classes directly
facing each other: Bourgeoisie and Proletariat.

From the serfs of the Middle Ages sprang the chartered
burghers of the earliest towns. From these burgesses the first
elements of the bourgeoisie were developed.

The discovery of America, rounding the Cape, opened up
fresh ground for the rising bourgeoisie. The East-Indian and
Chinese markets, the colonisation of America, trade with the
colonies, the increase in the means of exchange and in
commodities generally, gave to commerce, to navigation, to
industry, an impulse, never before known, and thereby, to the
revolutionary element in the tottering feudal society, a rapid
development.

The feudal system of industry, under which industrial
production was monopolised by closed guilds, now no longer
sufficed for the growing wants of the new markets. The
manufacturing system took its place. The guildmasters were
pushed on one side by the manufacturing middle class; division
of labour between the different corporate guilds vanished in
the face of division of labour in each single workshop.

Meantime the markets kept ever growing, the demand ever
rising. Even manufacture no longer sufficed. Thereupon, steam
and machinery revolutionised industrial production. The place
of manufacture was taken by the giant, Modern Industry, the
place of the industrial middle class, by industrial
millionaires, the leaders of whole industrial armies, the
modern bourgeois.

Modern industry has established the world-market, for
which the discovery of America paved the way. This market has
given an immense development to commerce, to navigation, to
communication by land. This development has, in its turn,

24

reacted on the extension of industry; and in proportion as industry, commerce, navigation, railways extended, in the same proportion the bourgeoisie developed, increased its capital, and pushed into the background every class handed down from the Middle Ages.

We see, therefore, how the modern bourgeoisie is itself the product of a long course of development, of a series of revolutions in the mode of production and of exchange.

Each step in the development of the bourgeoisie was accompanied by a corresponding political advance of that class. An oppressed class under the sway of the feudal nobility, an armed and self-governing association in the mediaeval commune;(5) here independent urban republic (as in Italy and Germany), there taxable "third estate" of the monarchy (as in France), afterwards, in the period of manufacture proper, serving either the semi-feudal or the absolute monarchy as a counterpoise against the nobility, and, in fact, corner-stone of the great monarchies in general, the bourgeoisie has at last, since the establishment of Modern Industry and of the world-market, conquered for itself, in the modern representative State, exclusive political sway. The executive of the modern State is but a committee for managing the common affairs of the whole bourgeoisie.

The bourgeoisie, historically, has played a most revolutionary part.

The bourgeoisie, wherever it has got the upper hand, has put an end to all feudal, patriarchal, idyllic relations. It has pitilessly torn asunder the motley feudal ties that bound man to his "natural superiors," and has left remaining no other nexus between man and man than naked self-interest, than callous "cash payment." It has drowned the most heavenly ecstacies of religious fervor, of chivalrous enthusiasm, of philistine sentimentalism, in the icy water of egotistical calculation. It has resolved personal worth into exchange value, and in place of the numberless indefeasible chartered freedoms, has set up that single, unconscionable freedom - Free Trade. In one word, for exploitation, veiled by religious and political illusions, it has substituted naked, shameless, direct, brutal exploitation.

The bourgeoisie has stripped of its halo every occupation hitherto honoured and looked up to with reverent awe. It has converted the physician, the lawyer, the priest the poet, the man of science, into its paid wage-labourers.

The bourgeoisie has torn away from the family its sentimental veil, and has reduced the family relation to a mere money relation.

The bourgeoisie has disclosed how it came to pass that the brutal display of vigour in the Middle Ages, which Reactionists so much admire, found its fitting complement in the most slothful indolence. It has been the first to show what man´s activity can bring about. It has accomplished wonders far surpassing Egyptian pyramids, Roman aqueducts, and Gothic cathedrals; it has conducted expeditions that put in the shade all former Exoduses of nations and crusades.(6)

The bourgeoisie cannot exist without constantly revolutionising the instruments of production, and thereby the relations of production, and with them the whole relations of society. Conservation of the old modes of production in unaltered form, was, on the contrary, the first condition of existence for all earlier industrial classes. Constant revolutionising of production, uninterrupted disturbance of all social conditions, everlasting uncertainty and agitation distinguish the bourgeois epoch from all earlier ones. All fixed, fast-frozen relations, with their train of ancient and venerable prejudices and opinions, are swept away, all new-formed ones become antiquated before they can ossify. All that is solid melts into air, all that is holy is profaned, and man is at last compelled to face with sober senses, his real conditions of life, and his relations with his kind.

The need of a constantly expanding market for its products chases the bourgeoisie over the whole surface of the globe. It must nestle everywhere, settle everywhere, establish connexions everywhere.

The bourgeoisie has through its exploitation of the world-market given cosmopolitan character to production and consumption in every country. To the great chagrin of Reactionists, it has drawn from under the feet of industry the national ground on which it stood. All old-established national industries have been destroyed or are daily being destroyed. They are dislodged by new industries, whose introduction becomes a life and death question for all civilised nations, by industries that no longer work up indigenous raw material, but raw material drawn from the remotest zones; industries whose products are consumed, not only at home, but in every quarter of the globe. In place of old wants, satisfied by the productions of the country, we find new wants, requiring for their satisfaction the products of distant lands and climes. In place of the old local and national seclusion and self-sufficiency, we have intercourse in every direction, universal inter-dependence of nations. And as in material, so also in intellectual production. The intellectual creations of individual nations become common

property. National one-sidedness and narrow-mindedness become
more and more impossible, and from the numerous national and
local literatures, there arises a world literature.

The bourgeoisie, by the rapid improvement of all
instruments of production, by the immensely facilitated means
of communication, draws all, even the most barbarian, nations
into civilisation. The cheap prices of its commodities are the
heavy artillery with which it batters down all Chinese walls,
with which it forces the barbarians´ intensely obstinate hatred
of foreigners to capitulate. It compels all nations, on pain
of extinction, to adopt the bourgeois mode of production; it
compels them to introduce what it calls civilisation into their
midst; i.e., to become bourgeois themselves. In one word, it
creates a world after its own image.

The bourgoisie has subjected the country to the rule of
the towns. It has created enormous cities, has greatly
increased the urban population as compared with the rural, and
has thus rescued a considerable part of the population from the
idiocy of rural life. Just as it has made the country
dependent on the towns, so it has made barbarian and
semi-barbarian countries dependent on the civilised ones,
nations of peasants on nations of bourgeois, the East on the
West.

The bourgeoisie keeps more and more doing away with the
scattered state of the population, of the means of production,
and of property. It has agglomerated population, centralised
means of production, and has concentrated property in a few
hands. The necessary consequence of this was political
centralisation. Independent, or but loosely connected
provinces, with separate interests, laws, governments and
systems of taxation, became lumped together into one nation,
with one government, one code of laws, one national
class-interest, one frontier and one customs-tariff.

The bourgeoisie, during its rule of scarce one hundred
years, has created more massive and more colossal productive
forces than have all preceding generations together.
Subjection of Nature´s forces to man, machinery, application of
chemistry to industry and agriculture, steam-navigation,
railways, electric telegraphs, clearing of whole continents for
cultivation, canalisation of rivers, whole populations conjured
out of the ground - what earlier century had even a
presentiment that such productive forces slumbered in the lap
of social labour?

We see then: the means of production and of exchange, on
whose foundation the bourgeoisie built itself up, were
generated in feudal society. At a certain stage in the

27

development of these means of production and of exchange, the
conditions under which feudal society produced and exchanged,
the feudal organisation of agriculture and manufacturing
industry, in one word, the feudal relations of property became
no longer compatible with the already developed productive
forces; they became so many fetters. They had to be burst
asunder; they were burst asunder.

Into their place stepped free competition, accompanied by
a social and political constitution adapted to it, and by the
economical and political sway of the bourgeois class.

A similar movement is going on before our own eyes.
Modern bourgeois society with its relations of production, of
exchange and of property, a society that has conjured up such
gigantic means of production and exchange, is like the
sorcerer, who is no longer able to control the powers of the
nether world whom he has called up by his spells. For many a
decade past history of industry and commerce is but the history
of the revolt of modern productive forces against modern
conditions of production, against the property relations that
are the conditions for the existence of the bourgeoisie and of
its rule. It is enough to mention the commercial crisis that
by their periodical return put on its trial each time more
threateningly, the existence of the entire bourgeois society.
In these crises a great part not only of the existing products,
but also of the previously created productive forces, are
periodically destroyed. In these crises there breaks out an
epidemic that, in all earlier epochs, would have seemed an
asburdity – the epidemic of over-production. Society suddenly
finds itself put back into a state of momentary barbarism; it
appears as if a famine, a universal war of devestation had cut
off the supply of every means of subsistence; industry and
commerce seem to be destroyed; and why? Because there is too
much civilisation, too much means of subsistence, too much
industry, too much commerce. The productive forces at the
disposal of society no longer tend to further the development
of the conditions of bourgeois property; on the contrary, they
have become too powerful for these conditions, by which they
are fettered, and so soon as they overcome these fetters, they
bring disorder into the whole of bourgeois society, endanger
the existence of bourgeois property. The conditions of
bourgeois society are too narrow to comprise the wealth created
by them. And how does the bourgeois get over these crises? On
the one hand by enforced destruction of a mass of production
forces; on the other, by the conquest of new markets, and by
the more exploitation of the old ones. That is to say, by
paving the way for more extensive and more destructive crises,
and by diminishing the means whereby crises are prevented.

The weapons with which the bourgeoisie felled feudalism to

the ground are now turned against the bourgeoisie itself.

But not only has the bourgeoisie forged the weapons that bring death to itself; it has also called into existence the men who are to wield the weapons - the modern working class - the proletarians.

In proportion as the bourgeoisie, i.e., capital, is developed, in the same proportion is the proletariat, the modern working class, developed - a class of labourers, who live only so long as they find work, and who find work only so long as their labour increases capital. These labourers, who must sell themselves piecemeal, are a commodity, like every other article of commerce, and are consequently exposed to all the vicissitudes of competition, to all the fluctuations of the market.

Owing to the extensive use of machinery and to the division of labour, the work of the proletarians has lost all individual character, and, consequently, all charm for the workman. He becomes an appendage of the machine, and it is only the most simple, most monotonous, and most easily acquired knack, that is required of him. Hence, the cost of production of a workman is restricted, almost entirely, to the means of subsistence that he requires for his maintenance, and for the propagation of his race. But the price of a commodity, and therefore also of labour,(7) is equal to its cost of production. In proportion, therefore, as the repulsiveness of the work increases, the wage decreases. Nay more, in proportion as the use of machinery and division of labour increases, in the same proportion the burden of toil also increases, whether by prolongation of the working hours, by increase of the work exacted in a given time or by increased speed of the machinery, etc.

Modern industry has converted the little workshop of the patriarchal master into the great factory of the industrial capitalist. Masses of labourers, crowded into the factory, are organised like soldiers. As privates of the industrial army they are placed under the command of a perfect hierarchy of officers and sergeants. Not only are they slaves of the bourgeois class, and of the bourgeois State; they are daily and hourly enslaved by the machine, by the overlooker, and, above all, by the individual bourgeois manufacturer himself. The more openly this despotism proclaims gain to be its end and aim, the more petty, the more hateful and the more embittering it is.

The less the skill and exertion of strength implied in manual labour, in other words, the more modern industry becomes developed, the more is the labour of men superceded by that of

29

women. Differences of age and sex have no longer any
distinctive social validity for the working class. All are
instruments of labour, more or less expensive to use, according
to their age and sex.

No sooner is the exploitation of the labourer by the
manufacturer, so far, at an end, and he receives his wages in
cash, than he is set upon by the other portions of the
bourgeoisie, the landlord, the shopkeeper, the pawnbroker, etc.

The lower strata of the middle class - the small
tradespeople, shopkeepers, and retired tradesmen generally, the
handicraftsmen and peasants - all these sink gradually into the
proletariat, partly because their dimunitive capital does not
suffice for the scale on which Modern Industry is carried on,
and is swamped in the competition with the large capitalists,
partly because their specialised skill is rendered worthless by
new methods of production. Thus the proletariat is recruited
from all classes of the population.

The proletariat goes through various stages of
development. With its birth begins its struggle with the
bourgeoisie. At first the contest is carried on by individual
labourers, then by the workpeople of a factory, then by the
operatives of one trade, in one locality, against the
individual bourgeois who directly exploits them. They direct
their attacks not against the instruments of production
themselves; they destroy imported wares that compete with their
labour, they smash to pieces machinery, they set factories
ablaze, they seek to restore by force the vanished status of
the workman of the Middle Ages.

At this stage the labourers still form an incoherent mass
scattered over the whole country, and broken up by their mutual
competition. If anywhere they unite to form more compact
bodies, this is not yet the consequence of their own active
union, but of the union of the bourgeoisie, which class, in
order to attain its own political ends, is compelled to set the
whole proletariat in motion, and is moreover yet, for a time,
able to do so. At this stage, therefore, the proletarians do
not fight their enemies, but the enemies of their enemies, the
remnants of absolute monarchy, the landowners, the
non-industrial bourgeois, the petty bourgeoisie. Thus the
whole historical movement is concentrated in the hands of the
bourgeoisie; every victory so obtained is a victory for the
bourgeoisie.

But with the development of industry the proletariat not
only increases in number; it becomes concentrated in greater
masses, its strength grows, and it feels that strength more.

The various interests and conditions of life within the ranks of the proletariat are more and more equalised, in proportion as machinery obliterates all distinctions of labour, and nearly everywhere reduces wages to the same low level. The growing competition among the bourgeois, and the resulting commercial crises, make the wages of the workers ever more fluctuating. The unceasing improvement of machinery, ever more rapidly developing, makes their livelihood more and more precarious; the collisions between individual workmen and individual bourgeois take more and more the character of collisions between two classes. Thereupon the workers begin to form combinations (Trades´ Unions) against the bourgeois; they club together in order to keep up the rate of wages; they found permanent associations in order to make provision beforehand for these occasional revolts. Here and there the contest breaks out into riots.

Now and then the workers are victorious, but only for a time. The real fruit of their battles lies, not in the immediate result, but in the ever-expanding union of the workers. This union is helped on by the improved means of communication that are created by modern industry and that place the workers of different localities in contact with one another. It was just this contact that was needed to centralise the numerous local struggles, all of the same character, into one national struggle between classes. But every class struggle is a political struggle. And that union, to attain which the burghers of the Middle Ages, with their miserable highways, required centuries, the modern proletarians, thanks to railways, achieve in a few years.

This organisation of proletarians into a class, and consequently into a political party, is continually being upset again by the competition between the workers themselves. But it ever rises up again, stronger, firmer, mightier. It compels legislative recognition of particular interests of the workers, by taking advantage of the divisions among the bourgeoisie itself. Thus the ten-hours´ bill in England was carried.

Altogether collisions between the classes of the old society further, in many ways, the course of development of the proletariat. The bourgeoisie finds itself involved in a constant battle. At first with the aristocracy; later on, with those portions of the bourgeoisie itself, whose interests have become antagonistic to the progress of industry; at all times, with the bourgeoisie of foreign countries. In all these battles it sees itself compelled to appeal to the proletariat, to ask for its help, and thus, to drag it into the political arena. The bourgeoisie itself, therefore, supplies the proletariat with its own elements of political and general education, in other words, it furnishes the proletariat with weapons for fighting the bourgeoisie.

Further, as we have already seen, entire sections of the ruling classes are, by the advance of industry, precipitated into the proletariat, or are at least threatened in their conditions of existence. These also supply the proletariat with fresh elements of enlightenment and progress.

Finally, in times when the class struggle nears the decisive hour, the process of dissolution going on within the ruling class, in fact within the whole range of old society, assumes such a violent, glaring character, that a small section of the ruling class cuts itself adrift, and joins the revolutionary class, the class that holds the future in its hands. Just as, therefore, at an earlier period, a section of the nobility went over to the bourgeoisie, so now a portion of the bourgeoisie goes over to the proletariat, and in particular, a portion of the bourgeois ideologists, who have raised themselves to the level of comprehending theoretically the historical movement as a whole.

Of all the classes that stand face to face with the bourgeoisie today, the proletariat alone is a really revolutionary class. The other classes decay and finally disappear in the face of Modern Industry; the proletariat is its special and essential product.

The lower middle class, the small manufacturer, the shopkeeper, the artisan, the peasant, all these fight against the bourgeoisie, to save from extinction their existence as fractions of the middle class. They are therefore not revolutionary, for they try to roll back the wheel of history. If by chance they are revolutionary, they are so only in view of their impending transfer into the proletariat, they thus defend not their present, but their future interests, they desert their own standpoint to place themselves at that of the proletariat.

The "dangerous class," the social scum, that passively rotting mass thrown off by the lowest layers of old society, may, here and there, be swept into the movement by a proletarian revolution, its conditions of life, however, prepare far more for the part of a bribed tool of reactionary intrigue.

In the conditions of the proletariat, those of old society at large are already virtually swamped. The proletarian is without property; his relation to his wife and children has no longer anything in common with the bourgeois family-relations; modern, industrial labour, modern subjection to capital, the same in England as in France, in America as in Germany, has

stripped him of every trace of national character. Law,
morality, religion, are to him so many bourgeois prejudices,
behind which lurk in ambush just as many bourgeois interests.

All the preceding classes that got the upper hand, sought
to fortify their already acquired status by subjecting society
at large to their conditions of appropriation. The
proletarians cannot become masters of the productive forces of
society, except by abolishing their own previous mode of
appropriation, and thereby also every other previous mode of
appropriation. They have nothing of their own to secure and to
fortify; their mission is to destroy all previous securities
for, and insurances of, individual property.

All previous historical movements were movements of
minorities, or in the interests of minorities. The proletarian
movement is the self-conscious, independent movement of the
immense majority, in the interests of the immense majority.
The proletariat, the lowest stratum of our present society,
cannot stir, cannot raise itself up, without the whole
superincumbent strata of official society being sprung up into
the air.

Though not in substance, yet in form, the struggle of the
proletariat with the bourgeoisie is at first a national
struggle. The proletariat of each country must, of course,
first of all settle matters with its own bourgeoisie.

In depicting the most general phases of the development of
the proletariat, we traced the more or less veiled civil war,
raging within existing society, up to the point where that war
breaks out into open revolution, and where the violent
overthrow of the bourgeoisie lays the foundation for the sway
of the proletariat.

Hitherto, every form of society has been based, as we have
already seen, on the antagonism of oppressing and oppressed
classes. But in order to oppress a class, certain conditions
must be assured to it under which it can, at least, continue
its slavish existence. The serf, in the period of serfdom,
raised himself to membership in the commune, just as the petty
bourgeois, under the yoke of feudal absolutism, managed to
develop into a bourgeois. The modern labourer, on the
contrary, instead of rising with the progress of industry,
sinks deeper and deeper below the conditions of existence of
his own class. He becomes a pauper, and pauperism develops
more rapidly than population and wealth. And here it becomes
evident, that the bourgeoisie is unfit any longer to be the
ruling class in society, and to impose its conditions of
existence upon society as an over-riding law. It is unfit to
rule because it is incompetent to assure an existence to its

slave within his slavery, because it cannot help letting him
sink into such a state, that it has to feed him, instead of
being fed by him. Society can no longer live under this
bourgeoisie, in other words, its existence is no longer
compatible with society.

The essential condition for the existence, and for the
sway of the bourgeois class, is the foundation and augmentation
of capital; the condition for capital is wage-labour.
Wage-labour rests exclusively on competition between the
labourers. The advance of industry, whose involuntary promoter
is the bourgeoisie, replaces the isolation of the labourers,
due to competition, by their revolutionary combination, due to
association. The development of Modern Industry, therefore,
cuts from under its feet the very foundation on which the
bourgeoisie produces the appropriate products. What the
bourgeoisie, therefore, produces, above all, is its own
grave-diggers. Its fall and the victory of the proletariat are
equally inevitable.

II. Proletarians and Communists

In what relation do the Communists stand to the
proletarians as a whole?

The Communists do not form a separate party opposed to
other working-class parties.

They have no interests separate and apart from those of
the proletariat as a whole.

They do not set up any sectarian principles of their own,
by which to shape and mould the proletarian movement.

The Communists are distinguished from the other
working-class parties by this only: (1) In the national
struggles of the proletarians of the different countries, they
point out and bring to the front the common interests of the
entire proletariat, independently of all nationality. (2) In
the various stages of development which the struggle of the
working class against the bourgeoisie has to pass through, they
always and everywhere represent the interests of the movement
as a whole.

The Communists, therefore, are on the one hand,
practically, the most advanced and resolute section of the
working-class parties of every country, that section which
pushes forward all others; on the other hand, theoretically,
they have over the great mass of the proletariat the advantage
of clearly understanding the line of march, the conditions, and
the ultimate general results of the proletarian movement.

The immediate aim of the Communists is the same as that of all the other proletarian parties: formation of the proletariat into a class, overthrow of the bourgeois supremacy, conquest of political power by the proletariat.

The theoretical conclusions of the Communists are in no way based on ideas or principles that have been invented, or discovered, by this or that would-be universal reformer.

They merely express, in general terms, actual relations springing from an existing class struggle, from a historical movement going on under our very eyes. The abolition of existing property relations is not at all a distinctive feature of Communism.

All property relations in the past have been subject to historical change consequent upon the change in historical conditions.

The French Revolution,(8) for example, abolished feudal property in favor of bourgeois property.

The distinguishing feature of Communism is not the abolition of property generally, but the abolition of bourgeois property. But modern bourgeois private property is the final and most complete expression of the system of producing and appropriating products, that is based on class antagonisms, on the exploitation of the many by the few.

In this sense, the theory of the Communists may be summed up in the single sentence: Abolition of private property.

We Communists have been reproached with the desire of abolishing the right of personally acquiring property as the fruit of a man´s own labour, which property is alleged to be the groundwork of all personal freedom, activity and independence.

Hard-won, self-acquired, self-earned property! Do you mean the property of the petty artisan and of the small peasant, a form of property that preceded the bourgeois form? There is no need to abolish that; the development of industry has to a great extent already destroyed it, and is still destroying it daily.

Or do you mean modern bourgeois private property?

But does wage-labour create any property for the labourer? Not a bit. It creates capital, i.e., that kind of property which exploits wage-labour, and which cannot increase except upon condition of begetting a new supply of wage-labour for fresh exploitation. Property in its present form, is based on the antagonism of capital and wage-labour. Let us examine both sides of this antagonism.

To be a capitalist, is to have not only a purely personal, but a social status in production. Capital is a collective product, and only by the united action of many members, nay, in the last resort, only by the united action of all members of society, can it be set in motion.

Capital is, therefore, not a personal, it is a social power.

When, therefore, capital is converted into common property, into the property of all members of society, personal property is not thereby transformed into social property. It is only the social character of the property that is changed. It loses its class-character.

Let us now take wage-labour.

The average price of wage-labour is the minimum wage, i.e., that quantum of the means of subsistence, which is absolutely requisite to keep the labourer in bare existence as a labourer. What, therefore, the wage-labourer appropriates by means of his labour, merely suffices to prolong and reproduce a bare existence. We by no means intend to abolish this personal appropriation of the products of labour, an appropriation that is made for the maintenance and reproduction of human life, and that leaves no surplus wherewith to command the labour of others. All that we want to do away with, is the miserable character this appropriation, under which the labourer lives merely to increase capital, and is allowed to live only in so far as the interest of the ruling class requires it.

In bourgeois society, living labour is but a means to increase accumulated labour. In Communist society, accumulated labour is but a means to widen, to enrich, to promote the existence of the labourer.

In bourgeois society, therefore, the past dominates the present; in Communist society, the present dominates the past. In bourgeois society capital is independent and has individuality, while the living person is dependent and has no individuality.

And the abolition of this state of things is called by the bourgeois, abolition of individuality and freedom! And rightly so. The abolition of bourgeois individuality, bourgeois independence, and bourgeois freedom is undoubtedly aimed at.

36

By freedom is meant, under the present bourgeois conditions of production, free trade, free selling and buying.

But if selling and buying disappears, free selling and buying disappears also. This talk about free selling and buying, and all the other "brave words" of our bourgeoisie about freedom in general, have a meaning, if any, only in contrast with restricted selling and buying, with the fettered traders of the Middle Ages, but have no meaning when opposed to the Communistic abolition of buying and selling, of the bourgeois conditions of production, and of the bourgeoisie itself.

You are horrified at our intending to do away with private property. But in your existing society, private property is already done away with for nine-tenths of the population; its existence for the few is solely due to its non-existence in the hands of those nine-tenths. You reproach us, therefore, with intending to do away with a form of property, the necessary condition for whose existence is the non-existence of any property for the immense majority of society.

In one word, you reproach us with intending to do away with your property. Precisely so; that is just what we intend.

From the moment when labour can no longer be converted into capital, money, or rent, into a social power capable of being monopolised; i.e., from the moment when individual property can no longer be transformed into bourgeois property, into capital, from that moment, you say, individuality vanishes.

You must, therefore, confess that by "individual" you mean no other person than the bourgeois, than the middle-class owner of property. This person must, indeed, be swept out of the way, and made impossible.

Communism deprives no man of the power to appropriate the products of society; all that it does is to deprive him of the power to subjugate the labour of others by means of such appropriation.

It has been objected that upon the abolition of private property all work will cease, and universal laziness will overtake us.

According to this, bourgeois society ought long ago to have gone to the dogs through sheer idleness; for those of its members who work, acquire nothing, and those who acquire anything, do not work. The whole of this objection is but

37

another expression of the tautology; that there can no longer be any wage-labour when there is no longer any capital.

All objections urged against the Communistic mode of producing and appropriating material products, have, in the same way, been urged against the Communistic modes of producing and appropriating intellectual products. Just as, to the bourgeois, the disappearance of class property is the disappearance of production itself, so the disappearance of class structure is to him identical with the disappearance of culture.

That culture, the loss of which he laments, is, for the enormous majority, a mere training to act as a machine.

But don´t wrangle with us so long as you apply, to our intended abolition of bourgeois property, the standard of your bourgeois notions of freedom, culture, law, etc. Your very ideas are but the outgrowth of the conditions of your bourgeois production and bourgeois property, just as your jurisprudence is but the will of your class made into law for all, a will, whose essential character and direction are determined by the economical conditions of existence of your class.

The selfish misconception that induces you to transform into eternal laws of nature and of reason, the social forms springing from your present mode of production and form of property - historical relations that rise and disappear in the progress of production - this misconception you share with every ruling class that has preceded you. What you see clearly in the case of ancient property, what you admit in the case of feudal property, you are of course forbidden to admit in the case of your own bourgeois form of property.

Abolition of the family! Even the most radical flare up at this infamous proposal of the Communists.

On what foundation is the present family, the bourgeois family, based? On capital, on private gain. In its completely developed form of this family exists only among the bourgeoisie. But this state of things finds its complement in the practical absence of the family among the proletarians, and in public prostitution.

The bourgeois family will vanish as a matter of course when its complement vanishes, and both will vanish with the vanishing of capital.

Do you charge us with wanting to stop the exploitation of children by their parents? To this crime we plead guilty.

But, you will say, we destroy the most hallowed of relations, when we replace home education by social.

And your education! Is not that also social, and determined by the social conditions under which you educate, by the intervention, direct or indirect, of society, by means of schools, etc.? The Communists have not invented the intervention of society in education; they do but seek to alter the character of that intervention, and to rescue education from the influence of the ruling class. The bourgeois clap-trap about the family and education, about the hallowed co-relation of parent and child, becomes all the more disgusting, the more, by the action of Modern Industry, all family ties among the proletarians are torn asunder, and their children transformed into simple articles of commerce and instruments of labour.

But you Communists would introduce community of women, screams the whole bourgeoisie in chorus.

The bourgeois sees his wife a mere instrument of production. He hears that the instruments of production are to be exploited in common, and, naturally, can come to no other conclusion than that the lot of being common to all will likewise fall to the women.

He has not even a suspicion that the real point aimed at is to do away with the status of women as mere instruments of production.

For the rest, nothing is more ridiculous than the virtuous indignation of our bourgeois at the community of women which, they pretend, is to be openly and officially established by the Communists. The Communists have no need to introduce community of women; it has existed almost from time immemorial.

Our bourgeois, not content with having the wives and daughters of their proletarians at their disposal, not to speak of common prostitutes, take the greatest pleasure in seducing each other's wives.

Bourgeois marriage is in reality a system of wives in common and thus, at the most, what the Communists might possibly be reproached with, is that they desire to introduce, in substitution for a hypocritically concealed, an openly legalised community of women. For the rest, it is self-evident that the abolition of the present system of production must bring with it the abolition of the community of women springing from that system, i.e., of prostitution both public and private.

39

The Communists are further reproached with desiring to abolish countries and nationalities.

The working men have no country. We cannot take from them what they have not got. Since the proletariat must first of all acquire political supremacy, must rise to be the leading class of the nation, must constitute itself the nation, it is, so far, itself national, though not in the bourgeois sense of the word.

National differences and antagonisms between peoples are daily more and more vanishing, owing to the development of the bourgeoisie, to freedom of commerce, to the world-market, to uniformity in the mode of production and in the conditions of life corresponding thereto.

The supremacy of the proletariat will cause them to vanish still faster. United action, of the leading civilised countries at least, is one of the first conditions of emancipation of the proletariat.

In proportion as the exploitation of one individual by another is put an end to, the exploitation of one nation by another will also be put an end to. In proportion as the antagonism between classes within the nation vanishes, the hostility of one nation to another will come to an end.

The charges against Communism made from a religious, a philosophical, and, generally, from an ideological standpoint, are not deserving of serious examination.

Does it require deep intuition to comprehend that man´s ideas, views and conceptions, in one word, man´s consciousness, changes with every change in the conditions of his material existence, in his social relations and in his social life?

What else does the history of ideas prove than that intellectual production changes its character in proportion as material production is changed? The ruling ideas of each age have ever been the ideas of its ruling class.

When people speak of ideas that revolutionise society, they do but express the fact, that within the old society, the elements of a new one have been created, and that the dissolution of the old ideas keeps even pace with the dissolution of the old conditions of existence.

When the ancient world was in its last throes, the ancient religions were overcome by Christianity. When Christian ideas succumbed in the 18th century to rationalist ideas, feudal society fought its death battle with the then revolutionary bourgeoisie. The ideas of religious liberty and freedom of conscience merely gave expression to the sway of free competition within the domain of knowledge.

"Undoubtedly," it will be said, "religious, moral, philosophical and juridical ideas have been modified in the course of historical development. But religion, morality, philosophy, political science, and law, constantly survived this change."

"There are, besides, eternal truths, such as Freedom, Justice, etc., that are common to all states of society. But Communism abolishes eternal truths, it abolishes all religion, and all morality, instead of constituting them on a new basis; it therefore acts in contradiction to all past historical experience."

What does this accusation reduce itself to? The history of all past society has consisted in the development of class antagonisms, antagonisms that assumed different forms at different epochs.

But whatever form they may have taken, one fact is common to all past ages, viz., the exploitation of one part of society by the other. No wonder, then, that the social consciousness of past ages, despite all the multiplicity and variety it displays, moves within certain common forms, or general ideas, which cannot completely vanish except with the total disappearance of class antagonisms.

The Communist revolution is the most radical rupture with traditional property relations; no wonder that its development involves the most radical rupture with traditional ideas.

But let us have done with the bourgeois objections to Communism.

We have seen above, that the first step in the revolution by the working class, is to raise the proletariat to the position of ruling class, to win the battle of democracy.

The proletariat will use its political supremacy to wrest, by degrees, all capital from the bourgeoisie, to centralise all instruments of production in the hands of the State, i.e., of the proletariat organised as the ruling class; and to increase the total of productive forces as rapidly as possible.

Of course, in the beginning, this cannot be effected except by means of despotic inroads on the rights of property, and on the conditions of bourgeois production; by means of

41

measures, therefore, which appear economically insufficient and untenable, but which, in the course of the movement, outstrip themselves, necessitate further inroads upon the old social order, and are unavoidable as a means of entirely revolutionising the mode of production.

These measures will of course be different in different countries.

Nevertheless in the most advanced countries, the following will be pretty generally applicable.
1. Abolition of property in land and application of all rents of land to public purposes.
2. A heavy progressive or graduated income tax.
3. Abolition of all right of inheritance.
4. Confiscation of the property of all emigrants and rebels.
5. Centralisation of credit in the hands of the State, by means of a national bank with State capital and an exclusive monoply.
6. Centralisation of the means of communication and transport in the hands of the state.
7. Extension of factories and instruments of production owned by the State; the bringing into cultivation of waste-lands, and the improvement of the soil generally in accordance with a common plan.
8. Equal liability of all to labour. Establishment of industrial armies, especially for agriculture.
9. Combination of agriculture with manufacturing industries; gradual abolition of the distinction between town and country, by a more equitable distribution of the population over the country.
10. Free education for all children in public schools. Abolition of children's factory labour in its present form. Combination of education with industrial production, &c., &c.

When in the course of development, class distributions have disappeared, and all production has been concentrated in the hands of a vast association of the whole nation, the public power will lose its political character. Political power, properly so called, is merely the organised power of one class for oppressing another. If the proletariat during its contest with the bourgeoisie is compelled, by the force of circumstances, to organise itself as a class, if, by means of a revolution, it makes itself the ruling class, and, as such, sweeps away by force the old conditions of production, then it will, along with these conditions, have swept away the conditions for the existence of class antagonisms and of classes generally, and will thereby have abolished its own supremacy as a class.

In place of the old bourgeois society, with its classes and class antagonisms, we shall have an association, in which the free development of each is the condition for the free development of all.

III. Socialist and Communist Literature

1. Reactionary Socialism
   A. Feudal Socialism. Owing to their historical position, it became the vocation of the aristocracies of France and England to write pamphlets against modern bourgeois society. In the French revolution of July 1830, and in the English reform(9) agitation, these aristocracies again succumbed to the hateful upstart. Thenceforth, a serious political contest was altogether out of the question. A literary battle alone remained possible. But even in the domain of literature the old cries of the restoration period(10) had become impossible.

In order to arouse sympathy, the aristocracy were obliged to lose sight, apparently, of their own interests, and to formulate their indictment against the bourgeoisie in the interest of the exploited working class alone. Thus the aristocracy took their revenge by singing lampoons on their new master, and whispering in his ears sinister prophecies of coming catastrophe.

In this way arose Feudal Socialism: half lamentation, half lampoon; half echo of the past, half menace of the future; at times, by its bitter, witty and incisive criticism, striking the bourgeoisie to the very heart´s core; but always ludicrous in its effect, through total incapacity to comprehend the march of modern history.

The aristocracy, in order to rally the people to them, waved to the proletarian alms-bag in front for a banner. But the people, so often as it joined them, saw on their hindquarters the old feudal coats of arms, and deserted with loud and irreverent laughter.

One section of the French Legitimists(11) and "Young England"(12) exhibited this spectacle.

In pointing out that their mode of exploitation was different to that of the bourgeoisie, the feudalists forget that they exploited under circumstances and conditions that were quite different, and that are now antiquated. In showing that, under their rule, the modern proletariat never existed, they forget that the modern bourgeoisie is the necessary offspring of their own form of society.

For the rest, so little do they conceal the reactionary

character of their criticism that their chief accusation against the bourgeoisie amounts to this, that under the bourgeois régime a class is being developed, which is destined to cut up root and branch the old order of society.

What they upbraid the bourgeoisie with is not so much that it creates a proletariat, as that it creates a revolutionary proletariat.

In political practice, therefore, they join in all coercive measures against the working class; and in ordinary life, despite their high-falutin phrases, they stoop to pick up the golden apples dropped from the tree of industry, and to barter truth, love, and honour for traffic in wool, beetroot-sugar, and potato spirits.(13)

As the parson has ever gone hand in hand with the landlord, so has Clerical Socialism with Feudal Socialism.

Nothing is easier than to give Christian asceticism a Socialist tinge. Has not Christianity declaimed against private property, against marriage, against the State? Has it not preached in the place of these, charity and poverty, celibacy and mortification of the flesh, monastic life and Mother Church? Christian Socialism is but the holy water with which the priest consecrates the heart-burnings of the aristocrat.

B. Petty-Bourgeois Socialism. The feudal aristocracy was not the only class that was ruined by the bourgeoisie, not the only class whose conditions of existence pined and perished in the atmosphere of modern bourgeois society. The mediaeval burgesses and the small peasant proprietors were the precursors of the modern bourgeoisie. In those countries which are but little developed, industrially and commercially, these two classes still vegetate side by side with the rising bourgeoisie.

In countries where modern civilisation has become fully developed, a new class of petty bourgeois has been formed, fluctuating between proletariat and bourgeoisie and ever renewing itself as a supplementary part of bourgeois society. The individual members of this class, however, are being constantly hurled down into the proletariat by the action of competition, and, as modern industry develops, they even see the moment approaching when they will completely disappear as an independent section of modern society, to be replaced, in manufactures, agriculture and commerce, by overlookers, bailiffs and shopmen.

In countries like France, where the peasants constitute

far more than half of the population, it was natural that writers who sided with the proletariat against the bourgeoisie, should use, in their criticism of the bourgeois régime, the standard of the peasant and the petty bourgeois, and from the standpoint of these intermediate classes should take up the cudgels for the working class. Thus arose petty-bourgeois Socialism. Sismondi was the head of this school, not only in France but also in England.

This school of Socialism dissected with great acuteness the contradictions in the conditions of modern production. It laid bare the hypocritical apologies of economists. It proved incontrovertibly, the disastrous effects of machinery and division of labour; the concentration of capital and land in a few hands; overproduction and crises; it pointed out the inevitable ruin of the petty bourgeois and peasant, the misery of the proletariat, the anarchy in production, the crying inequalities in the distribution of wealth, the industrial war of extermination between nations, the dissolution of old moral bonds, of the old family relations, of the old nationalities.

In its positive aims, however, this form of Socialism aspires either to restoring the old means of production and of exchange, and with them the old property relations, and the old society, or to cramping the modern means of production and of exchange, within the framework of the old property relations that have been, and were bound to be, exploded by those means. In either case, it is both reactionary and Utopian.

Its last words are: corporate guilds for manufacture patriarchal relations in agriculture.

Ultimately, when stubborn historical facts had dispersed all intoxicating effects of self-deception, this form of Socialism ended in a miserable fit of the blues.

C. German, or "True," Socialism. The Socialist and Communist literature of France, a literature that originated under the pressure of a bourgeoisie in power, and that was the expression of the struggle against this power, was introduced into Germany at a time when the bourgeoisie, in that country, had just begun its contest with feudal absolutism.

German philosophers, would-be philosophers, and beaux esprits, eagerly seized on this literature, only forgetting, that when these writings immigrated from France into Germany, French social conditions had not immigrated along with them. In contact with German social conditions, this French literature lost all its immediate practical significance, and assumed a purely literary aspect. Thus, to the German

45

philosophers of the eighteenth century, the demands of the first French Revolution were nothing more than the demands of "Practical Reason" in general, and the utterance of the will of the French bourgeoisie signified in their eyes the laws of pure Will, of Will as it was bound to be, of true human Will generally.

The work of the German _literati_ consisted solely in bringing the new French ideas into harmony with their ancient philosophical conscience, or rather, in annexing the French ideas without deserting their own philosophic point of view.

This annexation took place in the same way in which a foreign language is appropriated, namely by translation.

It is well known how the monks wrote silly lives of Catholic Saints _over_ the manuscripts on which the classical works of ancient heathendom had been written. The German _literati_ reversed this process with the profane French literature. They wrote their philosophical nonsense beneath the French original. For instance, beneath the French criticism of the economic functions of money, they wrote "Alienation of Humanity," and beneath the French criticism of the bourgeois State they wrote "Dethronement of the Category of the General," and so forth.

The introduction of these philosophical phrases at the back of the French historical criticisms they dubbed "Philosophy of Action," "True Socialism," "German Science of Socialism," "Philosophical Foundation of Socialism," and so on.

The French Socialist and Communist literature was thus completely emasculated. And, since it ceased in the hands of the German to express the struggle of one class with the other, he felt conscious of having overcome "French one-sidedness" and of representing, not true requirements, but the requirements of Truth; not the interests of the proletariat, but the interests of Human Nature, of Man in general, who belongs to no class, has no reality, who exists only in the misty realm of philosophical fantasy.

This German Socialism, which took its schoolboy task so seriously and solemnly, and extolled its poor stock-in-trade in such mountebank fashion, meanwhile gradually lost its pedantic innocence.

The fight of the German, and, especially, of the Prussian bourgeoisie, against feudal aristocracy and absolute monarchy, in other words, the liberal movement, became more earnest.

By this, the long wished-for opportunity was offered to

"True" Socialism of confronting the political movement with the
Socialist demands, of hurling the traditional anathemas against
liberalism, against representative government, against
bourgeois competition, bourgeois freedom of the press,
bourgeois legislation, bourgeois liberty and equality, and of
preaching to the masses that they had nothing to gain, and
everything to lose, by this bourgeois movement. German
Socialism forgot, in the nick of time, that the French
criticism, whose silly echo it was, presupposed the existence
of modern bourgeois society, with its corresponding economic
conditions of existence, and the political constitution adapted
thereto, the very things whose attainment was the object of the
pending struggle in Germany.

To the absolute governments, with their following of
parsons, professors, country squires and officials, it served
as a welcome scarecrow against the threatening bourgeoisie.

It was a sweet finish after the bitter pills of floggings
and bullets with which these same governments, just at that
time, dosed the Germans working-class risings.

While this "True" Socialism thus served the governments as
a weapon for fighting the German bourgeoisie, it, at the same
time, directly represented a reactionary interest, the interest
of the German Philistines. In Germany the petty-bourgeois
class, a relic of the sixteenth century, and since then
constantly cropping up again under various forms, is the real
social basis of the existing state of things.

To preserve this class is to preserve the existing state
of things in Germany. The industrial and political supremacy
of the bourgeoisie threatens it with certain destruction; on
the one hand, from the concentration of capital; on the other,
from the rise of a revolutionary proletariat. "True" Socialism
appeared to kill these two birds with one stone. It spread
like an epidemic.

The robe of speculative cobwebs, embroidered with flowers
of rhetoric, steeped in the dew of sickly sentiment, this
transcendental robe in which the German Socialists wrapped
their sorry "eternal truths," all skin and bone, served to
wonderfully increase the sale of their goods amongst such a
public.

And on its part, German Socialism recognised, more and
more, its own calling as the bombastic representative of the
petty-bourgeois Philistine.

It proclaimed the German nation to be the model nation,
and the German petty Philistine to be the typical man. To

every villainous meanness of this model man it gave a hidden,
higher, Socialistic interpretation, the exact contrary of its
real character. It went to the extreme length of directly
opposing the "brutally destructive" tendency of Communism, and
of proclaiming its supreme and impartial contempt of all class
struggles. With very few exceptions, all the so-called
Socialist and Communist publications that now (1847) circulate
in Germany belong to the domain of this foul and enervating
literature.(14)

2. Conservative, or Bourgeois, Socialism

A part of the bourgeois is desirous of redressing social
grievances, in order to secure the continued existence of
bourgeois society.

To this section belong economists, philanthropists,
humanitarians, improvers of the condition of the working class,
organisers of charity, members of societies for the prevention
of cruelty to animals, temperance fanatics, hole-and-corner
reformers of every imaginable kind. This form of Socialism
has, moreover, been worked out into complete systems.

We may cite Proudhon's Philosophie de la Misère as an
example of this form.

The Socialistic bourgeois want all the advantages of
modern social conditions without the struggles and dangers
necessarily resulting therefrom. They desire the existing
state of society minus its revolutionary and disintegrating
elements. They wish for a bourgeoisie without a proletariat.
The bourgeoisie naturally conceives the world in which it is
supreme to be the best; and bourgeois Socialism develops this
comfortable conception into various more or less complete
systems. In requiring the proletariat to carry out such a
system, and thereby to march straightway into the social New
Jerusalem,(15) it but requires in reality, that the proletariat
should remain within the bounds of existing society, but should
cast away all its hateful ideas concerning the bourgeoisie.

A second and more practical, but less systematic, form of
this Socialism sought to depreciate every revolutionary
movement, in the eyes of the working class, by showing that no
mere political reform, but only a change in the material
conditions of existence, in economical relations, could be of
any advantage to them. By changes in the material conditions
of existence, this form of Socialism, however, by no means
understands abolition of the bourgeois relations of production,
an abolition that can be effected only by a revolution, but
administrative reforms, based on the continued existence of
these relations; reforms, therefore, that in no respect affect
the relations between capital and labour, but, at the best,

lessen the cost, and simplify the administrative work, of bourgeois government.

Bourgeois Socialism attains adequate expression, when, and only when, it becomes a mere figure of speech.

Free trade: for the benefit of the working class. Protective duties: for the benefit of the working class. Prison Reform: for the benefit of the working class. This is the last word and the only seriously meant word of bourgeois Socialism.

It is summed up in the phrase: the bourgeois is a bourgeois - for the benefit of the working class.

3. Critical-Utopian Socialism and Communism

We do not here refer to the literature which, in every great modern revolution, has always given voice to the demands of the proletariat, such as the writings of Babeuf and others.

The first direct attempts of the proletariat to attain its own ends, made in times of universal excitement, when feudal society was being overthrown, these attempts necessarily failed, owing to the then undeveloped state of the proletariat, as well as to the absence of the economic conditions for its emancipation, conditions that had yet to be produced, and could be produced by the impending bourgeois epoch alone. The revolutionary literature that accompanied these first movements of the proletariat had necessarily a reactionary character. It inculcated universal asceticism and social levelling in its crudest form.

The Socialist and Communist systems properly so called, those of Saint-Simon, Fourier, Owen and others, spring into existence in the early undeveloped period, described above, of the struggle between proletariat and bourgeoisie (see Section I. Bourgeoisie and Proletariat).

The founders of these systems see, indeed, the class antagonisms, as well as the action of the decomposing elements, in the prevailing form of society. But the proletariat, as yet in its infancy, offers to them the spectacle of a class without any historical initiative or any independent political movemet.

Since the development of class antagonism keeps even pace with the development of industry, the economic situation, as they find it, does not as yet offer to them the material conditions for the emancipation of the proletariat. They therefore search after a new social science, after new social laws, that are to create these conditions.

Historical action is to yield to their personal inventive action, historically created conditions of emancipation to fantastic ones and the gradual, spontaneous class-organisation of the proletariat to an organisation of society specially contrived by these inventors. Future history revolves itself, in their eyes, into the propaganda and the practical carrying out of their social plans.

In the formation of their plans they are conscious of caring chiefly for the interests of the working class, as being the most suffering class. Only from the point of view of being the most suffering class does the proletariat exist for them.

The undeveloped state of the class struggle, as well as their own surroundings, causes Socialists of this kind to consider themselves far superior to all class antagonisms. They want to improve the condition of every member of society, even that of the most favoured. Hence, they habitually appeal to society at large, without distinction of class; nay, by preference, to the ruling class. For how can people, when once they understand their system, fail to see in it the best possible plan of the best possible state of society?

Hence, they reject all political, and especially all revolutionary, action; they wish to attain their ends by peaceful means, and endeavour, by small experiments, necessarily doomed to failure, and by the force of example, to pave the way for the new social Gospel.

Such fantastic pictures of future society, painted at a time when the proletariat is still in a very undeveloped state and has but a fantastic conception of its own position, correspond with the first instinctive yearnings of that class for a general reconstruction of society.

But these Socialist and Communist publications contain also a critical element. They attack every principle of existing society. Hence they are full of the most valuable materials for the enlightenment of the working class. The practical measures proposed in them - such as the abolition of the distinction between town and country, of the family, of carrying on of industries for the account of private individuals, and of the wage system, the proclamation of social harmony, the conversion of the functions of the State into a mere superintendence of production, all these proposals point solely to the disappearance of class antagonisms which were, at that time, only just cropping up, and which, in these publications, are recognised in their earliest, indistinct and undefined forms only. These proposals, therefore, are of a purely Utopian character.

The significance of Critical-Utopian Socialism and Communism bears an inverse relation to historical development. In proportion as the modern class struggle develops and takes definite shape, this fantastic standing apart from the contest, these fantastic attacks on it, lose all practical value and all theoretical justification. Therefore, although the originators of these systems were, in many respects, revolutionary, their disciples have, in every case, formed mere reactionary sects. They hold fast by the original views of their masters, in opposition to the progressive historical development of the proletariat. They, therefore, endeavor, and that consistently, to deaden the class struggle and to reconcile the class antagonisms. They still dream of experimental realisation of their social Utopias, of founding isolated "phalansteres," of establishing "Home Colonies," of setting up a "Little Icaeia"(16) - duodecimo editions of the New Jerusalem - and to realise all these castles in the air, they are compelled to appeal to the feelings and purses of the bourgeois. By degrees they sink into the category of the reactionary conservative Socialists depicted above, differing from these only by more systematic pedantry, and by their fanatical and superstitious belief in the miraculous effects of their social science.

They, therefore, violently oppose all political action on the part of the working class; such action, according to them, can only result from blind unbelief in the new Gospel.

The Owenites in England, and the Fourierists in France, repectively, oppose the Chartists(17) and the Réformistes.(18)

IV. Position of the Communists in Relation to the
Various Existing Opposition Parties

Section II has made clear the relations of the Communists to the existing working-class parties, such as the Chartists in England and the Agrarian Reformers in America.

The Communists fight for the attainment of the immediate aims, for the enforcement of the momentary interests of the working class; but in the movement of the present, they also represent and take care of the future of that movement. In France the Communists ally themselves with the Social Democrats,(19) against the conservative and radical bourgeoisie, reserving, however, the right to take up a critical position in regard to phrases and illusions traditionally handed down from the great Revolution.

In Switzerland they support the Radicals, without losing sight of the fact that this party consists of antagonistic elements, partly of Democratic Socialists, in the French sense, partly of radical bourgeois.

In Poland they support the party that insists on an agrarian revolution as the prime condition for national emancipation, that party which fomented the insurrection of Cracow in 1846.(20)

In Germany they fight with the bourgeoisie whenever it acts in a revolutionary way, against the absolute monarchy, the feudal squirearchy, and the petty bourgeoisie.

But they never cease, for a single instant, to instil into the working class the clearest possible recognition of the hostile antagonism between bourgeoisie and proletariat, in order that the German workers may straightway use, as so many weapons against the bourgeoisie, the social and political conditions that the bourgeoisie must necessarily introduce along with its supremacy, and in order that, after the fall of the reactionary classes in Germany, the fight against the bourgeoisie itself may immediately begin.

The Communists turn their attention chiefly to Germany, because that country is on the eve of a bourgeois revolution that is bound to be carried out under more advanced conditions of European civilisation, and with a much more developed proletariat, than that of England was in the seventeenth, and of France in the eighteenth century, and because the bourgeois revolution in Germany will be but the prelude to an immediately following proletarian revolution.

In short, the Communists everywhere support every revolutionary movement against the existing social and political order of things.

In all these movements they bring to the front, as the leading question in each, the property question, no matter what its degree of development at the time.

Finally, they labour everywhere for the union and agreement of the democratic parties of all countries.

The Communists disdain to conceal their views and aims. They openly declare that their ends can be attained only by the forcible overthrow of all existing social conditions. Let the ruling classes tremble at Communistic revolution. The proletarians have nothing to lose but their chains. They have a world to win.

WORKING MEN OF ALL COUNTRIES, UNITE!

Notes

1. Manifesto of the Communist Party - the first policy
document of scientific communism which provides an integral and
well-composed exposition of the fundamental principles of the
great teachings of Marx and Engels. "With the clarity and
brilliance of genius, this work outlines a new world
conception, consistent materialism, which also embraces the
realm of social life; dialectics, as the most comprehenisve and
profound doctrine of development; the theory of the class
struggle and of the world-historic revolutionary role of the
proletariat - the creator of a new, communist society" (V.I.
Lenin, Collected Works, Vol. 21, Moscow, 1964, p. 48). Written
by Marx and Engels in December 1847-January 1848. Originally
published in German in London in February 1848. Printed
according to the 1888 English edition.
2. By bourgeois is meant the class of modern Capitalists,
owners of the means of social production and employers of
wage-labour. By proletariat, the class modern wage-labourers
who, having no means of production of their own, are reduced to
selling their labour-power in order to live. [Note by Engels to
the English edition of 1888.]
3. That is, all written history. In 1847, the pre-history of
society, the social organisation, existing previous to recorded
history, was all but unknown. Since then, Haxthausen
discovered common ownership of land in Russia, Maurer proved it
to be the social foundation from which all Teutonic races
started in history, and by and by village communities were
found to be, or to have been the primitive form of society
everywhere from India to Ireland. The inner organisation of
this primitive Communistic society was laid bare, in its
typical form, by Morgan´s crowning discovery of the true nature
of the gens and its relation to the tribe. With the
dissolution of these primaeval communities society begins to be
differentiated into separate and finally antagonistic classes.
I have attempted to retrace this process of dissolution in:
"Der Ursprung der Familie, des Privateigenthums und des Staats"
[The Origin of the Family, Private Property and the State...
[Note by Engels to the English edition of 1888.]
4. Guild-master, that is, a full member of a guild, a master
within, not a head of a guild. [Note by Engels to the English
edition of 1888.]
5. "Commune" was the name taken, in France, by the nascent
towns even before they had conquered from their feudal lords
and masters local self-government and political rights as the
"Third Estate." Generally speaking, for the economical
development of the bourgeoisie, England is here taken as the
typical country; for its political development, France. [Note
by Engels to the English edition of 1888.]
    This was the name given their urban communities by the
townsmen of Italy and France, after they had purchased or

wrested their initial rights of self-government from their
feudal lords. [Note by Engels to the German edition of 1890.]
   6.   This refers to military colonialist expeditions to the
East by the West-European big feudal lords, knights and Italian
merchants in the eleventh-thirteenth centuries with the
religious goal of recovering shrines in Jerusalem and other
"holy places" from the Mohammedans.   The crusades were inspired
and justified by the Catholic Church and papacy which were
striving for world domination, while the knights made up their
main fighting force.   Peasants who sought liberation from the
feudal yoke also took part in the crusades.   The crusades
resorted to plunder and violence against both the Moslem and
Christian population of the countries through which they
marched.   The objects of their predatory aspirations were not
only the Moslem states in Syria, Palestine, Egypt and Tunisia,
but the orthodox Byzantine Empire.   Their conquests in the
Eastern Mediterranean area were, however, not lasting and soon
they were recovered by the Moslems.
   7.   In their later works Marx and Engels used the more exact
terms "the value of labour power" and "the price of labour
power" introduced by Marx instead of "the value of labour" and
"the price of labour"...
   8.   This refers to the French bourgeois revolution at the end
of the eighteenth century.
   9.   This refers to the movement for a reform of the electoral
law which, under pressure from the people, was passed by the
House of Commons in 1831 and was finally endorsed by the House
of Lords in June 1832.   This reform was directed against the
monopoly rule of the landed and financial aristocracy and
opened the way to Parliament for the representatives of the
industrial bourgeoisie.   The proletariat and the petty
bourgeoisie who were the main force in the struggle for the
reform were deceived by the liberal bourgeoisie and were not
granted electoral rights.
10.   Not the English Restoration 1660 to 1689, but the French
Restoration 1814 to 1830. [Note by Engels to the English
edition of 1888.]   The Restoration of 1660-89 - the period of
the second rule in England of the Stuart dynasty, which was
overthrown by the English bourgeois revolution of the
seventeenth century...
   The Restoration of 1814-30 - a period of the second reign in
France of the Bourbon dynasty.   The reactionary regime of the
Bourbons which supported the interests of the nobles and the
clericals was overthrown by the July revolution of 1830.
11.   The Legitimists - the adherents of the "legitimate"
Bourbon dynasty overthrown in 1830, which represented the
interests of the big landed nobility.   In their struggle
against the reigning Orleans dynasty (1830-48), which relied on
the financial aristocracy and big bourgeoisie, a section of the
Legitimists resorted to social demagogy and projected
themselves as defenders of the working people against

exploitation by the bourgeoisie.

12. "Young England" - a group of British Conservatives - men of politics and literature - formed in the early 1840s... While expressing the dissatisfaction of the landed aristocracy with the growing economic and political might of the bourgeoisie, the "Young England" leaders resorted to demagogic ruses in order to subjugate the working class to their influence and to turn it into a tool in their struggle against the bourgeoisie.

13. This applies chiefly to Germany where the landed aristocracy and squirearchy [i.e., in a narrow sense, landed nobility in East Prussia; in the broad sense this means a class of German landowners] have large portions of their estates cultivated for their own account by stewards, and are, moreover, extensive beetroot-sugar manufacturers and distillers of potato spirits. The wealthier British aristocracy are, as yet rather above that; but they, too, know how to make up for declining rents by lending their names to floaters of more or less shady joint-stock companies. [Note by Engels to the English edition of 1888.]

14. The revolutionary storm of 1848 [i.e., the bourgeois-democratic revolution of 1848-49 in Germany] swept away this whole shabby tendency and cured its protagonists of the desire to dabble further in Socialism. The chief representative and classical type of this tendency is Herr Karl Grun. [Note by Engels to the German edition of 1890.]

15. Jerusalem - famous city and religious centre in Palestine, a Christian and Judaean holy place.

   New Jerusalem is a synonym of Paradise according to the Christian tradition.

16. Phalanstères were Socialist colonies on the plan of Charles Fourier; Icaria was the holy name given by Cabet to his Utopia and, later on, to his American Communist colony. [Note by Engels to the English edition of 1888.]

   "Home colonies" were what Owen called his Communist model societies. Phalanstères was the name of the public palaces planned by Fourier. Icaria was the name given to the Utopian land of fancy, whose Communist institutions Cabet portrayed. [Note by Engels to the German edition of 1890.]

17. Chartism - a political movement of the British workers in the period from the thirties to the middle fifties of the nineteenth century which arose as a result of the hard economic conditions of the workers and their lack of political rights. The watchword of the movement was the struggle for the implementation of the People's Charter... which included the demand for universal suffrage and a number of provisions guaranteeing this right for the workers. Lenin said that Chartism was "the first broad, truly mass and politically organised proletarian revolutionary movement" (V.I. Lenin, Collected Works, Vol. 29, Moscow, 1965, p. 309.)

18. This refers to petty-bourgeois republican democrats and petty-bourgeois socialists who were adherents of the French

newspaper La Réforme. They came out for a republic and democratic and social reforms.

19. The party then represented in Parliament by Ledru-Rollin, in literature by Louis Blanc, in the daily press by the Réforme [i.e., French daily newspaper published in Paris from 1843 to 1850]. The name of Social-Democracy signified, with these its inventors, a section of the Democratic or Republican party more or less tinged with Socialism. [Note by Engels to the English edition of 1888.]

The party in France which at that time called itself Socialist-Democratic was represented in political life by Ledru-Rollin and in literature by Louis Blanc; thus it differed immeasurably from present-day German Social-Democracy. [Note by Engels to the German edition of 1890.]

20. In February 1846, preparations were made for an insurrection throughout the Polish territories with the aim of achieving national liberation. Polish revolutionary democrats (Demkowski and others) were the main inspirers of the insurrection. However, as a result of the betrayal by a section of the Polish gentry and the arrest of the leaders of the insurrection by the Prussian police, only isolated risings broke out. Only in Cracow, which from 1815 onwards was jointly controlled by Austria, Russia and Prussia, did the insurgents gain a victory on February 22 and establish a national government, which issued a manifesto repealing obligatory services to the feudal lords. The Cracow uprising was crushed early in March 1846. In November 1846 Austria, Prussia and Russia signed a treaty according to which Cracow was annexed to the Austrian Empire.

THE STATE AND REVOLUTION
THE MARXIST THEORY OF THE STATE AND THE TASKS
OF THE PROLETARIAT IN THE
REVOLUTION

V. I. Lenin

Class Society and the State

1. The State--A Product of the Irreconcilability of Class
Anatgonisms

What is now happening to Marx´s theory has, in the course
of history, happened repeatedly to the theories of
revolutionary thinkers and leaders of oppressed classes
fighting for emancipation. During the lifetime of great
revolutionaries, the oppressing classes constantly hounded
them, received their theories with the most savage malice, the
most furious hatred, and the most unscrupulous campaigns of
lies and slander. After their death, attempts are made to
convert them into harmless icons, to canonise them, so to say,
and to hallow their names to a certain extent for the
"consolation" of the oppressed classes and with the object of
duping the latter, while at the same time robbing the
revolutionary theory of its substance, blunting its
revolutionary edge and vulgarising it. Today, the bourgeoise
and the opportunists within the labour movement concur in this
doctoring of Marxism. They omit, obscure or distort the
revolutionary side of this theory, its revolutionary soul.
They push to the foreground and extol what is or seems
acceptable to the bourgeoise. All the social-chauvinists are
now "Marxists" (don´t laugh!). And more and more frequently
German bourgeois scholars, only yesterday specialists in the
annihiliation of Marxism, are speaking of the "national-German"
Marx, who, they claim, educated the labour unions which are so
splendidly organised for the purpose of waging a predatory war!

In these circumstances in view of the unprecedentedly
widespread distortion of Marxism, our prime task is to
re-establish what Marx really taught on the subject of the
state. This will necessitate a number of long quotations from
the works of Marx and Engels themselves. Of course, long
quotations will render the text cumbersome and not help at all
to make it popular reading, but we cannot possibly dispense
with them. All or at any rate all the most essential passages

Excerpt from: Lenin - Selected Works. 1977 Progress Publishers,
Moscow.

in the works of Marx and Engels on the subject of the state must by all means be quoted as fully as possible so that the reader may form an independent opinion of the totality of the views of the founders of scientific socialism, and of the evolution of those views, and so that their distortion by the "Kautskyism" now prevailing may be documentarily proved and clearly demonstrated.

Let us begin with the most popular of Engels's works, The Origin of the Family, Private Property, and the State, the sixth edition of which was published in Stuttgart as far back as 1894. We shall have to translate the quotations from the German originals, as the Russian translations, while very numerous, are for the most part either incomplete or very unsatisfactory.

Summing up his historical analysis, Engels says:

The state is, therefore, by no means a power forced on society from without; just as little is it `the reality of the ethical idea,´ `the image and reality of reason,´ as Hegel maintains. Rather, it is a product of society at a certain stage of development; it is the admission that this society has become entangled in an insoluble contradiction with itself, that it has split into irreconcilable antagonisms which it is powerless to dispel. But in order that these antagonisms, these classes with conflicting economic interests might not consume themselves and society in fruitless struggle, it became necessary to have a power, seemingly standing above society, that would alleviate the conflict and keep it within the bounds of `order´; and this power, arisen out of society but placing itself above it, and alienating itself more and more from it, is the state. (Pp. 177-78, sixth German edition.)(1)

This expresses with perfect clarity the basic idea of Marxism with regard to the historical role and the meaning of the state. The state is a product and a manifestation of the irreconcilability of class antagonisms. The state arises where, when and insofar as class antagonisms objectively cannot be reconciled. And, conversely, the existence of the state proves that the class antagonisms are irreconcilable.

It is on this most important and fundamental point that the distortion of Marxism, proceeding along two main lines, begins.

On the one hand, the bourgeois, and particularly the

58

petty-bourgeois, ideologists, compelled under the weight of indisputable historical facts to admit that the state only exists where there are class antagonisms and a class struggle, "correct" Marx in such a way as to make it appear that the state is an organ for the <u>reconciliation</u> of classes. According to Marx, the state could neither have risen nor maintained itself had it been possible to reconcile classes. From what the petty-bourgeois and philistine professors and publicists say, with quite frequent and benevolent references to Marx, it appears that the state does reconcile classes. According to Marx, the state is an organ of class <u>rule</u>, an organ for the <u>oppression</u> of one class by another; it is the creation of "order," which legalises and perpetuates this oppression by moderating the conflict between the classes. In the opinion of the petty-bourgeois politicians, however, order means the reconciliation of classes, and not the oppression of one class by another; to alleviate the conflict means reconciling classes and not depriving the oppressed classes of definite means and methods of struggle to overthrow the oppressors.

For instance, when, in the revolution of 1917, the question of the significance and role of the state arose in all its magnitude as a practical question demanding immediate action, and, moreover, action on a mass scale, all the Socialist-Revolutionaries and Mensheviks descended at once to the petty-bourgeois theory that the "state" "reconciles" classes. Innumerable resolutions and articles by politicians of both these parties are thoroughly saturated with this petty-bourgeois and philistine "reconciliation" theory. That the state is an organ of the rule of a definite class which cannot be reconciled with its antipode (the class opposite to it) is something the petty-bourgeois democrats will never be able to understand. Their attitude to the state is one of the most striking manifestations of the fact that our Socialist-Revolutionaries and Mensheviks are not socialists at all (a point that we Bolsheviks have always maintained), but petty-bourgeois democrats using near-socialist phraseology.

On the other hand, the "Kautskyite" distortion of Marxism is far more subtle. "Theoretically," it is not denied that the state is an organ of class rule, or that class antagonisms are irreconcilable. But what is overlooked or glossed over is this: if the state is the product of the irreconcilability of class antagonisms, if it is a power standing <u>above</u> society and "alienating itself <u>more and more</u> from it," it is clear that the liberation of the oppressed class is impossible not only without a violent revolution, but <u>also without the destruction</u> of the apparatus of state power which was created by the ruling class and which is the embodiment of this "alienation." As we shall see later, Marx very explicitly drew this theoretically self-evident conclusion on the strength of a concrete

historical analysis of the tasks of the revolution. And - as
we shall show in detail further on - it is this conclusion
which Kautsky has "forgotten" and distorted.

2. Special Bodies of Armed Men, Prisons, Etc.

Engels continues: "As distinct from the old gentile
[tribal or clan] order,(2) the state, first, divides its
subjects according to territory..." This division seems
"natural" to us, but it cost[s] a prolonged struggle against
the old organisation according to generations or tribes.

The second distinguishing feature is the establishment of a public power which no longer directly
coincides with the population organising itself as
an armed force. This special, public power is necessary because a self-acting armed organisation of the
population has become impossible since the split into
classes... This public power exists in every state;
it consists not merely of armed men but also of material
adjuncts, prisons, and institutions of coercion of
all kinds, of which gentile [clan] society knew
nothing...

Engels elucidates the concept of "power" which is called
the state, a power which arose from society but places itself
above it and alienates itself more and more from it. What does
this power mainly consist of? It consists of special bodies of
armed men having prisons, etc., at their command.

We are justified in speaking of special bodies of armed
men, because the public power which is an attribute of every
state "does not directly coincide" with the armed population,
with its "self-acting armed organisation."

Like all great revolutionary thinkers, Engels tries to
draw the attention of the class-conscious workers to what
prevailing philistinism regards as least worthy of attention,
as the most habitual thing, hallowed by prejudices that are not
only deep-rooted but, one might say petrified. A standing army
and police are the chief instruments of state power. But how
can it be otherwise?

From the viewpoint of the vast majority of Europeans of
the end of the nineteenth century whom Engels was addressing,
and who had not gone through or closely observed a single great
revolution, it could not have been otherwise. They could not
understand at all what a "self-acting armed organisation of the
population" was. When asked why it became necessary to have
special bodies of armed men placed above society and alienating
themselves from it (police and a standing army), the

West-European and Russian philistines are inclined to utter a few phrases borrowed from Spencer or Mikhailovsky, to refer to the growing complexity of social life, the differentiation of functions, and so on.

Such a reference seems "scientific," and effectively lulls the ordinary person to sleep by obscuring the important and basic fact, namely, the split of society into irreconcilably antagonistic classes.

Were it not for this split, the "self-acting armed organisation of the population" would differ from the primitive organisation of a stick-wielding herd of monkeys, or of primitive men, or of men united in clans, by its complexity, its high technical level, and so on. But such an organisation would still be possible.

It is impossible because civilised society is split into antagonistic, and, moreover, irreconcilably antagonistic, classes, whose "self-acting" arming would lead to an armed struggle between them. A state arises, a special power is created, special bodies of armed men, and every revolution, by destroying the state apparatus, shows us the naked class struggle, clearly shows us how the ruling class strives to restore the special bodies of armed men which serve it, and how the oppressed class strives to create a new organisation of this kind, capable of serving the exploited instead of the exploiters.

In the above argument, Engels raises theoretically the very same question which every great revolution raises before us in practice, palpably and, what is more, on a scale of mass action, namely the question of the relationship between "special" bodies of armed men and the "self-acting armed organisation of the population." We shall see how this question is specifically illustrated by the experience of the European and Russian revolutions.

But to return to Engel's exposition.

He points out that sometimes – in certain parts of North America, for example – this public power is weak (he has in mind a rare exception in capitalist society, and those parts of North America in its pre-imperialist days where the free colonist predominated), but that, generally speaking, it grows stronger.

It [the public power] grows stronger, however, in proportion as class antagonisms within the state become more acute, and as adjacent states become larger and more populous. We have only to look at

61

our present-day Europe, where class struggle and
rivalry in conquest have tuned up the public power
to such a pitch that it threatens to swallow the
whole of society and even the state.

This was written not later than the early nineties of the
last century, Engel´s last preface being dated June 16, 1891.
The turn towards imperialism - meaning the complete domination
of the trusts, the omnipotence of the big banks, a grand-scale
colonial policy, and so forth - was only just beginning in
France, and was even weaker in North America and in Germany.
Since then "rivalry in conquest" has taken a gigantic stride,
all the more because by the beginning of the second decade of
the twentieth century the world had been completely divided up
among these "rivals in conquest," i.e., among the predatory
Great Powers. Since then, military and naval armaments have
grown fantastically and the predatory war of 1914-17 for the
domination of the world by Britain or Germany, for the division
of the spoils, has brought the "swallowing" of all the forces
of society by the rapacious state power close to complete
catastrophe.

Engels could, as early as 1891, point to "rivalry in
conquest" as one of the most important distinguishing features
of the foreign policy of the Great Powers, while the
social-chauvinist scoundrels have ever since 1914, when this
rivalry, many times intensified, gave rise to an imperialist
war, been covering up the defence of the predatory interests of
"their own" bourgeoisie with phrases about "defence of the
fatherland," "defence of the republic and the revolution,"
etc.!

3.   The State--An Instrument for the Exploitation of the Oppressed Class

The maintenance of the special public power standing above
society requires taxes and state loans. "...Having public
power and the right to levy taxes," Engels writes, "The
officials now stand, as organs of society, above society. The
free, voluntary respect that was accorded to the organs of the
gentile [clan] constitution does not satisfy them, even if they
could gain it..." Special laws are enacted proclaiming the
sanctity and immunity of the officials. "The shabbiest police
servant" has more "authority" than the representatives of the
clan, but even the head of the military power of a civilised
state may well envy the elder of a clan the "unrestrained
respect of society.

The question of the priveleged position of the officials as
organs of the state power is raised here. The main point
indicated is: what is it that places them above society? We
shall see how this theoretical question was answered in

practice by the Paris Commune in 1871 and how it was obscured
from a reactionary standpoint by Kautsky in 1912.

> ...Because the state arose from the need to hold class
> antagonisms in check, but because it arose, at the
> same time, in the midst of the conflict of these
> classes, it is a rule, the state of the most
> powerful, economically dominant class, which, through
> the medium of the state, becomes also the politically
> dominant class, and thus acquires new means of holding
> down and exploiting the oppressed class...

The ancient feudal states were organs for the exploitation of
the slaves and serfs; likewise,

> the modern representative state is an instrument of
> exploitation of wage labour by capital. By way of
> exception, however, periods occur in which the warring
> classes balance each other so nearly that the state
> power as ostensible mediator acquires, for the
> moment, a certain degree of independence of both...

Such were the absolute monarchies of the seventeenth and
eighteenth centuries, the Bonapartism(3) of the First and
Second Empires in France, and the Bismarck regime in Germany.

Such, as we may add, is the Kerensky government in
republican Russia since it began to persecute the revolutionary
proletariat, at a moment when, owing to the leadership of the
petty-bourgeois democrats, the Soviets have _already_ become
impotent, while the bourgeoise are not _yet_ strong enough simply
to disperse them.

In a democratic republic, Engels continues, "wealth
exercises its power indirectly, but all the more surely,"
first, by means of the "direct corruption of officials"
(America); secondly, by means of an alliance of the government
and the Stock Exchange" (France and America).

At present, imperialism and the domination of the banks
have "developed" into an exceptional art both these methods of
upholding and giving effect to the omnipotence of wealth in
democratic republics of all descriptions. Since, for instance,
in the very first months of the Russian democratic republic,
one might say during the honeymoon of the "socialist" S.R.s and
Mensheviks joined in wedlock to the bourgeoisie, in the
coalition government, Mr. Palchinsky obstructed every measure
intended for curbing the capitalists and their marauding
practices, their plundering of the state by means of war
contracts; and since later on Mr. Palchinsky, upon resigning
from the Cabinet (and being, of course, replaced by another

quite similar Palchinsky), was "rewarded" by the capitalists with a lucrative job with a salary of 120,00 rubles per annum - what would you call that? Direct or indirect bribery? An alliance of the government and the syndicates, or "merely" friendly relations? What role do the Chernovs, Tseretelis, Avksentyevs and Skobelevs play? Are they the "direct" or only the indirect allies of the millionaire treasury-looters?

Another reason why the omnipotence of "wealth" is more certain in a democratic republic is that it does not depend on defects in the political machinery or on the faulty political shell of capitalism. A democratic republic is the best possible political shell for capitalism, and, therefore, once capital has gained possession of this very best shell (through the Palchinskys, Chernovs, Tseretelis and Co.), it establishes its power so securely, so firmly, that no change of persons, institutions or parties in the bourgeois-democratic republic can shake it.

We must also note that Engels is most explicit in calling universal suffrage as well an instrument of bourgeois rule. Universal suffrage, he says, obviously taking account of the long experience of German Social-Democracy, is "the gauge of the maturity of the working class. It cannot and never will be anything more in the present-day state."

The petty-bourgeois democrats, such as our Socialist-Revolutionaries and Mensheviks, and also their twin brothers, all the social-chauvinists and opportunists of Western Europe, expect just this "more" from universal suffrage. They themselves share, and instil into the minds of the people, the false notion that universal suffrage "in the present-day state" is really capable of revealing the will of the majority of the working people and of securing its realisation.

Here we can only indicate this false notion, only to point out that Engels's perfectly clear, precise and concrete statement is distorted at every step in the propaganda and agitation of the "official" (i.e., opportunist) socialist parties. A detailed exposure of the utter falsity of this notion which Engels brushes aside here is given in our further account of the views of Marx and Engels on the "present-day" state.

Engels gives a general summary of his views in the most popular of his works in the following words:

The state, then, has not existed from all eternity.
There have been societies that did without it, that
had no idea of the state and state power. At a
certain stage of economic development, which was necessarily bound up with the split of society into
classes, the state became a necessity owing to this
split. We are now rapidly approaching a stage in the
development of production at which the existence of
these classes not only will have ceased to be a necessity, but will become a positive hindrance to
production. They will fall as inevitably as they
arose at an earlier stage. Along with them the state
will inevitably fall. Society, which will reorganise
production on the basis of a free and equal association of the producers, will put the whole machinery
of state where it will then belong; into a museum
of antiquities, by the side of the spinning-wheel
and the bronze axe.

We do not often come across this passage in the propaganda
and agitation literature of the present-day Social-Democrats.
Even when we do come across it, it is mostly quoted in the same
manner as one bows before an icon, i.e., it is done to show
official respect for Engels, and no attempt is made to gauge
the breadth and depth of the revolution that this relegating of
"the whole machinery of state to a museum of antiquities"
implies. In most cases we do not even find an understanding of
what Engels calls the state machine.

4. The "Withering Away" of the State, and Violent Revolution

Engels´s words regarding the "withering away" of the state
are so widely known, they are so often quoted, and so clearly
reveal the essence of the customary adaptation of Marxism to
opportunism that we must deal with them in detail. We shall
quote the whole argument from which they are taken.

The proletariat seizes state power and turns the means
of production into state property to begin with. But
thereby it abolishes itself as the proletariat, abolishes
all class distinctions and class antagonisms, and abolishes
also the state as state. Society thus far, operating amid
class antagonisms, needed the state, that is, an organisation of the particular exploiting class, for the maintenance of its external conditions of production, and, therefore, especially, for the purpose of forcibly keeping the
exploited class in the conditions of oppression determined
by the given mode of production (slavery, serfdom
or bondage, wage-labour). The state was the official
representative of society as a whole, its concentration in
a visible corporation. But it was this only insofar as it
was the state of that class which itself represented, for

65

its own time, society as a whole; in ancient times, the
state of slave-owning citizens; in the Middle Ages, of the
feudal nobility; in our own time, of the bourgeoisie. When
at last it becomes the real representative of the whole of
society, it renders itself unnecessary. As soon as there
is no longer any social class to be held in subjection, as
soon as class rule, and the individual struggle for
existence based upon the present anarchy in production,
with the collisions and excesses arising from this
struggle, are removed, nothing more remains to be held in
subjugation - nothing necessitating a special coercive
force, a state. The first act by which the state really
comes forward as the representative of the whole of
society - the taking possession of the means of production
in the name of society - is also its last independent act
as a state. State interference in social relations becomes,
in one domain after another, superfluous, and then dies
down of itself. The government of persons is replaced by
the administration of things, and by the conduct of
processes of production. The state is not `abolished.´
It withers away. This gives the measure of the value
of the phrase `a free people´s state,´ both as to
its justifiable use for a time from an agitational point of
view, and as to its ultimate scientific insufficiency;
and also of the so-called anarchists´ demands
that the state be abolished overnight. (Herr
Eugen Dühring´s Revolution in Science [Anti-
Dühring], pp. 301-03, third German edition.)(4)

It is safe to say that of this argument of Engels´s, which
is so remarkably rich in ideas, only one point has become an
integral part of socialist thought among modern socialist
parties, namely, that according to Marx the state "withers
away" - as distinct from the anarchist doctrine of the
"abolition" of the state. To prune Marxism to such an extent
means reducing it to opportunism, for this `interpretation´
only leaves a vague notion of a slow, even, gradual change, of
absence of leaps and storms, of absence of revolution. The
current, widespread, popular, if one may say so, conception of
the "withering away" of the state undoubtedly means obscuring,
if not repudiating, revolution.

Such an "interpretation," however, is the crudest
distortion of Marxism, advantageous only to the bourgeoisie.
In point of theory, it is based on disregard for the most
important circumstances and considerations indicated in, say,
Engels´s "summary" argument we have just quoted in full.

In the first place, at the very outset of his argument,
Engels says that, in seizing state power, the proletariat
thereby "abolishes the state as state." It is not done to

66

ponder over the meaning of this. Generally, it is either ignored altogether or is considered to be something in the nature of "Hegelian weakness" on Engels's part. As a matter of fact, however, these words briefly express the experience of one of the greatest proletarian revolutions, the Paris Commune of 1871, of which we shall speak in greater detail in its proper place. As a matter of fact, Engels speaks here of the proletarian revolution "abolishing" the bourgeois state, while the words about the state withering away refer to the remnants of the proletarian state after the socialist revolution. According to Engels, the bourgeois state does not "wither away," but is "abolished" by the proletariat in the course of the revolution. What withers away after this revolution is the proletarian state or semi-state.

Secondly, the state is a "special coercive force." Engels gives this splendid and extremely profound definition here with the utmost lucidity. And from it follows that the "special coercive force" for the suppression of the proletariat by the bourgeoisie, of millions of working people by handfuls of the rich, must be replaced by a "special coercive force" for the suppression of the bourgeoisie by the proletariat (the dictatorship of the proletariat). This is precisely what is meant by "abolition of the state as state." This is precisely the "act" of taking possession of the means of production in the name of society. And it is self-evident that such a replacement of one (bourgeois) "special force" by another (proletarian) "special force" cannot possibly take place in the form of "withering away."

Thirdly, in speaking of the state "withering away," and even the more graphic and colorful "dying down of itself," Engels refers quite clearly and definitely to the period after "the state has taken possession of the means of production in the name of the whole of society," that is, after the socialist revolution. We all know that the political form of the "state" at that time is the most complete democracy. But it never enters the head of any of the opportunists, who shamelessly distort Marxism, that Engels is consequently speaking here of democracy "dying down of itself," or "withering away." This seems very strange at first sight. But it is "incomprehensible" only to those who have not thought about democracy also being a state and, consequently, also disappearing when the state disappears. Revolution alone can "abolish" the bourgeois state. The state in general, i.e., the most complete democracy, can only "wither away."

Fourthly, after formulating his famous proposition that "the state withers away," Engels at once explains specifically that this proposition is directed against both the opportunists and the anarchists. In doing this, Engels puts in the

67

forefront that conclusion, drawn from the proposition that "the state withers away," which is directed against the opportunists.

One can wager that out of every 10,000 persons who have read or heard about the "withering away" of the state, 9,990 are completely unaware, or do not remember, that Engels directed his conclusions from that proposition not against the anarchists alone. And of the remaining ten, probably nine do not know the meaning of a "free people's state" or why an attack on this slogan means an attack on the opportunists. This is how history is written! This is how a great revolutionary teaching is imperceptibly falsified and adapted to prevailing philistinism. The conclusion directed against the anarchists has been repeated thousands of times; it has been vulgarised, and rammed into people's heads in the shallowest form, and has acquired the strength of a prejudice, whereas the conclusion directed against the opportunists has been obscured and "forgotten"!

The "free people's state" was a programme demand and a catchword current among the German Social-Democrats in the seventies. This catchword is devoid of all political content except that it describes the concept of democracy in a pompous philistine fashion. Insofar as it hinted in a legally permissible manner at a democratic republic, Engels was prepared to "justify" its use "for a time" from an agitational point of view. But it was an opportunist catchword, for it amounted to something more than prettifying bourgeois democracy, and was also failure to understand the socialist criticism of the state in general. We are in favour of a democratic republic as the best form of state for the proletariat under capitalism. But we have no right to forget that wage slavery is the lot of the people even in the most democratic bourgeois republic. Furthermore, every state is a "special force" for the suppression of the oppressed class. Consequently, every state is not "free" and not a "people's state." Marx and Engels explained this repeatedly to their party comrades in the seventies.

Fifthly, the same work of Engels's, whose argument about the withering away of the state everyone remembers, also contains an argument of the significance of violent revolution. Engels's historical analysis of its role becomes a veritable panegyric on violent revolution. This "no one remembers." It is not done in modern socialist parties to talk or even think about the significance of this idea, and it plays no part whatever in their daily propaganda and agitation among the people. And yet it is inseparably bound up with the "withering away" of the state into one harmonious whole.

68

Here is Engels's argument:

...That force, however, plays yet another role [other
than that of a diabolical power] in history, a revolutionary role; that, in the words of Marx, it is the mid-
wife of every old society which is pregnant with a new
one, that it is the instrument with which social movement forces its way through and shatters the dead, fos-
silised political forms - of this there is not a word in
Herr Duhring. It is only with sighs and groans that
he admits the possibility that force will perhaps be
necessary for the overthrow of an economy based on
exploitation - unfortunately, because all use of force
demoralises, he says, the person who uses it. And this
in spite of the immense moral and spiritual impetus
which has been given by every victorious revolution!
And this in Germany, where a violent collision - which
may, after all, be forced on the people - would at least
have the advantage of wiping out the servility which
has penetrated the nation's mentality following the
humiliation of the Thirty Years' War.(5) And this person's
mode of thought - dull, insipid and impotent - presumes to
impose itself on the most revolutionary party that
history has known! (P. 193, third German edition, Part
II, end of Chap. IV.)(6)

How can this panegyric on violent revolution, which Engels
insistently brought to the attention of the German
Social-Democrats between 1878 and 1894, i.e., right up to the
time of his death, be combined with the theory of the
"withering away" of the state to form a single theory?

Usually the two are combined by means of eclecticism, by
an unprincipled or sophistic selection made arbitrarily (or to
please the powers that be) of first one, then another argument,
and in ninety-nine cases out of a hundred, if not more, it is
the idea of the "withering away" that is placed in the
forefront. Dialectics are replaced by eclecticism - this is
the most usual, the most widespread practice to be met with in
present-day official Social-Democratic literature in relation
to Marxism. This sort of substitution is, of course, nothing
new; it was observed even in the history of classical Greek
philosophy. In falsifying Marxism in opportunist fashion, the
substitution of eclecticism for dialectics is the easiest way
of deceiving the people. It gives an illusory satisfaction; it
seems to take into account all sides of the process, all trends
of development, all the conflicting influences, and so forth,
whereas in reality it provides no integral and revolutionary
conception of the process of social development at all.

We have already said above, and shall show more fully

later, that theory of Marx and Engels of the inevitability of a violent revolution refers to the bourgeois state. The latter cannot be superseded by the proletarian state (the dictatorship of the proletariat) through the process of "withering away," but, as a general rule, only through a violent revolution. The panegyric Engels sang in its honour, and which fully corresponds to Marx's repeated statements (see the concluding passages of The Poverty of Philosophy and the Communist Manifesto,(7) with their proud open proclamation of the inevitability of a violent revolution; see what Marx wrote nearly thirty years later, in criticising the Gotha Programme of 1875, when he mercilessly castigated the opportunist character of that programme) - this panegyric is by no means a mere "impulse," a mere declamation or a polemical sally. The necessity of systematically imbuing the masses with this and precisely this view of violent revolution lies at the root of the entire theory of Marx and Engels. The betrayal of their history by the now prevailing social-chauvinist and Kautskyite trends expresses itself strikingly in both these trends ignoring such propaganda and agitation.

The suppression of the bourgeois state by the proletarian state is impossible without a violent revolution. The abolition of the proletarian state, i.e., of the state in general, is impossible except through the process of "withering away."

A detailed and concrete elaboration of these views was given by Marx and Engels when they studied each particular revolutionary situation, when they analysed the lessons of the experience of each particular revolution. We shall now pass to this, undoubtedly the most important, part of their history.

II.   The State and Revolution. The Experience of 1848-51

1.   The Eve of the Revolution
The first works of mature Marxism - The Poverty of Philosophy and the Communist Manifesto - appeared just on the eve of the revolution of 1848. For this reason, in addition to presenting the general principles of Marxism, they reflect to a certain degree the concrete revolutionary situation of the time. It will, therefore, be more expedient, perhaps, to examine what the authors of these works said about the state immediately before they drew conclusions from the experience of the years 1848-51.

In The Poverty of Philosophy, Marx wrote:

...The working class, in the course of development, will substitute for the old bourgeois society an association which will preclude classes and their antagonism, and there will be no more political power proper, since political power is precisely the official expresssion of class antagonism in bourgeois society. (P. 182, German edition, 1885.)(8)

It is instructive to compare this general exposition of the idea of the state disappearing after the abolition of classes with the exposition contained in the Communist Manifesto, written by Marx and Engels a few months later - in November 1847, to be exact:

... In depicting the most general phases of the develop- ment of the proletariat, we traced the more or less veiled civil war, raging within existing society up to the point where that warbreaks out into open revolution, and where the violent overthrow of the bourgeoisie lays the foundation for the sway of the proletariat... ...We have seen above that the first step in the revolution by the working class is to raise the proletariat to the position of ruling class, to win the battle of democracy. The proletariat will use its political supremacy to wrest, by degrees, all capital from the bourgeoisie, to centralise all instruments of production in the hands of the state, i.e., of the proletariat organised as the ruling class; and to increase the total of productive forces as rapidly as possible. (Pp. 34 and 37, seventh German edition, 1906.)(9)

Here we have a formulation of one of the most remarkable and most important ideas of Marxism on the subject of the state, namely, the idea of the "dictatorship of the proletariat" (as Marx and Engels began to call it after the Paris Commune); and also, a highly interesting definition of the state, which is also one of the "forgotten words" of Marxism: "the state, i.e., the proletariat organised as the ruling class."

This definition of the state has never been explained in the prevailing propaganda and agitation literature of the official Social-Democratic parties. More than that, it has been deliberately ignored, for it is absolutely irreconcilable with reformism, and is a slap in the face for the common opportunist prejudices and philistine illusions about the "peaceful development of democracy."

The proletariat needs the state - this is repeated by all the opportunists, social-chauvinists and Kautskyites, who assure us that this is what Marx taught. But they "forget" to add that, in the first place, according to Marx, the proletariat needs only a state which is withering away, i.e., a state so constituted that it begins to wither away immediately, and cannot but wither away. And, secondly, the working people need a "state, i.e., the proletariat organised as the ruling class."

The state is a special organisation of force: it is an organisation of violence for the suppression of some class. What class must the proletariat suppress? Naturally, only the exploiting class, i.e., the bourgeoisie. The working people need the state only to suppress the resistance of the exploiters, and only the proletariat can direct this suppression, can carry it out. For the proletariat is the only class that is consistently revolutionary, the only class that can unite all the working and exploited people in the struggle against the bourgeoisie, in completely removing it.

The exploiting classes need political rule to maintain exploitation, i.e., in the selfish interests of an insignificant minority against the vast majority of the people. The exploited classes need political rule in order to completely abolish all exploitation, i.e., in the interests of the vast majority of the people, and against the insignificant minority consisting of the modern slave-owners - the land-owners and capitalists.

The petty-bourgeois democrats, those sham socialists who replaced the class struggle by dreams of class harmony, even pictured the socialist transformation in a dreamy fashion - not as the overthrow of the rule of the exploiting class, but as the peaceful submission of the minority to the majority which has become aware of its aims. This petty-bourgeois utopia, which is inseparable from the idea of the state being above classes, led in practice to the betrayal of the interests of the working classes, as was shown, for example, by the history of the French revolutions of 1848 and 1871, and by the experience of "socialist" participation in bourgeois Cabinets in Britain, France, Italy and other countries at the turn of the century.

All his life Marx fought against this petty-bourgeois socialism, now revived in Russia by the Socialist-Revolutionary and Menshevik parties. He developed his theory of the class struggle consistently down to the theory of political power, of the state.

The overthrow of bourgeois rule can be accomplished only by the proletariat, the particular class whose economic conditions of existence prepare it for this task and provide it

72

with the possibility and the power to perform it. While the
bourgeoisie break up and disintegrate the peasantry and all the
petty-bourgeois groups, they weld together, unite and organise
the proletariat. Only the proletariat - by virtue of the
economic role it plays in large-scale production - is capable
of being the leader of all the working and exploited people,
whom the bourgeoisie exploit, oppress and crush, often not less
but more than they do the proletarians, but who are incapable
of waging an independent struggle for their emancipation.

The theory of class struggle, applied by Marx to the
question of the state and the socialist revolution, leads as a
matter of course to the recognition of the political rule of
the proletariat, of its dictatorship, i.e., of undivided power
directly backed by the armed force of the people. The
overthrow of the bourgeoisie can be achieved only by the
proletariat becoming the ruling class, capable of crushing the
inevitable and desperate resistance of the bourgeoisie, and of
organising all the working and exploited people for the new
economic system.

The proletariat needs state power, a centralised
organisation of force, an organisation of violence, both to
crush the resistance of the exploiters and to lead the enormous
mass of the population - the peasants, the petty bourgeoisie,
and semi-proletarians - in the work of organising a socialist
economy.

By educating the workers´ party, Marxists educate the
vanguard of the proletariat, capable of assuming power and
leading the whole people to socialism, of directing and
organising the new system, of being the teacher, the guide, the
leader of all the working and exploited people in organising
their social life without the bourgeoisie and against the
bourgeoisie. By contrast, the opportunism now prevailing
trains the members of the workers´ party to be the
representatives of the better-paid workers, who lose touch with
the masses, "get along" fairly well under capitalism, and sell
their birthright for a mess of pottage, i.e., renouce their
role as revolutionary leaders of the people against the
bourgeoisie.

Marx´s theory of "the state, i.e., the proletariat
organised as the ruling class," is inseparably bound up with
the whole of his doctrine of the revolutionary role of the
proletariat in history. The culmination of this role is the
proletarian dictatorship, the political rule of the
proletariat.

But since the proletariat needs the state as a special
form of organisation of violence against the bourgeoisie, the

following conclusion suggests itself: it is conceivable that
such an organisation can be created without first abolishing,
destroying the state machine created by the bourgeoisie for
themselves? The Communist Manifesto leads straight to this
conclusion, and it is of this conclusion that Marx speaks when
summing up the experience of the revolution of 1848-51.

2. The Revolution Summed Up
      Marx sums up his conclusions from the revolution of
1848-51, on the subject of the state we are concerned with, in
the following argument contained in The Eighteenth Brumaire of
Louis Bonaparte:

> ...But the revolution is thoroughgoing. It is still
> journeying through purgatory. It does its work
> methodically. By December 2, 1851
> [the day of Louis Bonaparte´s coup
> d´etat], it had completed one half of its preparatory work.
> It is now completing its other half. First it perfected
> the parliamentary power, in order to overthrow it.
> Now that it has attained this, it is perfecting the
> executive power, reducing it to its purest expression,
> isolating it, setting it up against itself as the sole
> object, in order to concentrate all its forces of
> destruction against it [italics ours]. And when it
> has done this second half of its preliminary work,
> Europe will leap from its seat and exultantly exclaim:
> well grubbed, old mole!
> This executive power with its enormous bureaucratic
> and military organisation, with its vast and ingenious
> state machinery, with a host of officials numbering
> half a million, besides an army of another half million,
> this appalling parasitic body, which enmeshes the
> body of French society and chokes all its pores, sprang
> up in the days of absolute monarchy, with the
> decay of the feudal system, which it helped to hasten.

The first French Revolution developed centralisation, "but at
the same time" it increased "the extent, the attributes and the
number of agents of governmental power. Napolean completed
this state machinery." The legitimate monarchy and the July
monarchy

> added nothing but a greater division of labour...
> ...Finally, in its struggle against the revolution, the
> parliamentary republic found itself compelled to strengthen,
> along with repressive measures, the resources and centrali-
> sation of governmental power. All revolutions perfected
> this machine instead of smashing it [italics ours]. The
> parties that contended in turn for domination regarded the

possesion of this huge state edifice as the principal spoils of the victor. (The Eighteenth Brumaire of Louis Bonaparte, pp. 98-99, fourth edition, Hamburg, 1907.)(10)

In this remarkable argument Marxism takes a tremendous step forward compared with the Communist Manifesto. In the latter the question of the state is still treated in an extremely abstract manner, in the most general terms and expressions. In the above-quoted passage, the question is treated in a concrete manner, and the conclusion is extremely precise, definite, practical and palpable: all previous revolutions perfected the state machine, whereas it must be broken, smashed.

This conclusion is the chief and fundamental point in the Marxist theory of the state. And it is precisely this fundamental point which has been completely ignored by the dominant official Social-Democratic parties and, indeed, distorted (as we shall see later) by the foremost theoretician of the Second International, Karl Kautsky.

The Communist Manifesto gives a general summary of history, which compels us to regard the state as the organ of class rule and lead us to the inevitable conclusion that the proletariat cannot overthrow the bourgeoisie without first winning political power, without attaining political supremacy, without transforming the state into the "proletariat organised as the ruling class"; and that this proletarian state will begin to wither away immediately after its victory because the state is unnecessary and cannot exist in a society in which there are no class antagonisms. The question as to how, from the point of view of historical development, the replacement of the bourgeois by the proletarian state is to take place is not raised here.

This is the question Marx raises and answers in 1852. True to his philosophy of dialectical materialism, Marx takes as his basis the historical experience of the great years of revolution, 1848 to 1851. Here, as everywhere else, his theory is a summing up of experience, illuminated by a profound philosophical conception of the world and a rich knowledge of history.

The problem of the state is put specifically: How did the bourgeois state, the state machine necessary for the rule of the bourgeoisie, come into being historically? What changes did it undergo, what evolution did it perform in the course of bourgeois revolutions and in the face of the independent actions of the oppressed classes? What are the tasks of the proletariat in relation to this state machine?

The centralised state power that is peculiar to bourgeois society came into being in the period of the fall of absolutism. Two institutions most characteristic of this state machine are the bureaucracy and the standing army. In their works, Marx and Engels repeatedly show that the bourgeoisie are connected with these institutions by thousands of threads. Every worker's experience illustrates this connection in an extremely graphic and impressive manner. From its own bitter experience, the working class learns to recognise this connection. That is why it so easily grasps and so firmly learns the doctrine which the petty-bourgeois democrats either ignorantly or flippantly deny, or still more flippantly admit "in general," while forgetting to draw appropriate practical conclusions.

The bureaucracy and the standing army are a "parasite" on the body of bourgeois society - a parasite created by the internal antagonisms which rend that society, but a parasite which "chokes" all its vital pores. The Kautskyite opportunism now prevailing in official Social-Democracy considers the view that the state is a <u>parasitic organism</u> to be the peculiar and exclusive attribute of anarchism. It goes without saying that this distortion of Marxism is of vast advantage to those philistines who have reduced socialism to the unheard-of disgrace of justifying and prettifying the imperialist war by applying to it the concept of "defence of the fatherland"; but it is unquestionably a distortion, nevertheless.

The development, perfection and strengthening of the bureaucratic and military apparatus proceeded during all the numerous bourgeois revolutions which Europe has witnessed since the fall of feudalism. In particular, it is the petty bourgeoisie who are attracted to the side of the big bourgeoisie and are largely subordinated to them through this apparatus, which provides the upper sections of peasants, small artisans, tradesmen and the like with comparatively comfortable, quiet and respectable jobs raising their holders <u>above</u> the people. Consider what happened in Russia during the six months following February 27, 1917. The official posts which formerly were given by preference to the Black Hundreds(11) have now become the spoils of the Cadets, Mensheviks and Socialist-Revolutionaries. Nobody has really thought of introducing any serious reforms. Every effort has been made to put off "until the Constituent Assembly meets," and to steadily put off its convocation until after the war!(12) But there has been no delay, no waiting for the Constituent Assembly, in the matter of dividing the spoils, of getting the lucrative jobs of ministers, deputy ministers, governors-general, etc., etc.! The game of combinations that has been played in forming the government has been, in essence,

only an expression of this division and redivision of the
"spoils," which has been going on above and below, throughout
the country, in every department of central and local
government. The six months between February 27 and August 27,
1917, can be summed up, objectively summed up beyond all
dispute, as follows: reforms shelved, distribution of official
jobs accomplished and "mistakes" in the distribution corrected
by a few redistributions.

But the more bureaucratic apparatus is "redistributed"
among the various bourgeois and petty-bourgeois parties (among
Cadets, Socialist-Revolutionaries and Mensheviks in the case of
Russia), the more keenly aware the oppressed classes, and the
proletariat at their head, became of their irreconcilable
hostility to the whole of bourgeois society. Hence the need
for all bourgeois parties, even for the most democratic and
"revolutionary-democratic" among them, to intensify repressive
measures against the revolutionary proletariat, to strengthen
the apparatus of coercion, i.e., the state machine. This
course of events compels the revolution "to concentrate all its
forces of destruction" against the state power, and to set
itself the aim, not of improving the state machine, but of
smashing and destroying it.

It was not logical reasoning, but actual developments, the
actual experience of 1848-51, that led to the matter being
presented in this way. The extent to which Marx held strictly
to the solid ground of historical experience can be seen from
the fact that, in 1852, he did not yet specifically raise the
question of what was to take place of the state machine to be
destroyed. Experience had not yet provided material for
dealing with this question, which history placed in the agenda
later on, in 1871. In 1852, all that could be established with
the accuracy of scientific observation was that the proletarian
revolution had approached the task of "concentrating all its
forces of destruction" against the state power, of "smashing"
the state machine.

Here the question may arise: is it correct to generalise
the experience, observations and conclusions of Marx, to apply
them to a field that is wider than the history of France during
the three years 1848-51? Before proceeding to deal with this
question, let us recall a remark made by Engels and then
examine the facts. In his introduction to the third edition of
The Eighteenth Brumaire, Engels wrote:

...France is the country where, more than anywhere
else, the historical class struggles were each
time fought out to a finish, and where, consequently,
the changing political forms within which they move and

77

in which their results are summarised have been
stamped in the sharpest outlines. The centre of feudalism
in the Middle Ages, the model country, since the
Renaissance, of a unified monarchy based on social estates,
France demolished feudalism in the Great Revolution and
established the rule of the bourgeoisie
in a classical purity unequalled by any other European land.
And the struggle of the upward-striving proletariat
against the ruling bourgeoisie appeared here in an
acute form unknown elsewhere. (P. 4, 1907 edition.)(13)

The last remark is out of date inasmuch as since 1871
there has been a lull in the revolutionary struggle of the
French proletariat, although, long as this lull may be, it does
not at all preclude the possibility that in the coming
proletarian revolution France may show herself to be the
classic country of the class struggle to a finish.

Let us, however, cast a general glance over the history of
the advanced countries at the turn of the century. We shall
see that the same process went on more slowly, in more varied
forms, in a much wider field: on the one hand, the development
of parliamentary power" both in the republican countries
(France, America, Switzerland), and in the monarchies (Britain,
Germany to a certain extent, Italy, the Scandinavian countries,
etc.); on the other hand, a struggle for power among the
various bourgeois and petty-bourgeois parties which distributed
and redistributed the "spoils" of office, with the foundations
of bourgeois society unchanged; and, lastly, the perfection and
consolidation of the "executive power," of its bureaucratic and
military apparatus.

There is not the slightest doubt that these features are
common to the whole of the modern evolution of all capitalist
states in general. In the three years 1848-51 France
displayed, in a swift, sharp, concentrated form, the very same
processes of development which are peculiar to the whole
capitalist world.

Imperialism - the era of blank capital, the era of
gigantic capitalist monopolies, of the development of monopoly
capitalism into state-monopoly capitalism - has clearly shown
an extraordinary strengthening of the "state machine" and an
unprecedented growth in its bureaucratic and military apparatus
in connection with the intensification of repressive measures
against the proletariat both in the monarchical and in the
freest, republican countries.

World history is now undoubtedly leading, on an
incomparably larger scale than in 1852, to the "concentration
of all the forces" of the proletarian revolution on the

"destruction" of the state machine.

What the proletariat will put in its place is suggested by the highly instructive material furnished by the Paris Commune.

3. The Presentation of the Question by Marx in 1852 (14)
In 1907, Mehring, in the magazine Neue Zeit (Vol. XXV,2, p. 164), published extracts from Marx´s letter to Weydemeyer dated March 5, 1852. This letter, among other things, contains the following remarkable observation:

> And now as to myself, no credit is due to me for discovering the existence of classes in modern society or the struggle between them. Long before me bourgeois historians had desribed the historical development of this class struggle and bourgeois economists, the economic anatomy of the classes. What I did that was new was to prove: 1) that the existence of classes is only bounded up with particular, historical phases in the development of production (historische Entwicklungsphasen der Produktion), 2) that the class struggle necessarily leads to the dictatorship of the proletariat, 3) that this dictatorship itself only constitutes the transition to the abolition of all classes and to a classless society...(15)

In these words Marx succeeded in expressing with striking clarity, first, the chief and radical difference between his theory and that of the foremost and most profound thinkers of the bourgeoisie; and, secondly, the essence of his theory of the state.

It is often said and written that the main point in Marx´s theory is the class struggle. But this is wrong. And this wrong notion very often results in an opportunist distortion of Marxism and its falsification in a spirit acceptable to the bourgeoisie. For the theory of the class struggle was created not by Marx, but by the bourgeoisie before Marx, and, generally speaking, it is acceptable to the bourgeoisie. Those who recognise only the class struggle are not yet Marxists; they may be found to be still within the bounds of bourgeois thinking and bourgeois politics. To confine Marxism to the theory of the class struggle means curtailing Marxism, distorting it, reducing it to something acceptable to the bourgeoisie. Only he is a Marxist who extends the recognition of the class struggle to the recognition of the dictatorship of the proletariat. This is what constitutes the most profound distinction between the Marxist and the ordinary petty (as well as big) bourgeois. This is the touchstone on which the real understanding and recogntion of Marxism should be tested. And it is not surprising that when the history of Europe brought

the working class face to face with this question as a
practical issue, not only all the opportunists and reformists,
but all the Kautskyites (people who vacillate between reformism
and Marxism) proved to be miserable philistines and
petty-bourgeois democrats repudiating the dictatorship of the
proletariat. Kautsky´s pamphlet, The Dictatorship of the
Proletariat, published in August 1918, i.e., long after the
first edition of the present book, is a perfect example of
petty-bourgeois distortion of Marxism and base renunciation of
it in deeds, while hypocrtically recognising it in words (see
my pamphlet, The Proletarian Revolution and the Renegade
Kautsky, Petrograd and Moscow, 1918).

Opportunism today, as represented by its principal
spokesman, the ex-Marxist Karl Kautsky, fits in completely with
Marx´s characterisation of the bourgeois position quoted above,
for this opportunism limits recognition of the class struggle
to the sphere of bourgeois relations. (Within this sphere,
within its framework, not a single educated liberal will refuse
to recognise the class struggle "in principle"!) Opportunism
does not extend recognition of the class struggle to the
cardinal point, to the period of transition from capitalism to
communism, of the overthrow and the complete abolition of the
bourgeoisie. In reality, this period inevitably is a period of
an unprecedentedly violent class struggle in unprecedentedly
acute forms, and, consequently, during this period the state
must inevitably be a state that is democratic in a new way (for
the proletariat and the propertyless in general) and
dictatorial in a new way (against the bourgeoisie).

Further. The essence of Marx´s theory of the state has
been mastered only by those who realise that the dictatorship
of a single class is necessary not only for every class society
in general, not only for the proletariat which has overthrown
the bourgeoisie, but also for the entire historical period
which separates capitalism from "classless society," from
communism. Bourgeois states are most varied in their form, but
their essence is the same: all these states, whatever their
form, in the final analysis are inevitably the dictatorship of
the bourgeoisie. The transition from capitalism to communism
is certainly bound to yield a tremendous abundance and variety
of political forms, but the essence will inevitably be the
same: The dictatorship of the proletariat.

Notes

1. Marx and Engels, Selected Works, Vol. 3, Moscow, 1973, pp. 326-27. Further below Lenin quotes from the same work (op. cit., pp. 327-30).
2. The gentile or clan organisation of society, i.e., the primitive communal system, was the first socio-economic formation in human history. It was a community of blood relatives united by economic and social ties. Its relations of production were founded on social ownership of the means of production and an egalitarian distribution of products. In the main, this conformed to the low level of development of the productive forces in that period.
3. Bonapartism (named after the two Bonaparte emperors) - a term used to designate a government that seeks to give the impression of being non-partisan and utilises the sharp struggle between the parties of the capitalists and the working class. While actually serving the interests of the capitalists, such a government, more than any other, deceives the workers with promises and paltry doles.
4. Marx and Engels, Anti-Dühring, Moscow, 1962, pp. 384-85.
5. The Thirty Years' War of 1618-48 - the first general European War caused by an aggravation of contradictions between various groups of European states. These contradictions took the shape of a struggle between Protestants and Catholics. Germany became the main arena of this struggle, an object of military plunder and predatory claims. The war terminated with the conclusion of the Peace of Westphalia, which legalised the political dismemberment of Germany.
6. Marx and Engels, Anti-Dühring, Moscow, 1962, pp. 253-54.
7. This was the programme adopted in 1875 by the Socialist Workers' Party of Germany at a Congress in Gotha where the two then existing German Socialist parties merged. These were the Eisenachers (led by Bebel and Liebknecht and ideologically influenced by Marx and Engels) and the Lassalleans. The programme suffered from eclecticism and was opportunist; on major issues the Eisenachers made concessions to the Lassalleans and accepted their formulations. Marx (in the Critique of the Gotha Programme) and Engels (in a letter to Bebel on March 18-28, 1875), levelled annihilating criticism at the draft Gotha Programme, regarding it as a considerable step backward compared with the Eisenach Programme of 1869.
8. Marx and Engels, The Poverty of Philosophy, Moscow, 1966, p. 151.
9. Marx and Engels, Selected Works, Vol. 1, Moscow, 1973, pp. 118-19, 126.
10. Marx and Engels, Selected Works, Vol. 1, Moscow, 1973, pp. 476-77.
11. Lenin refers to the bourgeois-democratic revolution in Russia of February 27 (March 12), 1917, which deposed the tsar and led to the formation of a bourgeois Provisional Government.

12.   In a statement made on March 2 (15), 1917 the Provisional
Government announced that it would convene a Constituent
Assembly. Elections were set for September 17 (30), 1917.
However, the elections were postponed until November 12 (25).
The Constituent Assembly was convened by the Soviet Government
in Petrograd on January 5 (18), 1918. The elections were held
according to the electoral lists drawn up before the Great
October Socialist Revolution. On January 6 (19), 1918, after
the Constituent Assembly refused to endorse the decrees of the
Second Congress of Soviets on peace, on land and on the
transfer of power to the Soviets, it was dissolved by decision
of the All-Russia Central Executive Committee.
13.   Marx and Engels, Selected Works, Vol. 1, Moscow, 1973, p.
396.
14.   Added in the second edition.
15.   Marx and Engels, Selected Correspondence, Moscow, 1965, p.
69.

FOUNDATIONS OF LENINISM(1)

J. Stalin

The Party

In the pre-revolutionary period, in the period of more or
less peaceful development, when the parties of the Second
International were the predominant force in the labour movement
and parliamentary forms of struggle were regarded as the
principal forms, the Party neither had nor could have that
great and decisive importance which it acquired afterwards in
the midst of open revolutionary battles. In defending the
Second International against the attacks that were made upon
it, Kautsky says that the parties of the Second International
are instruments of peace and not war, that for that very reason
they were powerless to take any far-reaching steps during the
war, during the period of revolutionary action by the
proletariat. That is absolutely true. But what does it prove?
It proves that the parties of the Second International are not
suitable for the revolutionary struggle of the proletariat,
that they are not militant parties of the proletariat leading
the workers to power, but an election apparatus suitable for
parliamentary elections and parliamentary struggle. This,
properly speaking, explains why, in the days when the
opportunists of the Second International were dominant, it was
not the Party but the parliamentary fraction that was the
fundamental political organisation of the proletariat. It is
well known that the Party at that time was really an appendage
or an auxiliary of the parliamentary fraction. It is
superfluous to add that under such circumstances and with such
a Party at its head, it was utterly impossible to prepare the
proletariat for revolution.

With the dawn of the new period, however, matters changed
radically. The new period is a period of open collisions
between the classes, a period of revolutionary action by the
proletariat, a period of proletarian revolution; it is the
period of the immediate mustering of forces for the overthrow
of imperialism, for the seizure of power by the proletariat.
This period confronts the proletariat with new tasks of
reorganising all Party work, revolutionary lines; of educating
the workers in the spirit of the revolutionary struggle for
power; of preparing and moving up the reserves; of establishing

From: Foundations of Leninism. 1935 Co-operative Publishing
Society of Foreign Workers in the U.S.S.R.

an alliance with the proletarians of neighboring countries; of
establishing durable contact with the liberation movement in
the colonies and dependent countries, etc., etc. To imagine
that these new tasks can be fulfilled by the old
Social-Democratic parties, brought up as they were in the
peaceful atmosphere of parliamentarism, can lead only to
hopeless despair and to inevitable defeat. To have such tasks
to shoulder under the leadership of the old parties is
tantamount to being left completely disarmed. It goes without
saying that the proletariat could not accept such a position.

Hence the necessity for a new party, a militant party, a
revolutionary party, bold enough to lead the proletarians to
the struggle for power, with sufficient experience to be able
to orientate itself in the complicated problems that arise in a
revolutionary situation, and sufficiently flexible to steer
clear of any submerged rocks on the way to its goal.

Without such a party it is futile to think of overthrowing
imperialism and achieving the dictatorship of the proletariat.

This new party is the party of Leninism.

What are the special features of this new party?

1. The Party as the Vanguard of the Working Class
    The Party must first of all constitute the vanguard of the
working class. The Party must absorb all the best elements of
the working class, their experience, their revolutionary spirit
and their unbounded devotion to the cause of the proletariat.
But in order that it may really be the vanguard, the Party must
be armed with a revolutionary theory, with a knowledge of the
laws of the movement, with a knowledge of the laws of
revolution. Without this it will be impotent to guide the
struggle of the proletariat and to lead the proletariat. The
Party cannot be a real Party if it limits itself to registering
what the masses of the working class think or experince, if it
drags along at the tail of the spontaneous movement, if it does
not know how to overcome the inertness and the political
indifference of the spontaneous movement, or if it cannot rise
above the transient interests of the proletariat, if it cannot
raise the masses to the level of the class interests of the
proletariat. The Party must take its stand at the head of the
working class, it must see ahead of the working class, lead the
proletariat and not trail behind the spontaneous movement. The
parties of the Second International which preach "tailism" are
the exponents of bourgeois politics which condemn the
proletariat to being a tool in the hands of the bourgeoisie.
Only a party which adopts the point of view of the vanguard of
the proletariat, which is capable of raising the masses to the

level of the class interests of the proletariat, is capable of diverting the working class from the path of craft unionism and converting it into an independent political force. The Party is the political leader of the working class.

I have spoken above the difficulties encountered in the struggle of the working class, of the complicated nature of this struggle, of strategy and tactics, of reserves and maneuvering operations, of attack and defence. These conditions are no less complicated, perhaps more so, than war operations. Who can understand these conditions, who can give correct guidance to the vast masses of the proletariat? Every army at war must have an experienced General Staff if it is to avoid certain defeat. All the more reason therefore why the proletariat must have such a General Staff if it is to prevent itself from being routed by its moral enemies. But where is this General Staff? Only the revolutionary party of the proletariat can serve as this General Staff. A working class without a revolutionary party is like an army without a General Staff. The Party is the Military Staff of the proletariat.

But the Party cannot be merely a vanguard. It must at the same time be a unit of the class, be part of that class, intimately bound to it with every fibre of its being. The distinction between the vanguard and the main body of the working class, between Party members and non-Party workers, will continue as long as classes exist, as long as proletariat continues replenishing its ranks with newcomers from other classes, as long as the working class as a whole lacks the opportunity of raising itself to the level of the vanguard. But the Party would cease to be a party if this distinction were widened into a rupture: if it were to isolate itself and break away the non-Party masses. The Party cannot lead the class if it is not connected with the non-Party masses, if there is no close union between the Party and the non-Party masses, if these masses do not accept its leadership, if the Party does not enjoy moral and political authority among the masses. Recently, two hundred thousand new workers joined our Party. The remarkable thing about this is that these workers did not come into the Party, but were rather sent there by the mass of other non-Party workers who took an active part in the acceptance of the new members and without whose approval no new member was accepted. This fact proves that the broad masses of non-Party workers regard our Party as their Party, as a Party near and dear to them, in the expansion and consolidation of which they are vitally interested and to whose leadership they willingly entrust their destinies. It goes without saying that without these intangible moral ties connecting the Party with the non-Party masses, the Party could never become the decisive force of its class. The Party is an inseparable part of the working class.

85

We are the party of a class - says Lenin - and
therefore almost the entire class (and in times of war,
during the period of civil war, the entire class) must
act under the leadership of our Party, must link
itself up with our Party as closely as possible. But
we would be guilty of Manilovism and `khvostism´ if
we believed that at any time under capitalism nearly
the whole class, or the whole class, would be
able to rise to the level of the class consciousness
and degree of activity of its vanguard, of its
socialist party. No sensible Socialist has ever
yet doubted that under capitalism even the trade union
organisations (which are more primitive and more
accessible to the intelligence of the undeveloped strata)
are unable to embrace nearly the whole, or the whole,
working class. To forget the distinction between
the vanguard and the whole of the masses gravitating
towards it, to forget the constant duty of the vanguard
to raise these increasingly widening strata
to this advanced level, only means deceiving oneself,
shutting one´s eyes to the immensity of our tasks
and narrowing them.(2)

2. The Party as the Organised Detachment of the Working Class
     The Party is not only the vanguard of the working class.
If it desires really to lead the struggle of the class it must
at the same time be the organised detachment of its class.
Under the capitalist system the Party´s tasks are huge and
varied. The party must lead the struggle of the proletariat
under the exceptionally difficult circumstances of inner as
well as outer development; it must lead the proletariat in its
attack when the situation calls for an attack, it must withdraw
the proletraiat from the blows of a powerful opponent when the
situation calls for retreat; it must imbue the millions of
unorganised non-Party workers with the spirit of discipline and
system in fighting, with the spirit of organisation and
perserverance. But the Party can acquit itself of these tasks
only if it itself is the embodiment of discipline and
organisation, if itself is the organised detachment of the
proletariat. Unless these conditions are fulfilled it is idle
to talk about the Party really leading the vast masses of the
proletariat. The Party is the organised detachment of the
working class.

     The conception of the Party as an organised whole has
become firmly fixed in Lenin´s well-known formulation of the
first point of our Party rules in which the Party is regarded
as the sum total of the organisations and the Party member as a
member of one of the organisations of the Party. The
Mensheviks, who had objected to this formulation as early as

86

1903, proposed to substitute for it a "system" of self-enrolment in the Party, a "system" of conferring the "title" Party member upon every "professor" and "high school student," upon every "sympathiser" and "striker" who gave support to the Party in one way or another, but who did not belong and had no inclination to belong to any one of the Party organisations. We need not stop to prove that had this odd "system" become firmly entrenched in our Party it would have been inundated with professors and students, it would have degenerated into a widely diffused, amorphous, disorganised "body" lost in a sea of "sympathisers," that would have obliterated the line of demarcation between the Party and the class and would have frustrated the aim of the Party to raise the unorganised masses to the level of the vanguard. It goes without saying that under such an opportunist "system" our Party would not have been able to accomplish its mission as the organising nucleus of the working class during the course of our revolution.

From Martov´s point of view - says Lenin - the boundary line of the Party remains absolutely unfixed inasmuch as `every striker could declare himself a member of the Party.´ What advantage is there in this diffuseness? Spreading wide a `title.´ The harmfulness of it lies in that it introduces the disruptive idea of identifying the class with the Party.(3)

But the Party is not merely the sum total of Party organisations. The Party at the same time represents a single system of these organisations, their formal unification into a single whole, possessing higher and lower organs of leadership, with submission of the minority to the majority, where decisions on questions of practice are obligatory upon all members of the Party. Unless these conditions are fulfilled the Party is unable to form a single organised whole capable of exercising systematic and organised leadership of the struggle of the working class.

Formerly - says Lenin - our Party was not a formally organised whole, but only the sum total of separate groups. Therefore, no other relations except that of ideological influence were possible between these groups. Now, we have become an organised Party, and this implies the creation of a power, the conversion of the authority of ideas into the authority of power, the subordination of the lower Party bodies to the higher Party bodies.(4)

The principle of the minority submitting to the majority, the principle of leading Party work from a centre, has been a subject of repeated attacks by wavering elements who accuse us

of "bureaucracy," "formalism," etc. It hardly needs to be
proved that systematic work of the Party, as one whole, and the
leadership of the struggle of the working class would have been
impossible without the enforcement of these principles. On the
organisational question, Leninsim stands for the strict
enforcement of these principles. Lenin terms the fight against
these principles "Russian nihilism" and "gentleman's anarchism"
which deserve only to be ridiculed and thrown aside.

This is what Lenin has to say about these wavering
elements in his book entitled One Step Forward, Two Steps
Backward:

The Russian nihilist is especially addicted
to this gentleman's anarchism. To him the Party organisation appears to be a monstrous "factory," the
subordination of the part to the whole and the
submission of the minority to the majority appears
to him to be `serfdom...the division of labour
under the leadership of a centre evokes tragi-comical
lamentations about people being reduced to mere
`cogs and screws'...the bare mention of the
Party rules on organisation calls forth a contemptuous
grimace and some disdainful...remark to the effect
that we could get along without rules... It seems
clear, however, that these outcries against the alleged
bureaucracy are an attempt to conceal the
dissatisfaction with the personnel of these centres, a
fig leaf... `You are a bureaucrat because you were
appointed by the Congress without my consent and
against my wishes; you are a formalist because
you seek support in the formal decision of the
Congress and not in my approval; you act in a
crudely mechanical way because your authority is the
`mechanical' majority of the Party Congress and you
do not consult my desire to be co-opted; you
are an autocrat because you do not want to deliver
power into the hands of the old gang.'(5 and 6)

3. The Party as the Highest Form of Class Organisation of the Proletariat

The Party is the organised detachment of the working
class. But the Party is not the only organisation of the
working class. The proletariat has in addition a great number
of other organisations which are indispensable in its correct
struggle against the capitalist system - trade unions,
co-operative societies, factory and shop organisations,
parliamentary fractions, non-Party women's associations, the
press, cultural and educational organisations, youth leagues,
military revolutionary organisations (in times of direct
revolutionary action), soviets of deputies as the State form of

organisation (where the proletariat is in power), etc. Most of
these organisations are non-Party and only a certain part of
these adhere directly to the Party, or represent its offshoots.
All these organisations, under certain conditions, are
absolutely necessary for the working class, as without them it
is impossible to consolidate the class position of the
proletariat in the diversified spheres of struggle, and without
them it is impossible to steel the proletariat as the force
whose mission it is to replace the bourgeois order by the
socialist order. But how unity of leadership becomes a reality
in the face of such a multiplicity of organisations? What
guarantee is there that this multiplicity of organisations will
not lead to discord in leadership? It might be argued that
each of these organisations carries on its work in its own
field in which it specialises and cannot, therefore, interfere
with the others. That, of course, is true. But it is likewise
true that the activities of all these organisations ought to be
directed into a single channel, as they serve one class, the
class of the proletariat. The question then arises: who is to
determine the line, the general direction along which the work
of all these organisations is to be conducted? Where is that
central organisation which is not only able, having the
necessary experience, to work out such a general line, but also
capable, because of its authority, of prevailing upon all these
organisations to carry out this line, in order to attain unity
of direction and preclude the possibility of working at cross
purposes?

This organisation is the party of the proletariat.

The party possesses all the necessary qualifications for
this purpose because, in the first place, it is the common
meeting ground of the best elements in the working class that
have direct connections with the non-Party organisation of the
proletariat and very frequently lead them; because, secondly,
the Party, as the meeting ground of the best members of the
working class, is the best school for training leaders of the
working class, capable of directing every form of organisation
of their class; because, thirdly, the Party, as the best school
for training leaders of the working class, is, by reason of its
experience and authority, the only organisation capable of
centralising the leadership of the struggle of the proletariat
and in this way of transforming each and every non-Party
organisation of the working class into an auxiliary body, a
transmission belt linking it with the class. The Party is the
highest form of class organisation of the proletariat.

This does not mean, of course, that non-Party
organisations like trade unions, co-operative societies, etc.,
must be formally subordinated to Party leadership. It means

simply that the members of the Party who belong to these organisations and doubtless exercise influence in them should do all they can to persuade these non-Party organisations to draw nearer to the Party of the proletariat in their work and voluntarily accept its political guidance.

That is why Lenin says that "the Party is the highest form of class association of the proletarians" whose political leadership ought to extend to every other form of organisation of the proletariat.(7)

That is why the opportunist theory of the "independence" and "neutrality" of the non-Party organisations, which theory is the progenitor of independent parliamentarians and publicists who are isolated from the Party, and of narrow-minded trade unionists and co-operative society officials who have become petty bourgeois, is wholly incompatible with the theory and practice of Leninism.

4. The Party as the Weapon of the Dictatorship of the Proletariat

The Party is the highest form of organisation of the proletariat. The Party is the fundamental leading element within the organisations of that class. But it does not follow by any means that the Party can be regarded as an end in itself, as a self-sufficing force. The Party is not only the highest form of class association of the proletarians; it is at the same time a weapon in the hands of the proletariat for the achievement of the dictatorship where that has not yet been achieved; for the consolidation and extension of the dictatorship where it has already been achieved. The Party would not rank so high in importance and it could not overshadow all other forms of organisation of the proletariat if the latter were not face to face with the question of power, if the conditions of imperialism, the inevitability of wars and the presence of a crisis did not demand the concentration of all the forces of the proletariat on one point and the gathering together of all threads of the revolutionary movement in one spot, to overthrow the bourgeoisie and to establish the dictatorship of the proletariat. The proletariat needs the Party first of all as its General Staff, which it must have for the successful seizure of power. Needless to say, the Russian proletariat could have never established its revolutionary dictatorship without a Party capable of rallying around itself the mass organisations of the proletariat and of centralising the leadership of the entire movement during the progress of the struggle.

But the proletariat needs the Party not only to achieve the dictatorship, it needs it still more to maintain, consolidate and extend its dictatorship in order to attain complete victory for socialism.

Certainly almost everyone now realises - says
Lenin - that the Bolsheviks could not have maintained
themselves in power for two and a half years, and not
even for two and a half months, without the strictest
discipline, the truly iron discipline, in our
Party, and without the fullest and unreserved support
rendered it by the whole mass of the working class,
that is, by all those belonging to this class who
think, who are honest, self-sacrificing,
influential, and capable of leading and attracting the
backward masses.(8)

Now what is meant by "maintaining" and "extending" the
dictatorship? It means imbuing these millions of proletarians
with the spirit of the discipline and organisation: it means
creating among the proletarian masses a bulwark against the
corrosive influences of petty-bourgeois spontaneity and
petty-bourgeois habits; it means that the organising work of
the proletarians in re-educating and remoulding the
petty-bourgeois strata must be reinforced; it means that
assistance must be given to the masses of the proletarians in
educating themselves so that they may become a force capable of
abolishing classes and of preparing the ground for the
organisation of socialist production. But it is impossible to
accomplish all this without a Party, which is strong by reason
of its cohesion and discipline.

The dicatorship of the proletariat - says
Lenin - is a persistent struggle - sanguinary and
bloodless, violent and peaceful, military and
economic, educational and administrative -
against the forces and traditions of the old society.
The force of habit of millions and of tens of millions
is a terrible force. Without an iron party steeled
in the struggle, without a party enjoying the
confidence of all that is honest in the given class,
without a party capable of keeping track of and
influencing the mood of the masses, it is impossible
to conduct such a struggle successfully.(9)

5. The Party as the Expression of Unity of Will,
    Which is Incompatible With the Existence of Factions
    The achievement and maintenance of the dictatorship of the
proletariat are impossible without a party strong in its
cohesion and iron discipline. But iron discipline in the Party
is impossible without unity of will and without absolute and
complete unity of action on the part of all members of the
Party. This does not mean, of course, that the possibility of
a conflict of opinion within the Party is thus excluded. On

91

the contrary, iron discipline does not preclude but presupposes criticism and conflicts of opinion within the Party. Least of all does it mean that this discipline must be "blind" discipline. On the contrary, iron discipline does not preclude but presupposes conscious and voluntary submission, for only conscious discipline can be truly iron discipline. But after a discussion has been closed, after criticism has run its course and a decision has been made, unity of will and unity of action of all Party members become indispensable conditions without which Party unity and iron discipline in the Party are inconceivable.

In the present epoch of intensified civil war - says Lenin - the Communist Party can discharge its duty only if it is organised with the highest degree of centralisation; ruled by iron discipline bordering on military discipline, and if its Party centre proves to be a potent authoritative body invested with broad powers and enjoying the general confidence of the Party members.(10)

This is the position in regard to discipline in the Party in the period of struggle preceding the establishment of the dictatorship.

The same thing applies, but to a greater degree, to discipline in the Party after the establishment of the dictatorship. In this connection, Lenin said:

Whoever in the least weakens the iron discipline of the party of the proletariat (especially during its dictatorship) actually aids the bourgeoisie against the proletariat.(11)

It follows that the existence of factions is incompatible with Party unity and with its iron discipline. It need hardly be emphasised that the existence of factions leads to the creation of a number of centers, and the existence of a number of centres connotes the absence of a common centre in the Party, a breach in the unity of will, the weakening and disintegration of the dictatorship. It is true that the parties of the Second International, which are fighting against the dictatorship of the proletariat and have no desire to lead the proletariat to power, can permit themselves the luxury of such liberalism as freedom for factions, for they have no need whatever of iron discipline. But the parties of the Communist International, which organise their activities on the basis of the task of achieving and strengthening the dictatorship of the proletariat, cannot afford to be "liberal" or to permit the formation of factions. The Party is synonymous with unity of will, which leaves no room for any factionalism or division of authority in the Party.

Hence Lenin´s warning on the "danger of factionalism from the point of view of Party unity and of the realisation of unity of will in the vanguard of the proletariat as the primary prerequisite for the success of the dictatorship of the proletariat," which is embodied in a special resolution of the Tenth Congress of our Party, On Party Unity.

Hence Lenin´s demand for the "complete extermination of all factionalism" and the "immediate dissolution of all groups without exception, that had been formed on the basis of this or that platform" on pain of "unconditional and immediate expulsion from the Party."(12)

6. The Party is Strengthened by Purging Itself of Opportunist Elements

The opportunist elements in the Party are the source of Party factionalism. The proletariat is not an isolated class. A steady stream of peasants, small tradesmen and intellectuals, who have become proletarianised by the development of capitalism, flows into the ranks of the proletariat. At the same time the upper strata of the proletariat - principally the trade union leaders and labour members of parliament - who have been fed by the bourgeoisie out of the super-profits extracted from the colonies, are undergoing a process of decay.

This stratum of the labour aristocracy or of workers who have become bourgeois - says Lenin - who have become quite petty-bourgeois in their mode of life, in their earnings, and in their outlook, serve as the principal bulwark of the Second International, and, in our days, the principal social (not military) support of the bourgeoisie. They are the real agents of the bourgeoisie in the labour movement, the labour lieutenants of the capitalist class, channels of reformism and chauvinism.(12)

All these petty-bourgeois groups somehow or the other penetrate into the Party into which they introduce an element of hesitancy and opportunism, of disintegration and lack of self-confidence. Factionalism and splits, disorganisation and the undermining of the Party from within are principally due to them. Fighting imperialism with such "allies" in one´s rear is as bad as being caught between two fires, coming both from the front and rear. Therefore, no quarter should be given in fighting such elements, and their relentless expulsion from the Party is a condition precedent for the successful struggle against imperialism.

The theory of "overcoming" opportunist elements by

ideological struggle within the Party; the theory of "living down" these elements within the confines of a single Party are rotten and dangerous theories that threaten to reduce the Party to paralysis and chronic infirmity, that threaten to abandon the Party to opportunism, that threaten to leave the proletariat without a revolutionary party, that threaten to deprive the proletariat of its main weapon in the fight against imperialism. Our Party could not have come out on the high road, it could not have seized power and organised the dictatorship of the proletariat, it could not have emerged victorious from the civil war, if it had had within its ranks people like Martov and Dan, Potresov and Axelrod. Our Party succeeded in creating true unity and greater cohesion in its ranks than ever before, mainly because it undertook in time to purge itself of opportunist pollution and expelled liquidators and Mensheviks from its ranks. The proletarian parties develop and become strong by purging themselves of opportunists and reformists, social-imperialists and social-chauvinists, social-patriots and social-pacifists. The Party becomes strong by ridding itself of opportunist elements.

With reformists and Mensheviks in our ranks - says Lenin - we cannot be victorious in the proletarian revolution nor can we defend it against attack. This is clearly so in principle. It is strikingly confirmed by the experiences of Russia and Hungary... Russia found itself in a tight corner many a time, when the Soviet regime would certainly have been overthrown had the Mensheviks, reformists or petty-bourgeois democrats remained within our Party... It is generally admitted that in Italy events are heading towards decisive battles of the proletariat with the bourgeoisie for the capture of State power. At such a time not only does the removal of the Mensheviks, reformists and Turatists from the Party become absolutely necessary, but it may even prove useful to remove certain excellent Communists who might and who do waver in the direction of desiring to maintain `unity´ with the reformists - to remove these from all responsible positions... On the eve of the revolution and in the midst of the desperate struggle for victory, the slightest hesitancy within the Party is apt to ruin everything, to disrupt the revolution and to snatch the power out of the hands of the proletariat, since that power is as yet insecure and the attacks upon it are still too violent. The retirement of wavering leaders at such a time does not weaken but strengthens the

Party, the labour movement and the revolution.(13)

Notes

1. This was a lecture delivered by Stalin at Sverdlov University, in April 1924.
2. V.I. Lenin, *Collected Works*, Russian edition, Vol. VI, pp. 205-206.
3. *Ibid.*, p. 211.
4. *Ibid.*, p. 291.
5. The "old gangs" here referred to is that of Axelrod, Martov, Potresov and others who would not submit to the decisions of the Second Congress and who accused Lenin of being a "bureaucrat." - J.S.
6. *Ibid.*, pp. 310, 287.
7. V.I. Lenin, "*Left-Wing*" Communism, etc., Chap. VI.
8. *Ibid.*, Chap. II.
9. *Ibid.*, Chap. V.
10. V.I. Lenin, *Conditions of Affiliation to the Communist International*.
11. V.I. Lenin, "*Left-Wing*" Communism, etc., Chap V.
12. Cf. the resolution, *On Party Unity*.
13. V.I. Lenin, *Imperialism*, Preface to the French and German editions.
14. V.I. Lenin, *Collected Works*, Russian edition, Vol. XXV, pp. 462-464.

SECRET SPEECH ON STALIN AND THE CULT OF THE INDIVIDUAL

Nikita S. Khrushchev

Superman and God

After Stalin's death the Central Committee of the party began to implement a policy of explaining concisely and consistently that it is impermissible and foreign to the spirit of Marxism-Leninism to elevate one person, to transform him into a superman possessing supernatural characteristics, akin to those of a god. Such a man supposedly knows everything, sees everything, thinks for everyone, can do anything, is infallible in his behavior.

Such a belief about a man, and specifically about Stalin, was cultivated among us for many years.

The objective of the present report is not a thorough evaluation of Stalin's life and activity. Concerning Stalin's merits, an entirely sufficient number of books, pamphlets and studies had already been written in his lifetime. The role of Stalin in the preparation and execution of the Socialist Revolution, in the Civil War, and in the fight for the construction of socialism in our country, is universally known. Everyone knows this well.

At present, we are concerned with a question which has immense importance for the party now and for the future - with how the cult of the person of Stalin has been gradually growing, the cult which became at a certain specific stage the source of a whole series of exceedingly serious and grave perversions of party principles, of party democracy, of revolutionary legality.

Because of the fact that not all as yet realize fully the practical consequences resulting from the cult of the individual, the great harm caused by the violation of the principle of collective direction of the party and because of the accumulation of immense and limitless power in the hands of one person, the Central Committee of the party considers it absolutely necessary to make the material pertaining to this

---

From: Secret Speech on Stalin and the Cult of the Individual (Twentieth Congress of the Communist Party of the Soviet Union, February 25, 1956). Translation released by the Department of State, June 4, 1956.

matter available to the 20th Congress of the Communist Party of the Soviet Union.

Physical Annihilation of Opponents

Stalin acted not through persuasion, explanation and patient cooperation with people, but by imposing his concepts and demanding absolute submission to his opinion. Whoever opposed this concept or tried to prove his viewpoint and the correctness of his position was doomed to removal from the leading collective and to subsequent moral and physical annihilation. This was especially true during the period following the 17th Party Congress, when many prominent party leaders and rank-and-file party workers, honest and dedicated to the cause of Communism, fell victim to Stalin's despotism.

Stalin originated the concept "enemy of the people." This term automatically rendered it unnecessary that the ideological errors of a man or men engaged in a controversy be proven; this term made possible the usage of the most cruel repression, violating all norms of revolutionary legality, against anyone who in any way disagreed with Stalin, against those who were only suspected of hostile intent, against those who had bad reputations. This concept "enemy of the people" actually eliminated the possibility of any kind of ideological fight or the making of one's views known on this or that issue, even those of a practical character. In the main, and in actuality, the only proof of guilt used, against all norms of current legal science, was the "confession" of the accused himself; and, as subsequent probing proved, "confessions" were acquired through physical pressures against the accused. This led to glaring violations of revolutionary legality and to the fact that many entirely innocent persons, who in the past had defended the party line, became victims.

We must assert that, in regard to those persons who in their time had opposed the party line, there were often no sufficiently serious reasons for their physical annihilation. The formula "enemy of the people" was specifically introduced for the purpose of physically annihilating such individuals.

It is a fact that many persons who were later annihilated as enemies of the party and people had worked with Lenin during his life. Some of these persons had made errors during Lenin's life, but, despite this, Lenin benefited by their work; he corrected them and he did everything possible to retain them in the ranks of the party; he induced them to follow him.

Arbitrary behavior by one person encouraged and permitted arbitrariness in others. Mass arrests and deportations of many thousands of people, execution without trial and without normal investigation created conditions of insecurity, fear and even desparation.

This, of course, did not contribute toward unity of the party ranks and of all strata of working people, but, on the contrary, brought about annihilation and the expulsion from the party of workers who were loyal but inconvenient to Stalin.

Our party fought for the implementation of Lenin´s plans for the construction of socialism. This was an ideological fight. Had Leninist principles been observed during the course of this fight, had the party´s devotion to principles been skillfully combined with a keen and solicitous concern for people, had they not been repelled and wasted but rather drawn to our side, we certainly would not have had such a brutal violation of revolutionary legality and many thousands of people would not have fallen victim to the method of terror. Extraordinary methods would then have been resorted to only against those people who had in fact committed criminal acts against the Soviet system.

Liquidation of Top Communists
Having at its disposal numerous data showing brutal willfulness toward party cadres, the Central Committee has created a party commission under the control of the Central Committee Presidium; it was charged with investigating what made possible the mass repressions against the majority of the Central Committee members and candidates elected at the 17th Congress of the All-Union Communist Party (Bolsheviks).

The commission has become acquainted with a large quantity of materials in the NKVD[1] archives and with other documents and has established many facts pertaining to the fabrication of cases against Communists, to false accusations, to glaring abuses of socialist legality, which resulted in the death of innocent people. It became apparent that many party, Soviet and economic activists, who were branded in 1937-1938 as "enemies," were actually never enemies, spies, wreckers, etc. but were always honest Communists; they were only so stigmatized and, often no longer able to bear barbaric tortures, they charged themselves (at the order of the investigative judges - falsifiers) with all kinds of unlikely crimes.

The commission has presented to the Central Committee Presidium lengthy and documented materials pertaining to mass repressions against the delegates to the 17th Party Congress and against members of the Central Committee elected at that Congress. These materials have been studied by the Presidium of the Central Committee.

It was determined that of the 139 members and candidates of the party's Central Committee who were elected at the 17th Congress, 98 persons, i.e., 70 percent, were arrested and shot (mostly in 1937-1938). (Indignation in the hall.) What was the composition of the delegates to the 17th Congress? It is known that 80 percent of the voting participants of the 17th Congress joined the party during the years of conspiracy before the Revolution and during the civil war; this means before 1921. By social origin the basic mass of the delegates to the Congress were workers (60 percent of the voting members).

For this reason, it was inconceivable that a congress so composed would have elected a Central Committee a majority of whom would prove to be enemies of the party. The only reason why 70 percent of Central Committee members and candidates elected at the 17th Congress were branded as enemies of the party and of the people was because honest Communists were slandered, accusations against them were fabricated, and revolutionary legality was gravely undermined.

The same fate met not only the Central Committee members but also the majority of the delegates to the 17th Party Congress. Of 1,966 delegates with either voting or advisory rights, 1,108 persons were arrested on charges of anti-revolutionary crimes, i.e., decidedly more than a majority. This very fact shows how absurd, wild and contrary to common sense were the charges of counterrevolutionary crimes made out, as we now see, against a majority of participants at the 17th Party Congress. (Indignation in the hall.)

We should recall that the 17th Party Congress is historically known as the Congress of Victors. Delegates to the Congress were active participants in the building of our socialist state; many of them suffered and fought for party interests during the pre-Revolutionary years in the conspiracy and at the civil-war fronts; they fought their enemies valiantly and often nervelessly looked into the face of death.

How, then, can we believe that such people could prove to be "two-faced" and had joined the camps of the enemies of socialism during the era after the political liquidation of Zinovievites, Trotskyites and rightists and after the great accomplishments of socialist construction? This was the result of the abuse of power by Stalin, who began to use mass terror against the party cadres.

What is the reason that mass repressions against activists increased more and more after the 17th Party Congress? It was because at that time Stalin had so elevated himself above the party and above the nation that he ceased to consider either the Central Committee or the party.

While he still reckoned with the opinion of the collective before the 17th Congress, after the complete political liquidation of the Trotskyites, Zinovievites and Bukharinites, when as a result of that fight and socialist victories the party achieved unity, Stalin ceased to an ever greater degree to consider the members of the party's Central Committee and even the members of the Political Bureau. Stalin thought that now he could decide all things alone and all he needed were statisticians; he treated all others in such a way that they could only listen to and praise him.

Order to Expedite Executions

After the criminal murder of Sergei M. Kirov, mass repressions and brutal acts of violation of socialist legality began. On the evening of December 1, 1934, on Stalin's initiative (without the approval of the Political Bureau - which was passed two days later, casually), the Secretary of the Presidium of the Central Executive Committee, Yenukidze, signed the following directive:

"1. Investigative agencies are directed to speed up the cases of those accused of the preparation or execution of acts of terror.

"2. Judicial organs are directed not to hold up the execution of death sentences pertaining to crimes of this category in order to consider the possibility of pardon, because the Presidium of the Central Executive Committee of the USSR does not consider as possible the receiving of petitions of this sort.

"3. The organs of the Commissariat of Internal Affairs are directed to execute the death sentences against criminals of the above-mentioned category immediately after the passage of sentences."

This directive became the basis for mass acts of abuse against socialist legality. During many of the fabricated court cases, the accused were charged with "the preparation" of terrorist acts; this deprived them of any possibility that their cases might be re-examined, even when they stated before the court that their "confessions" were secured by force, and when, in a convincing manner, they disproved the accusations against them.

Mystery of Kirov Killing

It must be asserted that to this day the circumstances surrounding Kirov's murder hide many things which are inexplicable and mysterious and demand a most careful examination. There are reasons for the suspicion that the killer of Kirov, Nikolayev, was assisted by someone from among the people whose duty it was to protect the person of Kirov.

A month and a half before the killing, Nikolayev was arrested on the grounds of suspicious circumstances that when the Chekist assigned to protect Kirov was being brought for an interrogation, on December 2, 1934, he was killed in a car "accident" in which no other occupants of the car were harmed. After the murder of Kirov, top functionaries of the Leningrad NKVD were given very light sentences, but in 1937 they were shot. We can assume that they were shot in order to cover the traces of the organizers of Kirov´s killing. (Movement in the hall.)

Mass repressions grew tremendously from the end of 1936 after a telegram from Stalin and [Andrei] Zhdanov, dated from Sochi on September 25, 1936, was addressed to Kaganovich, Molotov and other members of the Political Bureau. The content of the telegram was as follows:

"We deem it absolutely necessary and urgent that Comrade Yezhov be nominated to the post of People´s Commissar for Internal Affairs. Yagoda has definitely proved himself to be incapable of unmasking the Trotskyite-Zinovievite bloc. The OGPU is four years behind in this matter. This is noted by all party workers and by the majority of the representatives of the NKVD."

Strictly speaking, we should stress that Stalin did not meet with and, therfore, could not know the opinions of party workers.

This Stalin formulation that the "NKVD is four years behind" in applying mass repression and that there is a necessity for "catching up" with the neglected work directly pushed the NKVD workers on the path of mass arrests and executions.

The mass repressions at this time were made under the slogan of a fight against the Trotskyites. Did the Trotskyites at this time actually constitute such a danger to our party and to the Soviet state? We should recall that in 1927, on the eve of the 15th Party Congress, only some 4,000 votes were cast for the Trotskyite-Zinovievite opposition while there were 724,000 for the party line. During the 10 years which passed between the 15th Party Congress and the February-March Central Committee plenum, Trotskyism was completely disarmed; many former Trotskyites had changed their former views and worked in the various sectors building socialism. It is clear that in the situation of socialist victory there was no basis for mass terror in the country.

Stalin´s report at the February-March Central Committee

plenum in 1937, "Deficiencies of party work and methods for the liquidation of the Trotskyites and other two-facers," contained an attempt at theoretical justification of the mass terror policy under the pretext that as we march forward toward socialism, class war must allegedly sharpen. Stalin asserted that both history and Lenin taught him this.

This terror was actually directed not at the remnants of the defeated exploiting classes but against the honest workers of the party and of the Soviet state; against them were made lying, slanderous and absurd accusations concerning "two-facedness," "espionage," "sabotage," preparation of fictitious "plots," etc.

Confessions through Inhuman Torture

Using Stalin's formulation, namely, that the closer we are to socialism the more enemies we will have, and using the resolution of the February-March Central Committee plenum passed on the basis of Yezhov's report, the provocateurs who had infiltrated the state-security organs together with conscienceless careerists began to protect with the party name the mass terror against party cadres, cadres of the Soviet state and the ordinary Soviet citizens. It should suffice to say that the number of arrests based on charges of counterrevolutionary crimes had grown ten times between 1936 and 1937.

It is known that brutal willfulness was practiced against leading party workers. The party statute, approved at the 17th Party Congress, was based on Leninist principles expressed at the 10th Party Congress. It stated that in order to apply an extreme method such as exclusion from the party against a Central Committee member, against a Central Committee candidate and against a member of the Party Control Commission, "it is necessary to call a Central Committee plenum and to invite to the plenum all Central candidate members and all members of the Party Control Commission"; only if two-thirds of the members of such a general assembly of responsible party leaders find it necessary, only then can a Central Committee member or candidate be expelled.

The majority of the Central Committee members and candidates elected at the 17th Congress and arrested in 1937-1938 were expelled from the party illegally through the brutal abuse of the party statute, because the question of their expulsion was never studied at the Central Committee plenum.

Now, when the case of some of these so-called "spies" and "saboteurs" were examined, it was found that all their cases were fabricated: Confessions of guilt of many arrested and charged with enemy activity were gained with the help of cruel and inhuman tortures.

At the same time, Stalin, as we have been informed by members of the Political Bureau of that time, did not show them the statements of many accused political activists when they retracted their confessions before the military tribunal and asked for an objective examination of their cases. There were many such declarations, and Stalin doubtless knew of them.

The Central Committee considers it absolutely necessary to inform the Congress of many such fabricated "cases" against the members of the party´s Central Committee elected at the 17th Party Congress.

An example of vile provocation, of odious falsification and of criminal violation of revolutionary legality is the case of the former candidate for the Central Committee Political Bureau, one of the most eminent workers of the party and of the Soviet Government, Comrade Eikhe, who was a party member since 1905. (Commotion in the hall.)

Comrade Eikhe was arrested on April 29, 1938, on the basis of slanderous materials, without the sanction of the Prosecutor of the USSR, which was finally received 15 months after the arrest.

Investigation of Eikhe´s case was made in a manner which most brutally violated Soviet legality and was accompanied by willfulness and falsification.

Eikhe was forced under torture to sign ahead of time a protocol of his confession prepared by the investigative judges, in which he and several other eminent party workers were accused of anti-Soviet activity.

On October 1, 1939, Eikhe sent his declaration to Stalin in which he categorically denied his guilt and asked for an examination of his case. In the declaration he wrote: "There is no more bitter misery than to sit in the jail of a government for which I have always fought."

A second declaration of Eikhe has been preserved which he sent to Stalin on October 27, 1939; in it he cited facts very convincingly and countered the slanderous accusations made against him, arguing that this provocatory accusation was on the one hand the work of real Trotskyites whose arrests he had sanctioned as First Secretary of the West Siberian Krai [Territory] Party Committee and who conspired in order to take revenge on him, and, on the other hand, the result of the base falsification of materials by the investigative judges.

Eikhe wrote in his declaration:

"...On October 25 of this year I was informed that the
investigation in my case has been concluded and I was given
access to the materials of this investigation. Had I been
guilty of only one hundredth of the crimes with which I am
charged, I would not have dared to send you this pre-execution
declaration; however, I have not been guilty of even one of the
things with which I am charged and my heart is clean of even
the shadow of baseness. I have never in my life told you a
word of falsehood, and now, finding my two feet in the grave, I
am also not lying. My whole case is a typical example of
provocation, slander and violation of the elementary basis of
revolutionary legality...
   "...The confessions which were made part of my file are not
only absurd but contain some slander toward the Central
Committee of the All-Union Communist Party (Bolsheviks) and
toward the Council of People's Commissars, because correct
resolutions of the Central Committee of the All-Union Communist
Party (Bolsheviks) and of the Council of People's Commissars
which were not made on my initiative and without my
participation are presented as hostile acts of
counterrevolutionary organizations made at my suggestion...
   "I am now alluding to the most disgraceful part of my life
and to my really grave guilt against the party and against you.
This is my confession of counterrevolutionary activity... The
case is as follows: Not being able to suffer the tortures to
which I was submitted by Ushakov and Nikolayev - and especially
the first one - who utilized the knowledge that my broken ribs
have not properly mended and have caused me great pain, I have
been forced to accuse myself and others.
   "The majority of my confession has been suggested or
dictated by Ushakov, and the remainder is my reconstruction of
NKVD materials from Western Siberia for which I assumed all
responsibility. If some part of the story which Ushakov
fabricated and which I signed did not properly hang together, I
was forced to sign another variation. The same thing was done
to Rukhimovich, who was at first designated as a member of the
reserve net and whose name was later removed without telling me
anything about it; the same was also done with the leader of
the reserve net, supposedly created by Bukharin in 1935. At
first I wrote my name in, and then I was instructed to insert
Mazhlauk. There were other similar incidents.
   "...I am asking and begging you that you again examine my
case, and this is not for the purpose of sparing me but in
order to unmask the vile provocation which, like a snake, wound
itself around many persons in a great degree due to my meanness
and criminal slander. I have never betrayed you or the party.
I know that I perish because of vile and mean work of the

enemies of the party and of the people, who fabricated the provocation against me."

It would appear that such an important declaration was worth an examination by the Central Committee. This, however, was not done, and the declaration was transmitted to Beria while the terrible maltreatment of the Political Bureau candidate, Comrade Eikhe, continued.

On February 2, 1940, Eikhe was brought before court. Here he did not confess any guilt and said as follows:

"In all the so-called confessions of mine there is not one letter written by me with the exception of my signatures under the protocols, which were forced upon me. I have made my confession under pressure from the investigative judge, who from the time of my arrest tormented me. After that I began to write all this nonsense... The most important thing for me is to tell the court, the party and Stalin that I am not guilty. I have never been guilty of any conspiracy. I will die believing in the truth of party policy as I have believed it during my whole life."

On February 4 Eikhe was shot. (Indignation in the hall.)

It has been definitely established now that Eikhe´s case was fabricated; he has been posthumously rehabilitated.

Thousands Died Innocent
This is the kind of vile things which were practiced. (Movement in the hall.)

Even more widely was the falsification of cases practiced in the provinces. The NKVD headquarters of the Sverdlov Oblast "discovered" the so-called "Ural uprising staff" - an organ of the bloc of rightists, Trotskyites, Socialist Revolutionaries, church leaders - whose chief supposedly was the Secretary of the Sverdlov Oblast Party Committee and member of the Central Committee, All-Union Communist Party (Bolsheviks), Kabakov, who had been a party member since 1914. The investigative materials of that time show that in almost all krais, oblasts [provinces] and republics there supposedly existed "rightist Trotskyite, espionage-terror and diversionary-sabotage organizations and centers" and that the heads of such organizations as a rule - for no known reason - were first secretaries of oblast or republic Communist party committees or central committees.

Many thousands of honest and innocent Communists have died as a result of this monstrous falsification of such "cases," as a result of the fact that all kinds of slanderous "confessions"

106

were accepted, and as a result of the practice of forcing accusations against oneself and others. In the same manner were fabricated the "cases" against eminent party and state workers - Kossior, Chubar, Postyshev, Kosarev and others.

In those years repressions on a mass scale were applied which were based on nothing tangible and which resulted in heavy cadre losses to the party.

The vicious practice was condoned of having the NKVD prepare lists of persons whose cases were under the jurisdiction of the Military Collegium and whose sentences were prepared in advance. Yezhov would send these lists to Stalin personally for his approval of the proposed punishment. In 1937-1938, 383 such lists containing the names of many thousands of party, Soviet, Komsomol, Army and economic workers were sent to Stalin. He approved these lists.

A large part of these cases are being reviewed now and a great part of them are being voided because they were baseless and falsified. Suffice it to say that from 1954 to the present time the Military Collegium of the Supreme Court has rehabilitated 7,679 persons, many of whom were rehabilitated posthumously.

Mass arrests of party, Soviet, economic and military workers caused tremendous harm to our country and to the cause of socialist advancement.

Mass repressions had a negative influence on the moral-political condition of the party, created a situation of uncertainty, contributed to the spreading of unhealthy suspicion, and sowed distrust among Communists. All sorts of slanderers and careerists were active.

Resolutions of the January plenum of the Central Committee, All-Union Communist Party (Bolsheviks), in 1938 had brought some measure of improvement to the party organizations. However, widespread repression also existed in 1938.

Only because our party has at its disposal such great moral-political strength was it possible for it to survive the difficult events in 1937-1938 and to educate new cadres. There is, however, no doubt that our march forward toward socialism and toward the preparation of the country´s defense would have been much more successful were it not for the tremendous loss in the cadres suffered as a result of the baseless and false mass repressions in 1937-1938.

We are justly accusing Yezhov for the degenerate practices of 1937. But we have to answer these questions:

Could Yezhov have arrested Kossior, for instance, without the knowledge of Stalin? Was there an exchange of opinions or a Political Bureau decision concerning this?

No, there was not, as there was none regarding other cases of this type.

Could Yezhov have decided such important matters as the fate of such eminent party figures?

No, it would be a display of naivete to consider this the work of Yezhov alone. It is clear that these matters were decided by Stalin, and that without his orders and his sanction Yezhov could not have done this.

We have examined the cases and have rehabilitated Kossior, Rudzutak, Postyshev, Kosarev and others. For what causes were they arrested and sentenced? The review of evidence shows that there was no reason for this. They, like many others, were arrested without the prosecutor's knowledge.

In such a situation, there is no need for any sanction, for what sort of a sanction could there be when Stalin decided everything? He was the chief prosecutor in these cases. Stalin not only agreed to, but on his own initiative issued, arrest orders. We must say this so that the delegates to the Congress can clearly undertake and themselves assess this and draw the proper conclusions.

Facts prove that many abuses were made on Stalin's orders without reckoning with any norms of party and Soviet legality. Stalin was a very distrustful man, sickly suspicious; we know this from our work with him. He could look at a man and say: "Why are your eyes so shifty today?" or "Why are you turning so much today and avoiding to look at me directly in the eyes?" The sickly suspicion created in him a general distrust even toward eminent party workers whom he had known for years. Everywhere and in everything he saw "enemies," "two-facers" and "spies." Possessing unlimited power, he indulged in great willfullness and choked a person morally and physically. A situation was created where one could not express one's own will.

When Stalin said that one or another should be arrested, it was necessary to accept on faith that he was an "enemy of the people." Meanwhile, Beria's gang, which ran the organs of state security, outdid itself in proving the guilt of the arrested and the truth of materials which it falsified. And

what proofs were offered? The confessions of the arrested, and
the investigative judges accepted these "confessions." And how
is it possible that a person confesses to crimes which he has
not committed? Only in one way - because of application of
physical methods of pressuring him, tortures, bringing him to a
state of unconsciousness, deprivation of his judgment, taking
away of his human dignity. In this manner were "confessions"
acquired.

World War II

The power accumulated in the hands of one person, Stalin,
led to serious consequences during the Great Patriotic War.

When we look at many of our novels, films and historical
"scientific studies," the role of Stalin in the Patriotic War
appears to be entirely improbable. Stalin had foreseen
everything. The Soviet Army, on the basis of a strategic plan
prepared by Stalin long before, used the tactics of so-called
"active defense," i.e., tactics which, as we know, allowed the
Germans to come up to Moscow and Stalingrad. Using such
tactics, the Soviet Army, supposedly thanks only to Stalin's
genius, turned to the offensive and subdued the enemy. The
epic victory gained through the armed might of the land of the
Soviets, through our heroic people, is ascribed in this type of
novel, film and "scientific study" as being completely due to
the strategic genius of Stalin.

We have to analyze this matter carefully because it has a
tremendous significance not only from the historical, but
especially from the political, educational and practical point
of view. What are the facts of this matter?

Before the war, our press and all our
political-educational work was characterized by its bragging
tone: When an enemy violates the holy Soviet soil, then for
every blow of the enemy we will answer with three blows, and we
will battle the enemy on his soil and we will win without much
harm to ourselves. But these positive statements were not
based in all areas on concrete facts, which would actually
guarantee the immunity of our borders.

During the war and after the war, Stalin put forward the
thesis that the tragedy which our nation experienced in the
first part of the war was the result of the "unexpected" attack
of the Germans against the Soviet Union. But, comrades, this
is completely untrue. As soon as Hitler came to power in
Germany he assigned to himself the task of liquidating
Communism. The fascists were saying this openly; they did not
hide their plans.

In order to attain this aggressive end, all sorts of pacts

and blocs were created, such as the famous Berlin-Rome-Tokyo Axis. Many facts from the prewar period clearly showed that Hitler was going all out to begin a war against the Soviet state, and that he had concentrated large armed units, together with armored units, near the Soviet borders.

Documents which have now been published show that by April 3, 1941, Churchill, through his Ambassador to the USSR, Cripps, personally warned Stalin that the Germans had begun regrouping their armed units with the intent of attacking the Soviet Union.

It is self-evident that Churchill did not do this at all because of his friendly feeling toward the Soviet nation. He had in this his own imperialistic goals - to bring Germany and the USSR into a bloody war and thereby to strengthen the position of the British Empire.

Just the same, Churchill affirmed in his writings that he sought to "warn Stalin and call his attention to the danger which threatened him." Churchill stressed this repeatedly in his dispatches of April 18 and on the following days. However, Stalin took no heed of these warnigs. What is more, Stalin ordered that no credence be given to information of this sort, in order not to provoke the initiation of military operations.

We must assert that information of this sort concerning the threat of German armed invasion of Soviet territory was coming in also from our own military and diplomatic sources; however, because the leadership was conditioned against such information, such data was dispatched with fear and assessed with reservation.

When the fascist armies had actually invaded Soviet territory and military operations began, Moscow issued the order that the German fire was not to be returned. Why? It was because Stalin, despite evident facts, thought that the war had not yet started, that this was only a provocative action on the part of several undisciplined sections of the German Army, and that our reaction might serve as a reason for the Germans to begin the war.

The following fact is also known: On the eve of the invasion of the territory of the Soviet Union by the Hitlerite army, a certain German citizen crossed our border and stated that the German armies had received orders to start the offensive against the Soviet Union on the night of June 22 at 3 o'clock. Stalin was informed about this immediately, but even this warning was ignored.

As you see, everything was ignored: warnings of certain

Army commanders, declarations of deserters from the enemy army, and even the open hostility of the enemy. Is this an example of the alertness of the chief of the party and of the state at this particularly significant historical moment?

And what were the results of this carefree attitude, this disregard of clear facts? The result was that already in the first hours and days the enemy had destroyed in our border regions a large part of our Air Force, artillery and other military equipment; he annihilated large numbers of our military cadres and disorganized our military leadership; consequently we could not prevent the enemy from marching deep into this country.

Very grievous consequences, especially in reference to the beginning of the war, followed Stalin's annihilation of many military commanders and political workers during 1937-1941 because of his suspiciousness and through slanderous accusations. During these years repressions were instituted against certain parts of the military cadres beginning literally at the company and batalion commander level and extending to the higher military centers; during this time the cadre of leaders who had gained military experience in Spain and the Far East was almost completely liquidated.

The policy of large-scale repression against the military cadres led also to undermined military discipline, because for several years officers of all ranks and even soldiers in the party and Komsomol cells were taught to "unmask" their superiors as hidden enemies. (Movement in the hall.) It is natural that this caused a negative influence on the state of military discipline in the first war period.

And, as you know, we had before the war excellent military cadres which were unquestionably loyal to the party and to the Fatherland. Suffice it to say that those of them who managed to survive, despite severe tortures to which they were subjected in the prisons, have from the first war days shown themselves real patriots and heroically fought for the glory of the Fatherland; I have here in mind such comrades as Rokossovsky (who, as you know, had been jailed), Gorbatov, Maretskov (who is a delegate at the present Congress), Podlas (he was an excellent commander who perished at the front), and many, many others. However, many such commanders perished in camps and jails and the Army saw them no more.

All this brought about the situation which existed at the beginning of the war and which was the great threat to our Fatherland.

111

It would be incorrect to forget that, after the first severe disaster and defeat at the front, Stalin thought that this was the end. In one of his speeches in those days he said: "All that which Lenin created we have lost forever."

After this Stalin for a long time actually did not direct the military operations and ceased to do anything whatever. He turned to active leadership only when some members of the Political Bureau visited him and told him that it was necessary to take certain steps immediately in order to improve the situation at the front.

Therefore, the threatening danger which hung over our Fatherland in the first period of the war was largely due to the faulty methods of directing the nation and the party by Stalin himself.

However, we speak not only about the moment when the war began, which led to serious disorganization of our Army and brought us severe losses. Even after the war began, the nervousness and hysteria which Stalin demonstrated, interfering with actual military operation, caused our Army serious damage.

Stalin was very far from an understanding of the real situation which was developing at the front. This was natural because, during the whole Patriotic War, he never visited any section of the front or any liberated city except for one short ride on the Mozhaisk highway during a stabilized situation at the front. To this incident were dedicated many literary works full of fantasies of all sorts and so many paintings. Simultaneously, Stalin was interfering with operations and issuing orders which did not take into consideration the real situation at a given section of the front and which could not help but result in huge personnel loses.

The tactics on which Stalin insisted without knowing the essence of the conduct of battle operations cost us much blood until we succeeded in stopping the opponent and going over to the offensive.

The military know that already by the end of 1941, instead of great operational maneuvers flanking the opponent and penetrating behind his back, Stalin demanded incessant frontal attacks and the capture of one village after another.

Because of this, we paid with great losses - until our generals, on whose shoulders rested the whole weight of conducting the war, succeeded in changing the situation and shifting to flexible-maneuver operations, whch immediately brought serious changes at the front favorable to us.

All the more shameful was the fact that, after our great victory over the enemy which cost us so much, Stalin began to downgrade many of the commanders who contributed so much to the victory over the enemy, because Stalin excluded every possibility that services rendered at the front should be credited to anyone but himself.

In the same vein, let us take, for instance, our historical and military films and some literary creations; they make us feel sick. Their true objective is the propagation of the theme of praising Stalin as a military genius. Let us recall the film, The Fall of Berlin. Here only Stalin acts; he issues orders in the hall in which there are many empty chairs and only one man approached him and reports something to him - that is Poskrebyshev, his loyal shield-bearer. (Laughter in the hall.)

And where is the military command? Where is the Political Bureau? Where is the Government? What are they doing and with what are they engaged? There is nothing about them in the film. Stalin acts for everybody; he does not reckon with anyone; he asks no one for advice. Everything is shown to the nation in this false light. Why? In order to surround Stalin with glory, contrary to the facts and contrary to historical truth.

The question arises: And where are the military, on whose shoulders rested the burden of the war? They are not in the film; with Stalin in, no room was left for them.

Deportation of Whole Nations

Comrades, let us reach for some other facts. The Soviet Union is justly considered a model of a multinational state because we have in practice assured the equality and friendship of all nations which live in our great Fatherland.

All the more monstrous are the acts whose initiator was Stalin and which are rude violations of the basic Leninist principles of the nationality policy of the Soviet state. We refer to the mass deportations from their native places of whole nations, together with all Communists and Komsomols without any exception; this deportation action was not dictated by any military considerations.

Thus, already at the end of 1943, when there occurred a permanent break-through at the fronts of the Great Patriotic War benefiting the Soviet Union, a decision was taken and executed concerning the deportation of all the Karachai from the lands on which they lived.

In the same period, at the end of December 1943, the same lot befell the whole population of the Autonomous Kalmyk Republic. In March 1944, all the Chechen and Ingush peoples were deported and the Chechen-Ingush Autonomous Republic was liquidated. In April 1944, all Balkars were deported to faraway places from the territory of the Kabardino-Balkar Autonomous Republic and the Republic itself was named the Autonomous Kabardian Republic.

The Ukrainians avoided meeting this fate only because there were too many of them and there was no place to which to deport them. Otherwise, he would have deported them also. (Laughter in the hall.)

Not only a Marxist-Leninist but also no man of common sense can grasp how it is possible to make whole nations responsible for inimical activity, including women, children, old people, Communists and Komsomols, to use mass repression against them, and to expose them to misery and suffering for the hostile acts of individual persons or groups of persons.

The "Leningrad Affair"
After the conclusion of the Patriotic War, the Soviet nation stressed with pride the magnificent victories gained through great sacrifices and tremendous efforts. The country experienced a period of political enthusiasm. The party came out of the war even more united; in the fire of the war, party cadres were tempered and hardened. Under such conditions nobody could have even thought of the possibility of some plot in the party.

And it was precisely at this time that the so-called "Leningrad affair" was born. As we have now proven, this case was fabricated. Those who innocently lost their lives included Comrade Voznesensky, Kuznetsov, Rodionov, Popkov, and others.

As is known, Voznesensky and Kuznetsov were talented and eminent leaders. Once they stood very close to Stalin. It is sufficient to mention that Stalin made Voznesensky first deputy to the chairman of the Council of Ministers and Kuznetsov was elected Secretary of the Central Committee. The very fact that Stalin entrusted Kuznetsov with the supervision of the state-security organs shows the trust which he enjoyed.

How did it happen that these persons were branded as enemies of the people and liquidated?

Facts prove that the "Leningrad affair" is also the result of willfulness which Stalin exercised against party cadres. Had a normal situation existed in the party's Central Committee and in the Central Committee Political Bureau, affairs of this nature would have been examined there in accordance with party practice, and all pertinent facts assessed; as a result, such an affair as well as others would not have happened.

We must state that, after the war, the situation became even more complicated. Stalin became even more capricious, irritable and brutal; in particular, his suspicion grew. His persecution mania reached unbelievable dimensions. Many workers were becoming enemies before his very eyes. After the war Stalin separated himself from the collective even more. Everything was decided by him alone without any consideration for anyone or anything.

This unbelievable suspicion was cleverly taken advantage of by the abject provocateur and vile enemy, Beria, who had murdered thousands of Communists and Soviet people. The elevation of Voznesensky and Kuznetsov alarmed Beria. As we have now proven, it had been precisely Beria who had "suggested" to Stalin the fabrication by him and by his confidants of materials in the form of declarations and anonymous letters, and in the form of various rumors and talks.

The party's Central Committee has examined this so-called "Leningrad affair"; persons who innocently suffered are now rehabilitated and honor has been restored to the glorious Leningrad party organization. Abakumov and others who had fabricated the affair were brought before a court; their trial took place in Leningrad and they received what they deserved.

The question arises: Why is it that we see the truth of this affair only now, and why did we not do something earlier, during Stalin's life, in order to prevent the loss of innocent lives? It was because Stalin personally supervised the "Leningrad affair," and the majority of the Political Bureau members did not, at that time, know all of the circumstances in these matters and could not therefore intervene.

When Stalin received certain material from Beria and Abakumov, without examining these slanderous materials he ordered an investigation of the "affair" of Voznesensky and Kuznetsov. With this, their fate was sealed.

The Rift with Tito
The willfulness of Stalin showed itself not only in decisions concerning the internal life of the country but also in the international relations of the Soviet Union.

The July plenum of the Central Committee studied in detail the reasons for the development of the conflict with Yugoslavia. It was a shameful role which Stalin played here. The "Yugoslavia affair" contained no problems which could not have been solved through party discussions among comrades. There was no significant basis for the development of this "affair"; it was completely possible to have prevented the rupture of relations with that country. This does not mean, however, that the Yugoslav leaders did not make mistakes or did not have shortcomings. But these mistakes and shortcomings were magnified in a monstrous manner by Stalin, which resulted in a break of relations with a friendly country.

I recall the first days when the conflict between the Soviet Union and Yugoslovia began artificially to be blown up. Once, when I came from Kiev to Moscow, I was invited to visit Stalin, who, pointing to the copy of a letter lately sent to Tito, asked me, "Have you read this?"

Not waiting for my reply, he answered, "I will shake my little finger - and there will be no more Tito. He will fall."

We have dearly paid for this "shaking of the little finger." This statement reflected Stalin´s mania for greatness, but he acted just that way: "I will shake my little finger - and there will be no more Kossior"; "I will shake my little finger once more and Postyshev and Chubar will be no more"; "I will shake my little finger again - and Voznesensky, Kuznetsov and many others will disappear."

But this did not happen to Tito. No matter how much or how little Stalin shook, not only his little finger but everything else he could shake, Tito did not fall. Why? The reason was that, in this case of disagreement with the Yugoslav comrades, Tito had behind him a state and a people who had gone through a severe school of fighting for liberty and independence, a people which gave support to its leaders.

You see to what Stalin´s mania for greatness led. He had completely lost consciousness of reality; he demonstrated his suspicion and haughtiness not only in relation to individuals in the USSR, but in relation to whole parties and nations.

We have carefully examined the case of Yugoslavia and have found a proper solution which is approved by the peoples of the Soviet Union and of Yugoslavia as well as by the working masses of all the people´s democracies and by all progressive humanity. The liqidation of the abnormal relationship with Yugoslavia was done in the interest of the whole camp of socialism, in the interest of strengthening peace in the whole world.

The Affair of the "Doctors' Plot"

Let us also recall the "affair of the doctor-plotters." (Animation in the hall.) Actually there was no "affair" outside of the declaration of the woman doctor Timashuk, who was probably influenced or ordered by someone (after all, she was an unofficial collaborator of the organs of state security) to write Stalin a letter in which she declared that doctors were applying improper methods of medical treatment.

Such a letter was sufficient for Stalin to reach an immediate conclusion that there are doctor-plotters in the Soviet Union. He issued orders to arrest a group of eminent Soviet medical specialists. He personally issued advice on the conduct of the investigation and the method of interrogation of the arrested persons. He said that the academician Vinogradov should be put in chains, another one should be beaten. Present at this Congress as a delegate is the former Minister of State Security, Comrade Ignatiev. Stalin told him curtly, "If you do not obtain confessions from the doctors we will shorten you by a head." (Tumult in the hall.)

Stalin personally called the investigative judge, gave him instructions, advised him on which investigative methods should be used; these methods were simple - beat, beat and, once again, beat.

Shortly after the doctors were arrested, we members of the Political Bureau received protocols with the doctors' confessions of guilt. After distributing these protocols, Stalin told us, "You are blind like young kittens; what will happen without me? The country will perish because you do not know how to recognize enemies."

The case was so presented that no one could verify the facts on which the investigation was based. There was no possibility of trying to verify facts by contacting those who had made the confessions of guilt.

We felt, however, that the case of the arrested doctors was questionable. We knew some of these people personally because they had once treated us. When we examined this "case" after Stalin's death, we found it had to be fabricated from beginning to end.

This ignominious "case" was set up by Stalin; he did not, however, have the time in which to bring it to an end (as he conceived that end), and for this reason the doctors are still alive. Now all have been rehabilitated; they are working in the same places they were working before; they treat top individuals, not excluding members of the Government; they have our full confidence; and they execute their duties honestly, as

117

they did before.

In organizing the various dirty and shameful cases, a very base role was played by the rabid enemy of our party, an agent of a foreign intelligence service - Beria, who had stolen into Stalin´s confidence. In what way could this provocateur gain such a position in the party and in the state, so as to become the First Deputy Chairman of the Council of Ministers of the Soviet Union and a member of the Central Committee Political Bureau? It has now been established that this villan had climbed up the Government ladder over an untold number of corpses.

Self-Adulation

Comrades: The cult of the individual acquired such monstrous size chiefly because Stalin himself, using all conceivable methods, supported the glorification of his own person. This is supported by numerous facts. One of the most characteristic examples of Stalin´s self-glorification and his lack of even elementary modesty is the edition of his Short Biography, which was published in 1948.

This book is an expression of the most dissolute flattery, an example of making a man into a godhead, of transforming him into an infallible sage, "the greatest leader, sublime strategist of all times and nations." Finally, no other words could be found with which to lift Stalin up to the heavens.

We need not give here examples of loathsome adulation filling this book. All we need to add is that they all were approved and edited by Stalin personally and some of them were added in his own handwriting to the draft text of the book.

What did Stalin consider essential to write into this book? Did he want to cool the ardor of his flatters who were composing his Short Biography? No! He marked the very places where he thought that the praise of his services was insufficient. Here are some examples characterizing Stalin´s activity, added in Stalin´s own hand:

"In this fight against the skeptics and capitulators, the Trotskyites, Zinovievites, Bukharinites and Kamenevites, there was definitely welded together, after Lenin´s death, that leading core of party...that upheld the great banner of Lenin, rallied the party behind Lenin´s behests, and brought the Soviet people into the broad road of industrializing the country and collectivizing the rural economy. The leader of this core and the guiding force of the party and the state was Comrade Stalin."

Thus writes Stalin himself! Then he adds:

"Although he performed his task as leader of the party and
the people with consummate skill and enjoyed the unreserved
support of the entire Soviet people, Stalin never allowed his
work to be marred by the slightest hint of vanity, conceit or
self-adulation."

Where and when could a leader so praise himself? Is this
worthy of a leader of the Marxist-Leninist type? No.
Precisely against this did Marx and Engels take such a strong
position. This also was always sharply condemned by Vladimir
Ilyich Lenin.

In the draft of his book appeared the following sentence:
"Stalin is the Lenin of today." This sentence appeared to
Stalin to be too weak, so in his own handwriting, he changed it
to read: "Stalin is the worthy continuer of Lenin's work, or,
as it is said in our party, Stalin is the Lenin of today." You
see how well it is said, not by the nation but by Stalin
himself.

It is possible to give many such self-praising appraisals
written into the draft text of that book in Stalin's hand.
Especially generously does he endow himself with praises
pertaining to his military genius, to his talent for strategy.

I will cite one more insertion made by Stalin concerning
the theme of the Stalinist military genius. "The advanced
Soviet science of war received further development," he writes,
"at Comrade Stalin's hands. Comrade Stalin elaborated the
theory of the permanently operating factors that decide the
issue of wars, of active defense and the laws of
counteroffensive and offensive, of the cooperation of all
services and arms in modern warfare, of the role of big tank
masses and air forces in modern war, and of the artillery as
the most formidable of the armed services. At the various
stages of war Stalin's genius found the correct solutions that
took account of all the circumstances of the situation."
(Movement in the hall.)

And, further, writes Stalin: "Stalin's military
mastership was displayed both in defense and offense. Comrade
Stalin's genius enabled him to divide the enemy's plans and
defeat them. The battles in which Comrade Stalin directed the
Soviet armies are brilliant examples of operational military
skill."

In this manner was Stalin praised as a strategist. Who
did this? Stalin himself, not in his role as a strategist but
in the role of an author-editor, one of the main creators of

his self-adulatory biography. Such, comrades, are the facts. We should rather say shameful facts.

And one additional fact from the same Short Biography of Stalin. As it is known, The Short Course of the History of the All-Union Communist Party (Bolsheviks) was written by a commission of the party Central Committee.

This book, parenthetically, was also permeated with the cult of the individual and was written by a designated group of authors. This fact was reflected in the following formulation of the proof copy of the Short Biography of Stalin: "A commission of the Central Committee, All-Union Communist Party (Bolsheviks), under the direction of Comrade Stalin and with his most active personal participation, has prepared a Short Course of the History of the All-Union Communist Party (Bolsheviks)."

But even this phrase did not satisfy Stalin: The following sentence replaced it in the final version of the Short Biography: "In 1938 appeared the book, History of the All-Union Communist Party (Bolsheviks), Short Course, written by Comrade Stalin and approved by a commission of the Central Committee, All-Union Communist Party (Bolsheviks)." Can one add anything more? (Animation in the hall.)

As you see, a surprising metamorphosis changed the work created by a group into a book written by Stalin. It is not necessary to state how and why this metamorphosis took place.

A pertinent question comes to our mind: If Stalin is the author of this book, why did he need to praise the person of Stalin so much and to transform the whole post-October historical period of our glorious Communist party solely into an action of "the Stalin genius"?

Did this book properly reflect the efforts of the party in the socialist transformation of the country, in the construction of socialist society, in the industrialization and collectivization of the country, and also other steps taken by the party which undeviatingly traveled the path outlined by Lenin? This book speaks principally about Stalin, about his speeches, about his reports. Everything without the smallest exception to his name.

And when Stalin himself asserts that he himself wrote the Short Course of the History of the All-Union Communist Party (Bolsheviks), this calls at least for amazement. Can a Marxist-Leninist thus write about himself, praising his own person to the heavens?

120

Or let us take the matter of the Stalin Prizes. (Movement in the hall.) Not even the Czars created prizes which they named after themselves.

Where was the Central Committee?

Some comrades may ask us: Where were the members of the Political Bureau of the Central Committee? Why did they not assert themselves against the cult of the individual in time? And why is this being done only now?

First of all, we have to consider the fact that the members of the Political Bureau viewed these matters in a different way at different times. Initially, many of them backed Stalin actively because Stalin was one of the strongest Marxists and his logic, his strength and his will greatly influenced the cadres and party work.

It is known that Stalin, after Lenin's death, especially during the first years, actively fought for Leninism against the enemies of Leninist theory and against those who deviated. Beginning with Leninist theory, the party, with its Central Committee at the head, started on a great scale the work of socialist industrialization of the country, agricultural collectivization and the cultural revolution.

At that time Stalin gained great popularity, sympathy and support. The party had to fight those who attempted to lead the country away from the correct Leninist path; it had to fight Trotskyites, Zinovievites and rightists, and the bourgeois nationalists. This fight was indispensable.

Later, however, Stalin, abusing his power more and more, began to fight eminent party and Government leaders and to use terrorist methods against honest Soviet people. As we have already shown, Stalin thus handled such eminent party and Government leaders as Kossior, Rudzutak, Eikhe, Postyshev and many others.

Attempts to oppose groundless suspicions and charges resulted in the opponent falling victim of the repression. This characterized the fall of Comrade Postyshev.

In one of his speeches Stalin expressed his dissatisfaction with Postyshev and asked him, "What are you actually?"

Postyshev answered clearly, "I am a Bolshevik, Comrade Stalin, a Bolshevik."

This assertion was at first considered to show a lack of respect for Stalin; later it was considered a harmful act and consequently resulted in Postyshev´s annihilation and branding without reason as a "people´s enemy."

In the situation which then prevailed I have talked often with Nikolai Alexandrovich Bulganin; once when we two were traveling in a car, he said, "It has happened sometimes that a man goes to Stalin on his invitation as a friend. And, when he sits with Stalin, he does not know where he will be sent next - home or to jail."

It is clear that such conditions put every member of the Political Bureau in a very difficult situation. And, when we also consider the fact that in the last years the Central Committee plenary sessions were not convened and that the sessions of the Political Bureau occurred only occasionally, from time to time, then we will understand how difficult it was for any member of the Political Bureau to take a stand against one or another unjust or improper procedure, against serious errors and shortcomings in the practices of leadership.

Editors' Note

1. This is the former title of the KGB, the Soviet intelligence organization.

SOVIET POLITICS AND CULTURE

A political culture is a particular distribution of political values, attitudes feelings, information and skills. As an individual's values affect what he or she will do, a nation's political culture affects the conduct of its citizens and leaders throughout the political system. Each nation has its own particular mix which makes each unique. It is important to note the contours of this culture which determines the amount of latitude that leaders and citizens have in their behavior and how they perform their political duties and respond to political events.

It should be kept in mind that interpretation and acceptance of the expectations, attitudes, and values that make up a political culture are likely to vary widely in coherence and intensity among members of a community as a whole and especially among members of various religious, ethnic, regional, and occupational subcultures. In addition, in nations such as the Soviet Union that have undergone rapid industrialization, the political culture is in constant state of change as individual citizens define themselves and the state differently as their positions in society change.

Finally, the Soviet Union is a nation with a revolutionary ideology whose goal is no less than to remake man into a new ideal Soviet Man who is selfless and cooperative. As a result, the Soviet Government has undergone a concerted effort to socialize the young and re-socialize the adults through education, social organizations and the media into this new belief system.

In order to understand the politics of a nation, it is imperative to understand a nation's culture. In order to understand this culture it is necessary to survey the landscape of a nation. By this, it is meant the physical geography, the history, the composition of the various ethnic and religious groups along with the traditions and outlooks they represent. It is also important to look at the structure of its government and process by which it solves its political conflict and policy questions. For this important task, Frederick Barghoorn and Thomas Remington's article entitled, "Politics in the U.S.S.R." has been selected. Barghoorn and Remington give us an important overview of the Soviet Union which not only covers history, demographics, religious and ethnic compositions, the role of government and the role of the Party, but also explains how each element is interrelated to all other elements.

The second article is by Wayne DiFranceisco and Zvi Gitelman entitled, "Soviet Political Culture and `Covert Participation´ in Policy Implementation." This article examines Soviet Culture through the dimension of political participation. The study of political participation was based on interviews with recent emigres. The authors find that in the Soviet Union there is no meaningful participation in the development of public policy. The citizens are not surprised or shocked by this lack of participation in this level of public policymaking. However, there are meaningful forms of participation in the system, but they take place either outside the nominally participatory institutions or within those institutions but in nonproscribed ways. The Soviet citizen generally participates in a covert manner, utilizing unsanctioned or blatantly illegal methods in attempts to influence how policy is implemented as it affects the individual, but not policymaking. DiFranceisco and Gitelman conclude that Soviet citizens behave in a traditional and prerevolutionary mode of behavior with regard to interactions between citizen and state. And that these patterns are reinforced by Soviet socio-economic development and by a highly centralized and hierarchical administrative structure which itself, is a continuation of czarist patterns. The study describes how different educational groups view their degree of freedom and efficacy in changing public policy. It also describes the different techniques of power used by varying strata of Soviet citizens in an attempt to persuade bureaucracies to implement policy in a favorable manner to the individual. Finally, the study looks at how the varying bureaucracies, including education and housing, respond to various techniques used to influence its policy implementation.

This article gives an insight into Soviet culture and how Soviet society functions. It certainly demonstrates that the Socialist ideal is a long way from present reality, and in particular, the egalitarian ideal. The article also gives us a glimpse of citizens´ expectations of the system and how they cope with everyday life.

The third article is by Frank M. Sorrentino and is entitled, "Russian Political Culture and Socialization." It examines the Russians´ history under the czars and their legacy of power and authority.

The Russian people and their leaders developed a messianic mission of spreading the Orthodox religion and civilization to other nations. They saw Rome and Constantinople fall and perceive themselves as the third Rome which shall never fall

and hence a fourth Rome is not necessary. Rome and
Constantinople fell because of weakness and a lack of
steadfastness to their beliefs and principles. They have
absorbed these patterns into their culture. These cultural
dimensions have justified policies of expansionism and
authoritarianism.

Sorrentino also points out how the physical environment
has lead to a form of collectivism and further justified
authoritarianism. Life in the rugged terrain was difficult.
The cooperation of the entire village was essential to
survival. Each member of the village had to help the others
and share his resources if difficulty arose. The individual
did not know whether it would be he who needed the help the
next time. In addition, decisions had to be made and enforced.
A father disciplined his wife and children if they did not do
what was necessary on the farms. In turn, the father was
subject to his superiors and so on and so on, until the czar,
who was seen as the stern but wise father of all the Russian
people.

Sorrentino argues that while Communism is qualitatively
different from czarism and orthodoxy, there are strong
similarities - a utopian vision in which Russian people play an
essential role in bringing to the other people of the globe
strong and stern leadership to accomplish these goals and a
strong sense of collectivism. Sorrentino contends that
Communism was a philosophy that was congenial to the
traditional values of the Russian people. The last reign of
the czars and the brief democratic government were weak and had
to be replaced by stronger, more visionary leaders. Lenin and
his followers fulfilled these cultural and symbolic needs quite
effectively.

Sorrentino states that while Russian political culture
greatly assisted the ascendance of Communism in Russia, that
culture proves to be a difficult impediment for the Communist
Party to accomplish its goals, in particular, to develop a New
Soviet Man and to increase industrialization in the Soviet
Union.

Sorrentino concludes that the Soviet political culture is
a significant and persistent factor that must be taken into
consideration when one attempts to understand the Soviet Union.

The final article in this section is by David K. Shipler,
entitled, "The Willing Suspension of Disbelief," which is an
excerpt from his book, Russia: Broken Idols, Solemn Dreams.
This book was based on Shipler's experience as a correspondent
for The New York Times stationed in the Soviet Union.

In this article, Shipler discusses the process of education in the Soviet Union. He begins with a section called, "Teaching Political Values." Shipler describes his observations of several Soviet schools, in which he points out the extensive and propagandistic methods employed by the schools to teach the values of the regime and of Communism. In teaching English, teachers use such political documents as "The Draft Contitution of the USSR as their reading materials." Students are encouraged to parrot political slogans. Shipler points out that "Lenin is portrayed as the embodiment of goodness, the avuncular figure of kindness who sits and talks with little boys and girls as Jesus tended his flock." In fact, Shipler makes the analogy to American Catholic schools in which a picture of Jesus is the central focus of the class. In the Soviet schools it is a picture of Lenin that occupies the focal point.

Quotations from Lenin are used generously throughout textbooks on most subjects. Shipler suggests that if an author omits them he is advised to insert a few. Students also learn that a line or two from Lenin, Brezhnev and Andropov is a prerequisite for a good grade.

Politics pervades all aspects of education even in the apolitical subject of mathematics. Textbook authors sprinkle exercises and word problems designed to remind pupils of the superiority of the Soviet state and to sensitize them to the fundamental mechanics of a socialist society.

Shipler contends that the schools are learning grounds for hypocricy. Children routinely give the teachers what they expect in terms of slogans and correct opinions with parental encouragement. Students join organizations such as the Octobrists, Pioneers, and the Komsomol (Communist youth and party groups) because membership is important for admission to universities and for good jobs. Shipler also points out that there is widespread cheating and that this is rarely clamped down upon because teachers are under pressure to give good grades to indicate their own productivity. Students quickly learn that they can get away with most things if they maintain the proper political positions in public.

Shipler demonstrates through his own anecdotes the reluctance of students to criticize their government and its party line. He concludes through extensive indoctrination, clear economic and social incentives and a willingness to learn a degree of hypocricy, the Soviet Union and its citizens have learned to live with each other. Shipler, however, feels that there is a certain emptiness and lack of fulfillment in the process.

It is contended that the Soviet Political System is still significantly influenced by its prior history and culture and that the new regime is comprehensively and systematically attempting, and with some success, influencing its future. This section provides the reader with a series of articles which are intended to give an overview of the Soviet political system, Soviet political culture, and its socialization process. It focuses on how the Soviet political leaders use educational institutions to promote their political goals and the obstacles that they face.

POLITICS IN THE U.S.S.R.

Frederick C. Barghoorn and
Thomas Remington

Significance of the Russian Revolution

The influence of a revolution on human societies might be
likened to that of an earthquake on the natural environment, or
as Crane Brinton argued in The Anatomy of Revolution, to the
effect of acute but not mortal illness on a human being.(1)
Such events unleash forces that, if sustained long enough at
full power, bring total transformation or destruction.

Upheavals give way to new equilibria, however. Organisms,
species, and communities survive. The post-revolutionary state
of affairs, in political systems, is a combination of elements
and influences carried over from the prerevolutionary order,
with new ones created by the forces that upset the old
equilibrium. Thus, in both the French Revolution of the
eighteenth century and the Russian in the twentieth,
bureaucratic centralism seems to have survived stronger than
ever. In less-developed countries, however, many people
perceive the progress in industry and technology of modern
revolutionary regimes more positively than do most Westerners.
More than any other political experience, revolutions engage
the emotions of men and women, kindling commitment and hope for
a bright future in some, fear and loathing in others. These
observations apply with particular force to the irreconcilable,
intransigent challenge to establish authority and political
culture not only in Russia but of the whole capitalist world
posed by the Bolsheviks, led by Lenin (real name: Validimr
Ilich Ulyanov), when they seized power on November 6, 1917
(October 25, old-style calendar).

The ambitious Bolsheviks were seemingly boundless. Their
program demanded abolition of private property and even of a
money economy, smashing of the bourgeois state and its
replacement first by the dictatorship of the proletariat and

ultimately by a stateless, classless, coercionless society.
They went even further, calling for trasformation of human
beings into new, socialist men and women, purged of all the
defects and weaknesses produced by feudalism and capitalism.

The Bolsheviks brought to their task of transforming
Russia and the world the unique organizational weapon of the
elite vanguard political party.(2) Political strategy,
tactics, propaganda, and organization - above all, organization
- were the major tactics of Lenin as well as of those who have
ruled Russia in his name since his death. The vanguard,
Leninist hegemonic party embodied the organizational and
strategic knowhow Lenin distilled from his experience as a
revolutionary conspirator and political prisoner in Russia and
as an exile and polemicist in Europe. There was much diversity
of outlook among the Bolsheviks, though, and Lenin had to draw
heavily on his astuteness and strength of will to guide the
party, which came to power disastrously lacking in consensus on
specific policies.

Although Lenin's disciplined "party of a new type" was
designed to destroy the autocracy of the tsars, it absorbed
from the politics and environment against which it had
struggled an authoritarian-bureaucratic spirit. This strain
coexisted with other elements, including veneration for
technology and militant utopianism, derived from Marxism and
from native Russian radicals, such as Nikolai Chernyshevski.

Despite the two regimes' similar authoritarianism, the
Soviet elite, recruited on the basis of performance (including
loyalty) rather than inheritance, differs enormously from the
hereditary nobility and the rising middle classes who dominated
the political and social life of the empire. Even today, the
Soviet regime at least pays lip service to egalitarian,
plebeian, and populist values largely absent from the tsarist
political culture. On the other hand the Soviet culture,
heavily reliant on ritualistic conformity to authority and
deeply conscious of hierarchic differences in status, bears a
striking and increasing resemblance to that of tsarist Russia.

Obviously the Soviet regime has been more successful than
the old regime in generating military power and projecting
abroad. Here the centralized political machine created by
Lenin and perfected by Stalin has been invaluable. Also, the
Bolsheviks' enthusiasm for economic development, science, and
technology - expressed in recent years primarily in the
movement to effect the "scientific-technological revolution" -
has fed economic and military power. In foreign policy, the
Bolsheviks and their successors have benefitted from the
opportunity to side with oppressed classes and people

everywhere. As leaders of the first avowedly socialist state,
they seek to turn to their advantage social and national
tensions in a world in which modernization undermines
traditional values and institutions.

The Soviet regime's achievements are considerable, though
often overrated; certainly they have been costly in human life
and freedom. The Soviet record has been fairly strong - though
again often overstated - in such fields as mass access to
social services, public health, and education. But since the
1930s persons of high bureaucratic or professional status and
city dwellers have been heavily favored over workers, and the
latter over peasants. Moreover, for many the discrimination,
harassment, and persecution practiced by the regime against
religious believers has been a major source of suffering,
though the regime regards its militant atheist propaganda as a
vital means of instilling an enlightened modern outlook.

Still, these achievements and their costs have little in
common with the ideals that many Bolsheviks professed in the
War Communism era (1917-1920), when hopes were widespread that
a just, egalitarian, democratic society could be quickly
created. Many evils of Society that Lenin denounced, such as
ethnic discrmination, official corruption, and violation of
civil rights, often flagrant, persist.

Is it possible to explain the limited success of the
Russian Revolution? The following suggestions may be useful in
seeking an answer to this difficult question.

1. The Bolshevik political culture was, at its core, both
authoritarian and pragmatic. When choices had to be made
between ends and means, expedience took priority.
2. The attempt to impose an ambitious program of development
and transformation on the mainly tradition-bound population
generated fierce resistance. The new leaders believed that
suppression of resistance, maintenance of the regime's power,
and the prosaic but vital tasks of economic administration
required rapid construction of a centralized state machine,
possessing the capacity for massive coercion. After a time
this machine ceased to be regarded as a means; its preservation
became an end in itself.
3. Although pressure on the labor force was extreme during
the civil war period (1918-1921), it was enormously intensified
during Stalin's "revolution from above." Even more than the
civil war, the drives for industrialization and agricultural
collectivization after 1929 fostered the administrative methods
and attitudes that underlie contemporary Soviet policy. In
particular, Stalin's virtual reenserfment of the peasants on
collective farms and the deportation of millions of resistant
or suspect peasants to forced labor camps contributed to the

power and growth of the secret police.

4. The Bolsheviks' zeal to extend their system beyond Soviet borders and the hostility of foreign governments to the new regime, partly a response to Soviet revolutionary expansionism, spurred militarization of the Soviet economy and a militaristic mentality.

5. Leninist ideology, especially its downplaying of the role of law in favor of arbitrary coercion as an instrument of rule, and the enduring habit of justifying expedient actions by reference to noble goals, made it difficult squarely to face the problems at the center of the Western political tradition: how to limit the power of government over individuals and to establish the accountability of political leaders to citizens.

Political authorities in Russia not only have the powers by liberal governments but also control the economy - and thus the life chances of the population. Such concentrated power militates against freedom for individual and group action.

<u>Historical Background</u>
Soviet power was forged and acquired enduring characteristics in the crucible of revolution and civil war. Beginning with the abdication of Tsar Nicholas II in February 1917, the Russian empire rapidly disintegrated. A society already savagely battered by the German offensives of World War I endured four years of civil war. In an experienced provisional government, power passed from bourgeois liberals to the moderate vocalist Alexander Kerensky, but by November 1917 the Bolshevik faction of the Marxist Social Democrats, headed by Lenin, Lev Trotsky, Josef Stalin, Grigori Zinoviev, Lev Kamenev, Nikolai Bukharin, and other seasoned revolutionaries, was able to seize power. Thus began the most profound, radical, and world-shaking social revolution of our century. The ideals of equality and justice proclaimed by Lenin remains unrealized, but all Soviet leaders since Lenin have claimed legitimacy in his name and in that of the official creed, formulated under Stalin, of Marxism-Leninism.

The revolution's roots lie deep in Russia's past; its catalyst was catastrophic defeat in World War I. The earlier humiliating defeat in the Russo-Japanese war of 1904 and 1905 had produced a crisis viewed by Lenin as a dress rehearsal for the great revolution to come. But it was Russia's enormous losses in World War I that broke the back of the old regime. The war at first had popular support, but disastrous mismanagement of the fight with Germany led to disillusionment. Most of the tsar's subjects, including eventually most of the military, turned against the war; the Bolsheviks' promise to end it contributed powerfully to their victory.

An unpopular war was not the only reason for Lenin's

stunning conquest. Bolshevik land-reform slogans fanned a peasant uprising; many peasant-soldiers deserted the army and came home to seize their share of the land. In the cities were food shortages that brought to the boiling point the simmering antagonism between workers and employers. Another factor was dissatisfaction of the non-Russian nationalities that formed half the population. Pressures mounted in 1917 as diverse elements - radicalized soldiers, peasants, workers, and national minorities - were mobilized by the Bolsheviks, by far the best organized and most skillfully led of the revolutionary parties, into a force that brought a new form of government into the world, dedicated to abolishing capitalism and building socialism.

Bolshevik rule was consolidated and partly legitimatized by victory in the bitter civil war (1918-1920), in which moderate socialist parties, such as the Mensheviks and the Social Revolutionaries, and all nonsocialists were eliminated from contention. Battle lines were drawn between the "Reds" (Bolsheviks) and the "Whites" (forces loyal to the deposed Tsar Nicolas). Halfhearted, bungling intervention by France and Britain, in which the United States and Japan also took part, probably helped rather than hurt the communists, casting them as defenders of the homeland against foreign foes.

In the first years of the revolution, the Soviet regime moved ruthlessly against its enemies, expropriating the propertied classes and creating a political police (the Cheka) empowered to employ terror against opponents of the regime. The new leaders endeavored to centralize political power and to put into practice many of their theories of socialism. They expected that revolution in the advanced countries of Europe would bring the Western working classes to their aid. When these revolutions failed to materialize, and at home workers and peasants rose in opposition to Bolshevik dictatorship, the regime reversed itself early in 1921 and introduced a limited return to private enterprise.

The New Economic Policy (NEP) as it was called, facilitated economic recovery. New conflicts arose within the party, however, once Lenin died in 1924, Lenin's chief lieutenants vied to succeed the revered leader in a bitter struggle for power. Stalin, head of the administrative machinery of the party, skillfully manipulated policy issues while building up a corps of local party secretaries loyal to him. First outmaneuvering Trotsky and other leftists, then Bukharin and the right. Stalin achieved dominance by the late 1920s. He then saw to the rewriting of party history, portraying Trotsky as disloyal and himself as Lenin's trusted discipline and logical heir.

Stalin codified the doctrines of the party and named the official creed "Marxism-Leninism"; he was the dogma's official interpreter. In 1929 Stalin declared that the time was right to advance rapidly to socialism. Any opposition to his policies was equated with treason, and was dealt with accordingly. Exceeding the coercive practices of War Communism, Stalin mobilized millions of people to build new industries and create an administrative structure to run them; by violence he collectivized agriculture, exiling or killing millions of kulaks (better-off peasants, or any who opposed collectivization); he squeezed out private enterprise and brought the economy under control of five-year plans. When opposition to him formed at the top levels of the party, he imprisoned, exiled, or executed hundreds of thousands of party, government, and military officials and other "enemies of the people" in purges that reached their peak between 1936 and 1938. His ruthless dictatorship drastically limited participation in decision making and established rigid censorship and a terroristic political police, creating a pattern of centralized rule that has lasted, in modified form, to the present.(3)

Today the Soviet system presents the appearance of great stability. The most dysfunctional aspects of Stalin's rule have been dismantled, including mass terror and personal dictatorship. The adulation of Stalin was denounced by Khrushchev as a "cult of personality," antithetical to Leninist norms of party life. Greater personal security, legality, and tolerance for within-system policy debates have all been institutionalized. At the same time, however, many of the structural features of Stalin's rule have been retained. The official doctrine, Marxism-Leninism, remains the source of the myths and institutions that legitimate Soviet rule, and dissent from it is treated as a crime against the state. To create a semblance of logical completeness and consistency in the doctrine, history is falsified and alien ideas are excluded. The hypercentralization of economic administration continues. The articulation and particularly the aggregation of interests are carefully supervised by party officials to ensure that the party monopolizes the policy-making function.

Soviet Economy

The U.S.S.R. is continental in dimensions. With nearly 9 million square miles, extending from the Baltic Sea to the Pacific Ocean, it is the largest country in the world. Its 1981 population was 266.6 million. (See Table 1.) Comprising most of Northern Asia and Eastern Europe, the U.S.S.R. is endowed with vast human and natural resources. Modernization has affected the country unevenly, however. There are still wide gaps in cultural and economic development between city and country and between European and Asian regions. Well over a

Table 1

Population Growth, 1950–1981, and Doubling Times at 1980–1981 Growth Rate: U.S.S.R. and Republics

(population in thousands; estimate as of January 1, except 1980, as of January 15)

U.S.S.R. and republics	1950 population	1960 population	1950–60 annual percentage increase	1970 population	1960–70 annual percentage increase	1980 population	1970–80 annual percentage increase	1950–80 percentage increase (total)	1981 population	1980–81 percentage increase	Doubling time at 1980–81 growth rate (years)
U.S.S.R.	178,547	212,372	1.8	241,720	1.3	264,486	0.9	48.1	266,599	0.8	87
Slavic republics											
R.S.F.S.R.	101,438	119,046	1.6	130,079	0.9	138,365	0.6	36.4	139,165	0.6	121
Ukraine	36,588	42,469	1.5	47,126	1.1	49,953	0.6	36.5	50,135	0.4	194
Belorussia	7,709	8,147	1.3	9,002	1.0	9,611	0.7	24.7	9,675	0.7	105
Moldavia	2,290	2,968	2.6	3,569	1.9	3,968	1.1	73.3	3,995	0.7	103
Baltic republics											
Estonia	1,097	1,209	1.0	1,356	1.2	1,474	0.8	34.4	1,485	0.8	93
Latvia	1,944	2,113	0.8	2,364	1.1	2,529	0.7	30.1	2,539	0.4	175
Lithuania	2,573	2,756	0.7	3,218	1.3	3,420	0.9	32.9	3,445	0.7	96
Transcaucasus											
Armenia	1,347	1,829	3.1	2,492	3.1	3,074	2.1	128.2	3,119	1.5	48
Azerbaijan	2,859	3,816	2.9	5,117	3.0	6,112	1.8	113.8	6,202	1.5	48
Georgia	3,494	4,129	2.7	4,686	1.3	5,041	0.7	44.3	5,071	0.6	117
Kazakhstan	6,522	9,755	4.0	13,009	2.9	14,858	1.3	125.4	15,053	1.3	53
Central Asia											
Kirgiziya	1,716	2,131	2.2	2,933	3.3	3,588	2.0	109.1	3,653	1.8	39
Tadjikistan	1,509	2,015	2.9	3,900	3.7	3,901	3.0	158.5	4,007	2.7	26
Turkmenistan	1,197	1,564	2.7	2,159	3.3	2,827	2.7	136.2	2,897	2.5	28
Uzbekistan	6,264	8,395	3.0	11,799	3.5	15,765	2.9	154.5	16,158	2.5	28

Source: Murray Feshbach, "The Soviet Union: Population Trends and Dilemmas," Population Bulletin, 37:3 (August 1982). Reprinted by permission of Population Reference Bureau, Inc.

hundred nationalities make up the Soviet population, most speaking their native languages as well as Russian, which serves as the common language of this polyglot realm. The Russians themselves are the largest nationality group, but make up just over half of the population. Their numbers are falling as a proportion of the whole due to a lower rate of growth than that of the other nationalities.

From a primarily agricultural economy at the time of the 1917 revolution, the Soviet Union became the world's second largest industrial power, although it has recently been overtaken by Japan (the United States is first). Although much of its success in economic development can be attributed to its wealth of resources and population, and to the industrialization already under way when the Bolsheviks took power, the extraordinary pace of economic modernization in Russia since 1929 was mostly the consequence of social mobilization and the priority given to heavy industry over light industry and agriculture in the plans of economic growth. To a large extent, rapid economic development was achieved at the expense of the well-being of the working population. Moreover, the collectivization of agriculture and exploitation of the collective farmers for the sake of industry have left a legacy of very low agricultural productivity that the Soviet leaders are still struggling to overcome.

Communist Party of the Soviet Union
Under the Constitution, the Communist Party of the Soviet Union (CPSU) is the "nucleus" of the political system, guiding all state and public organizations. Because those who hold power in the party are not accountable to those they govern, the party's political monopoly contradicts the democratic facade of constitutional government. The party directs and coordinates the activities of all government, economic, social, and cultural organizations. The CPSU recruits, trains, and deploys executive personnel for all government and social agencies, guides them, monitors their performance, and controls their careers. The party mobilizes ordinary citizens for mass participation in carrying out policy. The soviets, as well as the courts, police, security units, armed forces, trade unions, professional unions, educational institutions, and mass media are controlled by party committees; in turn each party committee reports to higher-level party organizations. The party keeps a watchful eye on the military and police forces lest they threaten its power.

Unlike the state, the party is not federal even in form. It operates according to the Leninist principle of "democratic centralism": party members are theoretically permitted to discuss policy openly and to elect higher-level bodies but must

136

support an adopted decision without further question.

The present statutes of the party provide for its convening a congress every five years. The congress nominally holds ultimate power. It goes through the motions of electing a Central Committee to exercise power between congresses. In turn the Central Committee nominally elects a Politburo and Secretariat. In actuality, these lines of control operate in reverse. The congress meets to ratify the policies worked out by the Politburo and Secretariat. The Central Committee, which meets briefly twice a year, serves mainly as a forum for the announcement and approval of decisions made by the Politburo. The most recent Party Congress was the Twenty-sixth, held in February and March 1981. It elected a Central Committee consisting of 318 full (voting) and 151 candidate (nonvoting) persons. Among its members are the heads of party committees in the republics and provinces, together with prominent government, military, and cultural figures. In a sense, election to the Central Committee rewards them for loyal service. Rarely does the Central Committee play a policy-making role itself, but in 1957 it entered the political arena to support Khrushchev against his political enemies in the Politburo. Whether this incident could serve as a precedent in some future crisis is an intriguing question.

Staff work for the party leaders is performed by the Secretariat, which currently consists of ten secretaries who oversee the work of twenty-four departments. Each department coordinates and guides the performance of government ministries and lower party organizations in a specific sphere of public policy or administration. By tradition, the leading secretary ("first secretary," or "general secretary") heads the Politburo and hence the entire party.

The Politburo decides issues affecting general policy, such as the priority targets of economic growth, foreign policy, and changes in the ideological line. Its members, numbering eleven full and eight candidate members as of July 1983, include secretaries of the Central Committee, first secretaries of republican party organizations, and top government officials, such as the chairman of the Council of Ministers and the Defense and Foreign Ministers.(4)

Although in theory the Politburo operates collectively and by consensus, in practice the general secretary tends to dominate it; such was the pattern under Khrushchev, until his colleagues removed him, as well as under Brezhnev. This situation illustrates a tendency characteristic of the Soviet political system: concentration of power in an individual or a small group. Although it is hazardous to generalize about so few instances, Soviet successions seem to follow a pattern in which the collective power of a new leadership team is more or less gradually replaced by the domination of an individual, who must then find ways of maintaining his power - whether by terror or by building alliances with powerful groups and factions.(5) The rules governing this constant struggle for power are not written into law; once they have acquired power, Soviet leaders are not compelled to relinquish power and do not do so voluntarily. As the "Stalin generation" - men who rose to the top of the political ladder in the 1930s and 1940s and stayed in power through the 1970s - dies out, it will be replaced during the 1980s with a new generation of leaders.(6)

Although some social scientists apply the term "totalitarian" to the Soviet political system, this concept excludes some of the more important changes that have occurred since Stalin's death, particularly the relaxation of mass terror and the greater role for specialists in policy making. Therefore it may be more accurate to regard the Soviet system as a modernized variant of authoritarianism. In it open opposition is illegitimate. But extensive popular participation, initiated by the leadership and supervised by the party, is encouraged.

Social Structure and Political Subcultures

Official Soviet doctrine holds that Soviet society consists of two friendly classes (workers and collective farmers) plus a stratum formed by the working intelligentsia (those who earn their living by mental or nonmanual labor), but a number of subgroups or subcultures also take part in making public policy. Their demands sometimes shape alternative policy proposals through a political process that remains disguised, never officially recognized. Mostly because of rapid industrialization, the occupations of Soviet citizens are now significantly different from what they were even twenty or thirty years ago. Corresponding changes have occurred in patterns of residence and education. According to Soviet census figures, urban population exceeded rural for the first time in 1970. By 1980, of a total population of 264.5 million, 63 percent were classified as living in urban areas. Classified by employment, 76 percent of the working and retired persons derive their livelihoods from nonagricultural occupations.(7) The figures show the Soviet Union to be a relatively developed, urbanized society, although the proportion of the population employed in agriculture is still much higher than in the United States and Great Britain.

Education figures also show substantial changes (see Table 2). In 1939, fewer than 1.2 million Soviet citizens had received postsecondary education in some form. By 1970 the

138

Table 2

Levels of Education among the Soviet Population

A. Percentage of population over 10 years of age by educational
   level attained

	1970	1979
Higher and secondary (including incomplete)	48.3	63.8
Complete higher	4.2	6.8
Incomplete higher	1.3	1.5
Specialized secondary	6.8	10.7
General secondary	11.9	20.7
Incomplete secondary	24.1	24.1
Primary (including incomplete)	51.7	36.2

B. Percentage of urban and rural population over 10 years of age
   by educational level attained

	1939		1959		1970		1979	
	Urban	Rural	Urban	Rural	Urban	Rural	Urban	Rural
Higher[a]	1.9	.2	4.0	.7	6.2	1.4	9.3	2.5
Secondary[a]	19.9	5.0	42.0	24.9	53.0	31.8	63.0	46.7

Source: Naselenie SSSR: Po dannym vsesoiuznoi perepisi naseleniia
1979 goda (The Population of the U.S.S.R.: According to the Data
of the All-Union Census of 1979) (Moscow: Politizdat, 1980),
pp. 19-21.

[a]Includes incomplete.

number had grown to 9 million and by 1979, to more than 15
million. Many of these persons had received their degress
through correspondence or evening schools. Currently, although
the number of students entering postsecondary educational
institutions continues to grow, the rate of expansion has
slowed. Today, secondary education is universal and
obligatory, and, according to Soviet figures, 86.6 million -
80.5 percent of the employed population - have at least some
secondary education. (8)

Every year more and more educated citizens enter the work
force and earn their livings in nonmanual occupations requiring

mental labor. Overall, the share of the population formed by
"employees" - white-collar workers, both clerical and
intellectual - is now 25 percent, though this proportion varies
widely among nationalities. The intelligentsia is a smaller
section of the "employee" group, comprising perhaps 6 to 8
percent of the population.(9)

Groups and Strata in the Communist Party

The basic functions of the Communist party are leadership
and control of Soviet society. The keystone of this effort is
the inclusion in the disciplined party of adequate numbers of
the administrative and professional elites. As the society
becomes more complex and the level of education rises, party
control is reinforced by party workers specially trained to
deal with the tasks they are to supervise. The proportion of
party members with higher education has risen steadily, from
15.7 percent in 1966 to 28 percent in 1981. In the same period
the proportion of party members with no more than primary
schooling fell from 23.4 percent to 10.8 percent.
...(V)irtually all secretaries of party organizations above the
PPO level have postsecondary degrees.(10)

Party members are in three main categories. In the
highest ranks of the party command structure are the full-time,
paid professional functionaries, including party secretaries,
deputy secretaries, department and secretary chiefs, and staff
officials (called instructors) of the party committees. The
party committees are organized by levels, in descending order
from central, to regional, to local, and at each level the
full-time officials run party affairs. These party officials
are often referred to as apparatchniki - people of the
apparatus.

Soviet authorities do not disclose the size of the
full-time party apparatus, and its exact numbers can only be
estimated. Most Western scholars believe that there are from
100,000 to 200,000 party apparatchiki. Assisting them in their
work are many "nonstaff" or volunteer officials, who are
treated as a pool of replacements when the staff positions
become vacant. Information about the salaries and benefits
received by apparatchiki, like other information about the
party's budget or decision-making processes, is a closely
guarded secret.

The second category of members consists of the spare-time
secretaries at the lowest level, the primary party
organizations (PPOs). As of 1981, there were 414,000 of these.
Most are headed by volunteer, unpaid secretaries. They are
assisted by the leaders (secretaries and group organizers of
the smaller units into which the PPOs are divided. The party

secretaries in the enterprises and institutions supervise the work of the manager and employees, but are instructed not to meddle in management directly.

The final category consists of rank-and-file members (see Table 3). All party members are expected to take an active role in their places of work, and to serve as role models for their colleagues and friends. All are expected to take on unpaid social assignments, and most in fact have at least one regular spare-time task to perform, such as helping the PPO with its organizational work, giving rundowns of current events to their coworkers, or heading neighborhood committees. Many party members have more than one such assignment, and complement it with evening or weekend study in party schools. Apart from their social work, party members are called upon to supply information to local party organizations and to take the initiative in improving productivity. In return for these obligations, rank-and-file party members enjoy priveleges such as better career chances, better housing and material goods, and access to party channels of information.

Table 3

CPSU Membership, 1917-1981

Year	Members	Candidates	Total
1917	24,000	---	24,000
1920	611,978	---	611,978
1929	1,090,508	444,854	1,535,362
1940	1,982,743	1,417,232	3,339,975
1950	5,510,787	829,396	6,340,183
1960	8,017,249	691,418	8,708,667
1971	13,810,089	645,232	14,455,321
1981	16,763,009	717,759	17,480,768

Source: Reprinted by permission of Macmillan Publishing Co. from Handbook of Soviet Social Science Data, edited by Ellen P. Mickiewicz. Copyright © 1973 by the Free Press, a Division of Macmillan Publishing Co. Figures for 1981 from Partiinia zhizn' (Party Life), no. 14 (July 1981), p. 13.

It is ideologically important that there should always be a large proportion of factory workers in the party. During the Stalin era, preference in recruitment went to technical, managerial, and administrative personnel. Since then, however, the leaders have maintained a policy of limiting the recruitment of members of the intelligentsia and encouraging enrollment of workers. At the Twenty-sixth Party Congress in 1981, Brezhnev reported that 59 percent of new members since the previous congress in 1976 were workers, and that the overall percentage of workers in the party now stood at 43.4 percent. Another 12.8 percent are kolkhoz peasants, and 43.8 percent are of the intelligentsia.(11)

Priveleges and Problems of the Intelligentsia

The situation of the intelligentsia is complex. Members of this variegated group, access to which is based on higher education and, at its upper levels, extraordinary talent and skills, are, together with the highest-level party apparatchiki and state officials, the most priveleged members of Soviet society. Particularly among outstanding scientists and both creative and performing artists of high distinction, intellectuals have superior access to information, travel, and contact with foreign colleagues, as well as the prestige conferred by education and professional status. Moreover, the children of this elite have a far better chance of admission to the best institutions of higher learning than do the children of ordinary citizens. In return for these priveleges, however, political authorities demand not only appropriate professional performance but also ideological orthodoxy and political loyalty.

Among the occupational groups discernible within the intelligentsia, the economic intelligentsia is the largest (its members form about one-third of the party) and politically the most conservative. Its members direct the main branches of Soviet industry, the planning centers, and that large section of the state apparatus devoted to economic affairs. They are generally far more conformist than, say, the writers.

The natural scientists, even under Stalin, enjoyed great prestige and a superior standard of living, especially at the exalted level of the U.S.S.R. Academy of Sciences. Its members had high salaries, summer homes and government drivers. Relations between the party and natural scientists, especially physicists, whose work had obvious military applications, were less affected by ideological considerations than those between the regime and writers and artists. Demands among scientists for professional autonomy and even for a voice in making decisions that affected their interests were generally granted, but in return these priveleged strata were expected to refrain

142

from unauthorized political or ideological communication or activity.

Khrushchev's successors, interested as they were in economic and military development, pursued policies more acceptable to scientists than he did. Certainly Soviet scientists were pleased by events such as the celebration in 1966 of the sixieth anniversary of Einstein's theory of relativity, denounced by Stalin's era as "idealistic" and "bourgeois."

There have been, however, indications of rising concern among a few Soviet scientists over various policies. Many scientists shared the general alarm in intellectual circles over the end of de-Stalinization and the resumption of police methods for suppressing dissent. Toward the end of Brezhnev's reign even stiffer restrictions were imposed on contacts between Soviet citizens and the West.

Social scientists - historians, legal scholars, psychologists, and others - have enjoyed much less freedom of inquiry than natural scientists. Many fields, such as Freudian psychology, are still taboo. Moreover, social scientists must work within strict ideological guidelines. But if a social scientist does not stray from the ideological path and can make a good case for the practical value of a project (by showing that it will improve labor productivity, economic planning, or management), he or she will find it possible to obtain needed support for research. Indeed, during the 1970s, the U.S.S.R. underwent something of a sociological "boom," as officially sponsored opinion surveys on a variety of topics were conducted by professional and amateur sociologists. Although the professional standards of empirical research in social science have been rising, political constraints on the researchers have also increased. Much good research is left unpublished.

Among writers and artists the struggle sometimes takes on acute forms: the party wants to control creative expression and the artist seeks autonomy for his or her art. Nonrepresentational art is discouraged and not given mass exposure; artists who want to produce abstract or modernist works generally circulate them only among trusted friends. The 1966 trial of writers Andrei Sinyavsky and Yuli Daniel, who had published critical works abroad, marked the beginning of a new phase in relations between the party and the intelligentsia. It signified a shift in emphasis from Khrushchev's reliance on persuasion and political pressure to a policy of intimidation and selective repression of rebellious writers and other independent intellectuals.

Status of Workers

An important prop of the ideological legitimization of the Soviet system is the official claim that production workers in factories, mines, transport, and the like are the leading class of Soviet society. Always "objectively" a myth, except perhaps to some extent in the early heroic days of the revolution and civil war, this claim increasingly is being shattered by contemporary sociological research, both in the U.S.S.R. and abroad. There is no reason to believe, however, that this traditional claim will be abandoned by the regime, or even that its remoteness from objective reality will soon inspire widespread oppositionist stirrings in the ranks of the most fatalistic, regimented Soviet labor force.

Almost all wage earners and salaried employees belong to a network of industrial unions known as the All-Union Central Council of Trade Unions (AUCCTU). Its primary function is to stimulate workers to greater productive effort, but it also carries on welfare activities for the state, such as administering social insurance, arranging vacations, and operating cultural organizations, including clubs, evening education, and houses of culture. The main emphasis, however, is on the demand for higher production. The trade unions, like the party, keep up the pressure on workers to meet and exceed the plan targets.

In recent years the authorities have tried hard to involve as many workers as possible in the continuing managerial and governmental activities of their enterprises and localities. Although the nominal participation rates for workers are quite high - typically from a third to a half of the workers take part in organized spare time work - the executive positions in the party, the Komsomol, and the trade unions are generally occupied by members of "professional and higher status groups." Moreover, participation rates are higher among workers of higher skill and status levels. Lower-status workers tend to be relatively inactive and even apathetic about political matters.(12)

To be sure, there are many indications that the sense of political efficacy among workers is greater in local or enterprise matters, where "parochial contracts" or questions at workers´ meetings enable workers to voice their grievances directly. Local and parochial concerns are unlikely to place serious stress on the political system, however, because, first, workers separate themselves from "high politics," and second, such problems are often resolved through informal channels of influence and communication (Pravda, p. 23). Two factors may alter this pattern of relative political disengagement in the future. The first is the decline or even halt in the growth of living standards, which, as Seweryn

Bialer comments, is a "new experience for the very large majority of Soviet citizens who did not know the postwar years of hunger."(13) (On declining economic performance see Table 4.) The second factor is the drive by General Secretary Andropov to raise labor productivity and discipline. The newspapers have printed letters to the editor complaining about waste and mismanagement in the economy, some even going so far as to suggest that the worker's right to quit his job be abrogated. New laws have increased the penalities for drunkenness on the job. If these events herald a return to the draconian labor laws of the Stalin era, the working class may be roused to greater resistance.

Collective Farms
    The collective farm peasants (kolkhozniki) are the section of the population that is most underpriveleged, as in access to education and to cultural facilities, and the most poorly represented in the party and government. The situation of the collective farmers improved considerably under Khrushchev, however, and especially during Brezhnev's leadership. Their almost serflike status in freedom of movement away from the collective farms ended when they were granted internal passports, thus achieving at least equality in the limited, police-controlled mobility common to all Soviet citizens. Also, the farmers were brought within the Soviet social welfare system and granted a minimum wage. The Brezhnev leadership also raised the prices paid by the government for farm products sold to the state, increased the availability of farm machinery and, perhaps most important, loosened restrictions on the freedom of collective farmers to sell in special markets produce from their small but precious individual private plots, which are an indispensable source of fresh fruits and vegetables for Soviet consumers.

    Despite the priority given to agriculture under Brezhnev, the growth of cultural amenities in the countryside has been slow. General Secretary Andropov and many Soviet writers have commented favorably on the more successful "Hungarian model" of competitive cooperative farms, which rewards efficient production. Under Andropov, a new system of "collective contracts" with small-scale farm brigades is being widely introduced. It is intended to stimulate higher production by reducing the size and increasing the rewards and responsibilities of the agricultural production unit. Initial results have been encouraging, but it remains to be seen whether this and other features of the regime's current agricultural program will significantly improve the lot of the Soviet farmer.

Friendship of Peoples or Declining Empire: Soviet Nationality
   Policies and Problems
      Because of the difficulties they present to the Soviet
leaders and their potential future influence on the stability
of the Soviet system, nationality relations deserve close
attention. Our focus is mainly on the post-Stalin period.(14)
The most important line of cleavage in nationality relations in
the U.S.S.R., of course, is that which divides the dominant
Russians, and to a lesser degree the Russians and their fellow
Slavs (the Ukrainians and the Belorussians) taken together,
from the non-Slavic peoples of the U.S.S.R. There is, however,
evidence of ethnic tensions between or among Armenians and
Georgians, and in Cental Asia, "Europeans" (here meaning
non-"Moslem" peoples), and mainly Turkic, or "Moslem," peoples
of Central Asia and Kazakhstan, also between Jews and some
other national groups, and even between the "Moslems," exiled
Crimean Tartars and their fellow "Moslems," the Uzbeks.

      According to Article 70 of its third Constitution, adopted
in 1977, the U.S.S.R. is "a unitary, federal and multinational
state, formed on the basis of the principle of socialist
federalism and as a result of the free self-determination of
nations..." This language, and that of Article 6, which states
that "the Communist Party of the Soviet Union is the leading
and guiding force of Soviet society," indicate the
determination of the leadership and political elite that any
expression permitted national sentiments and interests will be
subordinate to norms and policies defined by the CPSU
leadership.(15) The Soviet authorities have always curbed,
sometimes with extreme harshness, manifestations of
"nationalsim" - usually on the part of non-Russians - that they
considered threatening to the unity of the U.S.S.R. The ruling
Politburo of the CPSU has always been dominated by Russians and
Russianized non-Russians.

      The Russians, according to the 1979 census, numbered
137,552,000, or 52.4 percent of the Soviet population of almost
262.5 million. This percentage was slightly smaller than the
53.4 percent shown by the 1970 census and the 54.6 percent of
1959. In the R.S.F.S.R. (Russian Soviet Federated Socialist
Republic) the Russians, with well over 82 percent of this
unit´s population, which accounts for 76 percent of the
U.S.S.R.´s area, enjoy enormous resources.

      To grasp the preponderance of sinews of power at the
disposal of the Russians, we must also remember that according
to the 1979 census, only seven nationalities numbered, in 1979,
more than five million. They were the Russians, the Ukrainians
(42.3 million), the Uzbeks (12.5), the Belorussians (9.5), the
Kazakhs (6.6), the Tatars (6.3), and the Azeris - usually
called Azerbaijanians in America - with 5.5 million. Moreover,

two other factors do add to their power. First, the Russians
have settled in large numbers in the non-Russian republics,
often taking key managerial and administrative positions.
Second, Russian is the language of politics, economics, and
science for the Soviet Union as a whole, giving native Russian
speakers an additional cultural advantage in social and
political mobility. Both the migration of Russians to
non-Russian regions and the dominance of the Russian language
have generated tensions between Russians and non-Russians.

This picture of the Russian predominance is slightly
misleading. Although the Russians still constitute more than
half the Soviet population, their rate of population growth has
lagged far behind that of the peoples of Moslem religious
backgound. This is a demographic trend of great political
significance. The most sensitive aspect of this trend is the
continuing (though now slightly declining) difference between
low birthrates among the Slavs and high birthrates among
Moslems. The share of "Moslem" peoples as a group - including,
besides the Kazakhs, the Uzbeks, Kirgiz, Tadjiks, Turkmens, and
one of the Transcaucasian peoples, the Azerbaijani, as well as
a number of small peoples of the Caucasus - in the Soviet
population increased between 1959 and 1979 from 11.6 percent to
16.5 percent. Between 1970 and 1979 the "Moslem" population
increased from some 35 million to about 43 million.(16)

Tensions in Nationality Relations

Among the most important sources of nationality tensions
in the U.S.S.R. are these: perceived threats to the ethnic and
cultural identity of non-Russian peoples stemming from policies
made in far-off Moscow; the tendency for peoples living in
areas bordering on foreign states to resent the "center´s"
policies as Russian policies; memories of the harsh methods
used by both tsarist and Soviet authorities to weld into one
the multinational state; and the belief among many non-Russians
that they are culturally superior to the Russians and the
conviction among the latter that they have carried an undue
share of the economic and military burden in providing for the
development and security of the non-Russian members of the
Soviet family of nations.

Soviet nationality policy was rather permissive in the
1920s, but Stalin´s prouncements increasingly reflected his
underlying Russian nationalist inclinations, as in his
declaration that Leninism was the highest expression of Russian
and world culture. Stalinist terror in the 1930s, visited even
more severely on non-Russians than on Russians, and with
special force on the Ukrainians and the nomadic peoples of
Central Asia, squashed non-Russian national resistance for a
long time; its memory even today keeps resentment alive but
helps impart a limited and cautious character to most active

147

non-Russian opposition.

In the Ukraine, indignation over a 1959 law on language education in the schools, which many parents regarded as a measure of linguistic Russification, erupted in overt protest against Russification and other policies of the central government. Ukrainian nationalist protest has resulted in arrests and repression by the central authorities. In fall 1965, thirty intellectuals were arrested in the Ukraine´s capital city of Kiev, and in the main city of Western Ukraine, Lvov (Lviv in Ukrainian), on charges of conducting anti-Soviet agitation and propaganda. In 1972 followed a much bigger wave of arrests. From 1978 to the present there have been still further arrests, especially of members of the Ukrainian Helsinki group.

Perhaps the best way to indicate the intellectual content of Ukrainian protest is to quote from literary critic Ivan Dzyuba´s major work, Internationalism or Russification? published in English in London in 1968. Writing from an avowedly Leninist perspective, Dzyuba denounced what he regarded as Moscow´s economic exploitation of the Ukraine. "Over-centralization," he said, "fetters the existing possibilities of development of a number of republics, the Ukraine in particular." He saw linguistic Russification as one instrument of a policy that threatened the Ukraine people with "denationalization."

In ethnic pride and sense of cultural distinctiveness, the Georgians rank on approximately the same level as the Lithuanians and Estonians, and in disposition to public protest behind only Crimean Tatars and the Jews. The widespread disaffection among the Georgians is evidence of an important general point: the material well-being of a nationality compared to other groups in the U.S.S.R. may not correlate with political contentment. Evidence is abundant that Jews, the Baltic peoples, and the Georgians and Armenians are much more "priveleged" peoples, as measured by the percentage of their group with higher education and other factors making social mobility, than are the majority, and politically dominant, Slavs. Probably the deterioration in recent years of the Georgians´ position in the pecking order of Soviet nationalities exacerbated well-established Georgian beliefs that their culture was superior to that of the Russians and that it was threatened by political and administrative pressures emanating from Moscow.

In 1978 new republic constitutions were drafted for the fourteen non-Russian republics. Traditionally, the three Transcaucasian republics (Georgia, Armenia, and Azerbaijan) - and only these three - had a clause in their constitutions declaring that the national language was the state language of the republic. The Georgians and Armenians also had been permitted to continue to write and publish in their own distinctive alphabets, though all the other major non-Russian languages had been converted to the Cyrillic alphabet used by Russians. In 1978 the local party and state authorities in the three Transcaucasian republics mounted campaigns purporting to show that public opinion favored eliminating the "state language" status of local languages. The effort met with an angry response in Georgia and Armenia. According to one report, "as many as 20,000 people demonstrated in Tbilisi, capital city of Georgia, on April 14, 1978, against the plan to drop Georgian as the republic´s state language. The first secretary of the Georgian communist party, Eduard Shevarnadze, finally stated, though not in the public media, that the nationality clause would remain in the Georgian constitution.(17)

The failure of the plan to deprive the three Transcaucasian republics of their state languages - though the issue was more symbolic than substantive - reflected both the touchiness of segments of the local populations, especially their most educated members, and a measure of flexibility in official policy.

Although the Armenians have been less vigorous than the Georgians in overt protest, they have produced a substantial body of dissent literature and have engaged in much protest activity, reported in such sources as the Chronicle of Current Events. Also, according to sources that we consider reliable, by spring 1982 some 15,000 Armenians had emigrated from the U.S.S.R. Moreover, (on a small scale to be sure), demands for separation of Armenia from the U.S.S.R. began to be raised in the 1970s.

Nationality discontent is perhaps even stronger in Soviet-ruled Lithuania than in Georgia. The attitudes of Lithuanians toward the Soviet Union resemble those of their fellow Roman Catholics, the Poles. As in Poland, religious and national resistance are partly fused. Lithuania is notable for the greatest profusion of samizdat journals (self-published tracts) anywhere in the Soviet Union. Also remarkable is the large number of signatures on protest petitions.(18)

Even more prosperous than the relatively well-off Lithuanians are the Estonians and the Latvians. The superior material conditions in this most "European" part of the U.S.S.R., however, are associated with perhaps as high a level of nationality discontent as anywhere in the U.S.S.R. Estonia and Latvia have the highest per capita income among the Soviet republics, yet Estonia, and to a lesser degree in Latvia, there has been open protest against the intrusive role of Russians. Russian migration to these republics, their dominant role in many sectors of the economy, and their insistence on a priveleged role for the Russian language have aroused resentment.

No group illustrates so well as the Jews the failure of Soviet nationality policy to achieve its goals of "friendship of peoples" and ultimate assimilation. Except for a few small nations, such as the Crimean Tatars, Soviet Jews are probably the most alienated Soviet nationality. In the 1920s and 1930s, despite Stalin's covert anti-Semitism, it was probably true that politically loyal Soviet Jews benefited more than any other ethnic group in the U.S.S.R. in gaining opportunities for education, social mobility, and other benefits of rapid economic development. With Stalin's - and his successors' - increasingly open appeal during and after World War II to Russian nationalism as means of tapping the loyalty of the largest Soviet ethnic group, the situation of the Soviet Jews deteriorated and their discontent increased.

Despite official Soviet obstacles, the catalyst for public and substantial emigration during the 1970s was the Arab-Israeli war of 1967. It raised ethnic consciousness and pride among Soviet Jews and triggered "anti-Zionist" propaganda by the regime, mostly a cover for crude anti-Semitism. The right of Soviet Jews to emigrate became a major theme in the appeals of Soviet human rights activists in the 1970s and a thorny issue in Soviet-Western relations. As of late 1982, about 250,000 Jews had left the U.S.S.R. Of all the Soviet peoples, and of all dissident groups, the Soviet Jews had been most successful in achieving their objectives, but, as emigration nearly halted by 1983, the future of some two million Jews still in the U.S.S.R. looked increasingly bleak.

Lest readers conclude that Soviet Jews have lost all status or influence, we recall that quite a few Jews, primarily of the older generation, still held high positions. As a group, the Jews' high average age helps explain their above-average representation in the Communist party and their high educational levels. This situation is not likely to persist, though, because younger Jews are subjected to restrictions on access to higher education and opportunities to work in "sensitive" fields.(19)

Soviet Moslems. For a variety of reasons, the nationalities within the Soviet Union that are of Moslem heritage form a particularly important group. The Azerbaijani, Tadjiks, Turkmens, Kirgiz, Kazakhs, and Uzbeks are the largest of these nationalities. Their Asian heritage and religion-defined cultural identity test the effectiveness and

universality of the Soviet model of ethnic integration.
Moreover, because of high birthrates, their numbers have grown
much faster than those of the other peoples. Because the
Soviet Union is currently experiencing an overall labor
shortage (with labor surpluses in the Central Asian region),
the Politburo must choose between increasing industrial
development in Central Asia, where most future additions to the
labor force will be located, or urging the Central Asians, who
unlike the Russians have been reluctant to settle outside their
native lands, to migrate nearer to the sources of energy and
raw materials. Another aspect of the problem is the leaders'
ability to maintain high levels of discipline and skill in
armed forces that, in the enlisted ranks, have a high
proportion of Central Asians (see Table 1).

With the resurgence of fundamentalist Islam in Iran,
Afghanistan, and other regions of the Middle East, many
observers have searched for evidence of similar trends among
the Soviet Moslems. Such evidence is scarce. The literary and
scholarly publications of Central Asian writers have reflected
the growth of cultural pride and self-awareness and have called
for loyalty to one's ethnic "roots," but little has been
published that could be considered specifically anti-Soviet,
even by implication. Compromises worked out between the Soviet
authorities and the Moslem religious leaders have satisfied the
needs of the faithful to observe the tenets of Islam (a
believer is relieved of the normal obligation to make the
pilgrimage to Mecca before his death; a few Soviet-approved
leaders go each year in his place).(20) Close observers of the
Central Asian cultural scene conclude that so long as some
cultural freedom is allowed, the Soviet Moslems can accomodate
their beliefs and customs to Soviet conditions without severe
conflict.(21)

Indeed, by some criteria, the Soviet model of development
has been relatively successful in Central Asia. Despite the
high birthrates, the spread of education and other benefits of
modernization have outpaced population growth. Illiteracy has
been virtually eradicated among the younger generations.
Between 1962-1963 and 1976-1977, the absolute numbers of
students in specialized secondary education from the six major
Moslem nationalities (Azerbaijani, Kazakh, Kirgiz, Tadjik,
Turkmen, and Uzbek) increased by nearly three times, and the
number in institutions of higher learning rose nearly two and
one-half times.(22) The proportion of specialists with
specialized secondary or higher education in each of these
republics has grown, although it is still below the rate for
the more highly developed republics. The network of
communications, retail shops and services, and schools and
preschool institutions has grown much more rapidly in the

Moslem republics than in the Soviet Union overall.(23) In part, of course, these high rates of growth reflect the low level of economic development from which Soviet-guided modernization began.

Moreover, when the relevant age groups are compared, the non-Russian nationalities are rather well represented in the Communist Party and other institutional hierarchies. It is at the central, all-union level of party and state bureaucracy that the underrepresentation of non-Slavic nationalities is pronounced.

The picture is not altogether positive. Conflicts between Islam and Soviet ideology remain to complicate Soviet efforts to win adherents for Soviet policies abroad. The invasion of Afghanistan may have antagonized Soviet Moslems and was particularly damaging to the image of the Soviet Union in the Middle East and Africa.(24) In addition, the pattern of economic development in Central Asia resembles in some respects the traditional Western-controlled "plantation" economics based on growing and processing cotton. The shortage of water is an acute problem. For more than a decade, a debate with major political implications has been raging over whether or not, and how soon, to undertake a grandiose project to divert the water from Siberian rivers into arid Central Asia. Despite substantial open opposition to this ambitious project, it has received high-level approval.

The relative success of the Soviet authorities in integrating the Soviet Moslems within the framework of Soviet political and ideological institutions reminds us that Soviet nationality policy is flexible in some ways. It tends to swing between the poles of pressure for assimilation into the official Soviet Russian culture and some tolerance for ethnic diversity. The former position is reflected in Soviet political jargon in assertions about desirability of the "coming together" (sblizhenie), or even "merging" (sliianie) of nations, the latter praising the "flourishing" (rastsvet) of non-Russian nations.(25)

Russian Nationalism. There are good reasons to believe that for most Soviet Russians the propaganda of "Soviet patriotism" - which official doctrine holds is not nationalist but "internationalist" - does not curb Russian ethnic self-awareness.(26) This does not mean that all Soviet Russians are satisfied with the current state of relations between Russians and non-Russians. Some Russians resent what they consider excessive generosity to the minority nationalities. Some exalt the role of Russia so unabashedly that they see in Russia and the Russians not only the major force in the life of the contemporary U.S.S.R., but even as the

152

true source of the impulses that led to Lenin's revolution of 1917. For varied reasons extreme forms of Russian nationalism, although not usually suppressed as harshly as their non-Russian counterparts, do arouse alarm in leadership circles.

In our view, nationality tensions are likely to pose gradually increasing difficulties, if traditional centralist economic policies continue to prevail, and if the growth in the relative weight of the Moslems in the Soviet population continues to rise rapidly, along with their educational level. They will doubtless seek a role in Soviet society commensurate with their increasing human resources. If non-Russian discontent grows substantially, Russian nationalism, as a defensive reaction, is also likely to intensify. If as a result of Russian-non-Russian, or other interethnic conflict, there are significant disturbances of public order and significant levels of repression are required to quell them, certainly domestic morale will suffer and so too will the prestige and authority of the U.S.S.R. abroad.

Political Participation and Recruitment

Recruitment of Elites
Although Soviet leaders and theorists do not claim that full equality has been achieved in Soviet society, they deny the existence of an elite of any kind. They assert that Soviet socialism offers talented and public-spirited people greater equality in opportunity for advancement to society's highest political, economic, and cultural positions than in capitalist societies. In fact, however, elite recruitment in the U.S.S.R. is determined only in part by equality of opportunity. In the Soviet Union, as elsewhere, those in positions of power and influence tend to obstruct the entry of newcomers into the establishment, especially newcomers whose perspectives differ from their own.

The tightly centralized system of Soviet recruitment tends to protect the mediocre and exclude much talent from participation in public life. Nevertheless, from the Kremlin's point of view the recruitment system has advantages, the most important being that it ensures that all strategic posts will be filled by politically reliable personnel.

The Soviet personnel system is controlled by the top leadership of the CPSU, working through the central party and state administrative organs. It is no surprise therefore that recruitment is planned and supervised by the executives who control the party's central organs and that the top leader devotes a good deal of time to this task.

In the Central Committee, a powerful secretary usually

acts as the leader's deputy in matters that are referred to as "organizational," which include selection of top-level personnel. Such a person is likely to be the second-ranking man in the political hierarchy, although no such position is explicitly identified. In Brezhnev's later years, responsibility for organizational matters and personnel became the particular province of Konstantin Chernenko. Nevertheless, his power was not sufficient to assure him selection as general secretary of the party when Brezhnev died November 10, 1982.(27)

A system of rekommendatsiia ("recommendation") for high political positions is used by the top leadership for the CPSU. Direct intervention by the party leaders in selections of high-level leadership is not openly acknowledged, but the rapid rise of certain proteges of top men indicates that this procedure persists.

The day-to-day business of elite recruitment is handled through the nomenklatura ("nomenclature") system, which refers to key job categories and descriptions that a specific party committee or governmental or other agency is responsible for filling. Each party committee has a list of positions in its jurisdiction, such as top management of local enterprises, editor of the newspaper, directors of the schools, and the like, and it names individuals to these positions from a list of eligible candidates. By controlling eligibility for these jobs, the party ensures that only politically reliable persons are named to sensitive leadership posts in society.(28)

Soviet law apparently makes no provision for the nomenclature system. Once an official is on a nomenclature list, he is usually assured of tenure for life, barring serious incompetence, flagrant political errors, or close involvement with a disgraced leader. Because access to command posts is controlled by top executives of major bureaucracies, it follows that a successful career depends on such factors as personal and organizational ties to rising and falling leaders. Thus Soviet elites often cultivate clientelistic relationships with powerful superiors, enjoying promotions as their patron's fortunes prosper and suffering declines when they fall from favor. Major upheavals at the center can devastate the political careers of elites based far from Moscow.

Under Brezhnev, however, security of tenure was much greater for political elites, especially those below the very high levels, than it was under Khrushchev or Stalin. Although this policy evidently won Brezhnev a good deal of support among middle-level officials, it also led to stagnation. Yuri Andropov cautiously but deliberately moved to replace some twenty senior officials, including three government ministers,

and a larger number of lower-ranking officials, in his first
two months in power.(29) Although the scope of change is still
something less than a wholesale purge, it seems clear that
Andropov intends to replace officials in poorly performing
areas and to reward politically trusted allies. During the
first half year of his leadership, however, it increasingly
appeared unlikely that his poor health would allow him to
achieve these goals.

   Recruitment Trends within the Apparatus. When the economy
was still underdeveloped and the political system not yet
consolidated, the party made do with cadres who were for the
most part Bolshevik apparatchiki, highly committed
ideologically but often poorly educated and lacking
professional skills. With industrialization, however, it
became necessary to bring into the party leadership more and
more specialists. The probelm for the party was how to harness
the precious skills of these people without allowing them to
acquire influence that might alter the direction of the
maturing socialist system.

   Stalin's answer was compulsion laced with terror, material
incentives, and a measure of autonomy for the state and
managerial bureaucracies. Khrushchev, because he did not use
terror as Stalin had, was less willing to grant bureaucratic
autonomy. He sought to cope with the problem by providing
attractive opportunities for specialists within the party
leadership. Although at first Khrushchev curbed the
technocrats on whom Stalin had conferred vast administrative
powers, his recruitment policy seemed to create conditions that
would allow industrial managers and other production
specialists to gain unprecedented influence within the party.
This prospect aroused resentment and opposition among the
less-specialized apparatchiki who feared for their own
influence. The Brezhnev regime in turn showed greater favor to
the traditional party members, to the professional
propagandists, and to the police, intelligence agencies, and
military.

   Role and Influence of the Apparatchiki. Even under Stalin
when intense insecurity was the lot of party cadres, positions
in the party were eagerly sought because of their power and
prestige. Through the Brezhnev era, the power of the party in
relation to government and other institutions steadily
increased. In lists of officials printed by the Soviet press,
the names of party secretaries always precede those of
highest-ranking government officials. In every city and town,
the best buildings are reserved for party headquarters and
offices. The leading role of the party in society was
especially emphasized in the 1977 Constitution. Perhaps a
counter trend, putting the power of state officials above that

155

of the party cadres, began with Andropov´s elevation to supreme leadership.

Within the party, the full-time paid functionaries, or apparatchiki, dominate the political elite. Among those recruited to the apparatus, however, a trend of recruiting individuals with specialized administrative or technical training is noticeable. So too is the tendency for apparatchiki to receive or advance their education once in office. Despite these trends, the largest group on the Central Committee and in the political elite are general-utility officials, promoted after lengthy service on the staffs of lower party committees. Konstantin Chernenko represents this type of leader in the post-Brezhnev leadership.

The modern political executive is likely to have the equivalent of a college education in engineering or other technical fields, not in the liberal arts. Many Soviet engineers who become political leaders either do not practice their profession after graduating from technical school or do so for only a short time. Often they have already, as students, given much time to Komsomol or party activity and were chosen for political careers while very young. Many party committees make it a practice to maintain a pool of volunteer activists, who gradually gain experience as organizers and leaders. When a vacancy on the staff of the party committee itself opens up, these activists are the first to be hired. Other individuals are brought into full-time party work from senior positions as factory managers and the like, having completed courses in party doctrine and social management in party schools.

The supremacy of party over government is illustrated in the careers of the men who have risen to the top of the Soviet power pyramid. Lenin created the party organization and then became head of the Soviet government. Stalin won power within the party apparatus that he himself had shaped. Khrushchev too had risen through the ranks of the party apparatus. When he was ousted from power, Leonid I. Brezhnev became head of the party while Aleksei N. Kosygin headed the Council of Ministers. Soon it became apparent that the old pattern of party superiority was reasserting itself as Brezhnev became unquestioned first among equals within the nominally collective leadership.

Even Andropov, though known best for having been KGB chairman between 1967 and 1982, made his political career in party work from 1936, when he left technical school. After World War II he rose in the party organization of the Karelo-Finnish Republic (which no longer exists) until, in 1951, he was transferred to a staff position on the Central

Committee Secretariat. Soon after, he entered diplomacy, serving as ambassador to Hungary from 1954 to 1957 and therefore as Moscow's representative in the field during the military suppression of Hungary's 1956 uprising. After returning again to Moscow in 1957 to reenter the central party apparatus, in 1962 he was made secretary in charge of relations with the East European regimes. Five years later he was elevated to candidate membership of the Politburo and named chairman of the KGB. He remained in that position (rising to full member of the Politburo in 1973) until May 1982 when he gave up the KGB in favor of a position, again, as Central Committee secretary. This move may well have been connected to the jockeying for position that all the potential rivals to Brezhnev's power were engaged in - no doubt the chairmanship of the political police was considered an unfavorable vantage point from which to claim the ultimate prize.(30)

Access to Elite Membership. For some large social groups - women, youth, farmers, and workers - opportunity to enter the party elite, and specially executive party bodies, is quite limited. Men, middle-aged functionaries with seniority, city dwellers, and politically reliable members of the intelligentsia have a far greater likelihood of being recruited.

Since the mid-1930s, when a trend favoring recruitment of women abruptly ended, a man's chances of becoming a party member have been about five times greater than a woman's. Although the proportion of women in the party has been rising, the share of women on the Central Committee has never exceeded 4 percent, and only one woman has ever served on the Politburo. A very high proportion of Soviet physicians, lawyers, engineers, and other professionals are women. But they tend not to occupy the senior positions in their professions, or to move over into political work. Both Soviet and non-Soviet observers attribute this disparity to the continuing problem of the "double burden": the need for many women to hold a job and simultaneously manage the household. On the average, men spend two to three times fewer hours on housekeeping and child-care than do women. The average workload of a mother in the labor force is 41 hours a week plus 36 hours of housework.

The party has made efforts to recruit workers and peasants into the ruling bodies of the party, but they continue to be underrepresented. Non-Russian and particularly non-Slavic minorities are also underrepresented. Although Russians comprise only about half the population, they make up about 60 percent of the party and even higher proportions of the central party leadership. Party leaders from the ethnic minorities tend to rise only within their own national region. David

Lane, who analyzed the 100 leading officials of the Soviet Union of February 1981, found that 69 were Russians and another 16 were either Ukrainian or Belorussian origin.(31)

Directed Political Participation

Running the national economy is the Soviet elite's most important task, as seen in the proportion of the party's leadership assigned to it. Other roles include overseeing national security policy, maintaining order, supervising education, culture, and communications, and directing the activities of public organizations. These organizations include the party itself, the trade unions, and the Komsomol, as well as hobby groups, neighborhood associations, and interest associations. These organizations are hierarchies under Moscow's political control. Their structures and processes conform to the regime's interpretation of the Leninist principle of democratic centralism. In fact, participation in the activities of these bodies consists not in influencing policy making, but in rendering various services to the state and demonstrating support and allegiance for the regime's doctrines and policies. Thus, "mass participation," as these activities are called, has little in common with political participation in Western democracies.

In keeping with the guided, mobilizational style of Soviet participation, the officials who direct it are assigned to their jobs by the CPSU. As a rule, political careers are not made by rising to high rank in public organizations (excepting, of course, the party itself); rather individuals who have already made a name for themselves in the party are assigned to high rank in the organizations. As indicated earlier, however, individuals who display leadership ability in Komsomol work sometimes become important party apparatchiki; Andropov is an example.

From the standpoint of the regime, political participation in the Soviet style is useful. Like the massive political socialization programs, which in some ways it supplements and reinforces, organized mass participation keeps the populace busy and out of mischief. Also, by involving them in regime-directed routines and rituals, it fosters habits of compliance in people and instills perception of the leadership's omnipotence. Some forms of participation, such as the "people's control" bodies, which check up on the performance of official organs and expose instances of abuse or corruption, may even help the central leaders spot and correct local problems.

Even for ordinary Soviet citizens, directed participation can sometimes be a source of psychological satisfaction. For one thing, its changeless routines may create a reassuring

sense of stability, even if this is offset for some by boredom
with official rituals and slogans and for others by anger at
the constant demands for displays of compliance. Pressure from
above to take part in such activities is mitigated, however,
according to recent émigrés, by the willingness of officials to
settle for minimal or nominal levels of conformity, provided it
does not blossom into open defiance or, still worse, organized
collective protest. Moreover, we should bear in mind that such
mass organizations as the trade unions provide for docile
members benefits such as cheap, subsidized trips to vacation
resorts.

        Soviet propagandists lay enormous stress on the democratic
nature of elections to the soviets, elections that are
uncontested and have little effect on the policy-making
process. But it would be unrealistic to expect most Soviet
citizens to be as irked by the controlled elections as we would
imagine ourselves to be. Political pluralism as it has been
known in Western democracies for a century or more existed in
Russia briefly between the 1905 revolution and the October
Revolution of 1917, and in a severely constrained form at that.
Unfavorable circumstances prevented it from sinking its roots
deep enough to implant habits of self-government and
responsible participation. In short, the political culture of
liberal democracy, which Gabriel Almond and Sidney Verba called
the "civic culture," did not replace the traditional Russian
authoritarianism.(32)

        To some extent, the bureaucratization of political life in
all modern, industrial societies has made the issue of popular
control and participation acute in both Western and socialist
systems. In both, economic development has created great
concentrations of power over which ordinary citizens have
little influence. It would be unwise to press the comparison
too far, though. By comparison to the liberal democracies, the
Soviet regime has a vastly more comprehensive and centralized
apparatus of control over its citizens. The channels of
directed participation by the general public are too thoroughly
penetrated and coordinated by the party to be even remotely
effective as a counterweight to the power of the state.

Political Culture, Socialization, and Communication

Official Political Culture
        There are striking similarities as well as dissimilarites
between Soviet political culture and that of nineteeth-century
Russia. The reigns of the highly authoritarian tsars Nicholas
I (1825-1855) and Alexander III (1881-1894), in particular,
were dominated by ideas suggested by the slogan," Orthodoxy,

Autocracy, and Nationality." A convenient equivalent way of describing Soviet political culture would characterize it as ideological, partisan, as subject-participatory. In addition - like that of tsarist Russia - Soviet political culture is elitist, despite the official fiction that calls Soviet workers the leading class of Soviet society.

Of course no historical comparison is entirely apt. One must be cautious in comparing the rural, overwhelming peasant Russia, in which the Orthodox Church played a major role in inculcating the tsar´s subjects devotion to the monarch and holy Russia, with the now heavily industrialized, urban, and officially atheist U.S.S.R. And one must not overlook the vast superiority in penetration, sophistication, and effectiveness of the Soviet socialization and political communication network compared to its ramshackle tsarist predecessor. It would be impossible to understand much in contemporary Soviet official political culture, however, especially its relatively high degree of at least passive acceptance by the Soviet peoples, without taking into account continuities between tsarist and Soviet Russian political cultures. Otherwise the acceptance of marked dominance by political authorities over rank-and-file citizens; lack of legal safeguards for citizens´ rights in relation to government; governmental intrusion into cultural life, and even into individuals´ private affairs; and harsh, often abitrary suppression of dissent is very difficult to understand for people brought up in democracies.

The authoritarianism, statism, and militarization of Soviet life has roots in harsh historical experience. Addressing an audience of Soviet industrial executives in 1931, Stalin characterized the history of old Russia as a history of defeats at the hands of people more advanced technologically - and declared that if this gap were not closed, the results could be disastrous for the Soviet Union. But economic, technological, and military development required belt-tightening. The Soviet people became accustomed to sacrificing standards of living, if necessary, to economic development and military preparedness. World War II, when the very existence of the Russian nation seemed to be at risk, undoubtedly strengthened acceptance of stern authority, as well as bolstering national pride, especially among the dominant Russian element in the population.

Characterizing the political culture as ideological reflects the persistent claim that Soviet political life is guided by the precepts of Marx and Lenin. Of course the Soviet authorities - at the very highest level - reserve the right to interpret Marxism-Leninism. The Leninist path is extolled as a blueprint of mankind´s future. There is no place in the offical creed for partial commitment to its goals. Doctrine and authority are closely associated. Power and ideology legitimize each other. This pattern is a source of strength, but it also creates problems. Because it endows rulers with a mystique based on ideological correctness, their errors go unchallenged. Dogmatic attachment to the doctrine can stifle innovation and creativity.

From the ideological conception of the citizen's obligation to the state flow demands for loyalty to the party - called "party-mindedness" (partiinost') - as well as for intellectual commitment, principled behavior, and other evidences of wholehearted devotion to Marxism-Leninism. Military party-mindedness is basic to the official political culture. Hence all Soviet leaders, from Lenin to Andropov, have rejected the concept of the coexistence of ideologies, though they frequently acknowledge the value of "peaceful coexistence of states with different social systems" to gain practical benefits such as trade and arms control.

The term subject-participatory refers to the subordination of Soviet citizens to superiors in one or more bureaucratic chains of command and to every citizen's obligation to participate in the work of the collective or organization to which he or she belongs. Soviet leaders attribute great value to the participatory and collective aspects of political life. At the Twenty-sixth Congress in 1981, General Secretary Brezhnev reported proudly on the large numbers of citizens who voluntarily participate in organizations such as the people's control committees and other social activities. Recently General Secretary Andropov was cited as saying that the decisive force of "our forward movement" consists in the individual's readiness to take responsibility for the cause.(33)

It would be a mistake to classify Soviet political culture as simply bureaucratic and authoritarian. But it is clear that participation occurs within a framework of values, directives, and controls emanating from a vast national bureaucracy that is subject to the commands of the party Politburo.

System of Political Socialization
The high priority assigned by Soviet leaders to formation of desired attitudes and values is reflected in the size and scope of the formal socialization program. Responsibility for initiating, proclaiming, and overseeing every major decision in the sphere of education lies with the party. It has set in motion one of the most systematic political indoctrination programs to which any population has ever been subjected. Through it, all citizens from early childhood are exposed to a coordinated array of influences intended to mold their character and determine their outlooks.(34)

161

The Schools. The most important instrument of political socialization in the Soviet Union has always been a tightly woven network of educational institutions, from the primary school through the university. After consolidation of the regime around 1921, and particularly after the start of rapid industrialization and agricultural collectivization in the late 1920s, Soviet educational institutions embarked on an elaborate effort to impart traits such as orderliness, punctuality, and discipline to a population that was (and to some extent still is) accustomed to the rough traditions of village life. Millions of peasant children were made conscious of national and international political issues and events. For students who advanced to secondary and higher levels of education, Soviet educators provided systematic instruction in the official version of Marxist-Leninist philosophy, social and economic theory, and history.(35)

In the early years of the revolution, educators, inspired by progressive and revolutionary theories of upbringing, tried out their ideas in a variety of experimental and model schools. Under Stalin, however, there was a backlash against experimentation. The new emphasis was to give all children standardized and highly disciplined education, emphasizing technical training in the skills needed to run an industrial society. Rote learning displaced experiments with progressive education. The curriculum of the schools gave a prominent place to political instruction, intended to build unquestioning loyalty to the party, the state, and above all, to Stalin personally.

The educational system that was set up under Stalin achieved notable success. It allowed millions to rise rapidly into the new industrial organizations and political bureaucracies. Almost overnight, it gave a backward population some awareness of world events. The emphasis on discipline and obedience, on patriotism and heroism, served the country well when it was put to the terrible test of World War II. On the other hand, the system created problems, which were left for Stalin's successors to solve. In particular, by the 1950s it had ceased to give working-class and village children a wide opportunity to rise to higher status. Universities and the better technical schools were filled with children of the new Soviet elite that had formed. A pervasive careerism had developed that seemed to put personal advancement ahead of the interests of the society, and thus deepened the gulf between those who had "made it" and the masses of the population. The result was widespread political apathy, even disaffection.

Khrushchev sought to overcome these problems by democratizing the school system and emphasizing labor education. Perhaps the most important reform he instituted was the requirement that all but the most gifted students would have to spend two years working after they graduated from secondary school before they could seek admission to institutions of higher education. This experience, Khrushchev hoped, would increase the chances that working-class children would have greater opportunities to obtain a higher education. Khrushchev´s reforms, however, were bitterly resisted by many educators and officials. It became apparent that the attempt to bring the educational system closer to practical labor was lowering the quality of education. Almost immediately after Khrushchev was ousted, his reforms were reversed.

Since Khrushchev, the educational system has combined the emphasis on shaping the "New Soviet Person" by memorization of the proper lessons from Lenin and other authorities, with the need to raise well-educated members for a modern society. The effort to create a "subject-participatory" political culture has continued through the intensive emphasis upon patriotism, collectivism, hostility toward states and movements the leadership designates as enemies, and loyalty toward the CPSU. The schools also seek to foster a moral code that is identified with the proclaimed values of communist society - selflessness, industriousness, personal integrity, and self-discipline.

Although in many respects the present educational system is the product of the Stalin era, it is no longer the laddar by means of which millions of working-class and peasant individuals can climb out of their class backgrounds. To a limited extent, the schools do enable children to move into more prestigious occupations - peasant children can go to schools training them as railroad engineers or skilled mechanics - but the scarcity of places in universities and good technical institutes means that schooling tends to allow those in higher-status strata to pass their privelege along to their offspring. David Lane, a British sociologist, predicts that the general slowing of upward mobility in Soviet society will continue.(36)

Khrushchev´s successors have also mostly ended the abrupt shifts in the official line that in the past required frequent overhauls of the curriculum. Criticism of Stalin´s policies is muted, as is criticism of Khrushchev´s reforms. Lenin is made the one unquestioned figure of universal respect; he is constantly referred to on every issue and his works are cited as if they were an inexhaustible source of guidance for the present. An intensive effort is made to instill love of homeland, along with a sense of "proletarian internationalism" (the idea of unity among working-class peoples and socialist societies), and respect for the nationalities that make up the Soviet Union. Passing marks in the mandatory courses on

Marxist-Leninist doctrine are required for graduation from all secondary and higher educational institutions. Thus, the political aspects of schooling under Stalin's successors have preserved the dogmatic and authoritarian elements of Stalinism.

The Komsomol and its Affiliates. The Soviet regime seeks to make all organized settings of social life into agencies of political socialization. To this end, not only the schools, but also the workplace, the mass media, public ceremonies and holidays, fine arts, armed forces, trade unions, courts, and youth organizations all play a role as "schools of communism." The Komsomol, the Pioneers, and the Octobrists are the sole legal youth groups. They are, therefore, important adjuncts of the schools in molding the consciousness of young people.

The All-Union Leninist League of Communist Youth - Komsomol - was founded in the heat of the civil war, in 1918. Since that time it has been officially named the reserve and helper of the party. As of early 1981, it had more than 40 million members. Serving as the official repository of youthful idealism and energy, it often contributes "volunteers" to major constructive projects. It is the major channel for the spare-time activities of youths in schools, the armed forces, farms, and factories, where Komsomol leaders, working closely with party officials, sponsor political study circles, field trips, and community service activities. Perhaps most important, it serves as a pool of potential recruits into the party, training young people in political knowledge as well as leadership skills. General Secretary Brezhnev reported at the Twenty-sixth Party Congress in 1981 that more than three-quarters of the new members of the party over the previous five years, or more than a million persons, entered from the Komsomol.(37)

At all levels of the educational system, the Komsomol and its junior affiliates, the Pioneers and the Octobrists, reinforce the political lessons taught in the regular curriculum. They also assist school officials in social control, discipline, and political surveillance. The Komsomol accepts youths of ages 14 to 28, the Pioneers 9 to 14, and the Octobrists 7 to 9. Officially, membership in all three organizations is voluntary. There is so much official and peer pressure to join, however, particularly for the younger organizations, that it is a rare boy or girl who is not a member. A good record in Komsomol is virtually a prerequisite to a university education and a political career. Expulsion from Komsomol is tantamount to expulsion from the university.

Some Pioneer activities, such as hiking, camping, and trips to famous historic sites, together with the quasi-military organization, suggest a resemblance to the Cub

164

Scouts or Brownies in the United States. (All three Soviet
youth groups are, however, coeducational.) But the insistent
political messages that underlie its teachings and activities,
its constant stress on collective rather than individual
achievement and on military training distinguish it from
American youth organizations. They also emphasize explicit
political instruction far more than do their American
counterparts. Their programs include organizing school
children to celebrate political holidays, establishing "Lenin
corners" for propaganda work among children, forming honor
guards at the tombs of war heroes, and initiating pen-pal
correspondence with children in other countries. Many Soviet
schoolchildren, especially from larger cities, spend several
weeks each summer in Pioneer camps. Under the guidance of
teachers and older youths in the Komsomol, many Pioneers´
groups also operate a wide range of hobby clubs and study
circles.

The stress is on political lessons appropriate to the age
group. The youngest children are urged to revere Lenin´s
memory, love their country, serve their society, and work hard
in school. They learn to take responsibility for each other as
members of a group, to watch and guide one another, and to turn
peer pressure into a force for moral upbringings. As they
enter their teens, they learn to await the chance to enter the
Komsomol, with its grownup duties, with eager anticipation.

Nearly all young people do enter the Komsomol, although
many, particularly when they have finished their schooling drop
out before reaching 28. The Komsomol continues many of the
same kinds of activities as the Pioneers, but gives them a more
explicit political focus. Komsomol members are all expected to
take on voluntary service, such as tutoring others, helping to
prepare for elections to the soviets, or writing for the school
newspaper. The Komsomol often sends members out at harvest
time, when extra hands are needed in the fields. A major
activity is sponsoring spare-time political study classes for
university students and young factory workers. The Komsomol
also organizes lectures on special topics, such as
international problems. Through the Komsomol, young people are
supposed to take on organizing duties, thus showing their
political loyalty and developing their ability as leaders. At
all times, they remain under the watchful scrutiny of party
members who are attached to their organizations.

The Komsomol is a major auxiliary instrument of political
socialization as well as political recruitment. Komsomol work
is taken very seriously by Soviet leaders to ensure that each
new generation will grow up loyal to the system and able to
take over its management. The Komsomol gives the party a way

of identifying and training activists, persons who distinguish themselves in organizational and service work, and who do a good job of keeping an eye on the political leanings of their fellow youths. It provides the party with a ready core of activists and leaders willing to take up party work.

On the other hand, the Komsomol´s success in producing outward conformity greatly exceeds its ability at instilling true ideological conviction. Many, perhaps most, Soviet youths participate in Komsomol activities knowing that they must do so if they wish to advance their careers, or simply because it is the thing to do. Many enter the Komsomol with high ideals but stay in only to avoid a black mark on their records. Komsomol leaders constantly exhort their members to overcome attitudes of passivity, indifference, and alienation, but often must settle for nominal compliance.

Role of the Family. Although in the early revolutionary years Soviet policy had the effect of weakening family ties (Marxists saw the family as an institution of bourgeois society), internal Soviet policy since the 1930s has assigned the family an honored place in the political upbringing of Soviet citizens. The family has been viewed as an important instrument for promoting social stability by teaching basic moral principles.

A good deal of evidence suggests, however, that the actual role of the family in socialization may not fit the regime´s wishes. The influence of parents and grandparents often contradicts the lessons taught by the schools and youth groups, particularly about religious and other moral values. The family reinforces pluralistic tendencies generated by economic and social stratification and by ethnic and regional differences. Among the most significant family influences at variance with offical ideology is the tendency of intelligentsia parents to try to guarantee for their children the advantages they gained by competitive struggle.

Among non-Russians, particularly Moslems, many parents interfere both consciously and unintentionally with the regime´s efforts to eliminate resistance to the obligatory adoption of the dominant urban, industrial, Russian communist culture. The result is perpetuation of traditional religious and national observances and customs, which often undercut beliefs and values taught by the regime. Soviet social scientists studying the prevalence of religious belief conducted a survey among fourth-year students at Samarkand University in the Uzbek Republic and found the continuing hold family religious ties had on the students, 9.4 percent of whom responded that they were still influenced by believing members of their families.(38) The same holds true for the persistent strength of various Christian denominations and other religious faiths.

The regime seeks to reduce the influence of religion both by frontal assault in the form of antireligious propaganda and by popularizing holidays and rituals that borrow from folk or religious traditions but emphasize modern and Soviet values. Wedding ceremonies often take place in secular "wedding palaces," where the vows reflect the view that marriage is an institution important to Soviet society; after the ceremony, newlyweds typically visit the local Tomb of the Unknown Soldier to lay a wreath, commemorating the sacrifices made by past generations of Soviet citizens to ensure the blessings of life for their heirs. Many similar customs, together with official holidays and votive symbols, have come into use, part of the effort to deflect the urges of citizens for expressive gratification onto an official "political religion."(39)

Even more difficult than assessing the Soviet family's influence in political socialization is evaluating the overall success of this gigantic effort to create a "Soviet person." Certainly it has not been fully successful, or criticism of the work of indoctrination and complaints against so many persisting survivals of capitalism would not be as prominent as they still are in the Soviet press. At the same time, and despite its serious shortcomings, political socialization in the U.S.S.R. has many formidable achievements to its credit. Objective Western scholars generally agree that although it has not created a uniform political culture, it has created a fairly high level of popular consensus around the regime's basic principles. Even though only a few Soviet youths have a profound knowledge of Marxist-Leninist doctrine, the youths shaped by the agencies described here, especially the student activists who are future leaders, are imbued with the peculiar mixture of anticapitalism and nationalism known as Soviet patriotism.

Adult Political Education. For more than five decades the CPSU has conducted a large-scale program of adult political instruction.(40) Today the system enjoys unprecedented scope. Altogether around 60 million individuals are enrolled in its courses, seminars and discussion groups; in some areas, particularly the large cities, three-quarters or more of the employed population may attend classes. The courses are organized by the party in each workplace (a good-sized factory might have fifty or a hundred such "schools") and at local Houses and Clubs of Political Education.

Classes are taught by volunteer activists, called propagandists, who work to fulfill a part of their obligation to the party. The propagandists themselves study in higher-level courses, where their knowledge of the Marxist-Leninist classics is deepened. They also learn how to relate current policy issues, such as economic management or nationality relations, to the theoretical doctrines of the party. Overall, about 2.5 million individuals, nearly all party members, work as propagandists.

The objectives of the adult political education system have changed with time. Early in the Soviet era, when most of the populace lacked even rudimentary political awareness, the systems sought to compensate for the politcal illiteracy of the workers and peasants. But, as the educational level of the Soviet population has risen, so too has the theoretical level of political instruction. Today the system seeks not only to provide thorough grounding in ideology for its listeners, but also to teach them ways of using theory to illuminate the political tasks of the moment as the party sees them. Thus, economic administrators attend courses relating political economy to their problems as managers; journalists, editors, and other communicators study more effective methods of ideological work.

The system has slowly grown more differentiated. Courses are specialized by the educational level, occupation, and political rank of their listeners. Along with a three-tiered system of party-run political instruction, a new network of economics courses was established in the 1970s. Although enrollment in these spare-time schools is enormous, their success in inculcating the desired familiarity with party doctrine is limited. The party frequently complains that the class sessions turn away from ideology and become discussions of purely practical subjects. From the standpoint of the party leaders, it is important to infuse the political education system with fresh and usable information, but not at the expense of the fundamentals of party doctrine.

This weakness suggests the difficulty of the task the party sets itself in its efforts at adult political socialization. In surveys of Soviet citizens, large proportions of respondents indicate that they attend political education courses out of a sense of obligation and that the quality of instruction leaves much to be desired. Many lack a solid grasp of some basic political doctrines. In the face of such findings, Soviet officials have pressed hard since the late 1970s to improve the entire propaganda system, by refining the methods of instruction and by raising the status of the propagandist (the party urges, for example, that the propagandist be exempted from all other spare-time duties).(41)

Both the forms and the content of adult political

168

education have undergone transformation since Stalin´s time. Then, political education presented a stark and simple picture of the world, filled with enemies abroad and cunning subversives and spies within, facing a glorious future but requiring great sacrifices in the short run. The textbooks used, particularly the notorious Short Course, were written in a dogmatic style and were riddled with factual distortions. History was reduced to a few fundamental lessons stressing the unceasing conflict between world imperialism and its servants and socialism - represented by the Soviet Union. All instruction fostered worshipful faith in Stalin. These methds, though crude, had several strengths, including sharpness of tone, intensity of mood, and simplicity of presentation. Bringing instruction up to date without losing any of the homogeneity and authority that characterized Stalinist propaganda has posed difficult problems for Stalin´s successors.

Today the population has been exposed to far more Western influences through radio broadcasts, tourists, and travel abroad than was thinkable thirty years ago. Increased knowledge about the non-Soviet world, combined with better education, has enabled citizens to make more independent judgments about the truth of party doctrine. To make propaganda credible and authoritative, therefore, the party must adapt its approach to the higher levels of knowledge among the population. At the same time, the party has sought to reach each section of society with propaganda tailored to its role. Finally, the party has broadened the reach of the system, seeking to draw in every member of the labor force. In sheer numbers, the system of adult political education has attained truly remarkable success. The challenge, however, as the party constantly observes, is to make effectivesness of the system equally high.

Media of Communication

Nowhere is the contrast between Soviet and American politics more striking than in their patterns of political communication, which is one reason citizens of either society feel uneasy about the other. Russians are shocked by the sensationalism and commercialism of the Western press. Americans are appalled by the massive effort to ensure that citizens see the world as rulers want them to. American society confronts citizens with a free choice among many sometimes contradictory facts and interpretations; the Soviet system bombards them with messages bent on reforming them and meant to reinforce official versions of truth.(42)

Criticism of the monotony and staleness of news supplied by Soviet press, radio, and television is inceasing. The electronic media, in particular, have made efforts to improve the appeal of their programming, using such formats as live phone-in programs that allow viewers and listeners to ask questions of expert guests directly. Despite the government's efforts to use television as a medium of instruction and edification, however, the most popular programs are movies and other shows meeting viewers' needs for relaxation and entertainment.(43) The press continues to be the dominant medium for commentary and analysis, but the regime demands that all the media serve its ideological goals. They must mold the consciousness of the population and at the same time combat inefficiency and other deficiencies in the system.(44)

In the U.S.S.R., all agencies that disseminate information are supervised by party functionaries and internal party units. The top policy-making body overseeing political communication is the Department of Propaganda, an arm of the apparatus of the party Central Committee. Its control extends down through party committees to the primary party organizations. Its principle duty is to lay down the correct ideological line to which all public communication must adhere, and to monitor compliance.

Party officials and activists supervise all elements of the political communication system. They discuss past and planned articles with newspaper editors; they check on the programming of television and radio broadcasts; they instruct writers and other intellectuals about the limits of permissible expression in the fine arts. At the base of the pyramid of the party organizations carrying out these functions stand the primary party organizations which comprise the party members in every workplace. These PPOs send out directives received from higher party authorities and receive citizens' complaints and reactions, which they then pass on up the pyramid. They must make certain that all patterns and instruments of communication are coordinated and attuned to current policy. They are expected to organize voluntary lectures and ceremonial meetings in the workplace, to oversee the enterprise's newspaper and radio station, and to select individuals to serve as editors and writers. They also see that clubs, hobby groups, and other cultural activities function properly and that the propaganda and agitation of the mass media are reaching their targets.

Oral Agitation. Soviet political communication is distinctive in relying on oral forms of communication between elites and masses in addition to the printed and broadcast media. One of the most important is oral agitation. Agitation arose in the revolutionary era, when most of the workers and peasants whom the revolutionaries sought to arouse were illiterate, and the socialist press had to operate underground. Agitators sent out by the revolutionary parties developed techniques of persuasion based on simple, emotional rhetoric,

guided discussion, and small-group settings. The aim of
agitation was to win over particular collectives, in factories,
villages, or mines, so as to direct opinion toward the party's
action goals. Thus agitation, in contrast to propaganda,
sought to focus attention on immediate issues, such as a
planned strike or demonstration. Propaganda was the term
reserved for more theoretical political instruction.

Oral agitation was a highly effective technique of
information and persuasion, for it enabled the party both to
reach the masses with its messages and to keep watch over
public attitudes and moods at close range. It provided a
two-way line of communication between the populace and the
local party organizations.

Today, the immense scope of the printed and broadcast
media provides the regime with multiple channels for
disseminating information. Yet oral agitation, and other oral
settings of communication, have not lost their usefulness.
Rather, their function has changed somewhat. Agitators today
seek to supplement newspapers, television, and radio by
providing additional explanation for a new government policy,
by answering questions, or by carrying out specialized
counseling with lawbreakers, alcoholics, or religious
believers. Agitators are also called upon to stimulate
interest in special events, such as elections to the soviets.

In the Brezhnev period, the regime found that the
curiosity of the population about domestic and international
affairs had outstripped the ability of agitators (many of whom
did not possess high levels of knowledge) to satisy it.
Accordingly, a new type of speaker, specializing in some field
of current events, such as economics or foreign affairs, was
established. The "political information specialist"
(politinformator) gives talks in the workplace much as the
agitator does, but is expected to be an authoritative source of
fresh information. Much of the content of the political
information specialist's talks consist of news of the sort that
would not normally be carried in the newpapers. Factual detail
builds credibility and helps to carry the political messages
home. Interest in the political information sessions is also
enhanced by the question-and-answer period, which may last
longer than the talk itself.

Agitation and political information sessions are added to
by yet other techniques of oral communication, such as
"political days" when officials from all over a province or
city fan out to address audiences in every workplace on a
common theme. Not only has the spread of printed and bradcast
media not made these oral settings of official communication
obsolete, but the continued encouragement the regime gives to

their development indicates the hopes the leadership attaches to them as a means of building mass support for its policies.

The Press. All Soviet newspapers are supervised by the party and its organs. Pravda (Truth), the most important Soviet newspaper, is published by the Party Central Committee. Izvestiia (News), the second-ranking daily, is the organ of the Supreme Soviet. The fifteen republics also have newspapers, produced jointly by party headquarters and the republican government, with most editorials reprinted from Pravda. The armed forces, trade unions, Komsomol, and other organizations also publish their own newspapers and periodicals. At times, local publications make it possible for liberal authors to publish works that Moscow would have censored. But in general, access to these newspapers is tightly controlled by the party.

The Soviet press might be described as the largest journalistic operation in the world under one management. The exceptionally uniform perspective and approach that party control ensures is reinforced by the special place that the major Moscow newspapers, especially Pravda, occupy in the press system. Pravda prints more than 10 million copies every day... It is printed simultaneously in many cities of the country, so that nearly every Soviet citizen can read it the day it appears. Its special authority derives from its being the principal press outlet for the central party leadership. Its editorials, articles, and commentaries are followed closely by foreign officials for evidence of shifts in national policy and other essential information.

Lower-level newspapers depend upon the central news agency, TASS, for much of their news. They also carry a large number of letters from readers, which are selected and rewritten by the newspaper´s staff. The perspective of the local newspapers upon local, national, and international events must be the same as that of the central newspapers, but they are encouraged to give more space to local problems and issues. Here they are expected to find ways of improving economic productivity and of responding to readers´ complaints about shortcomings in the operation of local facilities and services. There are tight limits, however, on the ability of the press to play a muckraking role. At all times, the press must assist the party in forming the "New Soviet Person" by showing that despite temporary difficulties, Soviet society is advancing steadily toward the eventual full triumph of communism. This requirement shapes the very definition of news. News, according to Soviet authorities, is agitation by means of facts.

Helping to ensure that the press and other media of communication do not inadvertently help to transmit incorrect messages is the system of censorship. Every issue of every newspaper and magazine, every book, play, or television program, everything, in fact, which is to be publicly disseminated, must be approved by the censors. Together, censorship and the self-censorship practiced by writers and editors prevent information on a wide range of subjects from reaching the public, including news of accidents, disasters, and epidemics, the private lives of political leaders, anything deemed prejudicial to state security, the party's internal budgetary and political processes, and censorship itself. The demands, that the press use information to indoctrinate citizens, combined with censorship, result in a press that, compared with Western publications, seems arid, pedantic, and often trivial.

Interest Aggregation and Policy Making: Stability and Change

The exercise of political power in the Soviet Union has always beem highly centralized and secretive. Its wielders have sought "unity" and conformity and have been extraordinarily intolerant of activities or attitudes they regard as incompatible with their goals. Despite rigidity and malcoordination generated by bureaucratic centralism, the Soviet system has displayed sufficient adaptiveness to adjust its policies to the exigencies of a seemingly endless series of crises. Although Marxist doctrine, which the Soviet leaders invoke as a major source of legitmacy for their power, rejects the role of "great men" in history, most of Soviet history can be written about the leadership exercised by four men: Lenin, Stalin, Khrushchev, and Brezhnev. Each of these men possessed the combination of energy, ambition, ruthlessness, and political skill necessary to grasp and maintain power and to cope with the challenges posed by changes in the domestic and foreign environments.

Lenin exercised leadership over the ruling party mainly by virtue of charisma, experience, and moral authority. He was ruthless in suppressing opposition. He did not hesitate to deprive non-Bolshevik socialists, not to mention "bourgeois" elements, of freedom of speech or of life itself, if in his opinion their activities threatened Soviet power. An important part of the political legacy bequeathed by Lenin to his successors consisted in the dread system of political police informants, jailers, and executioners known in his time as the Cheka and, since 1954, as the KGB (Committee of State Security).(45)

173

In his relations with communists whose opinions differed from his own, though, Lenin, unlike Stalin, resorted less to coercion than to debate and persuasion. Lenin´s greatest achievement was his creation of the cadre party, governed by the principle of "democratic centralism," the instrument by which he overturned Russian society and paved the way for the activities of Stalin and Stalin´s successors.

Stalin gained power not only by virtue of his considerable flair for administration and political intrigue, but also by skillfully presenting himself as Lenin´s most dedicated pupil. Once in power, he launched his "revolution from above" The major features of this coercive campaign were collectivization of agriculture and forced-draft industrialization. Stalin laid the foundations of Soviet economic and military power and led the U.S.S.R. to victory over Nazi Germany. The Soviet people paid an enormous price in fear, suffering, and tens of millions of lives for Stalin´s successes, although in the rather uninspiring atmosphere of recent years a good many Soviet citizens have looked back with nostalgia to the dictator´s stern rule. One of the most damaging consequences of Stalin´s rule was that it led to the establishment of patterns of economic development and administration ill-suited to dealing with today´s increasingly complex economy and the problem it generates.

The centralized patterns of policy making created by Lenin and greatly intensified by Stalin were carried over into the post-Stalin period. To be sure, both the Khrushchev and Brezhnev leaderships renounced mass terror, and under Khrushchev there were important legal reforms. Nevertheless, despite these and other significant changes, the traditional centralism of the Soviet system has basically persisted. It would not be much of a distortion to say that oligarchy replaced autocracy after Stalin´s death, even if there have been "cults" of Khrushchev and Brezhnev, though without the irrationality associated with Stalin worship. Only the approximately two dozen individuals who at any one time since 1952 have been members of the Politburo or the Secretariat or both have normally had significant parts in policy making at the national level, although the highest-ranking officials of other bureaucracies, such as the ministries, the KGB, the armed forces, and other agencies have important parts at times.

New Trends in Interest Articulation and Aggregation in Soviet
    Politics
    The death of Stalin set in motion significant loosening of the Soviet political system. During the period when Khrushchev sought ascendancy, and later as he fought to hold on to power, he instituted organizational reforms. Many were poorly conceived and hastily executed. Although some raised the hopes

of the young and the liberal intelligentsia, they also antagonized the central party and state bureaucracies, which supported the expulsion of Khrushchev and the accession of the stabilizing Brezhnev-Kosygin leadership. Nevertheless, many of the changes Khrushchev introduced, which broadened access to decision-making power and increased the security of masses and elites, have been institutionalized in the political system.

The de-Stalinization under Khrushchev opened opportunities to spokesmen of specialized bureaucratic interests, such as the legal specialists, who participated actively in formulating new codes of criminal law and criminal procedure to replace those of the Stalin era. Economists took part in debates over how to reform industrial management and planning. Writers and other creative intellectuals demanded greater freedom for their art. It became apparent that with the broadening of the policy arena, some group interest articulation and conflict was materializing. Scholars investigating group activity have found that the influence of a bureaucratic group is greatest when the party is divided or uncertain, when the group itself is united behind a demand, and when the issue calls for specialized expertise. Group participation has been especially important at the stages of deliberating policy issues and formulating alternatives for action.(46)

It would be incorrect to transplant the model of competitive interest group politics from liberal democracies to the Soviet system, however. Three features of Soviet group articulation make it distinctive. First, the bureaucratically organized functional groups are themselves frequently divided, so that coalitions favoring one policy option or another may cut across institutional lines. In this instance it may be more accurate to speak of issue "tendencies" rather than "groups."(47)

Second, the degree of influence enjoyed by specialist groups outside the party seems to depend on the party's willingness to open a policy debate to specialist participation, or disagreement within the leadership over how to resolve a problem. In a major study of policy making in agriculture, land use, and water, Thane Gustafson writes that although technical specialists in the Brezhnev period appeared to have a major role in formulating policy in their fields, they depended on the leadership to give legitimacy to policy ideas and to shape the policy agenda. Specialists advocating particular policies needed sponsors among the leadership who could provide them with political resources, such as research institutes and scholarly journals.(48)

Third, the major organization of interest aggregation remains the party, above all its permanent staff of officials.

By varied means they continue to exercise predominant control over policy making. They ensure representation of major bureaucratic interests on party committees and bureaus at each level of the system. They oversee the media through which specialists communicate with each other and the public. Through the nomenklatura system they set the criteria for appointments to leadership posts in the main bureaucracies and even supervise selection of appointees. The continued existence of these controls ensures that though the arena for policy making may broaden or shrink, depending on the leadership's receptivity to articulation of demands by specialist elites, the ultimate instrument for aggregating interests and making policy remains the one party.

Other forms of interest articulation exist. One is factional conflict among political leaders.(49) Because the system does not provide open channels of competition, personal and bureaucratic rivalry may take the form of covert maneuvers for power, manipulation of policy issues, and cultivation of networks of political clients. Factional conflict is personalized political conflict in a setting in which, under party rules, factional groupings are supposed to be strictly forbidden. Nevertheless, even in the placid Brezhnev era, events such as the "release" of Politburo members Petr Shelest in 1973, Aleksandr Shelepin in 1975, and Nikolai Podgorny in 1977 indicated tensions among the ruling few. Agreement among the party leadership on the need to preserve the fundamentals of the system mostly formed under Stalin has kept such internal conflict from threatening the formal unity of the party.

One of the ways in which the regime has responded to experts' proposals for reform to solve social and economic problems has been the conduct of various "social experiments." Social experiments are reforms carried out on a small scale, typically in one or a few enterprises. They enable the regime to test the effects of a new arrangement without upsetting entrenched bureaucratic interests. The much-publicized Shchekino experiment involved granting the enterprise director substantial freedom to reduce the size of the work force. It thus had radical implications. For the most part, however, despite publicity for successful experiments, they have not led to major economic reforms.(50)

Although a great deal of evidence suggests that on a wide variety of issues, specialists and groups do have a significant part in articulating interests, it would be misleading to regard the Soviet system as pluralistic.(51) Substantial doubt exists as to whether the system is evolving toward greater openness in interest articulation and policy making was more tolerant than was the Khrushchev leadership in permitting innovative, reformist proposals to be debated in the official press and in books, and that it displayed greater lenience toward dissenters than did Khrushchev. It is true that there has been a great deal of discussion, both under Khrushchev and under Brezhnev, of proposals designed to achieve increased efficiency, or to promote "democratization." Most of these proposals affected local government. This is an area of very real importance to Soviet citizens and, incidentally, the Soviet press has a profusion of criticism of neglect by local authorities of citizens, complaints about such matters as leaking roofs and discourteous sales personnel in shops. But relatively innovative proposals have generally been buried in obscure journals with tiny readership. What is more, they meet with almost no response, or even with condemnation, in the official press.(52)

     Outside the channels of legitimate interest articulation is a considerable body of "dissent": expression that the Soviet authorities consider subversive. Dissent here means articulation, especially in writing (and in the U.S.S.R., especially if transmitted abroad), of independent, critical opinions on matters political. Because the sphere of the political is so vast in communist systems, criticism not only of the government and the ruling CPSU and its justifying doctrines, but also of official policies in the arts and sciences, philosophy, and ethics is sometimes regarded as subversive by the Soviet authorities, as is presentation in fictional form of critical opinion on many topics.

     Dissent in the U.S.S.R. since Stalin differs so much from its earlier counterparts as to justify considering it virtually unprecedented in Soviet history. In the 1920s and 1930s dissent was mainly confined to disputes among factional groupings within the party, such as those led by Trotsky, Zinoviev, and Bukharin against one another and against Stalin. After Stalin became unchallenged leader in the Politburo, opposition, in the sense of organized efforts to change the leadership or policy of the state, was ruthlessly suppressed. From the early 1930s, particularly after the purges from 1936 to 1938, opposition and even dissenting opinions or merely belonging to a suspect social or ethnic group entailed agonizing anxiety and a high probability of arrest and sentence to a labor camp.(53)

     Stalin's death left the Soviet people both hopeful and fearful. There was hope that a new dawn of freedom and justice would follow the long night of terror and violence to which the dictator had subjected his subjects. Surviving victims of Stalin's terror, such as Aleksandr Solzhenitsyn, and relatives of those who had perished wrote powerful accounts of life in labor camps. The historian Roy Medvedev wrote, but could not publish in the Soviet Union, a history of the stunning

victories and horrifying crimes and blunders with which the
Stalin era was replete. Party leaders and bureaucrats
remembered with a shudder the years - vividly described by
Khrushchev in his famous "secret speech" at the Twentieth
Congress of the CPSU in February 1956 - when Stalin's closest
associates could not ever be sure that they would be at large
or alive on the morrow.

The Soviet elite, so many of whose members were implicated
in actions that Khrushchev bluntly characterized as crimes,
craved stability and security but feared that
"de-Stalinization" could, if carried too far, undermine the
legitimacy of the Soviet system and lead to their own
punishment for abuse of power. Khrushchev was, Stephen Cohen
writes, a "repentant Stalin," but he was also a shrewd
politician who exploited the Stalin issue against political
opponents such as Vyacheslav Molotov, Georgi Malenkov, and
Lazar Kaganovich. Khrushchev's attitude toward Stalin was
ambivalent. He would denounce him one day and call him a great
leader another day. But by giving the green light for
publication of Stolzhenitsyn's novella, One Day in the Life of
Ivan Denisovich, he struck a powerful blow for freedom of
artistic expression and historical truth. Ultimately the
pro-Stalinists proved more powerful than the anti-Stalinists
and their victory had a good deal to do with removing the
reformist but erratic Khrushchev leadership and its replacement
by the more cautious and stable, more consensual and somewhat
more efficient Brezhnev leadership in October 1964. Brezhnev
soon ended de-Stalinization and in 1965 began a campaign to
suppress expression of views and information on many topics
that had been articulated in official Soviet publications under
Khrushchev. To a large extent, this crackdown on anti-Stalinist
writings prompted the rise of the dissent movement.(54)

In the 1960s a group of intellectuals conceived the idea
of a "legal," nonviolent mode of dissent that involved acting
as if the Soviet Constitution and legal codes, with their
guarantees of freedom of speech, press, assembly, and the like,
could be taken at face value. Dissidents who adopted this
"legalist" approach, as it came to be called, demanded literal
compliance with the law by the Soviet authorities. They sought
to play on the embarrassment that could be caused the
authorities when in the trials of well-known dissidents,
especially in Moscow, it could be shown that the police, the
prosecutors, and the judges, not the dissidents, were violating
officially proclaimed legal principles and procedures. By
adhering strictly to formal legal norms they hoped to minimize
the risk of KGB repression. This strategy of legal and
nonviolent protest was adopted by Soviet "mainstream" groups of
dissidents, among whom the noted Academician Andrei Sakharov
was to become the leading figure in the early 1970s.(55)

The mainstream dissenters have most often been referred to
collectively as the Democratic Movement, but often also as
human rights and civil rights advocates or activists. They
were not really a movement. They shied away from
organizational discipline. Acting as like-minded individuals
with the common purpose of restraining the authorities from
arbitrarily harassing or arresting Soviet citizens who
advocated freedom of speech, freedom of religion, freedom of
movement inside the U.S.S.R., and freedom for Jews, Germans,
and members of ethnic groups who wanted to emigrate, they
joined forces from time to time to sign letters and petitions
to the authorities. Although the Democratic Movement was only
one of many currents of dissent - there were also important
reformist Marxist, religious, non-Russian, and Russian
nationalist currents - most of the more talented and thoughtful
participants in these groups were influenced by the legal,
nonviolent model offered by the civil rights activists. Of
great potential importance were the unofficial labor unions
that sprang up from 1977 on. They conducted a number of brief
strikes. So far, their influence has been marginal, but
judging by the speed with which the authorities moved to
suppress them (in several cases by committing their leaders to
mental institutions), they aroused great concern.(56)

In the period roughly from the late 1960s to the late
1970s, numerous small organizations were formed by the
dissidents, including the Initiative Group (often called Action
Group) for the Defense of Civil Rights, which was very active
then, the Moscow Human Rights Committee, founded in November
1970 by Academician Sakharov and his fellow physicists Valeri
Chalidze and Andrei Tverdokhlebov, and the Public Group to
Promote Fulfillment of the Helsinki Accords (CSCE). Organized
in 1976 by physicist Yuri Orlov, the Helsinki Group played a
much more visible role in East-West relations than any other
Soviet dissident organization. Four independent non-Russian
groups, centered in the capitals of the Ukrainian, Georgian,
Armenian, and Lithuanian Union Republics, affiliated their
activities with the Moscow Group. Other groups, concentrating
on such matters as the abuse of psychiatry for political
repression, the plight of handicapped persons, and persecution
of religious believers, sought out Orlov's group. Workers also
began coming to Moscow to talk to Orlov and other members of
the Helsinki Watch Group.(57)

As of late 1982, the KGB had decimated the ranks of
dissent. Its victory is tempered, however, by the continued
appearance of the Chronicle of Current Events and a stream of
other samizdat items. Moreover, although the volume of
"democratic" dissent has diminished, that of religious and
nationalist movements remains large, and in some areas such as

Lithuania and the Baltic area generally, samizdat, and an
impressive array of samizdat journals, still flourish. Several
times in the past the Democratic Movement has been pronounced
dead, only to rise again. It seems highly unlikely that
dissent can be snuffed out entirely, as long as the conditions
that give rise to it persist, and as long as the regime shrinks
from unleashing terror of the Stalin type.

Policy Making and Policies since Stalin: Tinkering With the Command Economy

Since Stalin, one of the principal intents of the
leadership has been to improve the performance of the economy.
All efforts to raise economic productivity must contend with
formidable obstacles inherent in the command economy that
developed under Stalin. That economy was a powerful instrument
of rapid development in basic industry and war production. It
slighted agriculture and production of consumer goods in order
to channel labor, managerial personnel, and capital into
activities necessary for building the "military-economic might"
of the U.S.S.R. Because of tight bureaucratic controls,
enterprise and farm managers are inhibited from engaging in the
innovative entrepreneurial behavior practiced by many of their
counterparts in the West.

Both Khrushchev and Brezhnev sought to increase the output
and efficiency of the economy, particularly in agriculture,
which had been so badly neglected under Stalin. Khrushchev´s
initiatives frequently were tied to his need for dramatic,
immediate successes in order to buttress his political
leadership. His Virgin Lands campaign, which opened to
cultivation the vast prairie lands of southeastern Russia and
Kazakhstan, mobilized hundreds of thousands of volunteers but
slighted the necessary infrastructure. In the long run,
because of inadequate irrigation, fertilization, and storage
and transport facilities, the campaign proved a costly
failure.(58) Similarly, Khrushchev´s frenzied drive to
overtake the United States in meat and dairy production raised
popular expectations to unrealistic heights and exposed the
leader to ridicule. Policy failures weakened his political
power as he ran out of "quick fixes."

Attacking the impetuous and personal manner of decision
making under Khrushchev, the Brezhnev leadership adopted a
blend of welfare and efficiency goals, innovating in policy
only to the extent that caution and prudence allowed. In many
ways they continued to follow trails blazed by Khrushchev.
Khrushchev´s successors, however, were more rational and
sophisticated than he. In general, though more intolerant of
experiment in the arts and literature than Khrushchev, the
Brezhnev regime was more receptive to advice from politically
loyal scientific and technological specialists.

The measures taken by the Brezhnev leadership after 1965 to modernize Soviet agriculture were impressive in scope. For the ebullient Khrushchev´s reliance on crash programs and rhetoric and reorganization, Brezhnev substituted a systematic program of heavy sustained investment in agriculture. Also, agronomists, livestock experts, and other agricultural specialists had a much more important role under Brezhnev than they had under Khrushchev. These specialists have only limited influence, however.(59)

Political factors also account for the half-hearted reforms of industrial administration that the Brezhnev regime enacted. In 1973 it announced that industrial "associations" would be formed by combining smaller enterprises and joining them with research institutes. Partly because individual ministries were made responsible for devising their own plans of reorganization, and were reluctant to lose control of their "own" enterprises, most mergers were effected within current ministerial boundaries. Ministry officials took advantage of the consultative nature of the reorganization to minimize actual organizational change. This tactic blunted the influence of the reform and helps explain the slowness of implementation.(60)

In 1979 another major reform was announced, consisting of measures designed to improve central planning and administration. Penalities for nonfulfillment of contracts by enterprises were raised, and a new "master indicator" of an enterprise´s performance was introduced. Overall, the reforms were, writes Nancy Nimitz, "a respectable third-best reform in a world where the first-best never comes and the second-best comes too late."(61) The reform reflected compromises among competing bureaucratic interests, and its implementation has been slow and halting. Media pressure designed to overcome bureaucratic resistance and "psychological barriers" has been ineffective in forcing adoption of the changes on unwilling ministries and enterprises.

The Andropov leadership signaled its impatience with the bureaucracy´s immobility. Andropov hinted at stronger measures in the future when he stated that "slogans alone will not get things done" in his first substantive address to the Central Committee on November 20, 1982.(62) It may at first seem paradoxical that a political system so centralized should also function so poorly in the formulation and execution of major policy initiatives. When we consider, however, the costs of mobilization under Stalin associated with creation of the state machinery that his successors inherited, we recognize that the power of a leader to make policy and carry it out without employing mass terror, personal dictatorship, and the other instruments of Stalinist rule depends upon his skill in forming a coalition of leaders and groups whose interests he must take into account. As a consequence, policy tends to be cautious rather than innovative. Bold new departures risk antagonizing major blocs of interests, which, however, have no recognized channels for articulating their interests except those sanctioned by the party. Successful policy making in the 1980s will require strong and skillful leadership to surmount the obstacles to change.

Policy Implementation

We have considered the critical role of the CPSU´s policy-making organs and leaders in generating and controlling political influence and power. Analysis of the Soviet system would be incomplete without giving attention to government institutions through which the party command translates its decisions into the directives, rules, and regulations that control citizens´ daily lives.

The party coordinates and controls a complex and interlocking network of governmental and bureaucratic structures, with duplication, or proliferation, of lines of command. There are several hierarchies of organizations with headquarters in Moscow and agencies in the field. There is also a powerful corps of "prefects," as Hough describes the party secretaries at middle levels, who ride herd on the field representatives of most other bureaucracies.(63) They serve as Moscow´s eyes, ears, and guiding hand in the field.

Soviet terminology divides all organizations into two main categories: public, mass, voluntary organizations (sometimes characterized in Soviet legal and social science literature as "representative"); and state organizations. The party, the trade unions, the Komsomol, and (though only partially) the soviets belong to the first category. State organizations include ministries, the military and police, and state committees and commissions. Official doctrine distinguishes between the structure and legal status of the two types of organizations. Leaders of state organizations and their personnel are generally appointed and have the lawful power to enforce their commands. Leaders of public organizations, by contrast, have no legal powers of compulsion over their members.

Structure of the Soviets

The soviets, which are organized in descending order from the national Supreme Soviet to the village soviets, are the backbone of the government´s structure. The elected soviets and their inner core of executive committee bureaucrats have some of the characteristics of both public and state

182

organizations. Deputies to the soviets at all levels, from village to Supreme Soviet, are elected by all voting citizens. All soviets are invested with legal powers. In fact, the U.S.S.R. Constitution vests in the Supreme Soviet the exclusive power of national legislation and designates it the "supreme organ of state power."

The Supreme Soviet is bicameral. Its two legislative chambers are the Soviet of the Union and the Soviet of Nationalities. The latter provides symbolic representation for ethnic minorities clustered in a geographic area. The Supreme Soviet normally meets for a few days twice a year. Legislation is passed unanimously, but standing commissions, which engage in "consultation with the public" and also draft legislation, have been increasingly important in lawmaking since Stalin. Nominally responsible to the Supreme Soviet is the Council of Ministers, which is so large that a smaller Presidium coordinates its work... The Council is headed by a chairman (currently Nikolai Tikhonov) whose functions roughly correspond to those of a premier or prime minister in parliamentary systems – but with the vital difference that he carries out policies determined by the permanently ruling CPSU. Subordinate to the chairman of the Council are first deputy chairmen and deputy chairmen, chairmen of state committees, the State Bank, and others. The numerous state committees, such as the State Committee for Science and Technology, the State Planning Committee (Gosplan), and the Committee of State Security (KGB), are probably more powerful than all but a few ministries, such as the Defense Ministry.

The structure of the soviets largely parallels or duplicates that of the party. Below the level of the national Supreme Soviet are the supreme soviets of each of the fifteen constituent republics. Below the republic level are the local organs of state power, consisting of soviets in <u>oblasti</u> (provinces), territories (<u>kraya</u>), urban and rural districts, and villages. There are, however, no counterparts in the hierarchy of soviets to party organizations in factories, scientific and educational institutions, government agencies, and the like.

The state bureaucracy includes three types of ministries: all-union, union-republic, and republic, in descending order of centralization of structure and jurisdiction. All-union ministries are in sole charge of one sphere of administration such as defense, coal, or iron, and are not accountable to any of the republic governments. Union-republic ministries have a central office in Moscow, but function through ministries in each republic capital. Republic ministries are the lowest rung of the ladder, responsible solely to the government of the republic in which they are located. The republic ministries handle two kinds of business - matters affected by the linguistic and ethnic composition of their republics (such as education, public health, and justice), and local economic activities using locally obtainable raw materials, labor, and so on. In comparison to all-union ministries, the republic ministries have small budgets and staffs.

Through the principle of dual subordination, many operations of the soviets are controlled by the agencies of appropriate ministries. According to this principle, each administrative subdivision of the local soviets (such as the department overseeing local schools) is accountable both to the executive committee of the soviet in that jurisdiction and to the ministry (in this case, the ministry of education) responsible for overseeing a function throughout the republic or country.

At all levels the structure of the soviets includes a "legislative" body (the soviet or Supreme Soviet itself made up of elected deputies) and an "executive" body (a council of ministers, or, at levels below that of the republic, an executive committee, or ispolkom). The chairman of the executive committee is the chief executive of his territorial unit - the equivalent of an American town mayor or state governor. Most of the deputies of the soviets hold other full-time jobs. Because of this, and because the soviets meet infrequently and briefly, ordinary deputies have little political power.

Still, limited as the legislative powers of the soviets are in view of their subordination to the party, it would be a mistake to underestimate their significance as agents of socialization and legitimation. They offer opportunities to millions of people for limited participation in political life that generates support for the state. Especially at lower levels, the soviets also perform a number of administrative tasks. Local soviets supervise provision of goods and services like food supplies, schools, social security payments, housing, and roads and transportation, as well as laundries, motion picture theaters, libraries, and clubs.

The democratic and participatory face of the soviets is best displayed during election of the deputies. Elections at the all-union and republic levels are held every five years, at the lower levels every two and one-half years. The candidates usually receive more than 99 percent of the vote. The Soviet voter is expected to vote for the party-selected candidate by dropping the ballot in a box outside the polling booth. The alternative is to enter the polling booth, cross out the candidate's name, and then drop the ballot in the box, thus attracting attention. Even riskier than this is failure to

vote at all, which can be construed as enmity toward the
regime.(64)

Party Control of the Bureaucracy

The intermeshing of the soviet and party networks can be
demonstrated in several ways (see Figure 1). The Constitution
states that the party "is the leading core of all organizations
of the working people, both public and state." Although party
guidance of the soviets´ work is generally effected indirectly
and unobtrusively by leading party members, party organizations
frequently interfere directly, even at times in purely
administrative functions such as street cleaning.

Although both in theory and in practice the Soviet system
assigns separate spheres of competence to the CPSU and the
state organs, the distinction has been fluid and shifting.
Generally speaking, party executives exercise political
leadership (rukovodstvo), and government officials engage in
actual administration (upravlenie). Decision, particularly
critical and innovative decision, is the prerogative of the
party; implementation and routine supervision are the jobs of
the soviets and ministries, though the party keeps a watchful
eye on how implementation is carried out. Direct party
involvement in administration increases during periods of
innovation (such as Stalin´s collectivization of 1929 to 1931),
when the survival of the system is at stake (as during the Nazi
invasion), and when revitalization is needed (as in
Khrushchev´s agricultural reorganization of 1953 to 1958).
Party involvement decreases when party-led campaigns seem to
have achieved their goals or are provoking antiparty
resentments, when party cadres are needed elsewhere, and when
the Kremlin fears that cadres may be getting so involved in
administration that they are in danger of losing sight of
ideological and political goals.

A prime source of party power over the bureaucracy lies in
its control over the assignment of executive and professional
personnel. Although it seems most interested in the top 15 or
20 percent of government posts, the party does not necessarily
confine its supervision to these higher reaches.

The party also influences administrators through its power
of oversight (kontrol) of their actions. Although the
Stalinist pattern of rampant terror is a thing of the past,
powerful mechanisms of surveillance persist. The party
enforces high standards of performance among state officials
with the help of a variety of inspection agencies, including,
besides the KGB, popular control committees and special state
agencies set up to combat bribery and embezzlement, illegal
disposal of land and apartments, violation of rules on

Figure 1

Hierarchic Structure of Government and Party Organs

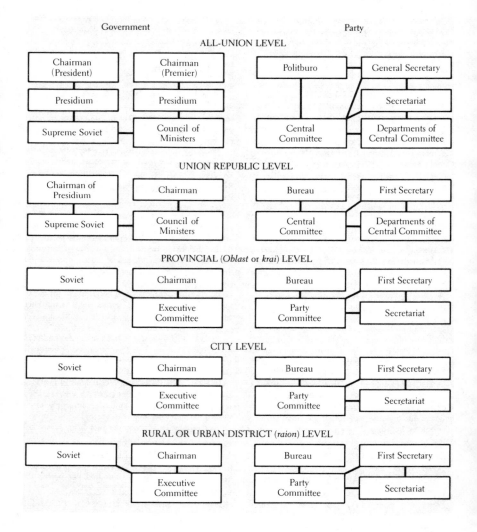

Government   Party

ALL-UNION LEVEL

Chairman (President)	Chairman (Premier)		Politburo	General Secretary
Presidium	Presidium			Secretariat
Supreme Soviet	Council of Ministers		Central Committee	Departments of Central Committee

UNION REPUBLIC LEVEL

| Chairman of Presidium | Chairman | | Bureau | First Secretary |
| Supreme Soviet | Council of Ministers | | Central Committee | Departments of Central Committee |

PROVINCIAL (*Oblast* or *krai*) LEVEL

| Soviet | Chairman | | Bureau | First Secretary |
| | Executive Committee | | Party Committee | Secretariat |

CITY LEVEL

| Soviet | Chairman | | Bureau | First Secretary |
| | Executive Committee | | Party Committee | Secretariat |

RURAL OR URBAN DISTRICT (*raion*) LEVEL

| Soviet | Chairman | | Bureau | First Secretary |
| | Executive Committee | | Party Committee | Secretariat |

admission to universities and granting diplomas, withholding by
farmers of produce due the state, and illegal relaxation of
quality controls by industry.

Law Enforcement and the Judicial Process

Law enforcement and legal scholarship are controlled by
the CPSU, though party control is less direct than it is over
the bureaucracy. Law and adjudication reflect the current
party line. When Khrushchev's populist approach was developing
in the late 1950s, public participation in the legal system
dramatically increased, though often in an amateurish and
vigilante style. At the same time, a campaign to increase
economic productivity led to new severity against "economic
crimes."(65)

Khrushchev's successors have tended to redress the balance
somewhat in favor of due process and against mass
participation. "Popular" forms of legal process, such as the
comrades' courts (see below), have been given a more codified
set of powers and limitations. On the other hand, some tactics
used against dissident intellectuals, such as beatings,
slanderous newspaper articles, and confinement to mental
institutions, are reminiscent of the Stalinist terror of the
1930s.

The party influences judicial decisions through the
doctrine of socialist legal consciousness, which requires that
judges be guided by party policy in deciding whether to apply a
statute to a case. As a result, a defendant's fate may be
decided on the basis of the regime's political preferences.

Under Soviet law, the range of activities defined as
criminal is enormous. Murder and theft are included among
private crimes. But the most severe penalities and the loosest
interpretation of law are reserved for numerous frequently
committed public crimes, crimes against the state, such as
production of poor quality, failure to supply products
according to plan, inefficiency, and poor performance. More
often enforced are yet harsher provisions covering political
crimes, such as anti-Soviet agitation, of which dissidents are
often accused.

Legal Profession: Judges, Advocates, Procurators. The
legal profession is thoroughly saturated and controlled by the
party, although in a few cases defense attorneys have been
known to resist party instructions. The three main components
of the profession are judges, who conduct court proceedings;
advocates, or attorneys; and procurators, comparable to
prosecutors, who prepare cases for trial.

187

Although elected by popular vote at the lowest level and by the soviets at higher levels, Soviet judges are essentially civil servants, promoted from lower to higher courts depending on ability. Almost all judges have some higher legal education. The U.S.S.R. Constitution states that "judges are independent and subject only to law"; direct interference by party organizations in particular cases is condemned. Even so, almost all Soviet judges are CPSU members and hence subject to party discipline.

The scope of the judicial function is narrower in the Soviet Union than in the Anglo-Amercian legal tradition. Soviet judges cannot refuse to enforce statutes on constitutional grounds, and they lack jurisdiction over major economic disputes. Few Soviet judges are politically prominent. In ability and prestige, it appears, the judge in the U.S.S.R. is outranked by the procurator.

The position of the advocate, or trial lawyer, is ambiguous. Most often they are better off financially than both judges and procurators and more than half the advocates are party members. On the other hand, because advocates are allowed to receive more than the official fee from clients, a capitalist shadow hangs over their public image.

Like everyone else, advocates are subject to party and government restrictions. A 1962 statute gave them governmental control over enforcement of professional standards and the schedule of fees and conditions for gratuitous services.(66) At the same time, the statute provided for colleges of advocates; the duly trained and qualified attorneys of an area were to elect a governing board to manage their own affairs, subject to state supervision. The colleges are given jurisdiction over organizational rights, duties, and compensation. Consultation offices working out of these colleges offer legal advice to the public, assist people in filling out petitions, and perform similar sevices.

Advocates, like judges and procurators, have been subjected to periodic social-pressure campaigns to punish criminals more severely. As a result, when advocates defend their clients in the courtroom, they often play a subdued role. The defense lawyer may not marshall all resources for the defense that are provided for by law. A concluding statement might be more a recitation of mitigating circumstances that a denial of guilt or a presentation of purely legal arguments.(67) The lawyer may, however, file an appeal to the higher courts.

Procurators outshine judges and advocates in training, organization, and power. In applying and interpreting the law, they are second only to the KGB in real power, and even the KGB cannot start an investigation or make an arrest without written permission from the appropriate officer of the procuracy.

The procuracy is a kind of bureaucratic and legal hydra. Its most important administrative function is to fight graft and corruption in the economy. In its legal aspect, the procuracy seeks to ensure that policy is carried out and that officials of middle and low rank do not exercise power arbitrarily. For this purpose it has departments charged with generally supervising the legality of all governmental operations, including the courts (except the U.S.S.R. Supreme Court) and other administrative and economic agencies. The Council of Ministers of the U.S.S.R. and the CPSU are not under its supervision. Procuracy officers conduct pretrial investigations in criminal cases, leaving the political cases to the KGB. They act as government prosecutors in court. Though they sometimes defend ordinary citizens whose rights have been violated by public officials, their principal work is to defend the interests of the party, both directly as criminal investigators and prosecutors and indirectly as administrators.

Pretrial investigations may last months. They are strictly controlled by the procuracy, or, in political crimes, the KGB. Prisoners are kept isolated and helpless. They may be told that failure to answer questions will result in imprisonment and that false answers will be punished by imposition of a prison sentence. Those accused are at a considerable disadvantage during this process because Soviet criminal law does not give them the right to counsel until the preliminary investigation has ended.

Because of its formidable role, efforts have been made to keep the procuracy free of local party and government links that might entangle it. The procurator-general of the U.S.S.R., according to the Constitution, is appointed by the Supreme Soviet of the U.S.S.R. for a five-year term. He in turn appoints the procurators of the union republics for five-year terms. They appoint procurators for the administrative regions within their republics (see Figure 2).

The Court System. There are two types of courts in the Soviet Union: the regular courts and the comrades´ courts.

The Regular Courts. The regular courts work at four levels. People´s courts have original jurisdiction over almost all cases, both civil and criminal. City and oblast courts have original jurisdiction over cases such as murder with aggravating circumstances, counterfeiting, and desertion. Supreme courts of the fifteen republics can review decisions of the intermediate courts. The Supreme Court of the U.S.S.R.,

the only all-union court, has original jurisdiction over some
important political cases and the power to reverse cases
appealed from decisions of republic supreme courts.

Most cases, both civil and criminal, are settled in the
people's courts, although appeal to higher courts is always
possible. People's courts have one elected judge, assisted by
two lay assessors elected from factories and nearby residential
areas. Higher courts have three judges, who, though formally
elected by the soviets, are in effect appointed, and there are
no lay assessors.(68)

Figure 2

Organization of the Procuracy of the U.S.S.R.

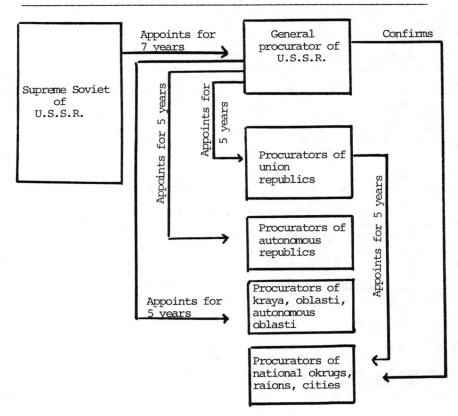

Comrades´ Courts. Comrades´ courts, staffed by
volunteers, rely on persuasive rather than coercive sanctions.
Although comrades´ courts may impose small fines and recommend
eviction from an apartment or other penalties, they do not
operate with conventional legal terminology. A person charged
with an offense is called not "the accused" but rather "the
person brought before the comrades´ court." The hearings are
informal and usually held in the common room of a factory,
collective farm, or apartment house. Lawyers do not usually
participate in the proceeding, and the judges are not civil
servants but neighbors or fellow workers, perhaps with
elementary legal training. The members of the comrades´ courts
are formally elected by open ballot meetings called by
trade-union committees, the boards of collective farms, or the
executive committees of local soviets.

Comrades´ courts consider a variety of cases, including
violations of labor discipline, small-scale theft of state or
farm property, hooliganism, petty speculation, public
drunkenness, and many other infractions against public order.
Cases may be brought before the comrades´ court by people´s
guard units, trade-union committees, executive committees of
local soviets, state agencies (including courts and procuracy),
and at the initiative of the comrades´ court itself. The court
has a range of penalties it may impose, such as a reprimand or
a fine. It may also turn the case over to the procurator for
criminal proceedings. The rough-and-ready trials held by the
comrades´ court relieve the regular courts of a variety of
minor offenses and also instruct and involve the public
directly in the administration of justice.

Police Agencies. Soviet police agencies fall into several
categories.

The Militia. The militia, or regular police, is
semimilitary in its training, organization, and ranks. It is
under strict party and government control, and is directed by
the Ministry of Internal Affairs. Its work includes regulating
traffic, maintaining public order, and apprehending criminals.
At the same time, both its functions and its organization have
some peculiarities. The militia administers crucial
instruments of social control, such as the internal passport
system. All citizens who have reached age 16 and who reside in
specified categories of urban communities must have an internal
passport and must, upon demand, present it to the militia and
other authorities.

The militia administers many other controls, including
procedures for obtaining permission to have and use printing,
mimeographing, photocopying, and other reproduction and

communicating equipment, as well as hazardous items such as firearms. Police controls over the means of disseminating information reinforce the party's political controls over communication.

The People's Guards. The people's guards (narodnye druzhinniki) are a kind of auxiliary police, assisting the regular police or militia, and made up of unpaid volunteers. First organized in 1958, the people's guards, like the comrades' courts, serve the dual function of supplementing regular state organs and of activating and educating the general citizenry. Units are formed through party, Komsomol, or trade-union organizations at workplaces. Duty as a "people's guard" is part of an individual's social obligation, and normally is rotated among the work force of an enterprise. Each unit works under a commander who supervises several units. The units are also supervised by a staff selected by the local party committee.

When on patrol, the people's guards wear identifying red armbands. They aid the regular police in traffic work, preventing or breaking up disorders in public places, apprehending criminals and turning them over to the police, and conducting raids on places of business to uncover illegal practices. They may demand to see the documents of citizens and may detain suspects. Although they carry no weapons, they are shielded because citizens know that harming a people's guard while on duty is nearly equivalent to assaulting a policeman and is punished severely.

The KGB. The KGB (Committee for State Security), or in Russian Komitet gosudarstvennoi bezopasnosti, is almost certainly the most politically powerful of the group administrative agencies charged with the duty that is known in Soviet terminology as "administration in the sphere of administrative-political activity." Besides the KGB, these include the armed forces, the Ministry of Internal Affairs, and the Ministries of Justice, Foreign Affairs, and Foreign Trade. These, according to Soviet doctrine, perform functions that in large measure constitute response to hostile pressures and actions emanating from the external environment. The KGB remains dominant in the sphere of detection and investigation of "state crimes," such as espionage, anti-Soviet agitation and propaganda, violation of laws governing separation of church and state, formation of "anti-state" organizations, and so on, as well as currency speculation, smuggling, and large-scale embezzlement of state property. It controls the vast and powerful border-guard troops and operates a network of special training schools. It also is the dominant agency in the conduct of Soviet foreign intelligence and espionage activities.

The rise of Yuri V. Andropov, Chairman of the KGB from 1967 to 1982, together with the promotion of Geidar Aliev to full membership in the Politburo and appointment of Vitali Fedorchuk as Minister of Internal Affairs, highlight the political significance of the KGB. Aliev made his career in the KGB in Azerbaijan before becoming first party secretary in that republic in 1969. Fedorchuk had been head cf the KGB in the Ukraine until he succeeded Andropov as chairman of the KGB cf the whole U.S.S.R. in May 1982; seven months later he was moved to the Ministry of Internal Affairs, which oversees the uniformed police. Though this reassignment appeared to be a demotion for Fedorchuk, it may well have been an important step in Andropov's effort to crack down on lax discipline within the regular police. Only time will tell whether these personnel changes, involving long-time KGB officials, represent a gain in the KGB's political weight as an institution.

Political Performance

Soviet secrecy makes it difficult to evaluate the performance of the Soviet political system. Matters are further complicated by the reality of candid communication between Soviet citizens and foreigners. Obstacles to communication include the sealing off of most of the U.S.S.R. to travel by foreigners, and the controls placed on information necessary for full comparison of the Soviet with other political systems. A good deal is known, however, about various aspects of Soviet political performance, and here we will summarize scholarly opinion on some vital matters.

We shall discuss Soviet performance in extraction of resources and services from the population, regulation and control by the political regime of the citizenry's activities, and distribution of goods to the people of the U.S.S.R. Some attention wil also be paid to symbolic performance. In a flood of propagandistic exhortations and commands in mass media and by way cf agitation, indoctrination, and mass political rituals, symbolic performance is pervasive in Soviet politics. Of course, the outputs and outcomes of performance capabilities are related: comparatively high development cf one capability may result in a relatively low level of other outcomes. Hypertrophy of the regulative capacity, a characteristic of the Soviet system, results in curtailment of personal and group initiative and liberty for all but a small number of the population, and may even render the ruling class prisoners of the immense bureaucracies.

Extractive Performance

In extracting resources from the population, the Soviet regime is effective, though as in all fields except perhaps police controls and military power, its efficiency is not outstanding. Through the centralized bureaucracy, closely supervised by the party, and more specifically by means of the "turnover tax" (a kind of sales tax) on most goods, the government derives enormous revenues. They are supplemented by other forms of taxation, which are relatively unimportant, and by the profits of state-operated enterprises. Members of the CPSU, the trade unions, and the other public organizations - and Soviet citizens are virtually required to belong to at least one - also pay dues. These, together with revenues from organization newspapers and other enterprises, are important sources of income for these organizations.

The Soviet state extracts labor in many ways other than in operating the state-run economy. The mass organizations require their members, as part of their obligations as citizens of a socialist society, to perform myriad tasks, such as assisting in child-care centers, auxiliary police work, agitation for getting out the vote in elections, and, for scientists and other professionals, delivering public lectures. A characteristic type of voluntary public service in the U.S.S.R., especially for industrial workers, consists of unpaid labor in an effort to fulfill or exceed the economic plans. This practice has apparently expanded in recent years. One of its aspects is the subbotnik (the Russian word for Saturday), a day of nominally voluntary labor donated to the state on weekends or holidays by workers whose efforts are praised as mainfestations of Leninist public spirit. Sometimes even top-flight scientists are mobilized to plant potatoes, and students spend part of their summers helping to harvest grain or raise vegetables, which are often in very short supply.

Military service in the U.S.S.R. is compulsory for young men. By the time a Soviet youth reaches the age of military service, he has already acquired a good deal of military training, some of it rather advanced. This training is received in school and in the Young Pioneers, the Komsomol, and the paramilitary program of the DOSAAF (Voluntary Society for Assistance to the Army, Air Force, and Navy). University students must participate in a reserve officers´ training program before receiving their commissions upon graduation. Most are then spared the necessity of entering active service.

An important type of extracted labor is punitive labor. According to recent CIA estimates, some 4 million Soviet citizens who are currently either in labor camps or are ex-convicts on probation or parole are obliged to perform some form of forced labor. Of these, 10,000 are estimated to be political prisoners.(69) Although this figure is minuscule in comparison with forced labor under Stalin, when the secret

194

police ran an empire of concentration camps that Solzhenitsyn called the "Gulag Archipelago," it is still not negligible. Also, this estimate is far lower than some cited by informed Soviet dissidents.(70)

The foregoing material suggests the vastness of the Soviet system's extractive performance. Although to some extent the activities it entails may be a source of satisfaction to Soviet people - and of course that is how they are portrayed in the Soviet mass media - there can be little doubt that one outcome is poverty for millions of citizens, especially for unskilled workers and collective farmers. The reason is that a disproportionate share of the resources extracted does not produce food and consumer goods, but is invested in capital goods, armaments, and military aid to "national liberation movements" abroad.

The mainfold techniques for extracting resources from the society, combined with the pervasive regulatory controls that prevent opposition distort and stunt political participation. Taking part in the formal channels of public activity under such circumstances loses much of its meaning and becomes a chore, to be evaded if possible and performed, when it must be, perfunctorily. Studies have shown that most of those engaged in voluntary social assignments carry out at least some of their tasks during work hours, despite rules against the practice. Clearly this practice cannot improve the quality of either participation or labor.

Regulative Performance
        Regulative performance is the output of the party, government, economic, cultural, and ideological rule-making bureaucacies, and that of the agencies for maintaining order such as the police, courts, and their mass auxiliaries. Behind the police of course, stand the armed forces, which may be called upon to suppress large disturbances of public order, and were indeed called upon during the strikes that broke out in Novocherkassk in 1962. Detailed discussion of the international aspects of regulative performance in the U.S.S.R. would take us far afield, but the Soviet leadership sees its task of maintaining orders as extending beyond the borders of the U.S.S.R., as shown when Soviet forces suppressed liberalization in Czechoslovakia in 1968 on the grounds that socialism throughout the bloc was threatened by Czechoslovak "counterrevolution."

At home the Soviet state's regulative capacity is immense. The multiplication of overlapping controls makes the regime's regulatory capacity topheavy and unwieldy, but it also ensures that the central leaders retain the power to set policy in an extremely wide area of social life. It has long sought the optimum mixture of control and tolerance that would preserve central direction of scientific research while allowing researchers to achieve success. Although the bureaucratic controls over science and technology are extensive, Soviet science has made impressive strides in some fields and in some high-prestige sectors, such as the space program. Similar challenges appear in the efforts to regulate cultural life. Cultural artists must belong to party-controlled unions that guide their activities and monopolize the commercial outlets for their products. They must adhere to the standards of "socialist realism," the prescribed style of Soviet arts, and must not engage in undue experimentation with new forms and techniques. Yet the regime also admonishes them to create a lively, convincing culture, in which Soviet official values are dramatized in a way that is both popularly accessible and artistically credible. This demand can produce zigzags in policy, as the regime defines and redefines the limits of the acceptable.

In the economy, regulative performance can claim both successes and failures. Strict rules about firing workers have contributed to a sense of job security for maual laborers (fostered as well by the shortages of labor in many occupations and regions of the country). Standing rules that reward managers for achieving high growth rates in physical output have achieved a respectable record of economic growth; the record is weakened, however, by the steady decline in the rate of economic growth. On the other hand, administrative methods have not improved productivity per worker in recent years: the productivity of both capital and labor is in fact falling (see Table 4). Perhaps the most dismal outcome of overabundant regulation is in agriculture. So worrisome are the continued failures in food production that the regime has relaxed its former restrictions on production from the subsidiary plots on which farmers and workers grow food for their family´s use and the surplus of which they may legally sell. These private plots, though they occupy a trifling proportion of the country´s arable land, account for a huge proportion of its fruits, vegetables, and other commodities.

A major failure of regulative performance is the vast underground complex of illegal and semilegal economic transactions, which is often called the "second economy." This is the marketplace of goods and services which are either illegal in themselves (such as stolen goods or moonshine liquor) or which are exchanged without heed to licensing or taxation rules. Often transactions of the second kind, such as the black market in automobile spare parts, are tacitly tolerated by the authorities, because they lubricate the sometimes sticky wheels of the official economy. At its best, the second economy imparts precious flexibility to an economy that would choke on its own red tape if its rigidity were not offset by these channels. One benefit is that in this way managers can procure scarce goods to meet the plan. At its worst, it siphons a great quantity of resources out of the official economy by illegal enrichment, fraud, and theft.

The ubiquity of regulatory controls imposes heavy pressure on Soviet citizens to conform with official norms of behavior and to meet goals set by the regime. Frustration with these pressures may take many forms. Some citizens comply with

Table 4

Average Annual Rates of Growth of Total GNP Production,
Inputs and Productivity, 1951-1980 (in percentages)

	1951-1955	1956-1960	1961-1965	1966-1970	1971-1975	1976-1980
Total GNP	6.0	5.8	5.0	5.5	3.8	2.7
Inputs						
Labor (man-hours), capital and land	4.5	3.9	4.1	3.9	4.1	3.6
Man-hours	1.9	.6	1.6	2.0	1.9	1.4
Capital	9.0	9.8	8.7	7.5	7.9	6.9
Land	4.0	1.3	.6	- .3	.9	0
Factor Productivity						
Labor (man-hours), capital and land	1.4	1.8	.9	1.5	- .2	- .8
Man-hours	4.6	5.1	3.4	3.4	1.8	1.3
Capital	-2.7	-3.6	-3.3	-1.9	-3.8	-3.9
Land	1.9	4.4	4.4	5.8	2.9	2.8

Source: Franklyn D. Holzman, "The Soviet Economy," Foreign Policy Association, Headline Series, no. 260 (September-October 1982). Reprinted by permission.

official expectations, identifying their interests with those
of the authorities. Others take their frustrations out in
drinking, a huge and growing problem in Soviet society.(71)
Others seek to emigrate from the country. Soviet leaders deal
with these problems with tactics that include repression,
propaganda, and efforts to displace blame for domestic problems
on to foreign targets, especially the United States and its
imperialist accomplices.

Distributive Performance

Distributive performance has been adversely affected in
recent years by a decline in the growth rate of the economy.
This does not mean that the pie to be divided among members of
society has shrunk; rather, the pie is growing more slowly from
year to year. Over the last twenty or so years, nonetheless,
the absence of domestic crises or foreign wars has permitted
the regime gradually to raise standards of living for
consumers. Necessities such as living space, electricity and
gas, and bread are heavily subsidized by the government in
order to keep them affordable for even the poorest households.
"Luxury" goods and services, such as jewelry, automobiles, and
air travel are very expensive.

The implicit promise of Soviet socialism is equality not
of condition, but of opportunity and security. But the
opportunity for upward mobility has narrowed considerably since
the social revolution of Stalin's day. Several measures
enacted under Brezhnev, such as providing for the first time a
minimum wage for collective farm peasants, along with
eligibility for pension and other benefits, have reduced
inequality. Income levels at the bottom end of the scale have
been raised. The system is severely hierarchic, though, in
allocation of income, status, and power. A hierarchic
distribution system of benefits and priveleges works to reward
those to whom the regime wishes to favor. A network of coupon
stores closed to ordinary citizens enables elite citizens to
shop for clothing, food, and other goods normally unavailable
in the regular stores. ELites also have access to better
medical care, housing, vacation resorts, and other
prerequisites. The highly controlled distributive apparatus
fosters support for Soviet rule among the elite members of its
governing bureaucracies, but leaves a life of shortages, long
lines, and low standards of living for the bulk of the
populace.

Distributive performance should also be assessed by the
capacity of the centrally planned economy to funnel resources
into the projects to which the leaders give especially high
priority. Traditionally, the Soviet regime has been most
effective either in mobilizing resources for a few massive

projects or in organizing serial production of a standardized, relatively simple good.(72) The space program is a conspicuous example of the former. Because the economy must meet the more varied needs of a complex society, however, variety and quality of assortment take precedence over sheer volume of production.

Meantime, there is some evidence that in important respects the regime's distributive capacity is declining. Mortality rates are growing in nearly every age category and have risen sharply among infants.(73) These findings, which contrast sharply with the trend toward reduced mortality rates in most of the world, suggest that the state of public health is falling.

The worsening of distributive performance is also attested to by the return to food rationing in many parts of the country as a means of coping with severe food shortages. A 1981 survey of 782 former residents of 102 Soviet cities discovered that such basic foodstuffs as bread, butter, cabbage, eggs, milk, and sausage were often reported to be only irregularly available in the state-run stores, although nearly all reported that vodka was regularly and universally available. And 90 percent and more of the respondents said that beef and pork were not available, or rationed. In many cities, products such as butter and even bread can be bought only in limited quantities at one time.(74)

Worsening distributive performance in some areas, however, should not blind us to the considerable strengths that the centralized economy continues to possess. For citizens with the ability and ambition to climb the ladder of success, the regime provides many opportunities for material as well as symbolic rewards and satisfactions. Citizens may take patriotic pride in the immense and growing military might of their country, the conquest of space, breakthroughs in science, and the promise of a prosperous socialist future.

On the other hand, where symbolic performance is not reinforced by successful distributive performance, popular discontent could result in political instability. Conscious that labor unrest in Poland developed into a national movement that has threatened the foundations of the regime, Brezhnev named the food question the major political, as well as economic, issue of the current Five-Year Plan, and Andropov has continued to emphasize the grandiose "Food Program" announced by Brezhnev in May 1982. One early initiative in Andropov's leadership is an increase in food supplies in the state-run stores in the major cities. Andropov is offering both positive incentives and the threat of penalties for slack performance in his attempt to reinvigorate economic production. The domestic tranquility of the regime in the 1980s may well hang on his success.

Soviet Foreign Policy:
Conflict and Coexistence

Driving Forces and Context

Even a chapter dealing mainly with the U.S.S.R.´s
"internal" politics requires some attention to external
affairs, which interact in many ways with domestic affairs.
The increasing significance of foreign policy is indicated by
the rising influence within the Soviet leadership of men such
as Foreign Minister Andrei Gromyko, Defense Minister Dmitri
Ustinov, and of course former KGB Chairman Yuri Andropov.

The conduct and influence of Soviet foreign policy of all
countries and of course prospects for the future welfare and
security of the peoples of the Soviet Union. The Soviet
standard of living is determined in part by the Soviet military
budget, the size of which in turn reflects Politburo
perceptions of threats and opportunities in the non-Soviet
world.

Since 1939 the U.S.S.R. has incorporated into itself
territories taken from Poland (1939), Finland (1940), Romania
(1940), China (Tannu-Tuva, 1944), Czechoslovkia (1945), Germany
(1945), and Japan (Southern Sakhalin and the Kurile Islands,
1945) and it incorporated as "republics" the whole of the
formerly independent states Latvia, Lithuania, and Estonia -
which, to be sure, had been ruled by the tsar until the
collapse of the Russian Empire in 1917. The U.S.S.R. has also
acquired preponderant power over the states of Eastern Europe,
except for Yugoslovia (which is careful to refrain from actions
that might excessively irritate Russia) and Albania. Of
course, by comparison to Stalin´s era, the East European allies
have acquired some autonomy, but, as demonstrated by such
events as the invasion of Czechoslovakia in 1968 and the
imposition of martial law in Poland in 1981. Moscow has
circumscribed their freedom of development. Cuba, since Fidel
Castro took power in 1959 and especially since the late 1960s,
has been a semiautonomous ally of the U.S.S.R., useful to its
mighty patron as an assistant in projecting and consolidating
Soviet influence in far-flung areas of the Third World.

In Afghanistan a revolutionary coup d´etat in April 1978
established a "socialist" republic, closely allied with Moscow.
In December 1979, after a new Afghan leader who had come to
power by murdering his predecessor lost the confidence of the
Politburo, the Soviet army moved in. At the time of writing
Soviet efforts to reestablish undisputed control remain
frustrated. Nonetheless, Afghanistan furnishes signficant
evidence of the persistent expansionary urge in Soviet foreign

policy. The Mongolian People´s Republic and the Democratic
Republic of Vietnam (and its Laotian and Kampuchean satellites)
round out the list of countries ruled by Soviet-oriented
"Marxist-Leninist" one-party states. Finally, there are the
"client" states: South Yemen (since 1970), Laos (since 1973),
Angola (since 1975) and Ethiopia (since 1976).

There have been retreats, of course, on the road to the
goal that contemporary Soviet doctrine calls the "revolutionary
transformation of the world." Soviet authorities, however,
declare it their obligation to provide economic, ideological,
and diplomatic aid to any Marxist or "progressive" regime that
opposes Western "imperialism." Moreover, the U.S.S.R. also
considers its duty defending socialism throughout the entire
socialist camp, often called the "Brezhnez Doctrine."
Moreover, Soviet sources assert with pride that there is no
part of the globe where problems in foreign relations can be
resolved without participation by the U.S.S.R.

Doctrinal claims that imperialism is retreating while
Soviet power is becoming more powerful may help the regime to
gain at least passive acceptance of the Soviet system among
Soviet citizens, despite the difficulties and frustrations of
daily life in the U.S.S.R. Thus, ideology is the servant of
Russian nationalism, but a servant, according to Adam Ulam, who
cannot be dismissed "without gravely imperiling the position of
the master."(75) Does Soviet influence in Angola, Ethiopia,
Mozambique, and South Yemen then really counterbalance reverses
since the mid-1960s in Indonesia, Egypt and Somalia?
Occasionally individual Soviet citizens express outright
hostility to Soviet Third World adventures on the grounds,
apparently that they waste resources that could better be
employed to raise the standard of living of the Soviet people.
Moreover, events such as casualties in, and foreign criticism
of, the "Soviet Vietnam" in Afghanistan, and the relatively
poor performance of Soviet arms in the Israeli-PLO and
Israeli-Syrian fighting in Lebanon in summer 1982 may well have
diminished any positive appeal Soviet foreign policy
expansiveness may have had for the ordinary Soviet citizen. As
for the Soviet elite, they know too much about the possible
dangers of East-West military conflict to take a positive
attitude toward a policy likely to provoke it. In fact, we
believe that both "elites" and "masses" in the U.S.S.R. desire
peace, and that Soviet propaganda on foreign affairs achieves
its greatest influence to the extent that it can persuade the
Soviet people that the Politburo is working for peace while
"imperialists" plot war. Nevertheless, chauvinistic
nationalism is a strong sentiment in some segments of Soviet
society, particularly in organizations connected with foreign
policy, intelligence, defense, heavy industry, and propaganda.

Soviet Foreign Policy in Action

Cold War, Detente, and Coexistence. The cold war was a
state of relations with minimal communication and hostile
propaganda exchanges between the United States and Soviet
Union. It was also a time when fear of direct Soviet-American
military clash was intense. The author of a recent study on
Soviet foreign policy in the Stalin era argues that both
"detente" and "cold war" were instruments of Stalin's policy.
This point appears to be valid still. A state approaching cold
war tends to develop when Western governments, after periods of
failed detente, become convinced that they must stiffen
resistance to Soviet efforts to take advantage of Western
accommodativeness, perceived by Moscow as weakness.(76) We do
not attribute to Soviet leaders a "grand design" for speedy
world conquest. In fact, we see in Soviet policy intense
determination and unlimited persistence, buttressed by
confidence that "history" is on the side of "socialism," as
interpreted by the Soviet Politburo, in the struggle against
the dangerous but waning forces of "imperialism."

It is crucial in understanding Soviet foreign policy
behavior to comprehend the Soviet approach to the concepts
"detente" and "peaceful coexistence of states with different
social systems," which are called the goals of Soviet foreign
policy. These concepts, as used today, differ little from
those applied by Lenin and Stalin. They are instruments for
convincing domestic and foreign audiences of the Soviet
leadership's desire for peace and ultimately for minimizing the
costs of preserving and expanding the U.S.S.R.'s influence
abroad. Under Khrushchev peaceful coexistence, which under
Lenin and Stalin had been regarded as a short-term tactic,
became the long-term strategy of Soviet foreign policy. In
reality it adapted to the new conditions of the nuclear age
Lenin's "dualistic" foreign policy approach, by which Lenin and
his successors simultaneously pursued both "revolutionary" and
"pragmatic" policies. Through agents of the CPSU, and by any
other overt or covert agencies that were available, they could
promote the "world revolutionary process," and through the
Foreign Ministry and other state agencies, they could practice
respectable, conventional diplomacy.(77)

Confrontation and Detente in Europe. According to an
often-quoted statement by Milovan Dijlas, a former close
associate of Yugoslav communist leader Josip Broz-Tito, Stalin
said in April 1945 that "this war is not as in the past:
whoever occupies a territory imposes his own social system."
The result of Stalin's policy was imposition of political and
social institutions of the Soviet type, over much of Eastern
Europe, including the zone of Germany occupied by Soviet forces
at the conclusion of World War II. The division of Germany has

been one of the most acute issues in East-West relations since 1945.

Moscow erected in its zone of Germany a regime known since 1949 as the German Democratic Republic (GDR). The GDR depended on Soviet military and diplomatic power to fend off pressures and blandishments from the far more populous, prosperous, and free Federal Republic of Germany in the West. This dependence and its enormous strategic importance to the U.S.S.R., indicated by the very large Soviet military strike forces always on duty in the GDR and by other signs, are among many reasons why the leadership of the GDR has usually worked more closely with the U.S.S.R. than that of any East European state, possibly excepting Bulgaria.

By the 1970s, a series of treaties and agreements, culminating in the Helsinki Conference on Security and Cooperation in Europe (CSCE) (in which, besides the United States and the U.S.S.R., thirty-three other Eastern and Western European countries and Canada took part) had led the West to accept Soviet hegemony over Eastern Europe. Ironically, by the time the Helsinki Final Act was signed in 1975, detente, which seemed for a time to represent the beginning of a new and higher stage of international relations, was already being viewed (especially in the United States) with a more and more jaundiced eye. The summit conferences between Brezhnev and Nixon in 1972 and 1973, and the signing of the SALT (Strategic Arms Limitation Talks) Agreement in 1972 probably marked the high point of Soviet-American detente. The Soviet invasion of Afghanistan in the week between Christmas and New Year´s Day, 1979, following other developments in the Third World, struck a mortal blow to detente.

Oddly, considering the deep Soviet suspicions and antipathy toward Germany in the 1940s, 1950s, and 1960s, detente between West Germany and the U.S.S.R. was stronger than the relationship achieved between the United States and Russia. Gradually the GDR experienced very rapid economic growth. Trade between West and East Germany, as well as between the Federal Republic and the U.S.S.R., grew rapidly. A somewhat similar pattern prevailed between France, under a succession of conservative governments, and the Soviets. In the 1970s, Western Europeans, though by no means unsympathetic to Soviet human rights defenders came to feel that something like a "live-and-let-live" relationship might develop between themselves and the Soviets.

Nevertheless, fear of the military power of the U.S.S.R., nowhere so massive and menacing as on the European continent, continued strong in the European consciousness. In fall 1979,

following a rapid buildup of Soviet missiles targeted on
Europe, the United States, at the behest of NATO, undertook to
deploy in Western Europe a force of modern nuclear missiles
unless the U.S.S.R. agreed to remove its SS-20 intermediate
long-range ballistic missiles (IRBMs). Opposition to
deployment of these missiles soon grew. The U.S.S.R. brought
to bear on the peoples and governments of the NATO and other
European countries its formidable arsenal of instruments of
propaganda and psychological warfare to persuade them that the
United States was planning to make them victims of an
American-Soviet war that, as Soviet propaganda presented the
story, Washington hoped could be fought in Europe. Though
Soviet propaganda undoubtedly played a part, the rapid growth
of the new antinuclear mood in both Europe and America can be
attributed in part to what appeared to be both incautious
rhetoric in Washington and the belief in some quarters that
American strategic weapons policy had shifted from deterrence
of nuclear war to a commitment to fighting and "winning" such a
war.

   Asia and the Third World. Since President Nixon´s
dramatic visit to China in 1972, the Soviet Union, China, and
the United States have formed a trianglar relationship.
Several issues have divided the two communist giants since
Khrushchev exposed the conflict to world view in 1960 by
abruptly withdrawing Soviet technical advisors from China:
disputes over their common border, expansion of Soviet
influence in Vietnam, and, most recently the Soviet invasion of
Afghanistan. The extreme hostility expressed by the Chinese
toward Soviet "social imperialism" and "hegemonism" during the
Cultural Revolution from 1966 to 1969 has abated, and no
repetition of the military clashes of 1969 has occurred.
Relations remain wary and occasionally tense, however, as when
China attacked the border provinces of Vietnam in spring 1979.

   Both the Soviet Union and China seek to retain the freedom
to improve relations with the United States should
circumstances be propitious. Also, despite Soviet signals of
interest in solving its "quagmire" in Afghanistan, few experts
expect the Soviet Union to find an aceptable solution in the
near future. To be sure, the Soviet Union appears overextended
in the country, capable of controlling only the major cities,
and suffering significant numbers of casualties. But the
current regime, under Babrak Karmal, is fractured by internal
dissension between its two factions, and is unlikely to be able
to rule without major assistance from the Soviet Union.

   Neither military aid, like that given the Soviet Union´s
Middle Eastern allies, nor military pressure, such as the
Soviets direct toward Japan, has been wholly successful in
generating significant political influence in the states that

neighbor the Soviet Union. Soviet foreign policy seeks opportunities for expanding Soviet influence, and strengthens the effect of diplomatic and propaganda instruments by a steady and substantial increase in its military power. Despite the slowdown in Soviet economic growth in the late 1970s and early 1980s, military spending is still estimated to rise by 3 to 4 percent each year. And since the mid-1960s, when the current phase began, the Soviet Union has acquired parity and, in some areas, superiority to American military power. The challenge for the Soviet Union has been to convert its vast nuclear and conventional force into commensurate political power.

Where possible, the Soviet Union has avoided direct military involvement in third countries, preferring instead to direct proxy forces, often Cubans and East Germans. That is how it has managed with Soviet support for the Marxist-Leninist forces in Angola and for insurgencies in Central America. The aim of such activity is to undermine and eliminate American influence and to establish footholds for further growth of Soviet influence.

It is obvious, however, that the enormous difficulties confronting less-developed countries, far more than Soviet politico-military activity, produce the political turmoil exploited by Soviet policy. A Western perspective focused primarily on Soviet designs will be costly and ultimately futile. As long as problems generated by vulnerability and instability in developing nations remain acute, the relatively wealthy industrial societies will face difficult choices. Their leaders and peoples will need all the sympathetic understanding, cultural sophistication, patience, and skill they can muster. For direct American-Soviet relations, an appropriate mixture of the same attributes, plus realism and firmness in coping with the challenge of Soviet power and discrimination, will be needed. We must realize that decades will be required to build an international order more tranquil and rational than the present international anarchy.

Notes

1. Crane Brinton, The Anatomy of Revolution, rev. ed. (NY: Vintage, 1965.
2. The Bolsheviks were one faction of the Russian Social Democratic Labor party, and the Mensheviks were their main rivals. After Lenin´s Bolshevik group seized group power in Russia they suppressed the Mensheviks and later took the names Russian Communist party (1918), All-Union Communist party (of Bolsheviks)(1925) and since 1952 have been known officially as

the Communist Party of the Soviet Union (CPSU).

3. See Robert C. Tucker, ed., Stalinism: Essays in Historical Interpretation (NY: Norton, 1977) and Sheila Fitzpatrick, ed., Cultural Revolution in Russia, 1928-1931 (Bloomington: Indiana University Press, 1978).

4. For a discussion of the history, composition, and functions of the Politburo, see John Lowenhardt, The Soviet Politburo, trans. Dymphna Clark (NY: St. Martin's Press, 1982).

5. See George W. Breslauer, Khrushchev and Brezhnev as Leaders: Building Authority in Soviet Politics (London: Allen & Unwin, 1982).

6. See Seweryn Bialer, Stalin's Successors: Leadership, Stability and Change in the Soviet Union (Cambridge University Press, 1980).

7. Narodnoe khoziaistvo SSSR v 1979 goda (The National Economy of the U.S.S.R. in 1979)(Moscow: Statistika, 1980, pp. 10-12.

8. Nasselenie SSSR: Po dannym vsesoiuznoi perepisi naseleniia 1979 goda (The Population of the U.S.S.R.: From the Data of the All-Union Census of the Population of 1979)(Moscow: Politizdat, 1980, p. 19).

9. Mervyn Matthews, Class and Society in Soviet Russia (NY: Walker, 1972),p. 146.

10. See "KPSS v tsifrakh" (The CPSU in Figures") Partiinaia zhizn' (Party Life), no. 14 (July 1981), pp. 17,25.

11. See Materialy XXVI s'ezda KPPS (Materials of the Twenty-Sixth Congress of the CPSU)(Moscow: Izdatel'stvo politicheskoi literatury (Political Literature Publishing House), (1981), p. 68; on party recruitment and composition in the Stalin and post-Stalin periods, see T.H. Rigby, Communist Party Membership in the USSR, 1917-1967 (Princeton: Princeton University Press, 1968).

12. See Alex Pravda, "Is There a Soviet Working Class?" Problems of Communism, 31 (November-December 1982), pp. 1-25.

13. S. Bialer, "The Andropov Succession," New York Review of Books, February 3, 1983, p. 27.

14. The material that follows is based in large part on: Helene Carrere d'Encausse, Decline of an Empire (NY: Newsweek Books, 1979, 1980); Zev Katz, Rosemarie Rogers, Frederic Harned, eds. Handbook of Major Soviet Nationalities (NY: Free Press, 1975); Edward Allworth, ed., Ethnic Russia in the USSR (NY: Pergamon Press, 1980); Teresa Rakowska-Harmstone, "The Nationalities Question," in Robert Wesson, ed., The Soviet Union, pp. 131-155; Frederick C. Barghoorn, "Soviet Dissenters on Soviet Nationality Policy," in Wendell Bell and Walter Freeman, eds., Ethnicity and Nation-Building (Beverly Hills, CA: Sage Publications, 1974); Ann Sheehy, comp., "The All-Union Census of 1979 in the USSR" (Munich: Radio Liberty Research Bulletin, September 1980). Background information on the Stalin and early post-Stalin periods available in Frederick

Barghoorn, Soviet Russian Nationalism (NY: Oxford University Press, 1956), and Vernon Aspaturian, "The Non-Russian Nationalities," in Allen Kassof, ed., Prospects for Soviet Society (NY: Praeger, 1968), pp. 143-200.
15. See Robert Sharlet, The New Soviet Constitution of 1977 (Brunswick, OH: King's Court, 1978), pp. 78, 96-97.
16. Sheehy, Radio Liberty Research Bulletin, 123/80, p. 3.
17. See The New York Times, April 15 and 18, 1978.
18. On Moscow's relations with Lithuania, see V. Stanley Vardys, The Catholic Church, Dissent and Nationality in Soviet Lithuania (NY: Columbia University Press, 1978).
19. See Carrere d'Encausse, Decline of an Empire, pp. 202-208; also Ellen Jones and Fred W. Grupp, "Measuring Nationality Trends in the Soviet Union: A Research Note," Slavic Review, 41:1 (Spring 1982), pp. 112-122.
20. Carrere d'Encausse, pp. 235-236.
21. See James Critchlow, "Uzbek Studies and Uzbekistan," Problems of Communism, 29:6 (November-December 1980), pp. 75-76; Daniel C. Matuszewski, "The Turkic Past and the Soviet Future," Problems of Communism, 31:4 (July-August 1982), pp. 76-82; Martha Olcott, "Soviet Islam and World Revolution," World Politics, 34 (July 1982), pp. 487-504.
22. John L. Scherer, ed. USSR Facts and Figures Annual, Vol. 6 (Gulf Breeze, FL: Academic International Press, 1982), pp. 302-303.
23. See Narodnoe khoziastvo SSSR v 1980g: Statisticheskii ezhigodnik (The National Economy of the U.S.S.R. in 1980: Statistical Annual) (Moscow: Finansy i statisika, 1981), pp. 29, 324, 371, 399, 450.
24. See Rasma Karklins, "The Nationality Factor in Soviet Foreign Policy," in Roger Kanet, ed. Soviet Foreign Policy in the 1980s (NY: Praeger, 1982) pp. 58-76, at pp. 68-73.
25. The classic discussion of zigs and zags between these poles, and the boundaries of permissible argument among Soviet theoreticians of nationality, is Grey Hodnett, "What's in a Nation?" Problems of Communism, 15:5 (September-October 1967), pp. 6-15.
26. Oleh Fedyshin, "The Role of Russians among the 'New, Unified' Soviet People," in Allenworth, ed. Ethnic Russia in the USSR, pp. 149-158.
27. See Jerry F. Hough, "Issues and Personalities," Problems of Communism, 31 (September-October 1982),pp. 29-31.
28. On tenure under Brezhnev, see Jerry F. Hough and Merle Fainsod, How the Soviet Union is Governed (Cambridge: Harvard University Press, 1979), pp. 260-264. A forthcoming publication of Bohdan Harasimyw, Political Elite Recruitment in the USSR, will be a major addition to the literature on that subject.
29. See Serge Schmemann, "Andropov Lights a Fire Under a Sleeping Nation," The New York Times, 7 February 1983.
30. Biographical details are drawn from John Lownhardt, The

Soviet Politburo, trans. Dymphna Clark (NY: St. Martin's
Press, 1982), pp. 110-111; and from Jerry F. Hough, "Issues and
Personalities," Problems of Communism (September-October 1982),
pp. 32-33. The news reports about Andropov personally - his
alleged tastes in music, books, and politics - are based on the
most doubtful evidence.
31. David Lane, The End of Social Inequality? Class, Status
and Power under State Socialism (London: Allen & Unwin, 1982),
p. 93.
32. Gabriel A. Almond and Sidney Verba, The Civic Culture
(Princeton: Princeton University Press, 1963); Stephen White,
"The USSR: Patterns of Autocracy and Industrialism," in Archie
Brown and Jack Gray, eds., Political Culture and Political
Change in Communist States, 2nd ed. (London: Holmes & Meier,
1979).
33. Pravda, January 30, 1983, p. 1.
34. Gayle Durham Hollander, Soviet Political Indoctrination
(NY: Praeger, 1972); Stephen White, Political Culture and
Soviet Politics (London: Macmillan, 1979).
35. A good up-to-date survey of the educational system is
Mervyn Matthews, Education in the Soviet Union: Policies and
Institutions since Stalin (London: Allen & Unwin, 1982).
36. David Lane, The End of Social Inequality? pp. 113-116.
37. Materialy XXVI s'ezda KPSS (Materials of the Twenty-Sixth
Congress of the CPSU) (Moscow: Izdatel'stvo politicheskoi
literatury [Political Literature Publishers House], 1981), p.
68.
38. A.B. Bazarov, "Osobennosti musulmanskikh religioznykh
perezhitkov" (Peculiarities of Moslem Religious Survivals")
Sotsiologicheskie isseldovaniia (Sociological Research), no. 2,
1982, p. 173.
39. See Christel Lane, The Rites of Rulers: Ritual in
Industrial Society - The Soviet Case (Cambridge: Cambridge
University Press, 1981).
40. See Ellen Mickiewicz, Soviet Political Schools (New Haven:
Yale University Press, 1967).
41. See Thomas Remington, "Soviet Public Opinion and the
Effectiveness of Party Ideological Work," The Carl Beck Papers
in Russian and East European Studies (Pittsburgh: Russian and
East European Studies Program, Universiy of Pittsburgh, 1983).
42. A major study of the uses of oral, printed, and broadcast
media for political indoctrination is Alex Inkeles, Public
Opinion in Soviet Russia: A Study in Mass Persuasion, rev. ed.
(Cambridge: Harvard University Press, 1958), which is, however,
based on materials dating from the 1940s and 1950s. A more
recent and highly comprehensive work is Gayle Durham Hollander,
Soviet Political Indoctrination: Developments in Mass Media and
Propaganda since Stalin (NY: Praeger, 1972).
43. Ellen Mickiewicz, Media and the Russian Public (NY:
Praeger, 1981).
44. Mark W. Hopkins, Mass Media in the Soviet Union (NY:

Praeger, 1970).
45. On the origins and early role of the political police, see George Leggett, The Cheka: Lenin´s Political Police (Oxford, England: Claredon Press, 1981).
46. See the important work on this subject by H. Gordon Skilling and Franklyn Griffiths, eds., Interest Groups in Soviet Politics (Princeton University Press, 1971). See also Philip D. Stewart, "Soviet Interest Groups and the Policy Process: The Repeal of Production Education," World Politics, 22:5 (October 1969), pp. 29-50.
47. See Skilling and Griffths, pp. 19, 370-372.
48. Thane Gustafson, Reform in Soviet Politics (Cambridge: Cambridge University Press, 1981), pp. 83 and passim.
49. Frederick C. Barghoorn, "Factional, Sectoral, and Subversive Opposition in Soviet Politics," in Regimes and Oppositions, Robert A. Dahl, ed. (New Haven: Yale University Press, 1973), pp. 27-87.
50. See Darrell L. Slider, "Social Experiments and Soviet Policymaking," Ph.D. dissertation, Yale University, 1981.
51. See Chapter 1 of Jerry F. Hough, The Soviet Union and Social Science Theory (Cambridge: Harvard University Press, 1979), p. 23; also Jerry F. Hough and Merle Fainsod, How the Soviet Union is Governed.
52. See, for example, Theodore H. Friedgut, Political Participation in the USSR and Ronald J. Hill, Soviet Politics, Political Science and Reform (NY: Martin Robertson and M.E. Sharpe, 1980).
53. See Robert Conquest, The Great Terror: Stalin´s Purge of the Thirties, rev. ed. (NY: Collier Books, 1973).
54. Stephen F. Cohen, "The Stalin Question since Stalin," in An End to Silence: Uncensored Opinion in the Soviet Union (NY: W.W. Norton, 1982), pp. 22-50, at p. 43. Also see Rudolf L. Tokes, "Dissent: The Politics for Change in the USSR," in Tokes and Henry Morton, eds., Soviet Politics and Society in the 1970s (NY: Free Press, 1974), pp. 3-60 at pp. 11-12; and in Joshua Rubenstein, Soviet Dissidents (Boston: Beacon Press, 1980), pp. 2-4; Ferdinand Feldbrugge, Samizdat (Leyden, the Netherlands: A.W. Sijthoff, 1975); and Frederick Barghoorn, Detente and the Democratic Movement in the USSR (NY: Free Press, 1976).
55. On the role of "legalism" in Soviet dissent, see Vladimir Bukovski, To Build a Castle (NY: Viking Press, 1979), pp. 234-241. The term "mainstream" was first applied to dissent and dissenters by Peter Reddaway in his landmark book, Uncensored Russia (NY: American Heritage, 1972).
56. Betsy Gidwitz, "Labor Unrest in the Soviet Union," Problems of Communism (November/December 1982), pp. 25-42.
57. On the activities of the Moscow Group, see, for example, Frederick Barghoorn, "Political Dissent," in Robert Wesson, ed., The Soviet Union (Stanford, CA: Hoover Institution Press, 1980), pp. 155-176; and Barghoorn,"Dissent in the USSR and

Soviet Foreign Relations," in Roger Kanet, ed., Soviet Foreign Policy in the 1980s, pp. 77-101. On the republic affiliates, see Yaroslav Bilinski and Tonu Parming, "Helsinki Watch Committees in the Soviet Republics," Nationalities Papers, 9:1 (Spring 1981), pp. 1-25.
58. See Roy and Zhores Medvedev, Khrushchev: The Years in Power (NY: Norton, 1978).
59. See Gustafson, Reform in Soviet Politics.
60. See Ellen Jones, "Representation of Organizational Interests in the USSR: Conflict and Consensus in Soviet Collegia," Paper presented at the annual meeting of the American Association for the Advancement of Slavic Studies, Washington, DC, October 1982.
61. Nancy Nimitz, "Reform and Technological Innovation in the 11th Five-Year Plan," in Seweryn Bialer and Thane Gustafson, Russia at the Crossroads: The 26th Congress of the CPSU (London: Allen & Unwin, 1982), p. 141.
62. Pravda, 23 November 1982.
63. Jerry F. Hough, The Soviet Prefects (Cambridge: Harvard University Press, 1969).
64. Max E. Mote, Soviet Local and Republic Elections (Stanford, CA: Stanford University Press, 1965), p. 78.
65. See Harold J. Berman, Justice in the USSR (NY: Vintage, 1968), pp. 81-88. This work is perhaps the most significant Western monograph in its field. Also outstanding is Peter Juviler, Revolutionary Law and Order (NY: Free Press, 1976).
66. See Lawrence M. Friedman and Zigurds L. Zile, "Soviet Legal Profession," Wisconsin Law Review, 1:1 (1964), pp. 32-77.
67. George Feifer, Justice in Moscow (NY: Simon & Schuster, 1964), p. 239.
68. A complete translation of the criminal code and code of criminal procedure for the Russian Republic is in Harold J. Berman and James W. Spindler, Soviet Criminal Law and Procedure, 2nd ed. (Cambridge: Harvard University Press, 1972).
69. See The New York Times, November 7, 1982.
70. Alexander I. Solzhenitsyn, The Gulag Archipelago, Vols. 1-3 (NY: Harper & Row, 1973-1978).
71. A study by economist Vladimir G. Treml estimates that per capita consumption of all forms of alcoholic beverages has risen sharply over the last two decades. He writes that, on the average, a strikingly high percentage of family budgets goes to purchase alcohol - as much as 13 percent of per capita income among persons 15 years old and older. See Vladimir G. Treml, Alcohol in the USSR: A Statistical Study (Durham, NC: Duke University Press, 1982).
72. Gustafson, Reform, pp. 138-139.
73. Christopher Davis and Murray Feshback, "Rising Infant Mortality in the USSR in the 1970s," U.S. Department of Commerce, Bureau of the Census, Series P-95, no. 74 (September 1980).
74. See D. Plumb et al., "Food Supply in the USSR: Evidence of

Widespread Shortages," Soviet Area Audience and Opinion Research, RFE/RL, AR #2-82 (April 1982).
75. Adam Ulam, "Russian Nationalism," in Seweryn Bialer, ed. The Domestic Context of Soviet Foreign Policy (Boulder, CO: Westview Press, 1981), p. 3.
76. See William Taubman, Stalin's American Policy: From Entente to Detente to Cold War (NY: Norton, 1982).
77. See Kurt London, "Soviet Foreign Policy: Fifty Years of Dualism," in Kurt London, ed., The Soviet Union - A Half Century of Communism (Baltimore: Johns Hopkins University Press, 1968), pp. 327-366.

SOVIET POLITICAL CULTURE AND
"COVERT PARTICIPATION" IN POLICY IMPLEMENTATION

Wayne DiFranceisco and Zvi Gitelman

The uneven, inconsistent thawing of the Soviet political
system over the last 30 years has drawn the attention of
Western scholars to interactions between state and society and
between elites and citizens. The view of the Soviet system as
a command polity, where political orders were given from above
to a completely subordinated population, has been modified. We
now think of more interactive politics with regularized,
legitimated exchanges, however, uneven, of political ideas and
influence between elites and non-elites. The roles of public
opinion, interest groups, and citizen participation in the
formulation of Soviet policies have been much discussed.(1)
Implicitly or explicitly comparing the Soviet system to Western
democracies, analysts of the Soviet system have tried to
determine the extent of political influence wielded by ordinary
citizens, specialist elites, political functionaries at
different levels, and broad social groupings such as workers or
ethnic groups. The focus has been on the input: in what ways
do Soviet people make demands of, and provide supports for, the
Soviet polity? The first instinct of Western political
scientists is to look for answers in the institutions of the
system and in the informal mechanisms of policymaking. It is
assumed that the crucial question is, "How and by whom is
policy made?" and so one turns to voting, interest group
activity, representative organs, or local government as the
locus of interaction between the leaders of the polity and its
rank-and-file members.

This article argues the question of policymaking is a
foregone conclusion to the great majority of Soviet people, and
that the more important question to them is, "How is policy
implemented?" Most Soviet people do not think they can make or
even influence policy and are not even interested in doing so.
A staunch Soviet patriot who was vigorously defending the
system to one of us said that "Policymaking is none of my
business - that's up to the Central Committee." He insisted
this was part of a quite reasonable division of labor. Even
among those who are interested in influencing policy, the

From: "Soviet Political Culture and 'Covert Participation' in
Policy Implementation," by Wayne DiFranceisco and Zvi Geitelman,
in The American Political Science Review, 1984, Volume 78. Used
by permission.

majority sees no realistic chance of doing so.

Western scholars are divided over the extent to which citizen participation in the formal institutions of policymaking has more than symbolic value. Hough has been the most consistent champion of the view that the scope of participation in the USSR is at least as great as that in many Western democracies, and its impact on policy may be significantly less. Hough is impressed by the growth in statistical indicators of citizens´ participation in the formal organs of the system. He also suggests that the increase in participation may be qualitative as well as quantitative. "How do we know that citizen participation in public policy discussions is not decisive in shaping major Soviet policies?" This "remains an open question...the fact is we really do not know," especially since our traditional image of the USSR as a "directed society" blinds us to "phenomena such as citizen input which do not correspond to the paradigm" (Hough, 1976, pp. 7, 15, 19). (One has to wonder about Hough´s own judgment when he says, in the same article (p. 13) that "there are few ideas that cannot be expressed in print in one form or another" in the USSR.)

Hough is somewhat more cautious in later formulations. He speaks of "large numbers of Soviet citizens" who "are engaged in activities that would seem to give them at least the potential of influence on some types of decisions" as well as of "organized group activity of a kind that can entail potential involvement in various levels of decision-making" (Hough & Fainsod, 1979, pp. 298-299; emphasis added). But the overall impression he conveys is of increasing and very large numbers of Soviet citizens participating meaningfully in political decisionmaking.

A different picture is drawn by Friedgut, who has studied Soviet political participation intensively and from several angles. Although not denying the quantitative indicators of participation adduced by Hough, Friedgut (1979, p. 302) imputes a very different qualitative nature to participation.

Wherever we have been able to examine empirical findings regarding the Soviet citizen´s public activity, whether from conversations with emigrants, from Soviet field surveys, or from some of the more frank and penetrating discussions published by Soviet scholars, we note a distinct lack of the dimension of citizen initiative. We find chronic recurrence of formal activity devoid of content... The activization of participatory institutions has not eliminated the subject element so prominent in

Soviet political culture. Conformity rather than
initiative still guides the Soviet citizen. Administrative
raison d´etat is served before community self-
determination and preserves its primacy through
control of both the form and content of the
participatory structures of the community.

Friedgut (p. 325) admits that the potential for "citizen, as
opposed to subject, participation," exists, but it has not been
realized for it would require "a basic change of political
values in the Communist Party leadership. Such changes are as
yet nowhere visible."(2)

Bialer (1980, pp. 166-167) offers a synthesis of the
positions. He distinguishes between "high politics" - the
major political issues and the actions of leaders - and "low
politics" - "the decisions that directly touch the citizen´s
daily life, the communal matters, and the conditions of the
workplace." The "average Soviet citizen" is indifferent to
"high politics" and feels that it´s none of his business. "The
average person considers politics a separate way of life, a
profession for which one is trained and paid." However, "low
politics" involves a "very high proportion" of the citzenry,
and it is "the very substance of the Soviet system of political
participation."

This is, no doubt, a useful and accurate distinction, but
it is an oversimplification. On one hand, a great many of the
intelligentsia who do not actively participate in high politics
seem to be intensely interested, as spectators, in the game as
it is played by the Communist Party elite. There are
discussions about politics at social gatherings, rumors are
circulated about the private and public lives of the verkhushka
(the men at the top), and there is substantial political
gossip. On the other hand, probably only a minority of the
population spontaneously involve themselves in low politics, at
least in those institutions whose ostensible function is to
make policy.(3)

As we shall see, in addition to high and low politics
there is a third dimension where policymaking is not the issue
but policy implementation is. Here politics become
individualized and privatized. People do not seek to promote
or retard policies that will affect large groups, but only to
have policies applied to themselves in the most beneficial way
possible. In order to do this, they enter into political
relationships either with input-side institutions, such as
soviets or the Party, or, more frequently, with government
officials on the output side - administrators or bureaucrats.
Soviet politics on this level is the interaction between the
citizen as client or supplicant looking for private benefit and

the representative of the system interpreting and implementing policy for this individual.

If Soviet political relationships are as we shall describe them, then conventional notions of Soviet political culture need to be revised. Neither the "parochial-subject-participant" trichotomy developed by Almond and Verba (1963), nor the idea of "subject-participatory" (Barghoorn, 1972, p. 25) political culture, where structures are designed for participation but the operative culture seems to treat the citizen as a subject, apply accurately to the Soviet case. This is not a subject political culture marginally affected by participatory institutions because there is a meaningful form of participation, but it takes place either outside the nominally participatory institutions or within those institutions but in nonprescribed ways. But because this participation is limited to affecting political outputs that concern the individual directly, it would be misleading to equate the Soviet kind of political culture with those that are conventionally thought of as largely participant. Moreover, the Russian-Soviet case (like others, especially in the Third World) demonstrates that there is no ineluctable progression from parochial to subject participant political cultures. The Soviet system, like many others, is syncretic, adapting traditional clientelist modes to what appear to be institutions for democratic participation.

One might expect a radical revolutionary regime not to adapt but to eliminate completely traditional political modes. But as Jowitt (1974) points out, Marxist-Leninist elites are induced by their ideology to select a set of system-building institutions which, ironically, reinforce traditional values and orientations toward politics. Jowitt cites three of these structural components of Communist system building and their ramifications for political beliefs at the mass level. The first component, the "dictatorship of the proletariat," with its stress on discipline, coercion, and Party control of both public and private sectors of the society, preserves much of the essence of traditional authority relationships - a bifurcation of society into the elite and a mistrusted populace. The second element involves the Leninist-Stalinist "commanding-heights" formula for development and a phenomenon that Jowitt (p. 1175) labels "revolutionary laissez-faire." Under this rubric, the emphasis is on rapid economic progress and mobilization such that the regime focuses on a rather limited set of priority areas, leaving vast segments of the society untransformed. "In return for performance in priority sectors...members of society are `allowed´ to manipulate non-priority sectors for their private benefit" This lack of development in nonpriority sectors allows, as we shall see in the Soviet case, for the perpetuation of traditional

216

clientelistic orientations toward officials, i.e., the use of blat (pull) or sviazy (connections) or even bribery. It is this pattern of interactions with public officials and institutions that we label covert participation.

A third component of Leninist system-building regimes is the elites´ production mentality. The leadership believes that political culture change will inevitably follow transformation in social and economic spheres, which in practice means that the Party tends to deemphasize cultural issues except where its primary goals of socioeconomic development are affected. Of course, the Soviet Union has long passed the system-building stage, and its intensive and extensive efforts at political socialization have narrowed the gap between political structures and political culture. (Even among our sample of émigrés described below, 47% acknowledge that they read agitation-propaganda material in the USSR, at least some of the time.)

Our observations on the nature of political participation and its implications for Soviet culture are based on Soviet writings and on our interviews with recent Soviet émigrés. These observations lead us to conclude that the way Soviet people relate to the political administrative system is to go through the motions of participation in the nominally democratic process of making decisions, but to put far more serious effort into trying to influence the way decisions are implemented. Thus the view of Soviet political culture as subject or subject-participant is misleading. Soviet political culture is neither a democratic nor a subject one, but an amalgam of traditional, pre-revolutionary modes of citizen-state relations and a superstructure of participatory institutions that superficially resemble those of Western democracies in many respects.

Sample and Method

A group of 1,161 ex-Soviet citizens who left the USSR from 1977 through 1980 were interviewed during 1980-1981 in Israel (n=590), the Federal Republic of Germany (n=100) and the United States (n=471). The sample was drawn as a quota, nonprobability sample, in line with hypotheses that led to a certain distribution of age, sex, education, nationality, and republic residence.(4) On some variables, such as age and sex, the proportions in the sample approximate those in the Soviet adult population rather closely. On the other hand, nearly half the respondents have had higher education (approximately 40% of all Soviet immigrants to Israel and the United States have come with higher education), 38% had secondary education, and only 15% had grade school education or less. Seventy-seven percent, of 899 people, had been registered as Jews on their

Table 1. Respondent's Area of Residence in the USSR[a]

RSFSR	Ukraine	Moldavia	Baltic	Georgia	Central Asia
330	247	120	174	120	165

[a]The area of residence of 5 respondents was not clear.

internal Soviet passports, 129 as Russians, 98 as Germans, 18 as Ukrainians, and 27 as other nationalities. The areas in which respondents had lived most of their lives are shown in Table 1.

Men and women are quite evenly distributed in age and regional categories, but men dominate blue collar and women white collar occupations, despite very similar educational levels. (Among the sample, 48% of the men and 46% of the women have higher education.) Educational levels are highest among those from the RSFSR, and, from the ethnic groups, among the Russians; 69% of the former and 72% of the latter have some higher education. The lowest educational levels are found among people from Central Asia (only 18% have higher education) and from Moldavia (23%). These people were interviewed in Russian or Georgian by native speakers. There were remarkably few refusals to be interviewed, although the average interview lasted between two and three hours. In addition to the standard questionnaire administered to the entire group, nearly 60 in-depth interviews were conducted with people who had been employees of the Soviet government agencies we inquired about, or who seemed to have unusually extensive knowledge about how citizens and government agencies operated in their respective republics.

The Problem of Bias

It cannot be claimed that the results obtained from any émigré sample are generalizable to the population in the Soviet Union, because not only are the émigrés demographically different from the population as a whole, but presumably their attitudes and assessments are different as well. Having chosen to leave the USSR, it is reasonable to assume that they were less pleased with the system than those who stayed behind. While accepting the inadmissibility of generalizing easily from the émigré to the original population, the assumption of émigré

bias can be exaggerated. First, the emigration is
demographically unrepresentative not because only certain
groups - Jews, Armenians, Germans - have chosen to leave the
country while others have chosen to remain, but because Soviet
policy in the last decade has made it possible for only those
groups to leave. Therefore, the ethnic imbalance of the
emigration is as much a product of Soviet emigration policy as
it is of special feelings of alienation on the part of those
who have left. Second, when questioned about their emigration,
our respondents cited a wide variety of reasons, many of them
having little or nothing to do with the Soviet political
system. Thus, 23% gave as their primary reason for leaving the
fact that they had relatives abroad or they were following
spouses, parents, or children who had decided to leave. Many
of these secondary migrants left reluctantly, and some resent
having been pulled along by the decisions of others. Another
23% cited their desire to live among people of their own ethnic
group. (Among the Germans, 51% cited this reason.) Despite
the possibility that some may have thought the interviewer was
eager to hear about their dislike of the USSR, only 15% cited
political reasons or hatred of the Soviet system as their
primary reason for leaving. The only reason cited as
frequently (15%) was a desire to escape anti-Semitism or
anti-German sentiment. Nearly one-fifth of the respondents
gave such varied answers as to defy coding under common
rubrics. These included numerous responses such as: "Soviet
life had become boring"; "My sister in Israel fell ill, and I
felt that I had to come and help her"; "I did not want to leave
but my children did, so what could I do"; "I thought the
Israeli climate would be good for my daughter's asthma";
"Everyone was going, so we went too"; "I was looking for
something new in my life." (Although some of these reasons may
seem trivial or frivolous, it should be remembered that travel
abroad is nearly impossible for most Soviet people, and
emigration becomes the only choice for people who in other
countries would have more options.) In sum, lacking any
reliable data on the Soviet population's attitude toward the
system, it cannot be assumed that the attitudes of the émigrés
are significantly more hostile, and in our sample, at least, we
see that alienation from the political system was by no means
the primary motivation for leaving it. Moreover, as in other
émigré studies, our respondents demonstrated considerable
support for many Soviet institutions and practices. One can
also assume that whatever biases may be present in the sample
as a whole, they are distributed fairly uniformly across
population subgroups. Therefore, we anticipate that any
differences observed across the subgroup strata are similar to
those characterizing the same groups within the Soviet
population.(5) As a further check on possible biases, we
developed a hostility/alienation index from questions that

solicited respondents´ opinion on the Soviet system and how the individual perceived his or her relationship to the regime. This index, whose construction is discussed in Appendix 1, allows us to determine whether hypothesized relationships are significantly affected by hostility toward the system.

In any case, even alienated citizens have no choice but to participate in many ways. They are not able to avoid some of the ritualistic forms of participation, such as voting, attending meetings, joining trade unions and, usually, the Komsomol. Because the state controls so many basic necessities, they must resort to official agencies, if only for the satisfaction of their private needs. The crucial question for us then becomes not whether they participate, but how they do so, and in this there seems no prima facie reason for thinking that they differ substantially from those who did not leave the country.

The Comparative Model of Political Culture and Soviet Politics

Attempts to classify the attitudinal and behavioral orientations of Soviet citizens toward political (input) institutions usually emphasize the predominantly "subject" nature of Soviet political culture.(6) This refers, in Almond and Verba´s model, to a political culture in which the typical citizen possesses an awareness of politics on the cognitive level but lacks the opportunity, the initiative, or both to influence the policymaking process (Almond & Verba, 1963, pp. 24-26). A participant culture, on the other hand, pertains to a political system in which citizens feel efficacious or politically competent and so believe that their actions to some extent affect policy decisions. Focusing on the political activities of Soviet citizens in formal settings, the conventional wisdom among Western scholars holds that participation Soviet-style tends to fulfill mainly support functions; i.e., it is primarily ritualistic and tutelary "involvement," (Sharlet, 1967). More important, it is claimed that Soviet citizens themselves recognize that their participation has little or no impact on the decisions of the verkushka (Friedgut, 1979; Gitelman, 1982). Thus, Friedgut (1979), Brown and Grat (1979), and others are inclined to accept Barghoorn´s characterization of Soviet political culture as a "subject-participant" hybrid in which mass participation serves as a mere facsimile of democratic activity and is devoid of emotional content. Its purpose is not to give citizens a voice in decision making - on this they and the regime are agreed - but to socialize them to the regime´s practices, promote their loyalty to it, demonstrate that loyalty to domestic and foreign audiences, and, perhaps, reassure the

220

leadership that its political house is in order.

When we restricted our investigation of Soviet political participation and culture to formal, conventional modes of political communication and interest articulation, our findings tended to support this view. Gitelman adapted several instruments from Almond's and Verba's The Civic Culture to his survey of Soviet émigrés which attempted to measure both the cognitive (awareness, knowledge) and affective (interest, competence) orientations of the respondents toward politics. Comparing these data with those from the Five-Nation samples, it was discovered that the former Soviets exhibited relatively high levels of awareness and knowledge of politics. Furthermore, even when we controlled for a putative distortion in the data resulting from the high proportion of college-educated men and women in the émigré sample, the results remained comparable to those from the Western countries studied by Almond and Verba (see Table 2). The ex-Soviet respondents were also reasonably well informed. Almost 62% of the sample correctly answered two out of three questions designed to test their knowledge of the Soviet system,(7) whereas only 16% could not correctly answer any of the questions that constituted the index.(8)

Our analysis of the results on several affective variables, however, demonstrated a markedly different pattern from that found on political cognitions. Although a majority (68.2%) of the respondents reported that they "regularly" or "sometimes" discussed politics with their families and friends in the Soviet Union, only 11.2% of them claimed that they felt completely free to talk about political and social issues with anyone in the USSR.(9) Even more striking was the negative relationship between this variable and education. Only 7.9% of the respondents with some college felt uninhibited about airing their political opinions openly, as opposed to 13.7% of those with secondary and 15.2% of those with only primary schooling.

This finding seems to indicate an intense interest in politics that is combined with a privatized pattern of political communication among Soviet citizens. Accordingly, a rigid distinction is preserved between one's inner beliefs and one's public actions.(10) The data also suggest that the participation of Soviet citizens lacks an element of interpersonal trust that is essential to cooperative public activity. The results from a series of "faith in people" indicators support this inference.(11) Even more remarkable, it seems, is the negative relationship between education and affect. Although the émigrés with higher education exhibit more political interest and knowledge (and also, as will be demonstrated below, a greater inclination toward participating) than others, they are the least emotionally attached to Soviet

Table 2. Following Politics Regularly and from Time to Time, by Education and Nation[a]

	Totals		Primary or Less		Secondary		Some College	
	%	N	%	N	%	N	%	N
USSR	76.3	1161	52.8	178	72.6	438	86.8	545
United States	80	970	67	339	84	442	96	188
United Kingdom	68	963	60	593	77	332	92	24
Federal Republic of Germany	72	995	69	790	89	124	100	26
Italy	36	995	24	692	58	245	87	54
Mexico	55	1007	51	877	76	103	92	24

[a]Includes data reprinted from Almond and Verba (1963, Table 10, p. 94).

Text of question: How frequently did you follow political and social events in the Soviet Union? Did you follow them regularly, from time to time, rarely or never?

Table 3. Perceived Ability to Do Something
about an Unjust Law
by Education and Nation (%)

	Total[a]	Primary	Secondary	College
USSR	6.9	2.8	5.0	9.7
Italy[b]	51	45	62	76

[a]Strata ns are the same as those reported in Table 2.

[b]Italian data are adapted from Almond and Verba (1963, Figure 1, p. 206).

political institutions and are less confident about their ability to influence policy decisions. To the statement, "People like me had no say about what the Soviet government did," 62% of the respondents with some college strongly agreed; the percentages for the primary and secondary school groups were 50.6 and 56.2, respectively.

Not surprisingly, levels of formal political competence among the émigré respondents were extremely low. Two Civic Culture questions on efficacy with respect to local-level (soviet) interest articulation were administered in the survey. Only 6.9% of the entire sample felt that it was possible to do something about an "unjust local law," and when probbed about the likelihood of changing that law, only a few more than half of the "competents" in the first question believed they would have had anything more than a remote chance of success.(12) We compared the findings on "local competence" among the émigrés to those in The Civic Culture. Although Italians possessed the lowest subjective competence levels of the five national groups studied by Almond and Verba, they greatly outdistance the Soviet sample at every level of education, as seen in Table 3.

Since these findings are based on a nonrepresentative émigré sample, we are obliged to be cautious in the inferences we draw from them. A scientific sample of the true Soviet population might well elicit higher levels of affect and competence. On the other hand, our data corroborate much of what has been shown by the current Western literature and personal observations of visitors to the USSR about the

characteric lack of enthusiasm of Soviet citizens toward the
official institutions of mass participation. According to
those sources, the typical Soviet accedes in the performance of
his civic obligations to a great extent out of ritualistic
habit, as well as in response to a variety of pressures, both
blatant and more subtle, to appear loyal to the regime.(13)
Further, our attempts to control for the possible biases of the
émigré respondents show no significant variation between
hostile and non-hostile groups in the sample on any of the
affect or competence variables.

Attitudes and Participation

The preliminary findings discussed above tended to support
the subject or subject-participant classification of Soviet
political culture. But an analysis of the recalled behavior of
the émigré casts doubt on its inference. A portion of the
sample could and did press its demands on the Soviet
authorities in a variety of ways. These activities ranged from
writing letters to newspaper editors to contacting Party and
government officials for help on personal and social problems.
Citizen-initiated modes of participation require high amounts
of motivation and effort by an individual (Verba & Nie, 1972,
p. 52); thus, it is not surprising that only a minority of the
respondents reported having engaged in such activities. More
important, as Verba and Nie stipulate, the usual purpose of
citizen-initiated contacts is private; the actor tends to seek
a particularized output rather than a change in legal or
administrative policy.(14)

A participation index was constructed from several of
these citizen-contact variables plus a few activities that
require some initiative, but which occur in more conventional
public settings, i.e., membership in the Communist Party,
membership in the Komsomol, or holding an elected office (see
Appendix 2). The participation scale was then tested against a
variety of cognition and affect measures discussed in the last
section. (For the sake of brevity we present the correlation
statistics, Tau-b, from the analysis in Table 4.) As expected,
the association measures between participation and political
cognitions were fairly robust. Also, given that education was
previously found to be an important indicator of a respondent's
political awareness and knowledge, it is not surprising that
the relationship between education and participation was strong
(Tau-b=.41).

The findings for the relationships between the
participation and the affect variables, however, did not
conform to the expectations of the "rational-activist" model of
political participation postulated by Almond and Verba (Almond,

Table 4. Correlations of Political Participation
with Cognitive Orientations, Affect toward
Inputs and Political Competence (in Tau-b's)

Cognitive Dimension	
Following Soviet politics	.28
Political knowledge	.22
Affect dimension	
Feeling free to discuss politics	-.22
Perceived influence in government policy	.06
Trust in other Soviet citizens[a]	.02
Efficacy in local politics	
Political competence[b]	.09

[a]This question asked the respondent if "most people in the USSR could be trusted."

[b]This variable was an index of the two local-competence measures discussed previously. See Appendix 3 for details on its construction.

1980, pp. 30-31). The negative association between participation and "feeling free to discuss politics" indicated that the most active Soviet émigrés were also the most guarded in their political communications. The other correlation statistics for participation-affect and participation-competence showed weak or non-existent relationships among the variables in general. Furthermore, the Tau-b correlation between participation and the hostility-alienation measure was a weak .09.

The paradoxical conclusion is that those Soviet citizens who are not sanguine about the viability of formal institutions of mass participation and who are hostile or neutral toward the system as a whole are precisely those who are most

self-initiated and active. We believe that this apparent
anomaly can be subsumed under a rational interest rubric, i.e.,
that self-interest and personal need induce the participant
Soviet citizen to unsolicited political activity. He eschews
the formal political institutions and focuses his attention
largely on the narrow issue of "Who Gets What." His
participation is direct and personalized, and it is motivated
by a desire for particularized outputs.

The data presented in Table 5 further illustrate the
unique aspects of Soviet political activity and hint at the
widespread persistence of clientelism in the political culture.
Table 5 lists the responses of the émigrés to a question about
"the best way to influence a Soviet government decision."
Despite the inclusion of the word "group" in the question,
fewer than 10% mentioned forming an interest group as a viable
option. The combined frequencies for officially sanctioned
methods of interest articulation - "writing letters to
officials" and "exerting influence through the Party" - account
for only 10.4% of the respondents. The modal response is
"personal or family connections (sviazy)," at 35.5%. It seems
likely that these individuals interpreted the phrase,
"government decision," in terms of its implementation or output
aspects - for example, the disposition of an individual case -
and not in the much broader sense of policymaking, a conversion
function, for which svaizy would be inappropriate. These
findings fit the proposition stated above, that the Soviet
citizen tends to avoid or denigrate cooperative activity and
formal channels of interest articulation. Where he does   .
participate he orients himself toward a specific individual or
agency in an informal, and often covert, manner.

Politics on the Output Side
Thus far we have discussed two types of participation:
ritualistic participation and citizen-initiated contacts with
people who hold positions in policymaking institutions. In
neither case is there much expectation of input into
policymaking, but in the second there is some hope that action
will be taken to benefit the individual, just as in the United
States a congressman is asked to render constituency service
without trying to influence legislation. Soviet citizens are
more oriented toward the administrative side of the system.
They are "subject competent," but not in the way described by
Almond and Verba, that is, trying to get legally prescribed
proper treatment. According to Almond and Verba (1963, p.
162), the competent subject obeys the law, does not help shape
it, and "if he is competent, he knows the law, knows what he
must do, and what is due him." In the Soviet system, however,
the "competent subject" is not content to demand fair play and
the universal application of the law, for he does not expect

226

Table 5. Best Way to Influence a Government Decision ($\underline{n}$=1,161)

Connections	Letters	Group	Party	Protest Demonstration	None	NR
35.5	4.5	9.9	5.9	3.4	25.8	15.2

Text of question: If a group of Soviet people were trying to influence some
government decision, which way would be most effective?

227

that of the system. Rather he takes matters into his own hands
when he is convinced that the routine workings of the system
will not automatically confer upon him the benefits he desires.
He does this by approaching those who implement policy, not
those who make it, and by following traditional ways of
handling administrators, adapted to the modern Soviet political
system. "Thus a premium is placed on informal adaptive
mechanisms...that allow for some stability and certainty in
response to what is often perceived as an abitrary and
threatening regime." These mechanisms "obstruct the
development of a political culture based on overt, public, and
cooperative relationships. Instead they reinforce the
traditional community and regime political cultures with their
stress on covert, personalized, hierarchical relationships
involving complicity rather than public agreements (Jowitt,
1974, p. 1183). It may well be that the Soviet development
process has actually reinforced clientelistic cultural
patterns. By raising society's overall level of education to
facilitate modernization, by focusing on heavy industry to the
detriment of the individual's standard of living, and by
failing to develop meaningful citizen participation and
emotional attachment to the policymaking process, the Communist
leadership has created a large number of "socialist
entrepreneurs" who are highly capable of and heavily
predisposed toward working nonpriority public sectors for their
own benefit. Our data suggest that Soviet citizens are open to
entering into informal or even illegal interactions with
officials. For example, we find that three-quarters of our
respondents believe that at least half of Soviet officials
"derive material benefit from citizens who approach them for
help," and 60% believe that a bribe could persuade a policeman
to overlook a minor traffic violation. Bribery is not a last
resort or an activity limited to society's marginal elements,
but seems to be accepted by a large number of people as a
common way of handling difficult situations. We posed an
open-ended question to our respondents: "If a government
official clearly lied to you or refused to give what you had
coming to you, what would be the best way of making him tell
the truth or giving you what was due you?" The modal response
was to "offer him a gift," with 46% of the total sample
mentioning this, and only 31% - the next largest group -
suggesting an appeal to the official's superior. A second open
question was, "What is the main precondition for success in
life in the USSR?" Two responses were coded, with 42%
mentioning "connections" as their first response and 64%
mentioning it either first or second. Clearly, informal, and
even illegal, means are those that immediately suggest
themselves to Soviet people who have to interact with the state
bureaucracy.

Working the Output Side

How Soviet citizens attempt to influence actively the implementation of policy seems to vary according to two factors: their own education and the particular agency involved. Regional differences are not as great as might be supposed. Sex and age are not important in differentiating styles of confronting and dealing with the bureaucracy. The influence of education is seen in response to the question. "Which type of government official would you prefer - the one who treats everyone equally regardless of circumstances or the one who treats each case individually, taking account of its special characteristics?"

The preference of the most educated people for a case-by-case differentiation is striking. As an engineer from Kharkov expressed it, "Taking each case on its own merits means that the opportunity to use blat (pull) or znakomstvo (connections) is present, and that's the only way to survive in the USSR. In the United States, on the other hand, I prefer that state employees treat everyone the same." In the country of immigration, in other words, the engineer felt disadvantaged vis-a-vis the rest of the population and no longer had confidence in his ability to swing things his way in bureaucratic encounters. But in the Soviet Union educated people may think their education gives them status greater than that conferred on the bureaucrat by his position. It also gives them savoir faire, which they can use to their advantage. Less-educated people have no such illusions. They defer to the status conferred on the official by his position, making no judgments about the person. The more educated look at the individual and figure they can handle him because they are better educated; the less educated look at the position and are not prepared to challenge it.

However, this does not mean that they will meekly accept whatever fate, speaking through the bureaucrat, will ordain. Many people, irrespective of their educational background, try to influence the implementation of policy and the decisions of administrators, although the more educated are more likely to take an activist posture even in rigid bureacracies such as the armed forces.

But the tactics of the more and less educated differ. Less-eduacted people are more inclined to bribery, whereas more-educated ones will use personal connections to extract what they want from a bureaucracy. Obviously, the highly educated are more likely to know people in high places, how to get them, and how to approach them. This tactical difference has probably been the pattern in Russia and elsewhere for centuries; the best that the peasant could do to gain the favor

Table 6. Bureaucrats Style Preferred,
by Education (n=1,113)

	Grade School %	Secondary %	Higher %
Equal treatment	21.9	14.8	5.9
Sometimes equal, sometimes differentiated	30.9	24.7	17.4
Differentiated	36.5	55.7	73.8
Don't know, no answer	10.7	4.8	3.0

of the all-mighty official was to bring him a chicken or some moonshine, whereas the educated and the wealthy were more likely to mix socially with the official and, probably, his superiors.

It is also quite clear that different agencies evoke different kinds of behavior on the part of the clients, probably not because of differences in the structure and personnel of the agencies so much as differences in the availability and nature of the services they provide, and in the importance they have been assigned by the regime.

In this study we found three categories of administrative agencies. The first category includes bureaucracies toward which citizen initiative is either unnecessary, because the agency will most likely produce the desired output without special efforts by the client, or it is useless, because the agency will not be responsive to such efforts. The great majority of respondents who had personal experience with pension agencies (gorsobes, raisobes) did not find it necessary to undertake any extraordinary initiatives in order to receive their pensions (although some "improved" their pensions by various means). Asked what a person should do if he did not receive a pension to which he was entitled, more than half the respondents said that a letter to a higher authority should suffice. Another 20% recommended that the person simply wait patiently, for he would surely get the pension. There was also widespread agreement that in the armed forces it would be useless to try to change one´s assignment and to get around orders.

Housing falls into a second category. Although some accept the routine workings of the official housing agencies, others try to influence those workings by illegal means, and still others choose to ignore the official agencies and opt for private, legal solutions to their housing problems.

The third category of agency includes admission committees in higher educational institutions, hiring departments of enterprises, and raspredelenie commissions, whose job it is to assign higher education graduates to their first post. In these institutions, it is widely felt, the routine workings of the system were highly unlikely to produce the desired result without a special "push" by the citizen which might involve semilegal or illegal measures. Thus, two-thirds of the respondents suggested bribery or using connections (sviazy) to avoid an undesirable job assignment, and three-quarters suggested the same tactics for gaining admission to a university or institute of higher education.

We arrived at this categorization partially on the basis of a battery of five open-ended questions consisting of hypothetical situations that asked what a (third) person could do in response to a negative decision by each of five Soviet institutions. Paraphrased versions of these questions are listed below.

Soviet Army: How could a Soviet Army officer in 1980, stationed in a good staff position in Leningrad, avoid being transferred to a unit headed for Afghanistan?
Pensions: What should a person do if he is entitled to a pension, has not received it, and is told by officials to "be patient"?(15)
Raspredelenie (assignment commission): What should a person do if he is assigned to work in a remote area after graduating from an institution of higher education?
University Admissions Committee: What should a woman do who wants to get her mediocre son into the mathematics department of a university?
Zhilotdel (local housing authority): What should a person do to get a better apartment, if the one he has is, by legal standards, large enough?

We observed that few respondents felt it advisable to resort to manipulative tactics in dealing with the army, but a large portion suggested covert measures in dealing with job assignments, university admissions, and housing. Moreover,

Table 7. Actions Suggested by Respondents (%) (n=1,161)

	Bribery	Connections[a]	Legal or Semi-Legal	Other	Nothing/Passive[b]
Soviet Army	2.9	11.1	10.2[c]	3.6	72.2
Raspredelenie	19.6	37.6	10.5[d]	11.6	20.6
University admissions committee	29.4	32.7	13.8[e]	3.5	20.6
Housing authority (zhilotdel)	18.4	14.1	39.5[f]	5.3	22.7

[a] Includes both protektsiia (patronage) and sviazy (connections).

[b] Those who responded that one could do nothing, or who could not think of anything to do.

[c] "Threaten to resign from the army" or "plead illness or family problems."

[d] "Marry someone with the right residence in one's home town" or "find a medical excuse.

[e] "Appeal to the committee," "apply to a different school," or "engage a private tutor."

[f] "Enter a cooperative," "exchange apartments with someone," or "buy a private apartment."

approximately 80% of the repondents were in the "active" range
of the three variables, suggesting that regime control of these
sectors is relatively lax and more willing to tolerate
flexibility in them. (As we shall see, there are legal
alternatives for those who fail to obtain satisfactory housing,
which explains the relatively low proportion of responses in
the covert range regarding housing.)

The final portion of our data analysis illustrates the
combined impact of structure and education on the preferred
strategy of the respondents. The findings in Table 8 follow
fairly closely from our predictions. First, the higher one´s
education, the greater his or her sense of competence and
resulting activity vis-a-vis Soviet allocative structures.
This can be discerned from a glance at the column headed
"passive": in every administrative setting there is a uniform
decline in passivity with increasing levels of education.
However, the results clearly indicate that the more powerful
and strategically located is the institution, the less is the
perceived opportunity to influence that institution by any
means, regardless of one´s social status. This is idicated by
the contrast between the frequencies for the military and those
for the other bureaucratic agencies.

There is ample evidence to confirm our hypothesis that the
modern Soviet system has tended to reinforce traditional
clientelistic orientations toward the structures of government.
Soviet citizens defer to the status or power of an official
and his agency as much for pragmatic as for normative reasons.
Where a bureaucratic encounter can be exploited for private
gain, the "competent" Soviet citizen, particularly if he or she
is highly skilled and educated, will attempt to do so. There
appears to be less confidence in legal rules and procedures as
a means of extracting services from the state, as demonstrated
by the fact that for every institution in Table 8 except the
housing authority, to which legal alternatives exist, the
proportions of respondents suggesting covert tactics (bribes
and connections) are higher than any other types of approach.
It should be also pointed out that all of the legal avenues
suggested in regard to housing were private (enter a
cooperative or exchange apartments) rather than public
solutions.

The data also confirm that, although covert forms of
participation appeal to all social classes in the Soviet Union,
different educational groups have different preferences for
strategies of influence. Bribery is (of necessity) the chosen
method of the less educated, whereas blat is the favored
instrument of the intelligentsia. In fact, for every
institution, the college-educated typically outdistanced the
low-status respondents in all spheres of specified activity

Table 8. Actions suggested by Respondents, by Education (%) (n=1,161)

	Bribery	Connections	Legal/Semi-Legal	Other	Nothing/Passive
Soviet army					
Primary or less	2.2	6.7	5.1	2.2	83.7
Secondary	3.7	8.2	8.2	3.9	76.0
Some college	2.2	14.9	13.4	3.9	65.3
Raspredelenie					
Primary or less	22.5	18.5	8.4	6.2	44.4
Secondary	22.1	37.7	9.6	8.2	22.4
Some college	16.7	43.9	11.9	16.1	11.4
College admissions					
Primary or less	34.8	15.7	6.2	4.5	38.8
Secondary	32.2	33.6	11.0	3.2	20.1
Some college	25.3	37.6	18.5	3.5	15.0
Housing Agency					
Primary or less	19.7	9.6	34.3	7.3	29.2
Secondary	18.5	11.6	41.6	5.9	22.4
Some college	18.0	17.6	39.6	4.0	20.7

except bribery. This finding confirms our hypothesis about the higher level of skills, and resources available to upper-status individuals and their more expansive repertoires of tactics for pulling the right strings in their dealings with the bureaucracy.

One must exercise caution in interpreting these data, since some of the hypothetical stories we presented to the respondents more often than not involve a character who is trying to get something to which he or she is not legally entitled in the first place. One could argue that, as such, they almost force the respondents to suggest illicit and unethical activities. On the other hand, the high rate of passive responses toward the military, in contrast to the willingnes of the émigrés to recommend covert and manipulative tactics with respect to the other institutions, supports the decision to utilize these variables in the analysis. Furthermore, in a total of 4,644 responses to the four questions there was not a single instance in which a former Soviet suggested that the character in the situation attempt individually or in a group to effect a change in the policy or procedure, thus corroborating the previous evidence that Soviet citizens concede that policymaking itself is a foregone conclusion. They are inclined instead to concentrate their efforts at political influence in the appropriate output sectors.

We turn now to the actual tactics used by citizens to extract their desiderata from the institutions, and observe how the nature of the institution influences the ways in which citizens will approach it. The agencies we investigated included those dealing with housing, employment, pensions, admission to higher education, the police and armed forces. Soviet sources provide ample evidence that the pension agencies are plagued by poorly trained personnel and inefficient procedures,(16) and yet we find that our respondents evaluate the agency and its personnel favorably, and that the great majority see no need to resort to any special tactics in order to receive their pensions. The apparent paradox is explained by the fact that almost all who are entitled to pensions receive them, whereas the housing problem is perhaps the most difficult one in the daily life of the Soviet citizen. Even though the USSR has been building 2.2 million housing units annually since 1957, in the mid-1970s the average per capita living space in urban areas was only 8 square meters (10 in Moscow). An estimated 30% of urban households still share apartments, and it is not uncommon for people to wait as long as 10 years to get an apartment (Morton, 1980, pp. 235-236). Even getting on the list is a problem, as only those with less than nine square meters of living space (a minimum standard set in the 1920s) are eligible. Twenty percent of our respondents had been on a waiting list for an apartment.

The scramble to obtain housing is fairly general, and not a few short stories, feuilletons, and even novels have been written on the subject.(17) Small wonder that the most imaginative tactics are devised to obtain even the most modest apartments. An informant who worked in two housing administrations in Moscow in the late 1940s and 1950s, when housing was especially short, notes that bribery to obtain an apartment was so widespread that "people did not ask each other `did you give´ but only `how much.´" Party officials, those with "responsible posts," those who had other favors to trade or simply had relatives and friends working in the housing administration were advantaged in the struggle for a dwelling. Although the situation has improved markedly in recent decades, nearly two-thirds of our respondents report that they tried to advance their position on the waiting list, either through appealing to a higher Soviet organ, or, less frequently, using illegal tactics. The intervention of one´s supervisor at work is often sought. Of those who went through the appeal process (n=129), just over half reported that the appeal was successful and they obtained the apartment. Those who do not appeal successfully use other tactics and enter what Morton (1980) calls the "subsidiary housing market" (private rentals, cooperatives, exchanges of apartments and private houses). Exchanging apartments is the remedy most often prescribed by our respondents for those who have been unsuccessful in getting one from the official lists, but bribery is the second best. The official list is quite "flexible," as Soviet sources explain. "Too often the decisive factor is not the waiting list," Pravda commented, "but a sudden telephone call [after which] they give the flats to the families of football players and the whole queue is pushed back."(18) Even to purchase a cooperative apartment involves waiting lists.

A Bukharan Jewish woman from Tashkent whom we interviewed grew up in an eight-room private house with her own room. After marriage, she applied for a co-op because all her mother´s children and grandchildren were registered as living in the big house, making it look like crowded conditions. The Uzbek clerk could not read Russian well and asked her to fill out the application for the co-op and then have it typed. "When I brought the typed version I put a bottle of vodka on the desk. He didn´t take money, only vodka. Uzbeks don´t take money. They are very humane people. He took vodka because, as an Uzbek, he is not allowed to drink. He can´t go into a store to buy vodka because the clerks are Uzbeks and it would be embarrassing. So they get vodka from us, the `foreigners.´"

Getting a pension rarely involves this much chicanery, although the press reports numerous instances of bureaucratic snafus connected with pensions, and there are occasional reports of pension officials making money from "dead souls" in the Gogolian tradition (Trud, 1980). But some pensioners also monkey with the system, especially since many pensions are very low. (We have reports from Central Asia of pensions as low as 24 rubles a month, and many instances in the European USSR of pensions of approximately 60 rubles, latter being roughly one-third the average urban wage in the 1970s.) A bookkeeper from a small town in Moldavia explained that since pensions are based on average salary in the last year of employment, "sometimes to help out a worker who was going on pension the administration would promote him to a vacancy with a higher pay scale, even if he was not qualified for the job." Bonuses and overtime pay would be calculated into the figures for average salary in order to inflate the pension. All of this, she claimed, was assumed to be legal.

Getting into an institution of higher education is a far more complicated matter especially for Jews, in the periods from 1945 to 1958 and from 1971 to the present. Although some respondents indicate that blat rather than bribery is used to gain entrance to higher education, two former members of admissions committees recall the widespread use of bribery, and one woman from the Ukraine frankly said that she was admitted only because her mother paid a 3,000 ruble bribe. Another person who was on the admissions committee of a polytechnic in Leningrad reports that in his institute the bribes ran about 500 rubles, but were into the thousands for the pediatric faculty and the First Medical Institute in Leningrad. But other forms of chicanery are more prevalent. A Georgian Jew tells how he paid 100 rubles in Kulashi to have his nationality changed from Jew to Georgian so that he would be admitted to the pediatric institute in Leningrad. This trick having worked, he returned as a pediatrician to Kulashi. But when he went to change his nationality back to Jew - "everyone knew me there and it was silly to be registered as a Georgian" - "the boys" demanded 200 rubles, for, they explained, because the Jews were getting out of the country, it was now worth more to be a Jew! Our Leningrad informant, who was himself helped in getting into the school of his choice because he was a basketball player, tells us that athletes and residents of Leningrad were favored for admission, as were children of faculty. Admissions committee members in Leningrad got written instructions not to admit anyone to the journalism faculty without recommendations from the Party raikom. Certain specialties even in the philological faculty were explicitly closed to Jews. In such cases, bribery, connections, and other tactics will not work, except very rarely, and people learn quickly to give up on these institutions.

The other side of this is an "affirmative action" program

designed to increase the number of natives in the republic´s higher educational institutions. Two Soviet authors assert that "It is understood that in socialist societies objectively there can be no discrimination against any national group. Soviet education practice knows no such examples." At the same time, they say that, "It must be assumed that the more the proportion of a nationality in higher education corresponds to its proportion in the population as a whole, the more the system of higher education lives up to the democratic ideal of equal educational opportunity for all people irrespective of nationality." To achieve this "one can permit...conditional influence of a variable such as the nationality of an individual" on admissions decisions (Prikhodko & Pan, 1974, pp. 70, 61). Indeed, informants from two cities in Moldavia reported independently that in the 1970s they were told quite openly not to bother applying to Kishinev Polytechnical Institute because that was being reserved for ethnic Moldavians. Central Asians respondents portray admissions officials desperately trying to fill ethnic quotas. One woman draws a perhaps exaggerated picture of Uzbek officials scouring the countryside for young Uzbek women who could be persuaded to attend a pedagogical institute training music teachers for elementary schools. Other informants report that in the Ukraine and Moldavia, at least, rural students were favored for admission to institutes and were eagerly recruited, and this is confirmed as policy by official sources.

For those departments and schools that are realistic possibilities for Jews, the way in is not always a direct one. A common practice is to hire a tutor for the applicant, not so much to prepare the applicant as to prepare the way with the admissions committee. Often, the tutor is a member of the faculty, and he will see to it that his student gets in, sometimes by turning over some of his fees to his colleagues (reported in Moscow, Kharkov, Leningrad). One operator told parents: "I´ll get your child into the institute for 1,000 rubles. Give me 300 now and the rest only if he gets in." The advance would be used to bribe clerks to put the child´s name on the list of those admitted, bypassing the admissions committee, and then the rest was pocketed by the fixer. One admissions committee member admitted frankly that he gave higher admission grades to students who had been tutored by his friends.(19)

If citizens and members of admissions committees fool with the system, so, of course, does the Party. A woman who taught in several pedagogical institutes reports that at the final meeting of the admissions committee a representative of the Party raikom and another of the obshchestvennost (usually someone working with the Party) would come and express their opinions freely. They would insure that certain ethnic distributions were achieved and that certain individuals were admitted or turned down. In Kharkov, it is claimed, that there are three lists of applicants: those who must be admitted, those who must not be, and the rest. In the Kharkovite´s experience, the Party did not directly participate in the admissions process, but did so indirectly by approving members of admissions committees, making up the above-mentioned lists, and providing written guidelines for admission policies.

The Soviet press does not hide the fact that the struggle for admission to higher education is a fierce one, and that all kinds of means are employed in it. "Every summer when the school-graduates boom starts and the doors of vuzy (higher educational institutions) are blocked by lines of applicants, ripples of that wave sweep over editorial staffs as well. Parents and grandparents of school graduates call up and come in person (the person who failed the exams never comes). With great inspiration they tell what profound knowledge their child has, how diligent he was, how well he replied to each question, but the perfidy of the examiner was beyond all expectations." The writer notes, however, that "the majority of complaints are quite just" (Loginova, 1980, p. 11).

The intelligentsia is especially anxious to have its children gain higher education. In Azerbaijan none other than the first secretary of the republic Party organization, now a member of the All-Union Politburo, Gaidar Aliev (1981, p. 10) complained that in the law faculty of the local university, "We discovered that the overwhelming majority of the students are children of the militia, procurators, judges, law professors and employees of Party and state organs... We were concerned with the threat of nepotism and `heredity´ within the administrative organs." He complained also about the fashion of the 1960s, when senior officials "arranged" to receive higher degrees, commenting sardonically on a popular saying that "A scholar you might not be, but a kandidat you surely must become."

If one gets into the institute or university and then graduates, a raspredelenie commission will normally assign the graduate his or her first job. Very often this is an undesirable position in an even less desirable location. For example, it is common practice to assign teachers or physicians, many of whom are single women, to rural areas in Siberia and Central Asia. To avoid such assignments, some will simply take a job outside their field, others arrange fictious marriages with spouses who have residence permits in desirable locations, and many will appeal the decision and try to get a "free diploma," that is, one without a specific job assignment, leaving them to their own devices. In only one instance were

239

we told of a bribe being used (in the West Ukraine) to get a
good assignment. Several informants report being assigned to
jobs in Central Asia, only to find upon arrival that there was
no need for them, that the local institutions had not requested
them, and the local authorities were not eager to have
nonnatives take jobs there. Despite the inconvenience, such
contretemps were welcomed because they freed the person from
the assignment. In 1979 nearly 30% of assigned jobs were not
taken (Uchitel´skaia gazeta, 1980, p. 2), and in some rural
areas the proportion of those who did not show up to their
assignments was higher.(20) Of course, some graduates try to
use blat, to try and pull strings with the job assignment
commission, and this is reported to work fairly well. The
other use of blat is to get some big boss to request the
graduate specifically as an employee of his institution.

The Use of Blat and Protektsiia
    Since blat and protektsiia are so commonly used, they are
frequently commented on by the Soviet press. One detailed
analysis raised both principled and pragmatic objections to
protektsiia. It is said to be objectionable because it
violates the socialist principle of "from each according to his
capabilities, to each according to his work." On the practical
level, protekitsiia is said to reward the incompetent,
discourage hard work and initiative, allow people to make
buying and selling favors their profession, and promote
calculations of self-interest "incompatible with communist
morality." The resort to protektsiia arises, it is suggested,
because social norms are not well defined and because of the
"underdevelopment of certain branches of our economy." The law
is said to be too vague for curbing the use of protektsiia.
Unlike bribery, using protektsiia is not generally considered a
crime except if "substantial harm is done to state or public
interests, or to the rights of individuals" (Kiselev, 1981, p.
152).(21)

    As this argument implicitly acknowledges, the use of
protektsiia - and in some areas and under certain circumstances,
even bribery - is socially acceptable and not discouraged by
law or custom. It is in line with age-old traditions in many
areas of the USSR. A Georgian author shows how traditional
birthdays, weddings, mourning rituals, the departure of young
men to the army, and even funerals are occasions for trading
influence and subtle forms of bribery (Dzhafarli, 1978, p. 72;
see also Verbitskii, 1981, p. 2). Soviet authors decry
"survivals of the past" which are said to contradict "socialist
morality and way of life." Some Western observers see not just
survivals but a Soviet failure to resocialize the population to
Marxist-Leninist norms. One student of Soviet political
culture asserts that "`New Soviet man,´ in short, does not yet
exist; Soviet citizens remain overwhelmingly the product of

240

their historical experience rather than of Marxist-Leninist ideological training" (White, 1979b, p. 49). This is an exaggeration - there has been successful resocialization in many areas of life - but it is true that prerevolutionary styles and practices survive in certain spheres, even among third and fourth generation Soviet citizens. The relationship between the government official and the citizen closely resembles pre-Communist forms in the USSR and other socialist countries. Jowitt's (1974, p. 1176) argument that traditional attitudes and behavior patterns survive the Communist revolution - and are even reinforced by it - is borne out by our investigation.

The prevalence of <u>blat</u> should not be attributed to some mystical staying power of prerevolutionary political culture. Rather, it is supported by present-day structural factors which are themselves continuations of tsarist practices. The highly centralized and hierarchical administrative structure of tsarist days has been continued and reinforced by its heirs, so the kind of tactics used to ameliorate the harshness of tsarist administration are well suited to the present day as well. In the light of weak rational-legal authority and of interest groups in both historical periods, the average citizen is without influence over policymaking and has little legal protection against administrative arbitrariness or even mindless application of what is construed as the law. He is left to devise individual strategies and tactics which will not change the making of the law, but will, he hopes, turn its implementation (or non-application) in his favor. Each person, then is reduced to being a special pleader, and not with those who make the rules but with those who are charged with applying and enforcing them.

Conclusion

Our analysis of the modes and meanings of participation in the Soviet system leads us to reject both Soviet claims for their system as well as Western characterizations of Soviet political culture as "subject" or "subject-participant." The three modes of participation in the Soviet political system have been identified: formal-ritualistic participation, which might better be labelled involvement citizen-initiated contacts with official persons and institutions whose task is, among other things, to represent, check up on (<u>kontrol'</u>), and run interference for people; and contacts with those whose task is to implement policies made elsewhere. Our sample of émigrés, and perhaps the Soviet population as well, shows little belief in the power of formal-ritualized participation to influence policy. Although a substantial number did contact official representatives and institutions, most were not greatly pleased with the outcome of these contacts, and many expressed

241

skepticism about their utility. More confidence was expressed
in the ability of the ordinary citizen to influence the process
of policy implementation. Although some bureaucracies were
judged quite impervious to citizen influence or manipulation,
and others were found to operate so routinely that such
manipulation was rarely necessary, several agencies were seen
as not producing outcomes favorable to the client unless he
made efforts to influence the way officials interpreted and
applied policy. The citizen approached the agency either as a
supplicant pleading for particular treatment, or as one who had
something to exchange - favors, influence, even money - in
return for favorable bureaucratic action.(22) How the citizen
approaches the organization and what he offers in return for
its favors depends largely on his educational background and on
the particular organization involved. Those with higher
education are more likely to take the initiative vis-a-vis the
bureaucracy and to mobilize connections to obtain a favorable
outcome. Those with less education are not as confident of
their ability to sway the bureaucracy by their own efforts, but
when they do so, they are more likely to resort to showing
their appreciation with gifts or money bribes. The attitudes
and behavior of the émigrés, and probably of the Soviet
citizenry, remain clientelistic and privatized, in contrast to
the nominally democratic structures and collectivist norms of
the official Soviet system. Our findings repeatedly suggest
that the dominant social ethos of Soviet citizens vis-a-vis
their government is one of private self-interest. Furthermore,
they display clear preference for informal access to and
influence on bureaucratic officials and a general disdain for
formal and legalistic procedures and norms. This observation
leads us to think of the Soviet political culture (or at least
the dominant subculture) as covert-participant. The
covert-participant individual is oriented toward system
outputs, but he exhibits few of the deferential, passive
attributes of the classic subject. Rather, he participates in
(or more precisely, attempts to manipulate) the implementation
process in whichever institutions he can, utilizing a varied
repertoire of assertive, creative, and illegal methods to
secure his private welfare from the extensive Soviet public
sector. Our research also indicates that covert orientations
are to be found in every stratum in the USSR, but that
different educational groups prefer different manipulative
strategies, and these variations are probably rooted in both
tradition and in the structure of the confrontation between
citizens and the state. In a critique of The Civic Culture, a
distinguished Polish scientist who has considerable firsthand
experience with the workings of his country´s political system
notes that "Some social groups feel...that their chances of
performing effectively within the system are minimal or nil; in
this case political apathy may be interpreted in terms of the
critical evaluation of the existing system rather than in terms

of the psychological characteristics of inactive citizens"
(Wiatr, 1980, pp. 116-117). He suggests that Almond and Verba
err in their "tendency to explain discrepancies between
normative standards of democracy and political reality in terms
of psychological deficiencies rather than structural conditions
within the system." Though Wiatr makes these points with
regard to Western democracies, they seem equally applicable to
the Soviet Union and other socialist countries. Rational
political behavior in the USSR should involve pro forma
participation in the system's rituals, occasional contracting
of approved agencies in approved ways in order to influence
policy implementation in individual cases, and more frequent
transactions with officials charged with policy implementation
for the same purpose. Ritualistic participation is rational,
not because it influences policy, but because it protects one
against charges of nonconformity and antisocial attitudes, and
for some it may provide emotional satisfaction. For others,
however, the effect is to emphasize the gap between rhetoric
and reality and to reinforce political cynicism.(23) Despite
the Khrushchevian rhetoric of the "state of the whole people"
succeeding the "dictatorship of the proletariat," only the
formal franchise has been broadened in the last decades. The
Soviet citizen participates politically in several ways, but,
except for a small elite, his (and especially her) ability to
influence policy decisions, even indirectly, is practically
nil. The citizen does have some ability to influence the
implementation of policy. But this can be done only on an ad
hoc and ad hominem basis, so that no systemic effects and
changes are felt. Despite the expansion of opportunities for
formal participation and the grudging increase in opportunities
for expressing opinions, the Soviet system remains
fundamentally directed from above. As Verba and Nie (1972, p.
113) comment in their analysis of political participation in
America:

> Particularized contacts can be effective for the
> individual contactor but they are inadequate as a
> guide to more general social policy... The
> ability of the citizen to make himself heard...
> by contacting officials...represents an im-
> portant aspect of citizen control. Though such contacts
> may be important in filling the policy gaps and
> in adjusting policy to the individual, effective
> citizen control over governmental policy would be
> limited indeed if citizens related to their government
> only as isolated individuals concerned with their
> narrow parochial problems. The larger political ques-
> tions would remain outside popular control. Therefore,
> though electoral mechanisms remain crude, they are the
> most effective for these purposes.

For the forseeable future the "larger political questions" will remain the domain of the _verkhushka_. Our respondents appear to be much more interested in private benefits than in democratic institutions. We infer from our analysis of respondents´ evaluations of Soviet bureaucracies and their dissatisfaction with its operations, that much of the Soviet population would probably be more interested in increasing levels of performance by the present system than in fundamental systemic change. Until such time as either of these comes about, the citizen is left to grapple as best he can with those small questions of daily life that he and those who administer the system must solve together.

<u>Notes</u>

1. Some of the better known works on these subjects are Connor and Gitelman (1977), Friedgut (1979), Hough (1976), Odom (1976), Oliver (1969), Schulz and Adams (1981), and Skilling and Griffiths (1971).
2. Falkenheim (1978, pp. 20-22) interviewed 37 émigrés from the People´s Republic of China and concluded that most saw political involvement as "time-consuming, competitve with attention to their personal interests, false, empty, and most often potentially dangerous." This did not make them passive or apathetic, for they did follow the media - "if you don´t grasp politics, politics will grasp you" - and engaged in the "rituals of support."
3. Bennett (1980) suggests that policy is not only the end result of decision-making processes; it also contributes to the process of reinforcing the dominant myths of the polity and preserving its social and economic arrangements.
4. Such a sample strategy might not be advisable for surveying in Western countries, but it must be borne in mind that a "randomized" method of sampling the Soviet émigré population would probably not result in a higher degree of inferential power with respect to the actual Soviet population than the quota technique used here. A more conventional sampling strategy could even have very adverse consequences, if, for example, the resulting random sample of the Soviet émigré population contained grossly disproportionate distributions of such variables as sex, age, region, and occupation.
5. For a thorough discussion of émigré research and controlling effects of sample bias see Inkeles and Bauer (1961, chap. 2). On the last point, see pp. 26-27.
6. See, for example, Friedgut (1979, p. 289); also Gray (1979, p. 260).
7. The "knowledge" or "information" index was composed of three questions which asked the respondent to identify the Soviet Minister of Defense (Ustinov), the First Secretary of

the Ukraine Communist Party (Shcherbitsky), and the approximate population of the Soviet Union. This latter measure was administered as a multiple-choice question in which the correct response was 225-270 million. The proportions of respondents with primary, secondary, and higher educations who correctly answered at least two questions were 52.8%, 72.6%, and 86.8%.

8. Comparing our data with those of Almond and Verba (1963) is problematic for two reasons: First, Almond and Verba´s (pp. 95-96) index of political information is not similar to that used in the Soviet émigré study; second, their data are not broken down according to education. We must contend, however, that the data do support the inference that Soviet citizens possess a relatively fair amount of information about their system.

9. The text of the question posed to the émigrés was, "Were there people in the USSR with whom you would not discuss political and social issues?"

10. See Friedgut (1979, p. 314). Also, see White´s (1979a, pp. 110-111) discussion of the Soviet citizen´s split personality, an identity for public rituals and a face shown only to his friends and family.

11. The questions asked (for example, Can most people be trusted? Would most people try to cheat you if they got the chance? Could you trust most people in the Soviet Union?) elicited similar results in all three cases; only 15 to 18% of the émigrés gave the unqualified trusting response to the questions.

12. The actual text of the question was, "Let´s assume that a local soviet is considering a new law which you feel is unjust - could you do anything about it?" "If you were to try to change this law on the local level, how likely is it that you would succeed?"

13. One of our respondents, an elderly woman from Leningrad, worked as a nonstaff instructor of a district executive committee (raiispolkom), and also served as secretary of the electoral commission for the raion soviet. She disliked the agitation work connected with elections. "It was most unpleasant, especially when people realized how absurd this show was." The commission was always headed by a Party member, and its members were told that their primary obligation was to see that every resident of the district would turn out to vote. Since the polls closed at midnight, at around 10 or 11 p.m. messengers would be dispatched to the homes of those who had not yet voted. Her old bedridden mother was the recipient of such a call. The messenger told the slightly deaf old lady, whose Russian was not very good in any case, that she had to fulfill her civic obligation (dolg)." The woman became furious: "I never borrowed any money in my life and I have no obligation (dolg) to any one!" But of course, she did owe the state her vote.

Voting is not the only activity of this nature.
Participation in political rallies and discussions or in some
of the voluntary associations which abound in Soviet life may
be similarly motivated, although the latter may offer symbolic
and material rewards which are the prime motivation for joining
and participating. See, for example, Odom (1973). On the
hollowness of membership in Polish organizations, see Sadowski
(1979).
14. The émigré data on "citizen-contact" variables confirm
this. The vast majority of the respondents who contacted
soviet deputies, control commission officials, and others
sought help in solving a personal or neighborhood problem, or,
more often, they were attempting to procure a government
service, such as employment or housing, that had not been
routinely granted by the bureaucracy.
15. Since the question concerning attitudes toward pension
agencies was asked only of those who had actually received a
Soviet pension, the data could not be incorporated into Table
7. However, the responses fell within the predicted range.
For example, more than 72% of those who answered advised
patience or writing a letter of appeal.
16. See, for example, Azarova (1979). She notes that more
than two-thirds of district and city social security inspectors
in the Russian republic have neither higher nor secondary
specialized education. She strongly criticizes red tape,
"illegal acts of employees," and the appeals process, whereby
citizens are supposed to get a hearing on the size of the
pensions. She goes so far as to imply quite clearly that the
administration of pensions to the USSR is inferior to that in
other socialist countries, citing specific examples.
Other articles along these lines are Tarasova (1976) and
Tosunian (1981). The latter (p. 11) describes some of the
pension officials: "Often the nature of the bureaucrat does
not depend on his appearance. For some, rudeness and
caddishness are the way they treat all visitors. Others are
polite, well-mannered, speak softly to everyone, but they are
nevertheless capable of confusing the simplest cases. Many
experienced employees are well versed in the nuances of their
job, but they use their knowledge, however strange it may
sound, not to benefit but to harm their clients."
17. Examples include Plekhanov, "Order na kvartiru,"
Literaturnaia gazeta, July 25, 1979, p. 12; Ia. Ianovskii, "O
sudebnoi grazhdanami i zhilishchnostroitel'nymi kooperatibami,"
Sovetskoe gosudarstvo i provo No. 1, 1967; "Fiancees with
Dowries," Pravda, January 20, 1979, translated in Current
Digest of the Soviet Press 31, 3 (February 14, 1979);
"Discussing an Urgent Problem: An Apartment for the Newlyweds,"
Sovetskaia Rossia February 14, 1979, translated in CDSP 31, 8
(March 21, 1979). A well-known novel on the subject is by the
recently emigrated Vladimir Voinovich, The Ivankiad (New York:
Farrar, Straus and Giroux, 1977).

18. Cited in Morton (1980, p. 250).
19. Corruption is involved in admissions even to military schools. Krasnaia zvezda reports a case where a general got his relatives admitted despite their poor grades and admits this is not an isolated case. "When applications to the military school are being considered the admissions committee is beseiged with phone calls... There are really two competitions for admission: the regular competition and the competition of relatives" (Filatov, 1980, p. 2).
20. In Orel province in 1979 only 179 of 323 graduates of agricultural institutes showed up to their assigned jobs. Some "`signed in´ only to vanish immediately afterward... In all fairness it must be said that not all farm managers create proper conditions under which young specialists can work...  In other cases they simply `forget´ to provide them with apartments...leave them on their own to solve all the problems of everyday life." See Troyan (1980).
21. See the frank article by the first secretary of the Georgian writers´ union, Tengiz Buachidze (1975, p. 12).
22. On the concept of the citizen-bureaucrat encounter as an "exchange relationship," see Hansenfeld and Steinmetz (1981). See also Hasenfeld (1978). More broadly, see Katz and Danet (1973).
23. Unger´s (1981, p. 122) interviews with 46 former Soviet political activitists of the Party and Komsomol lead him to conclude that "they did not believe their own participation to be effective... The combination of compulsion and formalism which characterizes participation in the Komsomol and party arenas clearly provides no scope at all for the development of a sense of efficacy. Indeed, one may well hypothesize that it has the opposite effect, that the induction of the individual into the `spectacle´ of Komsomol and party activities produces not a sense of efficacy but of inefficacy, not subjective competence but subjective incompetence."

Appendix 1. Construction of the
Hostility/Alienation Scale

The hostility/alienation scale comprises four measures that attempt to elicit the respondent´s overall evaluation of or affect toward the regime and its institutions. These questions are listed below:
1. "Sometimes oikutucs and government in the Soviet Union seemed so complicated that a person like me could not really understand what was going on." Do you agree strongly, agree, disagree, or disagree strongly with the statement?
2. "The Soviet press, radio, and television never tell the truth." Do you agree strongly, agree, disagree, or disagree strongly?
3. "Which of the following statements most accurately describes your relationship to the Soviet regime?" At one time

I was favorably disposed, but then became opposed ("mildly
hostile"). I was always opposed to the Soviet regime ("very
hostile"). I was always in favor of the Soviet regime ("very
favorable"). I once opposed the Soviet regime, but then became
favorable to it ("mildly favorable"). I was indifferent,
neutral, didn´t care (coded as missing).
   4. "To what extent did you consider the Soviet Union your
own country?" Always, sometimes, rarely, never?
The frequency distribution for the dichotomized
hostility/alienation scale is: Hostile Group, 36.1% (419);
Non-Hostile Group, 63.9% (742).

Appendix 2. Construction of the
Political Participation Scale

   The participation scale consists of variables which denote
two different styles or modes of political activity. The first
mode of participation is what Verba and Nie (1972) call
citizen-initiated contact. The second type of variable denotes
activity that is much more support-oriented than citizen
contacts. The variables used in the construction of the scale
are listed below:

Citizen-initiated activities
   writing a letter to the editor of a Soviet newspaper
   contacting ispolkom/raiispolkom official
   contacting a procurator
   contacting a People´s Control Commission
   contacting an elected soviet deputy

Support-related activities
   holding an elected office
   membership in the Communist Party
   membership in the Komsomol

   The scale itself is a simple summation of the number of
activities of both types that the individual engaged in.
Respondents who had not performed any activities were labeled
as Passives; those who performed either one or two acts were
low participants; those who reported three or four acts were
labeled Moderates, and those who engaged in more than four
activities were high participants. The frequencies for the
scale are: Passives, 23.9% (278); Low, 62.5% (726); Moderate,
11.5% (134); High, 2.0% (23).

Appendix 3. Construction of the
Local Political Competence Scale

   The political competence measure consists of two
instruments from Almond and Verba (1963) on local competence:
the perceived ability to "do something about an unjust law" and

248

the estimated likelihood of changing that law on the local
level. We recoded the variables so that response levels were
equivalent, and summed each respondent's scores on the two
variables. Those who were positive of their efficacy in both
questions were coded in the high range of the political scale;
those whose answers were mixed were placed in the medium
category; and those who responded negatively to both questions
were placed in the low range: Low, 91.8% (1018); Medium, 5.3%
(62); High, 2.8% (33).

References

Aliev, G. Interview. Literaturnaia gazeta, November 18,
    1981, p. 10.
Almond, G.A. The intellectual history of the civic cul-
    ture concept. In G.A. Almond & S. Verba (Eds.),
    The civic culture revisited. Boston: Little, Brown,
    1980, 1-36.
Almond, G.A., & Verba, S. The civic culture. Prince-
    ton, NJ: Princeton University Press, 1963.
Azarova, E. O zashchite pensionnykh prav grazhdan.
    Sovetskoe gosudarstvo i pravo, 1979, 2, 44-49.
Barghoorn, F.C. Politics in the USSR (2nd ed.).
    Boston: Little, Brown, 1972.
Bennett, W.L. Culture, communication, and political
    control. Presented at the Annual Meeting of the
    American Political Science Association, Washing-
    ton, D.C., August 18, 1980.
Bailer, S. Stalin's successors. NY: Cambridge
    University Press, 1980.
Brown, A., & Gray, J. (Eds.). Political culture and
    political change in Communist states (2nd ed.). NY:
    Holmes and Meier, 1979.
Buachidze, T. Protektsiia. Literaturnaia gazeta, Jan-
    uary 8, 1975, p. 12.
Connor, W.D., & Gitelman, Z. (Eds.). Public opinion
    in European socialist systems. NY: Praeger, 1977.
Dzhafarli, T.M. Izuchenie obshchestvennogo mneniia -
    neobkhdimoe uslovie priniatiia pravil'nykh
    reshenii. Sotsiologicheskie isseldovanie, 1978, 1,
    69-75.
Falkenheim, V. Political participation in China. Prob-
    lems of Communism, 1978, 27, 18-32.
Filatov, V. Plemianniki: k chemu privodit protektsiia
    pri prieme v voennoe uchilishche. Krasnaia zvezda,
    November 12, 1980, p. 2.
Friedgut, T.H. Political participation in the USSR.
    Princeton, NJ: Princeton University Press, 1979.
Gitelman, Z. Becoming Israelis: Political resocialization
    of Soviet and American immigrants. NY: Praeger,

1982.
Gray, J. Conclusion. In A. Brown & J. Gray (Eds.),
Political culture and political change in Communist
states (2nd ed.). NY: Holmes and Meier, 1979, 251-272.
Hasenfeld, Y. Client-organization relations: A systems
perspective. In R. Sarri & U. Hasenfeld (Eds.), The
management of human services. NY: Columbia
University Press, 1978, 184-206.
Hasenfeld, Y., & Steinmetz, D. Client-official encoun-
ters in social service agencies. In C. Goodsell (Ed.),
The public encounter: Delivering human services in
the 1980s. Bloomington: Indiana University Press,
1981, 83-101.
Hough, J. Political participation in the Soviet Union,
Soviet Studies, 1976, 28, 3-20.
Hough, J., & Fainsod, M. How the Soviet Union is
governed. Cambridge, MA: Harvard University
Press, 1979.
Inkeles, A., & Bauer, R. The Soviet citizen. Cambridge,
MA: Harvard Universitry Press, 1961.
Jowitt, K. An organizational approach to the study of
political culture in Marxist-Leninist systems.
American Political Science Review, 1974, 68, 1171-1191.
Katz, E., & Danet, B. Bureaucracy and the public.
NY: Basic Books, 1973.
Kiselev, V.P. O povyshenii deistvennosti prava v
bor´be s protektsionizmom. Sotsiologicheskie
Isseldovanie, 1981, 1, 151-154.
Loginova, N. Chervi kozyri. Literaturnaia gazaeta,
January 23, 1980.
Morton, H. Who gets what, when and how? Housing in
the Soviet Union. Soviet Studies, 1980, 32, 235-259.
Odom, W. A dissenting view on the group approach to
Soviet politics. World Politics, 1976, 28, 542-567.
Odom, W. The Soviet volunteers. Princeton, NJ:
Princeton University Press, 1973.
Oliver, J. Citizen demands and the Soviet political
system. American Political Science Review, 1969,
62, 465-475.
Prikhodko, D.N., & Pan, V.V. Obrazovanie i sot
sial´nyi status lichnosti: tendentsii internatsional-
izatsii i dukhovnaia kultura. Tomsk: izdatel´stvo
Tomskogo Universiteta, 1974.
Sadowski, C. The fragile link: Citizen voluntary associa-
tion and polity in People´s Poland. Unpublished
doctoral dissertation. Department of Sociology, The
University of Michigan, 1979.
Schulz, D., & Adams, J. Political participation in communist systems. NY: Pergamon Press, 1981.
Sharlet, R. Concept formation in political science and
communist studies: Conceptualizing political par-

ticipation. Canadian Slavic Studies, 1967, 1, 640-649.

Skilling, H.D., & Griffiths, F. Interest groups in Soviet politics. Princeton, NJ: Princeton University Press, 1971.

Tarasova, V.A. Okhrana subiektivnykh prav grazhdanin v oblasti pensionnogo obespecheniia. Sovet-skoe gosdarstvo i pravo, 1976, 8, 133-136.

Tosunian, I. Vot dozhivem do pensii. Literaturnaia gazeta. September 30, 1981.

Troyan, S. They never arrived for their assigned jobs. Izvestiia, June 11, 1980, 3. Translated in Current Digest of the Soviet Press, July 9, 1980, 32, 16-17.

Trud, October 16, 1980, p. 4.

Uchitel´skaia gazeta, January 15, 1980, p. 2.

Unger, A. Political participation in the USSR: YCL and CPSU. Soviet Studies, 1981, 33, 107-124.

Verba, S., & Nie, N. Participation in America. NY: Harper and Row, 1972.

Verbitsky, A. Vziatki, vziatki, vziatki. Novoe Russkoe slovo, August 4, 1981, p. 2.

White, S. Political culture and Soviet politics. NY: St. Martin´s Press, 1979(a).

White, S. The USSR: Patterns of autocracy and indus-trialism. In A. Brown & J. Gray (Eds.), Political culture and political change in Communist states (2nd ed.). NY: Holmes and Meier, 1979(b), pp. 25-65.

Wiatr, J. The civic culture from a Marxist-sociologial perspective. In G.A. Almond & S. Verba (Eds.), The civic culture revisited. Boston: Little, Brown, 1980, pp. 103-123.

RUSSIAN POLITICAL CULTURE AND SOCIALIZATION

Frank M. Sorrentino

Introduction

The purpose of this article is to explore, discuss and evaluate the Russian Political Culture. By Political Culture I mean the psychological orientation toward social objects; it refers specifically to political orientations - attitudes toward the political system and its various parts, and attitudes toward the role of the self in the system.(1)

This article will deal mostly with the peasants. The bearers of power in the Soviet Union are largely the children of peasants or those who are no more than two generations away from peasant background. It is assumed that there is continuity in a society from one generation to another. While the assumption is unprovable, it appears highly probable.

I will assume that the kind of experience a child has within his primary family group will be internalized to form the basis of his later expectations as to how the role of powerbearer and of subordinate, of leader and of lead, will be played in his wider social group.(2) I will also assume that "a given culture rests on an internalized and more or less unconscious system of mental images or models for the regulation and challenging of the psychological needs of individuals and for signaling what is sanctioned and approved, or forbidden and punished. The way authority rules are exercised within a society sharing such an internalized unconscious system will be conditioned by the qualities of this system - including its rigidities and irrationalities based on the cultural `myth´ concerning human nature."(3) The main mental mechanisms involved in transferring the internal system of the members to the interpretation of their external world are those of displacement and substitution, and of projection and identification. "It is precisely this shared regulation of biopsychological need systems and authority relations which impart to a culture its distinctive modal characteristic social rules."(4)

"A society does not make decisions solely on physiological rhythms and raw material available, it chooses some foods and rejects others as impure. For example, the people of England treat goat´s milk as disgusting whereas the people in Spain drink it regularly. Preference and avoidances are inculcated until children no longer question them but regard them as human nature."(5)

The transformation of physiological hunger into cultural
appetite is a particularly concrete illustration of how
psychological and emotional needs are patterned and modified by
culture. It is more difficult to demonstrate how love and
aggression are patterned and modified because it can only be
shown indirectly and by inference through prolonged observation
of many variables. There seems to be no inherent reason why a
political culture study cannot be made in regard to political
expectations and demands as any other set of political
variables.

     I have justified this study as both proper and of some
value. I would like to establish the primary hypothesis of
this paper. It is that the political culture of the particular
society will shape the way Communism takes form. Russia has
been and remains a peasant culture. The perspective is that
the minds of men and therefore their actions are seen to be
ruled by their total experience, not by ideas alone. "The
ideology that works is never precisely what its founders had in
mind: Communism as dogma is static but what a society may
think of as communistic - and that is their guide to action -
must change as the people, and more especially the leaders,
grow in experience and alter in outlook."(6)

     The Marxian view of man being members of a class and
history being determined by where they stood in regard to the
means of production is overly simplistic. In the case of the
Russians, "These peasants were poor but they were also as
people and as forces in history something much more: not just
men struggling for a meager living, not just inefficient
agricultural instruments, not just exploited members of the
lowest estate in the czar's empire but creators and creatures
of a distinctive culture which has been fashioned in rural
isolation and preserved against the otherwise pervasive changes
of the modern world. The man in the village was a human whole,
greater than his economic parts."(7)

     I will use a combination of psychological, anthropological
and historical methods to discuss this subject. It is my
belief that this is the most accurate way to understand this
phenomenon.

                    Russia: A Religious History

     About the middle of the 17th century Russian society split
into two. The city and the village had developed separate
cultures. While the cities modernized, the rural areas
remained in isolation. With the formation of the Soviet state,
Russian history became one again. It could not just continue
from the czarist days, but had to go back to its immediate
background - that of the history of the Muscovite state -

                              254

usually dated from the 14th century. The Muscovite society considered itself a religious rather than a national community and was organized politically as Ivan IV saw it, for the benefit of orthodox Christians. To be orthodox was to be Russian.

Orthodoxy and isolation molded cultural unity. The Muscovite state known as Holy Russia was "a land of innumerable churches and incessant chimes, of long services, pious prostrations and severe fasts."(8) It was a land "as uniform in religious ideas as only an uncultured nation can be."(9)

The czar and the patriarch representing the temporal and spiritual power ruled together sharing the title of "gosudar" sovereign. After the death of Patriarch Adrian in 1700, Peter the Great joined secular and ecclesiastical power in his own person.

The two powers in operation, nevertheless had always given effect to the same will like the "two arms of God."(10)

In the 15th century, after Constantinople fell to the Turks (1453) and the Russians threw off the Mongol yoke (1480), Muscovy found itself the only politically independent center of Eastern Christianity. In 1472 Ivan III married the niece of the last Byzantine emperor and thus acquired a claim to direct succession from Constantinople and Rome. He began to use the title "Czar" (from Caesar) and adopted the Byzantine double eagle as the symbol of Russian monarchy. Moscow then stood forth as the champion and guardian of the whole orthodox east, "the last and only refuge in the world for the true faith and right worship." According to the monk Philotheus, "the church of old Rome fell because of the apollinarian heresy; the gates of the second Rome, Constantinople, have been heavied down by the axes of the infidel Turks; but the present church of the Third Rome shines in the universe more resplendent than the sun. All of the empires of the Orthodox Christian faith have come together in a single empire. Thou art the sole emperor of all the Christians in the whole universe. For two Romes have fallen, but the Third stands and the Fourth shall never be."(11) The Russian began to view his local church as co-extensive with universal Christian consciousness which it alone embodied in all its original purity and completeness for all the Christians in the world. It alone possessed the whole truth and had therefore nothing more to learn, nothing to adopt in the matter of faith, but needed only carefully to preserve the treasure entrusted to it. History is regarded as working out Divine Providence through the czar with a messianic mission for the Russian people.

Under increasing western influence introduced by Peter the

Great, a new cultured elite was being formed. It was a product of a modernizing government but it developed into a tragic misfit, the Russian intelligentsia. It existed between an unenlightened government and the dark masses. Its capital, St. Petersburg, rivaled London, Paris and Vienna in its beauty and sophistication. But Russia westernized was Russia still. Its cultural and mental traits were un-European and uniquely Russian. In fact, they were more likely anachronistic reminiscences of an earlier cultural age. Nikolai Berdiaev has remarked: "There is the characteristically Russian search for an integral outlook which would give an answer to all questions of life, unite theoretical and practical reason and give a philosophical basis to the social idea."(12) This can be generally viewed as a manifestation of Russian messianism which might be explained as the subconscious memory when Russian society embraced a system of having an answer to all the questions of life. Again according to Berdiaev, "Russians are always inclined to take things in a totalitarian sense, among the Russian radical intelligentsia there existed an idolatrous attitude toward science (natural and social). What was a scientific theory in the west, a hypothesis, or in any case a relative truth, partial, making no claim to be universal, became among the Russian intelligentsia a dogma, a sort of religious revelation."(13)

In order to develop this point of how attitudes are carried from one generation to another, it is important to explain the religious training of children.

"Even before the child can speak it is likely to get its first training in the partly religious, partly magical practices of Orthodox Christianity from the babushka looking after it; it will learn to prostrate itself, to make the sign of the cross to avert the evil spirits and dark fears which threaten to take possession of human beings; and as it learns to speak it will learn the ritual prayers."(14)

"From age five it partakes as fully in the ritual of confession and absolution. An insight can be gained by describing this ritual, the priest stands while the penitent kneels at his feet; the penitent makes a ritual statement of his great sinfulness and the priest cross-examines the penitent, accusing him of sins he is not conscious of having committed. The penitent will usually confess because the priest may refuse absolution on the grounds of contumely and spiritual pride if the penitent persists in denying these sins." (15) This stems from the assumption of "the co-existence of both good and evil in all individuals and in the attitudes towards individuals, and expectation that friends could behave like enemies was combined with the expectation that this behavior could also be reversed - by confession,

repetance, and restoration of the former-state. Little
distinction was made between thought and deed, between the
desire to murder and murder itself. All men will be held
guilty, in some degree, of all human crimes."(16) At the end
of confession the penitents are in a highly emotional state,
weeping and beating their foreheads; the priest may impose
penances of fasts or other moritifications. Absolution gives a
feeling of great psychological relief and is highly valued. It
gives justification to sin in a widely quoted proverb, "If you
do not sin you cannot repent."(17) It, therefore, can be seen
that the Orthodox Church has had a great influence on the
people. The concepts of truth being one and the universal
sinfulness of man, coupled with Russian history´s messianic
role of acting God´s will in the preservation and expansion of
pure Christianity through God´s agent, the czar. "Yet powerful
the Orthodox Church has been in maintaining to some extent the
Russian community feeling, the Church could not be responsible
for it alone, or we could fix similar feelings in every
orthodox country."(18) It is for this reason that one must
look at the environmental factors and the social structures
that influenced the lives of the Russian peasants.

The Patriarchal System

"The striking fact of peasant life was its primary
communism. The basic social unit was not the person but the
household. The basic political unit was the village. To each
of these an individual inextricably belonged and could not act
or be thought of in his daily existence apart from them."(19)
Peasant life did not encourage individualism. Farming
techniques were so archaic and inefficient that it just barely
paid men to go to the trouble of cultivating the land. To
subsist the peasant needed continuous productive labor as well
as a reasonable share of good luck. One man cannot make it.
Even a man and a wife together could only hope to keep alive.
It thus can be seen how important children were. It was
primarily to produce workpower that peasants married. If she
proved unable to bear children the marriage was annulled.
Marriage was essentially a contract to establish a mutually
profitable association to multiply crops and workers. (20)

Evidently, the productive unit thus formed had to function
as a unit dedicated wholly to its objective and disciplined
effectively to the task. "The family was unified under the
absolute authority of the head. A totalitarian society in
miniature, it demanded ideally not only the obedience of all
members to the head of the group, but the dedication of each to
the purposes of the whole. He disposed the tasks, judged the
performance, flogged the recalcitrants. Nothing could take
place in the realm he controlled without his knowledge. Like a
modern dictator, a father was held to act as a trustee and

embodiment of the will of all. Right answers were found not by polling the members but by perceiving directly their higher good."(21)

The Russian peasants practiced Communist principles long before Karl Marx made ideals out of them. "From each according to his ability, to each according to his needs," has been pragmatic household doctrine for as long as the family existed. In practice, both peasant and modern communist have valued and therefore tended to reward the effective rather than merely the needy. The operative principle became, "To each according to his work."

"In rural society, father's authority was natural, not legal, and it had natural, not legal limitations. As an individual outside his household he was tightly bound by laws, regulations and customs. But within it he answered only to God, and even there rather for his devotion to proper ends than for the humane exercise of his power. If he failed the family it was too bad for the family."(22)

The patriarchal family developed to save the individual by suppressing him. Historians have missed the point when they say that the tyranny of the czars conditioned the Russians to despotism. It was the family structure that permitted both the czars and Communist rule. The autocrat was the image of authority which each child learned to accept in the family. "The physical superiority of the father is the child's first experience of authority, the father is the breadwinner, the father is bigger, stronger, wiser, and wealthier than the children. Conflicts with him have consequences. As a result of a long and painful pressure the individual learns in the family not merely to take account of authority but also to respect it. He adopts himself to circumstances by rationalizing his dependency and finding satisfaction therein."(23)

A person reared in the dependency of a patriarchal household is schooled to act only in ways explicitly permitted. He tends to abdicate his willpower and even his desires and to function as an agent of necessities for which he can feel no personal responsibilitiy. Once accustomed to mental dependence he can hardly escape it. This craving for command, it should be noted, was a craving only for command by a father or father figure. Lacking any abstract notion of institutionalized power, the peasant was loyal to God rather than to the Church, to the czar rather than to the imperial government, to Stalin rather than to the Party. Father was always right, not so his agents. He reasoned that if the father of all the Russians were not so far away and also knew the truth, he would repudiate those who acted harshly or unworthily in his name.

The Mir

It is interesting to note that "mir," the word for village, also means world.(24) The peasant village mir was a little orderly world, a federation of sovereign peasant households. "The mir held the land and distributed it, good and bad, in a patchwork intended to be as equitable as possible between families. The mir fixed the times of ploughing, sowing, and however much dispute and bad feelings there might be between individuals and families, no one rebelled against the authority of the mir."(25)

The meetings, many times heard heated discussions but the business of the mir was not to find consensus; it was to locate the collective will and activate collective authority. When objections were no longer heard a decision became unanimous and binding on all villagers, whether present or not.

Again this concept of truth being one and independent of what a majority believed was reinforced by this system. The peasant character developed out of this community. Primitive rural life has complications that overwhelmed primitive man with tension and anxiety. The peasant almost from birth is on the defensive against a hostile environment and typically develops traits that protect him against a hard father, a sharp neighbor, a powerful landlord, a meddling official and all the manifold castrophies of nature. He learns to practice caution, suspicion, shrewdness, ruthlessness and even treachery to endure or subvert the forces that are inherently stronger than he, yet must somehow overcome.(26).

The peasant´s fortitude had no flavor of equanimity. He submitted to the exactions of the Kulak or the lash of the police as he submitted to the seasons, only because he figured that by accomodating himself, like grass to wind, he might survive. He played the role of the lowly one, but would rather play the master. At the first opportunity he was ready to seize the whip of power and lay on. Because the habit of obedience was engrained in the mass, the whole of society was despotically organized. "The Tsar, in absolute command of the nation, was only the diadem of tyranny. Under him, by the interrelationship of command that made every man both slave and master - a linkage of arbitrary power which, historically, extended unbroken from the czar´s ministers to the peasants flogging his wife or work horse, each within limits imposed here by law, there by custom, was supreme and irresponsible. Difference in rank affected not the kind of power wielded by only its extent."(27) Nature is cruel, or rather is quite literally inhumane. The more tightly obedient man is to the compulsions and rhythms of nature, the less can he be expected

259

to exhibit the gentle human qualities called civilized because civilization alone is friendly to their exercise. Humanism and liberalism are urban, not rural products. In the village there was no view of mankind, only a number of men and women whom one knew well and of whom only too obviously were not worth a horse or a cow.

Birth and death belong to the routine of any form. A peasant lavished care on his animals to prepare them for slaughter; neither action could move him deeply. The Russian peasant prepared for his own death calmly. Survival was by numbers. Out of many born some would surely live, thus the family would survive and that was the most important thing. "Most men are likely to give back to their environment as good as they get - hardly anything better. Victimized by arbitrary power the peasant is perhaps drawn to exercise it where he can, if not revenge, at least in compensation. Having been humiliated he may wish to humiliate; having been subjected to brutality he may wish to torture. He undoubtedly acts simply as he is conditioned to act, without any kind of malice. He is cruel because he is himself inured to cruelty. He inflicts suffering as he takes it without emotions."(28)

The Russian Personality

The outstanding trait of the Russian personality is its contradictoriness - its ambivalence. "Russian behavior oscillates in large swings in relation to self, to primary love objects, authority figures, and outgroups. The quality of these serving is best understood in terms of an oral character: at one end the ominvorousness, the lust greed, the tendency to rush at things and to `swallow them whole,´ the overflowing vitality, spontaneity and anarchic demand for abolition of all bounds and limitations."(29)

"At the other end of the melancholy, dreary apathy, suspicion, the anxious and sullen submissiveness, moral masochism and grudging idealization of a strong and arbitrary authority were thought of as the only safeguard against the excesses of the Russian nature."(30) Whether in his bacchanalian mood or in his depression, he always needs direct, spontaneous, heart-to-heart contact and communication, and respects that need in others. He is intolerant of hauteur formalism, and bureaucratic protocol and hierarchy, preferring the direct, informal face-to-face handling of problems.(31)

At the other end of the spectrum is the expected role behavior of the elite. Since Peter the Great, the Russian elite has tried to wage war against the Russian character in order to catch up to the West. (32) As Erikson describes it,

Boleshivism is sort of a delayed Protestantism,(33) a sort of
Puritanism which would include the traits that are necessary
for an industrial society - neatness, orderliness, economy,
punctuality, cleanliness and the like. "By the standards
common in the Occident, the mass of Great Russians pay too
little attention to these compulsive traits; usual complaints
of people who have to work for them are that they are
chronically unpunctual, wasteful, careless and so on. These
compulsive traits have been consistently found in people who
have had childhood where early and severe cleanliness training
took place. This is one area where the contrast between the
Soviet elites and the mass population is most marked. The
Soviet leaders consider these traits of great social value and
demand them and, when possible, impose them on the rest of the
population."(34) This is often referred to by psychoanalysts
as the oral-anal conflict in Russian society.

In regard to authority, I have already stated that in the
patriarchal family, there exists certain images of authority
which would eventually be used to interpret the world beyond
the family. "The child's own image of immediate adults is of a
people subject to higher authority and filled with ambivalent
sentiment and submissive love for the authority figure. A
little later he learns that even grandfather is but a serf and
can be bullied and humiliated by his brain or the police.
There is indeed a series of infinite regresses leading over
grandfather to the brain and so to the Tsar and to God."(35)
Sons identify themselves with grandfather's arbitrary power and
play their own role in due course in a like manner. Aggression
passes down the family structures, the grandmother coerces and
torments her daughter-in-law, the adult sons assert their
status by beating their wives and children.(36)

The typical childhood of a Russian peasant was spent in
helpless participation in scenes of his elders - crude
emotional oscillation between tenderness and brutality. His
perceptions of his own father are strong and good as well as
cowardly and weak, his mother as lovable but despised, and
himself as powerless and dependent. This experience also
develops a capacity to tolerate silently the most contradictory
and powerful emotions.(37) The nature of the identification
made is highly paradoxical. The little boy will tend to
identify himself with the victim's position - with the tender,
persecuted, suffering mother. There is much evidence that this
theme is later elaborated into the hero fantasy of rescuing the
oppressesd, suffering mother figure. But it makes for a kind
of despair about weak tender emotions which can never lead to
happy endings. These are covered over by a defensive
identification with the power and cruelty of the male line, by
repression of the inner mother's boy in favor of rugged,
swaggering masculine behavior. The mother figure is treated

with sadistic contempt in fantasy and also revered, pitied and idealized.(38) Girls will harbor much hostility toward men and rebellion against the marital role as a fate not much worse than death. Love is always tragic in Russia; the strong independent woman is admired.(39)

In 1917 the Revolution was thus very culturally congenial. "The authorities whom the Russians had thrown off had been weak and ineffective men, though remote in status, were too much like themselves; unorganized, lazy and greedy. Into the power vacuum stepped Lenin, a father, speaking in angry peasant tones yet in terms of Western `science,´ `promising bread and land and revenge on oppressors,´ a severe order and a material plenty." (40)

The Soviet mastery of Russia has given evidence of their Russian-ness and hate of their Russian-ness. Their aim was to create an industrialized society which was to change the life style of the people in a fundamental way. The individual would move to the city, away from the farm and patriarchal society, and move into an urban society where there would be less dependency on the climate and family structure. In the process, however, this would require that the citizen would have to develop traits that would serve the new demands of the industrialized state. It is here where their difficulty began and remains. It was their Russian-ness that allows them to ride the storm. There was their wholesale, uncompromising acceptance of Western patterns of socialism but with their paranoid lack of discrimination of finer shades between black and white. They had a magical faith in the entirely scientific rational nature of their system supplanting the sense of mission of the Orthodox Russian Christianity, ever watchful of the least error which would enable "the devil to get in." It was thus consistent with the deepest modal fantasies that before long they re-established the persistent authority model inherent in the Russian mind. An absolute power which is the sole repository of truth and which cannot be questioned or deviated from.

Conclusion

In the exposition and analysis of the Russian political culture several points can be made. The Russian culture has a long history of strong authoritarian rule and the major source of this rule is the authoritarian father. It is this figure that conditions and socializes the young into dependency to the arbitrary will of the father and faith. The Russians view man as having original sin, therefore, the father disciplines the son to deal with evil that lies inside him.

Russians have also viewed themselves as having a unique

262

role in the history of the world – that of bringing the Orthodox religion to everyone. The messianic role has remained while the cause has changed.

The basic challenge, however, is that of modernization. The Russian political culture was congenial to Marxism and the development of the Communist State. The belief of a utopian vision of society coupled with strong authoritarian leadership to accomplish this goal in their society and in spreading it to the rest of the world is firmly entrenched in the Russian political culture. However, the Marxian tenet of industrialization pose some problems. Industrialization is generally desired by the population, however, to accomplish this goal successfully requires the adaptation of such anal traits such as punctuality, orderliness and hard work. These traits are resisted in the primary oral culture of the Russian people that emphasizes dependence, acceptance of authority and the belief that fate determines the future. Thus it can be seen that there is a paradox within the culture. It allows for Marxism-Leninism to be accepted yet it seriously hampers its ability to succeed. Soviet leaders have had to adjust their policies and their emphasis on varying aspects of their ideology to adapt to these realities.

It therefore can be concluded that the Russian political culture significantly affects the form that Communism has taken in Soviet Russia.

Notes

1. Gabriel Almond & Sidney Verba, The Civic Culture, (Princeton, NJ: Princeton University Press, 1963), pp. 13-14.
2. Henry V. Dicks, "Some Notes on the Russian National Character," in The Transformation of Russian Society, ed. by Cyril E. Black (Cambridge, MA: Harvard University Press, 1960), p. 637.
3. Ibid.
4. Ibid.
5. Geoffrey Gorer & John Rickman, The People of Great Russia: A Psychological Study, (NY: W.W. Norton, 1962), p. xi.
6. Nicholas P. Vakar, The Taproot of Soviet Society, (NY: Harper, 1962), p. 3.
7. Ibid., p. 5.
8. A. Kornilov, Modern Russian History, (NY: A.A. Knopf, 1917), Vol. 1, p. 40.
9. S. Kravchinsky, The Russian Peasantry: The Agrarian Conditions, Social Life and Religions, (London, 1888), p. 2.
10. Vakar, p. 20.
11. Ibid.
12. Nickolai Brediaev, The Origin of Russian Communism,

(London, 1955), p. 38.
13. Ibid., pp. 20-21.
14. Gorer, p. 101.
15. Ibid.
16. Margaret Mead, Soviet Attitudes Toward Authority, (Santa Monica: Rand Corporation, 1951), p. 67.
17. Gorer, p. 102.
18. Wright Miller, Russians as People, (NY: Dutton, 1961), p. 80.
19. Vakar, p. 32.
20. Ibid., p. 33.
21. Ibid.
22. Ibid., p. 38.
23. Max Horkheimer, "The Problem and its Setting," in The Family, Past and Present, ed. by Sten (NY, 1938), pp. 905-907.
24. Eric Erikson, Childhood and Society, (NY: W.W. Norton, 1963), p. 361.
25. Miller, p. 81.
26. Vakar, p. 81.
27. Ibid.
28. Ibid., p. 72.
29. Clyde Kluckhorn, "Recent Studies of the National Character," in The Transformation of Russian Society, ed. by Cyril E. Black (Cambridge, MA: Harvard University Press, 1960), p. 45.
30. Dicks, p. 640.
31. Ibid.
32. Ibid.
33. Erikson, p. 393.
34. Ibid.
35. Gorer, p. 39B.
36. Dicks, pp. 69, 642.
37. Dicks, p. 642.
38. Ibid.
39. Vera Dunham, "The Strong Women Motif," in The Transformation of Russian Society, ed. by Black, (Cambridge, MA: Harvard University Press, 1960), pp. 469-483.
40. Dicks, p. 644.

THE WILLING SUSPENSION OF DISBELIEF

David K. Shipler

Teaching Political Values
On the eleventh day of April no hint of spring had yet
reached Moscow. Snow covered the ground, and the frosty cold
kept the children heavily bundled as they walked up Yermolova
Street to a school next to our apartment house. This school
specialized in teaching English, and inside a third-grade class
of nine-year-olds the teacher was writing a poem on the
blackboard. When she had finished, she had the whole class
read it aloud:

> April, April, are you here?
> Oh, how fresh the wind is blowing,
> See the sky is bright and clear.

They huddled over their desks, writing the lines in their
copy books. Along the walls were the usual red and white
slogans and posters, except that they were in English, an
English far too complicated for these youngsters to understand:
"The Draft Constitution of the USSR"; "A New Step on the Road
of Communism"; and below, long texts headed "Brezhnev's
Commentary"; "All Education Available"; "Nationwide
Discussions"; "Internal Commentary." When they had finished
copying the poem, the teacher began drilling them with
questions.

"Is it spring or winter?" she asked, nodding through the
windows at the snow.
"It is spring," said the child she had called on.
"Yes. All together."
"It...is...spring." No trace of irony.

The children had read the parable of the fox and the
crane, and as the teacher held up a picture, she called on a
girl to retell the story. It was Aesop's fable. The fox
invites the crane to dinner, serves soup in a shallow dish, and
thinks it very funny that the crane, with its long beak, cannot
drink the soup. So the crane invites the fox in return, serves
soup in a tall, narrow jar that the fox cannot get its snout
into, and says to the fox, "I am so glad to be able to return

your courtesy. I hope you enjoy your dinner every bit as much
as I did mine when I visited you." The girl in class stood and
stumbled haltingly through the tale while her deskmate prompted
her in whispers that the teacher could not possibly have failed
to hear. But the teacher made no effort to silence the
deskmate, and when the girl had finished, she received a
khorosho ("good") from the teacher, as if she had done it all
without help.

"What is this?" the teacher asked, holding up a bugle tied
with a red pennant.
"A Pioneer bugle," said the class in unison.
"And this?"
"A Pioneer drum," said the class. "A Pioneer flag."

Children whispered to one another, talked, drew funny
pictures and giggled. A boy played with a small mirror at his
desk.

"All of you have Pioneer ties," the teacher continued,
ignoring the misbehavior and pointing to the red neckerchiefs
the children were wearing.
"Do you have a Pioneer tie, Andryusha?"
"Yes, I have a Pioneer tie," the boy replied.
"Are you a Pioneer?"
"Yes, I am."
"Is he a Pioneer, Peter?"
"Yes, he is."

Then she asked them to open their notebooks and write down
new words. "Slogan," she said, translating it into Russian,
lozung, so they would understand. "Have you slogans in your
class? How many slogans have you in your class?" The kids
looked around the room and counted.
A girl rose to her feet. "We have eleven slogans in the
class."
Then the teacher wrote on the board, "Long Live!"
"Write it please. `Long Live!´ The transaltion is Da
Zdravstvuet!" It may not come in very handy when these
children are speaking English, but the expression in Russian is
ubiquitous, strewn around the streets on banners and posters.
"Long live our Pioneer organization!"
A boy in the front row piped up irreverently, "Long live
the fox!" Titters.

It seemed to me when I had finished sitting through this
class that it contained most of the main ingredients of Soviet
teaching. It was spring by the calendar, and the poem of the
day talked of clear skies and a fresh breeze, and therefore,
cold facts outside the window could be stared down with the

266

supreme reality of the lesson, without so much as a smirk. It
was a good metaphor for the political dimension of education,
in which reality and truth are not investigated but
constructed. A small girl could be praised for parroting the
whispers of her classmate, a style of cheating widely ignored
by Soviet teachers, who express and reinforce concern for the
façade rather than the substance. Slogans obviously designed
for older grades could be hung on walls to meet some superior's
requirement, regardless of the children's inability to
comprehend them. The trinkets and props of political
orientation could be laced inextricably into the lessons; the
only fresh wind that day was the small boy's sudden,
spontaneous statement "Long live the fox!"

But the atmosphere in the classroom was warm despite the
dull material, fairly disciplined despite the buzz of talking
and wriggling in seats, and aimed at serious learning. Sincere
praise came from quick students. "Bob got up early," said the
teacher. "What does `early´ mean?"
   "Rano," said a little girl with the correct Russian word.
"Umnitza!" The teacher beamed. "Smart little one."

Americans who have gone to Catholic schools at home
invariably see parallels between the political and religious
instruction, between the inevitable portrait of Lenin and the
painting of Jesus on the wall. "It's like parochial school,
with catechism," said Kevin Klose. "The Young Pioneers in war
are like the martyrs of the church."

His wife, Eliza, added, "You have your picture of Christ
up there, and you say your prayers, but the important thing is
that you do your work well and learn."

To live contentedly within the intricate construction of
political attitude that schools build carefully for children,
it is also important never to confront whatever disbelief may
stir inside you, lest the spell be broken. This, I came to
feel, was one of the earliest lessons of Soviet childhood, and
it helps keep many, perhaps most, adults in a spirit of
political comfort with their country and their system. To
disbelieve is to destroy.

The academic levels of Soviet schools are uneven and
inconsistent, somewhat less impressive in many cases than the
formidable image invented by the American inferiority complex
in the years after the first Soviet Sputnik beat us into space.
The specter of ordinary Russian teenagers doodling brilliantly
in mathematical formulas on the tablecloths of Leningrad cafés
has faded now, partly as the society has opened slightly and
the official press has displayed more candor. One discovers
quickly that there are good schools and bad, just like

everywhere else in the world, and that parents plot and scheme to get into the main cities and escape the dreadful rural schools. Well-educated men and women from Moscow and Kiev, working for a few years as engineers on railroad and oil-drilling projects in the Siberian wilderness, told me of their dissatisfaction with the local village schools and their decision to leave their children back home with grandparents for a decent education, much as American parents might sacrifice to send their youngsters off to fine boarding schools. A teacher´s journal, <u>Uchitelskaya Gazeta</u>, reported in 1978 that such low-level high school graduates were being admitted to pedagogical institutes that these future teachers had to spend the first two semesters or more learning how to write grammatically.

Yet the basic three R´s are the main stuff of the classroom, supplemented by what might be called the three P´s - politics, party and patriotism. The relationship between the two dimensions is complex, one intertwined with the other. In high school years the courses in chemistry, physics, languages, history, and the like are so demanding that teenagers who emigrate to Israel and the United States often find the load suddenly lighter - to their relief and their parents´ dismay. But political orientation is an integral part of the diet as well, like bread with meals, and while it does not appear to detract from the seriousness of learning the lean scholastic skills, it makes an ample contribution to the stout convictions by which Russians view themselves and the world.

The nucleus of the creed is not Marx but Vladimir Ilyich Lenin, whose saintly wisdom and moral vision become the original introduction for all children to the blended reverence for communism and country that guides their growth. Lenin is portrayed as the embodiment of goodness, the avuncular figure of kindness who sits and talks with little boys and girls as Jesus tended His flock. Lenin´s name is used today to inject righteousness into the most unlikely places. I once came across a flower show in Baku adorned with a huge banner proclaiming, "For a Leninist Attitude Toward Nature!"

Every class in every kindergarten has its portrait of Lenin, usually in a special corner of the room where drawings and picture books portray his life. In one kindergarten´s holiday show a cute little girl with ribbons in her hair recited a small verse about "Dear Lenin, he taught us how to live in a friendly way." Parents and grandparents chuckled warmly and burst into applause. In elementary and high schools the corner is often located in the room set aside for Pioneer and Komsomol meetings, and it is called the Red Corner, a term usurped from earlier tradition when Russian Orthodox families had, in their homes, a Red Corner for the icons and the oil lamps or candles, often backed by a swath of material the color krasny ("red"), of the same root as krasivy ("beautiful"). Indeed, krasny itself meant "beautiful" in antiquated usage, so Red Corner was Beautiful Corner and Red Square, Beautiful Square.

On page 310 of the reading book for the third grade, a section of poems and stories about Lenin is headed "Lenin Lived, Lenin Lives, Lenin Will Live." Quotations from Lenin are sprinkled generously through textbooks on most subjects (if an author omits them, he is usually advised by his editor to insert a few, and college students quickly learn that a line or two from Lenin, Brezhnev, and Andropov is a prerequisite for a good grade). On the other hand, I came across a zoology textbook for sixth and seventh grades that contained not a single reference to Lenin. It fulfilled its obligation by opening with a dissertation on the sinister effects of religion in retarding zoological research. And many middle-aged Russians who grew up under Stalin discern some relaxation of the Lenin cult. "Children's propaganda about Lenin used to be crude and massive," said a loyal Soviet citizen in his forties. "Now I just don't see it anymore. He was portrayed like a saint, halo around his head. He could do no wrong. Once, the story went, he broke a pitcher. At first he lied about it, then two hours later was bothered by his conscience and declared that he had done it. It was nauseating, you know. And nobody believed it. Everybody laughed at it."

But not aloud. The most solemn place in all the vast reaches of the Soviet Union is the glazed brown-red granite mausoleum in front of the high brick Kremlin walls, where Lenin and Stalin once lay side by side and now Lenin lies alone, embalmed or waxed so that thousands upon thousands of pilgrims, who wait for hours in freezing long lines and are admonished by guards to stand erect and straighten their clothes, file silently into the darkened tomb and around its interior walkway to gaze upon the face of greatness. A friend said he once saw an old Russian woman cross herself as she came into view of the body.

Even the rich political humor by which Russians preserve their sanity rarely indicts Lenin himself. A joke that comes about the closest involves the famous artist commissioned to do a painting entitled "Lenin in Zurich." After weeks of work the painter lugs his huge work into the Kremlin, where the Politburo assembles for the unveiling. But when the cloth is pulled aside, there is a gasp of horror. There, lying in bed together, are Lenin's wife, Nadezhda Krupskaya, and Trotsky.
"Where's Lenin?" someone demands.
"Lenin's in Zurich," says the artist.

Then there's the one about Lenin coming to life and showing up at a Thursday morning Politburo meeting. Andropov and his cohorts are fawning, obsequious, asking what they can do for him. Lenin says that all he wants is a room and a supply of all the issues of Pravda since his death. This is duly done, and he locks himself in for weeks of reading. As time passes, concern grows, and finally someone is dispatched to enter the room to see what has happened. All the Pravdas have obviously been thoroughly read, and the room is in disarray. But Lenin is gone. There, on his desk, is a note in his hand: "You have made a mess of it. I've gone back to Zurich to start again."

The famous joke about the train to communism exempts Lenin from its bitter wit. Stalin, Khrushchev, and Brezhnev are on the train when it stops. When it does not go again, Stalin orders the crew taken out and shot. That done, the train still does not go. So Khrushchev orders the crew rehabilitated posthumously. Still, the train doesn't move. So Stalin and Khrushchev turn to Brezhnev. He pulls down the shades and says, "Now let's pretend the train is moving." It remains to be seen how this will be updated by Andropov's vulnerable qualities.

Late one night in our office, at the end of a tedious day covering the Twenty-fifth Party Congress, my colleague Chris Wren began speaking whimsically to the ceiling, which we imagined to be crammed with microphones. "Think I'll go see Yuri Zhukov tomorrow," Chris said loudly. Zhukov was a crusty cold warrior and Central Committee member who wrote table-thumping polemics for Pravda and delivered anti-American diatribes on television, a thoroughly distasteful character to anyone with an open mind. "I like old Yuri," Chris continued. "The only trouble is those Lenin jokes he's always telling. They're really embarrassing. But I guess once you get to be on the Central Committee, you can get away with anything."

It was a delicious prank, and we both were doubled up in hysteria, but a couple of months later Chris began to have trouble with the authorities. He was among three American correspondents - including Alfred Friendly, Jr., of Newsweek and George Krimsky of the Associated Press - accused in the Soviet weekly Literaturnaya Gazeta (frequently a KGB outlet) of working for the CIA. Official interviews started getting a bit more difficult to line up, and trips outside the Moscow area, requiring Foreign Ministry approval, encountered obstacles. There was no hard evidence that his joke was the cause, but it was a possible contribution. Lenin remains surrounded with taboos.

When Ina Rubin and her husband, Vitaly, were granted

permission to emigrate to Israel, she took boxes of books to
the post office to mail to her new home. They were heavy and
required lots of stamps, many of which bore Lenin's portrait.
She was sticking them on quickly in great numbers, pasting them
in whatever way would fit best, when a woman clerk ran
shrieking out from behind a counter. "What are you doing?" the
clerk yelled. "What are you doing?"
    "I´m pasting on stamps," Ina replied calmly.
    "But - you are putting our dear Lenin on upside down!"
shouted the woman, out of control. She demanded that Ina
remove the stamps and put them right side up. Ina refused, and
so the clerk painstakingly did it herself. In Stalin's day
this would have been cause for arrest; Ina, however, did not
hesitate to tell me about the incident while she was still in
Moscow, and it did not foil the Rubin's plans to leave.

    Lenin's birthday is an occasion in schools for canceling
lessons and holding pompous ceremonies and lectures at which
the memory of the Boleshevik leader becomes as much a patriotic
theme as an ideological vehicle. At a practice session in a
kindergarten in the Cental Asian city of Dushanbe a small boy
in a sailor's costume held a bouquet of white carnations and
sang:

In many countries children live,
And everywhere all children love Lenin.

    The song went on for a while about Lenin. Then, as other
children joined, the verses moved smoothly into adoration of
the motherland:

We children live better than anybody on earth,
Our country is happy and lucky.

    There was a song called "Beloved Motherland," exactly the
same one I heard back in Moscow, where Debby, Laura,(1) and I
attended a show at Kindergarten No. 104 celebrating the
anniversary of the Bolshevik Revolution. These were evidently
centrally planned pageants. "We get the songs from books," one
teacher said.

    At 4:00 P.M. a few days before the holiday the Moscow
kindergarten's music room began to fill up with mothers and
grandmothers and a few grandfathers, one of whom was armed with
a stillcamera and a jury-rigged light (he had no flash
attachment) that he was fumbling with, trying to plug into a
wall socket. At the lower right-hand corner of the Lenin
portrait that dominated the front wall a puffy red ribbon had
been tied in a fancy bow.

    First the girls skipped in, wearing red skirts, red

271

ribbons in their hair, holding a red flag in each hand. Then
came the boys in olive drab helmets with big red stars on the
fronts, reciting and singing songs about the Revolution, the
"glorious holiday." Other children were dressed in blue and
yellow, holding bunches of plastic autumn leaves, chanting,
"Glory to our great motherland, let her future be stronger and
redder." Then the whole group broke into song as a teacher
played the piano:

Our motherland guards the peace,
Victorious Red Army,
Our motherland is strong,
She guards the peace.

"Long live the Great October!" shouted a teacher.
"Hoorah!" yelled the tiny voices.
"Long live our great motherland!" the teacher shouted.
"Hoorah!"

Boys in helmets and a girl in a nurse's outfit then
marched with the drawn swords to martial music, shouting,
"Forward!" and "Hoorah!" Two contests were held. In the
first, two boys sat on chairs. When the whistle was blown,
they had to run to a rocking horse, put on a helmet, put on a
sword, sit on the horse, and draw the sword into the air.
Whoever did it first won. A teacher asked the children to give
a critique of the loser, to tell what he had done wrong. They
replied inexplicably that he had put the sword on first, when
he should have started with the helmet. Then two girls tried,
running to the rocking horse, putting on the helmet and the
sword, drawing the sword. The second contest began with a
recited verse by two girls and a boy about the harvest,
followed by a song about growing things in a garden. Two
youngsters then raced each other back and forth to pick a
cabbage, a handful of potatoes, and some carrots from two
chairs and put them into a truck. The teacher let the other
children judge the winner.

After the contests came a song about rain and wind and
flowers. A boy, dressed up as rain, did a dance with girls
carrying red and white parasols. Other children danced with
tambourines. A couple of poems about nature were recited.
Finally, a buxom teacher, dressed as a farm woman with a basket
over her arm and a scarf tied around her head, announced
greetings from the collective farm "where we live gaily and
sing." She did a little dance with a handkerchief, then stood
behind a big pot, singing about making soup from a potato,
cabbage, carrot, peas, and beets. When she was finished, she
dipped a spoon into the pot as if to ladle out soup - but the
spoon came up heaped with candy, which she scooped into bowls

272

and passed to the children. The program ended, and as people got up to leave, the director of the kindergarten sent two small boys over to present Laura, then six, with a little brown teddy bear.

The children's show represented fairly well the variety of themes that are woven together in these younger years; Lenin, the motherland, the military, nature, the virtue of work on the land. In a classroom for six-year-olds one bookshelf was devoted to a row of folders containing pictures, which the children would talk about to improve their diction. All but two of the nine folders had political or patriotic overtones: "Our Army," "Pioneers," "Collective Farm Labor," "Our Moscow," "V.I. Lenin," and so on. The only exceptions were "Times of the Year" and "Transport." The same was true of a middle school's library in Riga, the capital of Soviet Lativa. The shelves reserved for first and second graders learning to read contained the following sections: "Lenin," "The Great Patriotic War," "How Children Lived Before the Revolution," "Life of Children Abroad," "Our Motherland," "About the Lives of Noteworthy Communists," "About Plants," "About Animals," "About Cosmonauts in Space," "About Science and Technology," "I Want to Know Everything," "Being Strong, Brave, and Agile," "Cheerful Books," and "Children of the Soviet Land."

There is no escaping the political message. It pervades every dimension of education, becoming so ordinary that it seems as natural and unremarkable as chalk on a blackboard. Even in the apolitical subject of mathematics, textbook authors sprinkle exercises with word problems designed to remind pupils of the superiority of the Soviet state and to sensitize them to the fundamental mechanics of a socialist economy. In the third-grade math book, for example:

The first cosmonaut was a citizen of the Soviet Union, Communist Yuri Gargarin. He made a flight around the earth in 108 minutes. How many hours and how many minutes did the first flight around the earth last?

In our country the world's first atomic icebreaker, Lenin, was built. What is the length and width of this icebreaker if it is known that 1/8 of its length consists of 16 meters 75 centimeters, and 1/5 of its width is equal to 5 meters 52 centimeters?

A brigade of oil workers must drill 6 kilometers 650 meters per year. In the first year it drilled 4 kilometers 900 meters, and in the second 1 kilometer 50 meters less. Did the brigade fulfill its annual plan? If it overfulfilled it, but how much?

A sovkhov [state farm] pledged itself to give the
state 3,350 tons of cotton. But it gave 4,200 tons,
then added another 1/10 of this quantity. By how
many tons did the sovkhoz overfulfill its obligation?

If the authors' political instincts lapse, there are
always authorities to issue clear reminders. Roy Medvedev, the
dissident historian who worked in a textbook publishing house
during Khrushchev's era, told me of some amusing encounters
with the censors that revealed principles he said were
unchanged today. "The censor comes to us and says, `Comrades,
what is happening in your office? You have a Russian-language
textbook, with exercises: "Write here, co___ism." And the
children must put in the missing letters, "communism." Or
"so___ism," and the children must put in the missing letters,
"socialism." Or take "pa__y." The children must write,
"party." These sacred words, and you don't write them in
full!'" Roy declared, imitating the censor's pompous tones.
"We say," Roy replied, quoting himself and his colleagues,
"`That is the method of teaching the Russian language. We must
teach the children to write these words correctly. And if they
write "communism" with one m instead of two? And if they write
"party" not with an a but an o? That will be worse. How are
we going to teach children to write these words unless we teach
them the same way we teach other words?'
"`No, dear comrades,' the censor replies. `You don't need
to mutilate these words. You may not mutilate such important
words.' So as a result of this dialogue, in all textbooks the
words `communism,' `party,' `socialism,' all words connected
with ideology, are written in full.

"Or," Roy continued, "they come to us and say, `In
Russian-language textbooks, thirty percent of the text must be
political text.' It means that you must cite Khrushchev and
Lenin - then it was Khrushchev, now Brezhnev [and today
Andropov] - and other political figures. We said, `Dear
comrades, we can't. The children will end up knowing the
Russian language more poorly because political figures speak
badly. Pushkin, after all, was better, and Lermontov, or
Gogol, or Tolstoy. That is why all Russian-language textbooks
are made up from the classics. We wrote dictations.
Schoolchildren are not going to be interested in taking
dictation on excerpts from speeches by Khrushchev, right?'
"`No,' they said to us. `One-third of the text must be
political compostitions. They don't have to be from
Khrushchev, but about politics. For example: "The Soviet
economy is the best economy in the world."' We said, `Let
geography deal with that. Let history deal with that. What
does that have to do with Russian language and literature?'
They made us do it."

There were times when the wind blew in the opposite direction, Roy said, and orders came down that Russian-language texts were not to include so many political passages because children speaking ungrammatically would make mistakes and pronounce stupidities. But generally a high political content was required, and "security" matters were examined with farcical scrutiny.

"Suddenly a directive arrived: Change the precise measurements, the lengths and widths, of the cities of the Soviet Union. But we all know that Moscow has such and such a width and such and such a length, and textbooks have published the dimensions for a hundred years. Now we were supposed to change the widths and lengths in textbooks that had published them for a hundred years. We said that in regard to new cities, it was understandable. OK, foreigners don´t know about them. The censor said, `In the textbooks you must move Moscow, Leningrad, Kiev one degree north or one degree south.´ And we had to obey that. Then an order came to prohibit the mention in all textbooks of bridges. Because a bridge is a strategic structure that could be used in an invasion by adversaries, bridges must be secret. It is understood that new bridges can be secret. But they told us, `Exclude photographs of all bridges.´ In our textbooks we have pictures of Krimsky Bridge, the Kamenny Bridge in Moscow, in Leningrad the bridge of the Winter Palace. This was funny. I took the censor some stamps, postage stamps. `Look, please: bridges.´"

When Yuri Gargarin became the first human being to fly into space, Roy called, an order came to insert a page devoted to the flight in every textbook. "That was just," he said. "It was a particularly important event. But the country is large, textbooks are stable. The printing plants are all over the Soviet Union, and the time Gargarin flew in space was April, and printing had already started for the next year. The printers work all year. You can´t print that many books in two days. It was impossible. They said to me, `No. A decree has come down that Gargarin will be in all textbooks.´ So what to do? The mat with the Gargarin page was delivered to all printers in May, Roy said, but books printed previously didn´t have it. "So there were perhaps twenty million books without Gargarin and three million books with Gargarin. The twenty million books we distributed in the provinces - Kazakhstan, Novosibirsk - and the three million we put in Moscow, the Moscow Oblast, Leningrad. And everybody was pleased. Nobody knew about it."

It is the inflated regard for country that stands as the centerpiece of all that can be called political in Soviet education. Lenin may be idolized to small children as a naive combination of George Washington and Jesus Christ, and older

275

students may be immersed in detailed studies of the history of the Communist Party, of the principles of class struggle and internationalism as seen through the ideological amalgam that the Russians call Marxism-Leninism. But ultimately the power of these ideas to move Soviet citizens lies in their patriotic content, in their association with the adoration of country. As a concept of righteousness, a vehicle of analysis, and a focus of loyalty, the nation rises above competing elements of Soviet doctrine and shapes the teaching of political values.

This is accomplished first by preposterous boasts, as in the kindergarten song, "We children live better than anybody on earth,´ then by a mixing of patriotic and communist symbols so that the difference between the Soviet Union as a country and communism as an ideology is blurred into near invisibility, and finally by mystical appeals to the sanctity of the motherland in bold contrast with the frightening, alien, hostile world outside. A synthetic history is an essential ingredient of the process.

The reading book for nine-year-olds, for example, opens with a passage declaring, "The world´s first socialist country has become the world´s first country for children´s happiness. `All the best for the children´ - that has become law in our country." Page 105 of the book carries with a color picture of a welder and a construction worker surrounded by a network of steel girders. "Soviet People Build a New Life" is the caption. It is followed by one poem extolling the motherland, and another about the Soviet flag, and a passage on "the emblem of the Soviet land," the hammer and sickle. Further along is a reading entitled "Our Goal - Communism." The passage asks:

> Is it possible to find, in our current life,
> the first examples of how communism begins? Look
> carefully and see: There is already in our life a
> considerable amount that the people receive by the
> rule and law of communist society. Under communism
> each will receive not according to his work, as under
> socialism, but according to his needs. Thus, for
> example, in our country today everyone can already
> receive as much free medical care as needed. All
> children are taught free of charge - all equally,
> whether their parents earn much or little. This is
> also done according to communism. But the most
> important way in which communism is beginning is in
> the work of our people.

The paragraph continues on the theme of labor´s high productivity.

Sometimes the tone is one of simple boosterism, chamber of

commerce style, as in another textbook used in all schools to teach Russian to Russian children. A paragraph about "Our City" and how it grows each year, how "beautiful cars and buses go throughout the city" is full of italicized words that are to be put into the right number and case. Another paragraph reads: "Our scientists, engineers, and workers invent and manufacture ever more wonderful cars, machine tools, equipment. Electricity has long lit the gay lights of the cities and towns. Our people will build new rockets and spaceships. Cosmonauts will fly to other planets."

Here also, the deeper invocations to patriotism emerge. "Read the sentences. 1. We have a huge beautiful, excellent motherland. 2. The most beautiful, the warmest and dearest name - motherland. 3. Motherland - this place, where we live, where we were born, where we grew up."

And some pages later: "An exercise on the word zemlya ["land´]. 1. On all sides spread the land of the sovkhoz. 2. There is no end to the expanse of this land. 3. There is no land richer than ours. 4. In the sky shines the sun, and on the land walks the wind. 5. Spring, summer, and fall the machine operators work the land. 6. They are pleased with the land; it gives a good harvest."

One exercise probes the root of the word for motherland - rodina, which has as its core the original building block for the verb "to be born," the nouns "parents" and "relatives," the adjective "native," and the concept of one´s own, something integral to oneself. Rodina-Mat ("Motherland-Mother) the exercise is called, and it touches a point of fondest emotion in both children and adults. "We call our country rodina ["motherland"] because we were rodilis ["born´] in her, because in her our rodnoi ["native"] language is spoken, and everything in her is, for us, rodnoye ["our own"]." For any Russian, and certainly for those of nine, the sentence evokes strong feelings. "When we pronounce the word `motherland,´" reads an exercise in another text, "before us opens endless open space - woods, fields, mountains, snow, sand, rivers, seas, islands."

For older children, there are attempts to resolve the obvious contradictions of the high-pitch nationalism that grips Soviet society with the internationalism that lies almost dormant in the ideology of Marxism. High school seniors - that is, those in the Soviet tenth grade - age sixteen - get a social studies course whose textbook of communist ethics and social morality includes the following section, under the heading "Social Duty":

Patriotism is the deep social feeling consolidated by
centuries and millenia of the existence of isolated
native lands. In it is found the expression of love
for the country in which we were born and grew up, for
its history, people, inseparably linked with what we
feel ourselves part of. Patriotism concerns the best
manifestations of human nature, motivating people
toward active efforts in the name of their countrymen.
Socialist patriotism is linked with the selfless
devotion to progressive social construction, the
business of communism, with the feeling of great
pride in the Soviet people, which is building for
all humanity a road with a bright future. More than
once, poets and writers have described how a person,
confronted with the face of death, remembers the
motherland, his native house, the weeping willow or
the birch. For the Soviet people, the motherland
embodies not only the sweet picture of nature. We
find her form in recollections of Pioneer meetings
and Komsomol youth; she personifies for us a unique
atmosphere of comradeship, which defines the life of
the Soviet collective. The motherland and socialist
construction merge in the consciousness of the Soviet man.

In other words, it is OK to be both a nationalist and a
Communist; in fact, is it desirable because since the Soviet
Union is at the vanguard of the Communist movement, devotion to
the country becomes devotion to the cause. There is no
suggestion that a true Marxist might ever question the behavior
of the Soviet Union as a national entity or that the
government´s conduct in support of its state interests might
not always coincide with communist ideals. The two forces are
fused. This is more than just a curious and rather boring
piece of pedantry in an obscure tract: This textbook is used
by every graduating secondary school student in the country.
It is the best distillation of the party´s notions of how the
emerging "Soviet man" is supposed to think. And although there
is usually slippage between the printed word and the reality,
in my experience of talking with young people I found general
acceptance of the textbook view on the blurring of nationalism
and communism. In fact, the issue is rarely examined, even by
disaffected young adults in private conversation.

"Socialist patriotism" is presented as more mature than
plain patriotism; students are warned away from "blind feeling"
and are informed that "to Communists, so-called `kvas
patriotism´ - the unrestrained extolling of everything that we
have - is deeply alien." Kvas is a malty, beerlike drink made
from burned bread and served at curbside from dirty yellow
rolling tanks into widely shared glass mugs. It can be good if

you're really hot and parched, but otherwise its stale
bitterness is an acquired taste, symbolic of the tough, earthy
simplicity of the peasant in harmony with unthinking reflex.
The textbook declares:

> The kvasnoi patriot is ready to brag even about the
> quantity of shortcomings... Real love for the motherland
> is love with open eyes. We are rightly proud of
> our remarkable success, but we uncover shortcomings
> bold and apply all our strength to eliminate them.
> We are not ashamed of imitating the better achieve-
> ments of other peoples, and can learn something from
> the capitalists as well... To the Soviet people,
> national egotism and chauvinism are alien... In the
> future Communist society, all peoples of the world
> will stand as one friendly family. And then patriotism
> and internationalism will dissolve into one great
> feeling of love for all humanity and for its cradle
> - the planet Earth.

Still, kvas patriotism is precisely what is taught in the
lower grades, in those songs and stories that children feed on
from their earliest days in kindergartens and that foster
unquestioning love of country and denigration of others.
Esteem for the military is an important concomitant, beginning
with the themes of war that run through holiday pageantry;
moving into the first reading books, which are sprinkled with
drawings of heroic soldiers flanked by imposing missiles;
ending in the high school social studies texts with their
precise passages on the military obligations of every citizen.
For the little ones, the soldier is portrayed melodramatically,
with a sappy romanticism that would make most Westerners wince.
He is the defender of all that is dear, protector of goodness
and truth, and his exploits from war to war are mixed up into
the present so that time and history dissolve into the moment.
And children are heroes.

"Young drummer. The war was on," begins a passage in the
third-grade reading text, accompanied by a color drawing of a
drummer and men on horseback, riding with drawn swords beneath
a red flag. "The enemy encircled the division. In the
division there served a young drummer. At night he stood at
his post. Suddenly a light shadow appeared. Enemy! But the
fighters slept. The drummer with all his might beat the drum.
The fighters awoke, grabbed their rifles and beat off the
attack."

In an eighth-grade civics book entitled The Basis of the
Soviet State and Rights, the military section, called "Defense
of the Fatherland - Sacred Duty of the Citizen of the USSR," is

replete with religious terminology. "Our youth fervently love the Soviet Army and Navy," the chapter begins, "and preserve the holy memory of the wars, of those who perished for the freedom and independence of the motherland." A clear distinction is drawn between the Soviet armed forces and "the armies of bourgeois countries, which exist in the hands of the exploiters of violence with arms, terror with arms, imperialist agression and war. The Soviet armed forces laid down a glorious path of battle from the first heroic victory the hordes of counterrevolutionaries and interventionists in the years of the civil war to the full, utter defeat of German fascism and Japanese militarism in 1945... Our army is a united, friendly family, a school of internationalism, a school for the teaching of brotherhood, solidarity, and mutual respect for all nations and peoples." And so forth.

Elementary school classrooms are visited regularly by military lecturers, usually retired officers, who give chauvinistic pep-talks on the need for preparedness in an alien world. Civil defense drills include training with gas masks, usually primitive, homemade affairs of thick cotton and window glass for eyepieces; the effect is probably more psychological than practical. During the ninth and tenth grades, the last two years of high school, a compulsory military training course is given twice a week, and for several weeks the boys go to a military summer camp, where they learn many of the skills of boot camp. At fourteen they can join a repository of super-patriotism and infatuation with all things military, called the Voluntary Committee for Assistance to the Armed Forces, or DOSAAF by its Russian initials. In centers and clubhouses across the country, the youngsters and adults study military history and tactics, learn to shoot and to maintain truck engines and electrical equipment, and engage in other hobbies with military overtones. The theme continues into higher education. A friend in the prestigious Institute of Foreign Languages, whose graduates often go into diplomatic service, told me that all students were required to take a military course that met three times a week. "We study the American military," he said. "How many battalions, methods of defense. The whole institute is frighteningly militarized."

All this expresses and enhances the Russian's sense of isolation and adversity in relation to the world outside, a state of mind no more vividly conveyed and encouraged than in a third-grade book of readings. Beneath a drawing of a soldier in battle helmet, a caption says, "The soldier of the Soviet Army stands guarding peace, happiness, and freedom." There follows a short composition:

280

THE BORDER IS NEAR!

The soldier walked down the road. Along the dirt road of the border camp.

The soldier walked, not alone. He walked with his son. A big son - Pioneer, thirteen years old. He had come to his father on vacation.

A division of cavalrymen galloped by. A detail of frontier guards marched past; in the front, a great grey sheepdog.

"Our Rex," said the soldier. "Good boy! Twenty infiltrators to his credit!"

"We also train dogs for frontier duty! exclaimed the son.

"A job will also be found for you youngsters."

But all around bloomed apple trees and cherry trees. Bees and butterflies circled above the blossoms. And birds in the orchards sang clearly.

"Good," said the son.

"The border is nearby," said the soldier.

On the soccer field off-duty frontier guards pursued a ball. They used a horizontal bar on wheels.

In the woods a magpie flew out, flitting to the side away from the soccer players and suddenly landing calmly on one of the wheels as if nothing were happening. The magpie felt like drinking. She lowered her beak to a puddle - and drank.

Again she lowered her beak - and drank again. Then she spread her wings and flew back to the woods. And there, in the woods, stood tanks and armored cars. On the edge of the woods artillery was deployed. But the magpie was not afraid. Apparently she was used to it.

In the distance there were reeds, and beyond them a river. Not wide, calm, the water shining in the sun. Along the river runs the border. This bank is ours, and the other - not ours, alien.

"Quiet," said the son.

"The border is nearby," repeated the father. "Well, it's time for me to go on duty! Till evening!"

The soldier left for his post. The post was nearby. Along the side of the border.

On the bank of the river, the frontier guards stood stockstill in the bushes. The soldier stood still. He looked through binoculars at the reeds, on the nearby alien shore.

The border is near!

Learning Hypocrisy

Shura Sverdlova was nine years old when her teacher in Leningrad gave her class a thoroughly routine assignment. They were to read a story called "Vanya the War Hero," of a boy who spied against Germans and helped attack rural villages that served as German bases. Vanya came through to Shura as a very tough, very bad, rather mean boy, not a pleasant character

281

despite his heroic exploits. So when she and her classmates
were told to write an essay entitled "Why Do You Like Vanya?"
(not, of course, "Do You Like Vanya?"), Shura came home in
great distress. Her mother, Mira, knew quite well what was
expected: some high-brown platitudes on sacrifice and devotion
to the motherland, on fearlessness in defense of the sacred
soil. She herself was a teacher, and her field - college-level
history of the "bourgeois countries" - required finely tuned
political antennae. But Shura did not like the Vanya character
and just could not write that she did. Her mother backed her
up.

Even a decade later, after both mother and daughter had
emigrated to Israel, Mira´s recollections were full of the
anxiety of that evening, remembering how her small, sensitive
girl confronted the question of her own integrity and sat down
and wrote honestly why she did not like the war hero Vanya.
How would the teacher react? Would there be a low grade, a
public condemnation before the entire class? Would Mira be
called in? Would a report be made to her institute, casting a
shadow on her reliability? These were the tense uncertainties
that wound tightly through the evening and the next day, as
Shura was sent off with her heretical little manuscript.

The teacher was a young woman, bright and perceptive, who
responded in a fashion so unpredictable that Mira and Shura
were both amazed. She gave the essay a 5, the top grade, read
it to the entire class, and praised it for its honest
reflection of Shura´s real feelings. Then she asked how many
pupils shared Shura´s dislike of Vanya. Half the class raised
their hands. All but Shura had written lies.

Truth telling is not the forte of Soviet education. In
the structure of values the façade is more important than what
stands behind it; a smooth, unbroken surface of acceptance
comforts both teacher and pupil, political leader and citizen.
To crack the veneer is to violate the basic ethic of hypocrisy
and to embrace utter loneliness. There are few parents like
Mira Sverdlova to lend support, and few teachers like Shura´s.

Indeed, hypocrisy is taught as a virtue in effect. As
children learn what to say regardless of what they think, they
grow more responsive to outer form than to inner conviction.
There is not always a difference between the two: The
incessant saying and hearing of untruth have a numbing impact
on thought. But many Russians with their wits about them also
find that they must exist on disparate levels, keeping their
common sense to themselves, nurturing a careful schizophrenia.

Shura Sverdlova learned this in kindergarten, after she
had come home one day saying, "I´m lucky I was born in the

Soviet Union."

"Why?" her mother asked.

"Because children are starving in America." Her mother explained that it wasn't so. And she then began to teach her four-year-old not to talk outside the house about what was discussed at home. A four-year-old boy had absorbed the caution so well that it carried over to Israel, where he warned his father one morning to stop telling a Bible story because they were getting closer to the kindergarten and the teacher might hear.

Some teenagers master the slick technique of hypocrisy. "We had a boy who wanted to be a journalist," recalled Irina McClellan, the former high school teacher. "He started writing articles for some youth newspapers and magazines. He realized very quickly what would work in this society, what was permitted. In conversations he was open, but in writings he knew the formula. You see how they are corrupted so young. He was a careerist already, at the age of sixteen."

I saw a few such cases on a bulletin board in a school in Lativa, where tenth graders had been presented with questions to which they were expected to reply with firm expressions of disdain for material goods. This was a lot to ask of urban teenagers in a society that craves consumer items and whose most fad-conscious members will pay up to half the monthly wage of an average factory worker for a single pair of American jeans on the black market. But the kids performed as required. "Why do people try to surround themselves with things?" the questionnaire began. "Would you like to get an apartment, a dacha, many stylish clothes, and a car right after school, or would you prefer to earn them with your own labor?" The answers, hung there in a corridor for all to see, had a wonderful Sunday-school qualiy about them. Student after student renounced any desire for anything at all, condemning "thingism" as some malevolent disease foreign to their personal attitudes. "I, for example, hate things," wrote a boy named Igor Tarasov. "I think that the next ten years, with the approach of the ideals of communism, the materialist mania - thingism - will pass." An inventive girl commented that she would, actually, like to have a car - but just so she wouldn't be a burden on her parents.

The honest statement is such a novelty that younsters remember it for years. Mikhail, a lanky Moscow teenager, told me about a candid essay he once wrote in sixth grade, after a school celebration of a holiday devoted to "Young Antifascists." He had to write "about my general impressions of the day" and dealt with a story that had been told about a young Pioneer boy in wartime Estonia who had defied a fascist's command to take off his red neckerchief. Because he had refused, he had been killed. "I said the boy was foolish," Mikhail explained. "What did he accomplish? I didn't understand what was heroic about him. The teacher read the composition to the class, didn't say who wrote it, and asked for opinions. Somebody said that what was written was right. Somebody else said it wasn't right. You could feel that she wanted the class to denounce it, so a girl stood up and said it was all wrong." When the paper came back, however, it had been graded with a 5 for writing and a 4 for content. Mikhail judged her a good teacher because she had not been dictatorial but had merely nudged him gently in what she considered the proper direction. She had written on the composition, "Think about whether you're right."

Mira Sverdlova told me that she also tried, subtly, to nudge her classes on the history of "bourgeois countries," but in the opposite direction, "to put a positive accent, a nuance, to correct the official line," as she explained. "I thought there were informers in the class, so I had to be subtle, so much so that many students didn't understand." She drew a parallel between Nazi Germany and the Soviet Union, for example, by stressing that Germany had one party and that all newspapers said the same thing. "Some students saw it; you could tell by their eyes."

Few parents encourage political recalcitrance, however, preferring for their children the safer submissiveness to the line. "Parents say, `Don't talk too much,'" explained a Russian in his twenties whose father is a ranking party member. "They say it to defend themselves and the child. They say, `Quiet. Don't think about it.' They believe it is better to sit in a party meeting thinking about your lover, but with a serious face, raising your hand to vote at the right time – and everything is fine."

Russians often make fun of themselves on this score. There is a joke about the man who went to a clinic, looking for an eye and ear doctor. "We don't have an eye and ear doctor," said the receptionist, "only an eye doctor and an ear, nose, and throat doctor."
"I need an eye and ear doctor," the man insisted. "I keep hearing one thing and seeing another."

In Leningrad Debby and I saw an audience of mostly young adults go into excruciating laughter as a lanky pantomimist, Yuri Medvedev, impersonated a sleepy party member doing his duty at a "Mass Meeting," as the routine was entitled. The man sat in an imaginary audience (facing the real one), listening to an imaginary lecture. His eyes glazed over. With supreme effort he propped them open. His eyelids fluttered, then closed. His head fell back as he slept. Suddenly, at the right

284

moment, his hand popped up for a vote. He slept again, his
head lolling to the side. Another vote, and his hand came up
like a perfect machine. Again he slept, slumped forward, and
so on through every conceivable sleeping position, broken by
the obligatory votes. The crowd was in hysterics. Medvedev
then perked up as an imaginary superior sat down next to him.
Another superior sat on the other side, and one behind.
Fawning obsequiously, he catered to one and then the other,
trying to crouch and move so the official behind could see.
Finally he made his neck rubbery and held his head so far over
it seemed to sprout from his left shoulder, just so the
bureaucrat behind would not have to lean even slightly. Then
he began to figure out how he should react to what was being
said in the meeting. He took his first cue from the imaginary
superior on his left, glanced at the man, and laughed heartily
until he glanced to his right, saw a different response, and
abandoned his laugh for a glower. Back and forth he went, torn
between the superiors flanking him, laughing and frowning,
laughing and frowning until the meeting was over. At the end
he stood and walked slowly offstage, his head and shoulders
bowed in ignominy. In the audience the laughter ebbed into a
long moment of silence, before the applause.

A bitter moral on the loss of integrity, a therapeutic
release. But real life continues without the satire. In
classrooms it does not often matter how a child gets the right
answers, as long as he gets them. And because teachers are
judged partly by the performance of their pupils, cheating is
widely tolerated. "Yes, it´s very popular," said Irina
McClellan. "The year-end test is sent to the regional
committee. Teachers are afraid the tests will be badly done,
so they walk along the rows and help them. Sometimes they take
them into the corridors and give them notes. It is also done
in exit exams for the universities and institutes."

Cheating is so accepted and obvious that even visitors
can´t miss it, and Debby and I saw some ourselves. When a
teacher walked out of a sixth-grade physics class during a test
at Dushanbe´s School No. 35, the students, as if on signal,
turned to neighbors and whispered answers to each other. The
teacher could not have avoided noticing when she returned, but
she said nothing. In a corridor of a Moscow school, a class of
youngsters about to go into an exam prepared by writing answers
on their hands and folding crib sheets into accordion shapes
for easy concealment. In two classes at different schools we
watched as pupils were told one by one to close their books and
stand to recite lessons, all the while glancing down at their
deskmates´ books, left open within easy view.

Teachers have varied responses to this. "If she doesn´t

285

like you, she won't let you get away with it," said Mikhail.
"I went to a school for young workers. The teacher would walk
in the aisle, helping kids. But in a strong school there is
less cheating, and there are times when the teacher catches and
scolds kids. Students also know that you won't get a two [a
D]. You can say, `I don't know that, I don't know that, I
don't know that,´ and she'll say, "What do you know?´ `I know
that,´ and she'll give you a three."

Grades, as part of the façade, are constructed with
considerable bargaining among teachers, according to Irina
McClellan, and may have little to do with actual performance in
some cases. "At the end of the semester teachers´ meetings are
held to sum up results," she told me. "The mathematics and
literature teachers will say Ivanov is bad - 'I'll give him a
three if you give him a three´ - and they do it, like in the
market. They can't give bad marks because it's such a disgrace
for the school. I had two students who did not want to learn
English. I had to give them bad marks. At the teachers´
meeting I said I couldn't give them threes - they didn't know a
word. The director [principal] said, `I order you to give them
threes. Why do you care so much about your English? The main
subjects are literature and mathematics. Why do you try to
attract so much attention to yourself and your subject?´"

Pioneers and Komsomol
In the third year of elementary school, as children turn
nine, bright red neckerchiefs suddenly flare against the somber
brown and dark blue uniforms, signifying entry into the first
formal, institutionalized commitment to a political idea. The
children become Young Pioneers as naturally as they come of
age. They are inducted, in the illusion of having been
carefully selected, with fanfare and ceremony, with banners and
solemn oaths. But this passage is virtually automatic and
universal, like a puberty rite, a bar mitzvah, or a first
communion. Nobody is not a Pioneer. To refuse the oath and to
go without the neckerchief - that would be the lonely step into
a wilderness.

The induction ceremony has a military tone. Adult
commanders shout orders, and the children, scrubbed and neat,
march in precisely.
"Halt!"
"About...face!"
"Units, atten-tion! Eyes...left! Shun! Group commanders,
prepare to report! As you were!"
"Comrade Chief Pioneer Leader! The section of Pioneer
leaders of Class Three A, named after Feliks Edmundovich
Dzerzhinsky, is lined up for the ceremonial ritual formation!
All ten members are present for the ceremony of presentation of

286

the Pioneer scarf and badge."

Parents watch proudly. Children's eyes gleam as they take the oath. "I, Sulamsky, Aleksei, entering the ranks of the All-Union Pioneer Organization named after Vladimir Ilyich Lenin, solemnly promise before my comrades: to love my motherland fervently; to live, study, and fight as the great Lenin bequeathed us, as the Communist Party teaches. I promise always to observe the laws of the Pioneers of the Soviet Union."

The laws are as follows:

The Pioneer adheres to the motherland, the party, communism.
The Pioneer prepares to become a Komsomol member.
The Pioneer emulates the heroes of struggle and labor.
The Pioneer reveres the memory of the fallen fighters and prepares to become a defender of his motherland.
The Pioneer is persistent in studies, work, and sports.
The Pioneer is an honest and true comrade and always stands for the truth.
The Pioneer is a friend and leader of the Octobrists [members of a youth organization of younger children].
The Pioneer is a friend to other Pioneers and to the children of workers of all countries.

The adult commander concludes with a word of congratulation: "This day will be remembered throughout all your life. Ask your father, mother, or grandmother who was admitted to the Pioneers; they will always tell you about this because this is an unforgettable event. The Pioneer organization bears the name of Vladimir Ilyich Lenin from 1924, and according to our tradition, we always remember him on our brightest days and occasions. Atten-tion! A minute for Lenin's remembrance is announced! Place the wreaths!"

Valentin Vasiliev was nine, but he was not a Pioneer. He was a believer. Strictly speaking, in the cold irony of the Soviet lexicon, one cannot be both a believer and a Pioneer. The term "believer" (veruyushchii) is applied with official opprobrium to a believer in God, whose views are incompatible with the Pioneer's atheism. In practice, however, parents who are quietly religious rarely wish their sons and daughters friction in school and so encourage them to be overt Pioneers and secret believers. But Valentin Vasiliev came from a Pentacostalist family quite devout and fundamentalist in its conviction that there was only one God and that one should not worship Lenin.

The boy walked into School No. 36 in Vilnius, Lithuania,

one morning, took off his coat, and put it on the counter for
the old woman in the cloakroom. She reached for it in a weary
gesture of habit, then stopped as her eye caught something
strange. "Where is your Pioneer neckerchief?" she said
sharply. Valentin politely explained his remarkable failure to
become a Pioneer. The flabbergasted woman sputtered, wagged
her finger, and refused to hang up his coat, forcing it back
into his arms. The two stood at an impasse in the lobby,
children swirling into the building around them. The principal
was summoned, a haughty woman who knew the case all too well
and who told the boy sternly that of 2,000 eligible children in
the school, he was the only one who was not a Pioneer. "You
should wear a sign," she scolded," saying that you are a
believer."

More typically the neckerchief carries little political
emotion for children but is worn as a badge of pride in having
reached the appropriate age. The daughter of Jewish dissidents
recalled blushingly how pleased she felt to be seen walking to
and from school in her fresh neckerchief when she was nine and
how comfortable it became as she approached fourteen, the age
at which younsters move from the Pioneers into the Young
Communist League, Komsomol. The waning months in Pioneers
seemed endless, she remembered, and the neckerchief such a
garish advertisement of immaturity that she and her friends
used to take theirs off on the way home from school, just to
look older.

I once asked some young Western-oriented adults who were
mildly critical of the Soviet system what they saw as the most
important quality in a good Pioneer. "Honesty," said Natasha.
"To be devoted to your country," said Alyosha. "To defend the
young, respect the old." These are the Boy Scout, Girl Scout
ethics that occupy a large measure of the Pioneer
organization's mission. A revisionist cartoon of "Little Red
Riding Hood" on Soviet television, for example, had a young
Pioneer named Petya Ivanov as the hero. He tried to warn the
girl in the woods, but she took no heed. "Haven't you ever
read `Little Red Riding Hood´?" he asked. "No," she said, "I
myself am Little Red Riding Hood," and she went on her way. As
the wolf schemed, the boy scared him into thinking the hunter
was close at hand, pointed him toward a "shortcut" to
Grandmother's house that was really a long way around, and took
the shortcut himself, arriving there ahead of the wolf. He hid
Grandmother in the closet, put a jug with a hat and glasses in
bed, and tied his red scarf around his head to disguise himself
as Little Red Riding Hood. The wolf arrived, ate the jug, and
chased Petya around the house. But the boy was too quick for
him and held him off until the hunter turned up. Little Red
Riding Hood came along at the denouement, flapped her eyelashes
at Petya, and declared, "You are a real, a most real Pioneer."

Near the Caspian Sea I saw the fruits of a project by
Pioneers honoring the Soviet World War II spy Richard Sorge,
who had warned Stalin from Tokyo that Hitler would attack the
Soviet Union. The airy house where Sorge had lived until he
was three had been turned into a small museum; photographs and
documents collected and labeled by some Pioneers in the late
1960s told the story of the man who was executed by the
Japanese in 1944 and, twenty years later, awarded the title
Hero of the Soviet Union. Only one part of the story was
missing: the fact that Sorge's warning, which contained
precise information on the time and strength of the upcoming
attack, was ignored by Stalin.

The emphasis on political indoctrination through the
Pioneers varies somewhat from one region of the country to
another, but generally there seems to be more fun than politics
in everyday Pioneer activities. Every city has its Pioneer
Palace, usually an elaborate building fitted out with workshops
and classrooms for after-school instruction in modelmaking,
painting, sewing, weaving, folk dancing, drama, filmmaking,
stamp collecting, woodworking, ceramics, astronomy, and other
crafts and hobbies. The director of the Pioneer Palace in
Kiev, Lyubov Petrivna Ivanyuk, told me that most children come
every day after school and one or two days a week, for two
hours each, study Marx and Lenin. Political content is lighter
elsewhere, and in Moscow the central Pioneer Palace is a palace
indeed, spreading across a spacious campus at the edge of Lenin
Hills, overlooking the Moskva River. The sprawling complex,
built in 1962, resounds with the Russian love of immensity: a
total of 15,600 youngsters, up to 7,500 at any one time, come
here to pursue any of 162 different activities in groups of 10
to 20 each under 650 adult instructors. The operating budget
for this palace alone is $3 million a year, funded by the
government; the children pay nothing.

The facilities are sumptuous, and the instruction is
serious. As Debby and I were escorted through the maze of
corridors and classrooms, we came across chemistry and physics
labs better than in any school we had seen. In an astrophysics
lab, equipped with spectographic and other sophisticated
gadgets, thirteen children were studying Jupiter and Saturn.
In a small planetarium, adjacent to a room with huge globes and
models of the moon, Earth, and the solar system, eleven
ten-year-olds were being told about the movements of the
planets. The complex even has an observatory where older
students do telescopic photography. Soviet cosmonauts have
visited here to lecture.

Downstairs in a garage a group of boys hunched over the
open hood of a car, learning about engines. In a huge kitchen

paneled in dark wood, and an adjacent dining room outfitted with an attractive sideboard, a dining table, a tablecloth, and china, a cooking class for girls was going on. There was a weaving room with looms where girls were making sweaters and hangings, a sewing room where clothes were being produced, a set of large and well-lit studios for courses in sculpture and painting. In one workshop, boys were making model boats powered by electric motors and controlled by radio transmitters. In another, boys were coming several afternoons a week to make model airplanes from scratch out of balsa wood and paper - not from prefabricated kits - and learning the principles of aerodynamics en route. Then, equipping the models with little gasoline engines, they would take them outside to a circular arena built on the palace grounds especially for airplane competitions, where the youngsters would go up against each other periodically in acrobatics, dogfights, and races. I watched one of these on a Saturday afternoon, and as the planes buzzed around and around and leaped and looped to cut crepe streamers off the opponents' tails, I was struck by the intensity, the all-business and somewhat cheerless tone of it all, as if the boys had already learned to defer momentary joy for long-range, subdued satisfaction. There was no childlike laughter, no shout of happiness at a victory, just a professional polish and drive.

In its luxury, Moscow's cental Pioneer Palace may be the most extravagant institution for children anywhere in the world. It is also the most difficult for Soviet youngsters to get into. Moscow itself is a "closed city," where only those with special permission may live. And 98.7 percent of the capital's 1.2 million Pioneers are enrolled not in the central palace but in thirty-two Pioneer "houses" located in various neighborhoods. The "best" Pioneers from the neighborhoods are recommended to the central palace in a selection process that gives considerable weight to parental position and pull, with the result that the youngsters enjoying the richness of the elaborately equipped activities are the cream of the elite.

It was in that central palace that Debby and I had a remarkable encounter with a group of politically minded Komsomol activists, teenagers who had graduated from the Pioneers at the age of fourteen into the Young Communist League and had chosen and been chosen to participate in after-school study groups, "circles," on the United States, Africa, Latin America, the Middle East, and so on. These youngsters were part of the well-placed stratum of Soviet society that requires strict political orthodoxy in exchange for privelege, the sons and daughters of professors and scientists and diplomats, who were likely to follow their parents into party membership and relative comfort.

Komsomol is a mass organization like the Pioneers; it envelops virtually all children when they are fourteen. But since its members are of a thinking age, the tone is more heavily political, sometimes setting up silent conflicts in young minds that cannot help questioning. Most teenagers know - and if they don´t, their parents will explain - that failure to belong to Komsomol jeopardizes acceptance into institutions of higher learning and threatens careers.

"If they don´t get in, we push them a little," said the principal of a school in Vilnius, Lithuania. "We tell them it will be better for them if they join."

I came across one surprising exception in Estonia, whose cool Baltic population has resisted Russification since Soviet troops drove the Germans out in World War II and then stayed. A twenty-three-year-old woman named Rina, who had a sensitive job interpreting for foreign visitors, told me that she had never been a Komsomol member and had never been pressured to become one. "And that´s allowed me to see more pluses in the system than if I had been put under pressure," she said candidly. She even made it into Tartu University without Komsomol credentials, although she was asked by university officials why she had not joined. "I answered that I just didn´t go for being in any organization. I´m not a joiner," she said.

For Estonian intellectuals who have tried not to join Russian culture, such a reply may be appreciated as a sardonic metaphor. But in most of the rest of the country it would probably disqualify the ablest student. The outer trappings of political participation are more than obligations; they are as integral to the society´s mores as wearing clothes in public, no more easily shed than any mantle of decent behavior. So pervasive, so expected, so reflexive have these political gestures become that they have also been devalued. "To be a member of Komsomol is an empty formality," said a Russian woman with a penetrating eye. "It is like citizenship or age."

As a result, youngsters adopt varied levels of vigor or lassitude in their Komsomol activities, many showing up at meetings just to be warm bodies checked off on a list of names, others - often egged on by parents with ambitions for them - engaging more eagerly in the sorts of efforts that pass for political activism in the Soviet Union: circulating petitions for the release of Communists imprisoned in Latin America or holding rallies to support "national liberation movements" in the third world.

The group we met at the Pioneer Palace were activists of this latter breed, selected by officials in response to a

291

request I had made several months earlier. I had asked for a round-table discussion with four or five Komsomol members in their teens, knowing that the most orthodox would be produced. I wanted a glimpse of what made loyal Soviet youngsters tick, how they saw their own world and ours, what they cared about, what moved them. It was easy enough to talk on these themes with the sons and daughters of writers, scientists, and artists who were dissidents or independently minded enough to welcome friendships with Americans; it was more difficult to get to the more conformist or zealous, who were wary of contact with foreigners.

My request evidently caused some consternation in the party apparatus that handles Komsomol. Nothing happened for a long time, despite my badgering officials with phone calls and letters. When they finally decided to set up the meeting, I was not even told but was simply taken on a tour of the Pioneer Palace (which I had requested separately) and, midway through the walk through corridors and classrooms, was deposited at the head of a long table in a room with about fifty fifteen- to seventeen-year-olds. They had obviously been well prepared; I had not.

I sat at the table, staring at those young, scrubbed, earnest faces, and was asked by one of the few adults in the room to begin. As we talked over the next hour and a half on a late Friday afternoon, more people kept coming in until there were about a dozen adults and many more teenagers. I heard later from semiofficial Russians that such was unprecedented; nobody could remember an American correspondent´s ever having been permitted to sit with a group of Komsomol activists and talk about whatever he wished. The risk of contamination by alien ideas is usually considered too great, and youngsters of that age considered too impressionable. I thought that those few who spoke - most remained quiet and listened attentively - were pretty impervious to other viewpoints, and just to make sure they remained so, a middle-aged man at my left, the group´s chief ideological chaperone and watchdog and head of the astrophysics department, punctuated the discussion repeatedly with tendentious remarks.

I asked them first how they thought their lives would be different if they lived in the United States. Nobody ventured a response. They were a bit shy, and the watchdog was watching. So I called on a girl who had introduced herself as being from the "circle" specializing in the U.S.A. She said that it would depend on whether or not she was from a well-off American family. If so, her life would be about the same as in the Soviet Union, she thought. I prodded them to address the issue on some dimension other than material, the economic.

292

There were no takers.

"What's wrong in the world that you would want to set right?" I asked. There was a moment of hesitation; then the answers began to spill out, one after another, traveling down the grooves well worn by the Soviet press. Dictatorship, the denial of most elementary rights, as in Chile, Rhodesia, said one boy. Discrimination, as against the Palestinian people who do not have their rights, said another. War, said a girl. If it breaks out, it will annihilate all humanity. The colossal amount of American weaponry that nobody needs, said another, while at the same time people are perishing from hunger. Unemployment, said a boy, meaning unemployment in the "capitalist countries." Racial discrimination. The growth of crime in the U.S.A. - murder, robbery - people ought to do more useful things, another boy declared. "Fascism grows in America and Western Europe, where democratic reforms are needed," said another.

I pointed out that they had listed problems only in the West, not in their own country. "Is there anything in your own country you want to see right?" Silence. I pushed a bit. "Nothing that you want to do to make your own society better?" I asked of this future governing elite. Finally one boy said, "To build communism." But nobody else had a thing to say. Even after several adults had prompted them, they were silent. Debby, sitting beside me, searched their faces and saw no flicker of impulse to speak.

I asked what they did in their study circles. A girl in the Latin American group said they tried to understand the world, particularly economics, more deeply. She kept talking about solidarnost, solidarity with Latin American Communists. What did she and others do to further this solidarity? Kids had been selling souvenirs to raise money for Communists in Latin America, she said. Gifts were sent to a Communist festival in Havana, a boy explained. There had been a "campaign of solidarity" for Dean Reed, an American folk singer who is a celebrity in the Communist world and completely unknown in the United States. A supporter of Chilean Communists, he lives in East Berlin and travels through Eastern Europe and the Soviet Union, giving concerts of revolutionary songs that have teenagers nearly swooning over him. Whenever he visits the United States and gets himself arrested in some peace demonstration, he becomes a cause celebre in the pages of Pravda, further evidence of the American singer regime's oppression of dissenters. The singer had recently been jailed for several days on a trespassing charge in connection with a demonstration. "We collected ten thousand signatures for the freedom of Dean Reed," said one girl proudly. "We have a campaign of solidarity with Chilean Communists," she continued.

"In February we phoned Chile and conveyed our solidarity, our support."

Debby whispered a suggested question to me, and I asked it: Did they ever disagree with their parents on political issues? No, all the heads shook. And with their friends? No, never. Do they discuss politics? Yes, but they never disagree. I asked for a show of hands: Who ever disagreed? Not one. I laughed and told them they must be the only teenagers in the world who never had a difference with their parents.

"Who are your heroes?" I asked. A long silence stretched into embarrassed tension. Finally a boy, the same one who had announced his desire "To build communism," offered a name. "Lenin," he said. More silence followed. I looked around the room. The adults were uncomfortable. "Che Guevara and Fidel Castro," said the girl from the Latin American circle. Silence. Silence. "No more heroes?" I asked. Silence.

I invited them to ask me questions. Somebody began with a vague one on the state of the world. I said I thought both superpowers were playing a dangerous game by selling arms and competing for influence in the third world, magnifying local conflicts and doing nobody, least of all the local people, any good. The reaction to this was shocked and indignant, utter disbelief that I was equating the United States and the Soviet Union. The United States was doing those things, several youngsters asserted, but not we Russians. A boy with a fuzzy, new grown mustache lashed out: "The United States is an imperialist power that sucks the blood from smaller, weaker countries, taking their harvests and giving them nothing. The Soviet Union, by contrast, does what it does to help those countries. Look at American-supported countries, how backward they are - South Korea, for example, and the Philippines, which is nothing more than an American colony." The watchdog on my left sneered a word of praise for the boy - _molodetz_ ("good fellow"). I suggested that neither the Soviet Union nor the United States gave aid out of pure altruism. The boy countered that the Soviet Union got nothing in return for its help, except somtimes ingratitude. Look at Egypt, he said, which turned away and rejected the aid. He cited Cuba as a big expense. Perhaps the Soviet Union did get something in return from Cuba, I said. "Something?" the watchdog belched incredulously. Yes, I said. For example, a base where Soviet submarines can be repaired, air bases only ninety miles from the United States, and a source of troops for various operations in Africa.

My simple effort to maintain that neither of our countries always acted out of the noblest of motives ignited an

294

astonishment and rage that swept the entire room, twisting the
youngsters' faces into hurt and anger. Unwittingly I had
challenged a most fundamental vision of a world divided neatly
into good and bad, and the teenagers and adults were each
struggling, fighting to regain that vision and keep it intact.
It reminded me of the view from my teenage years in the 1950s,
when the world was cut unambiguously by an iron curtain, and
America still stood on the side of purity. Here was the mirror
image of that naïve and comfortable time, staring back at me in
complete incomprehension.

We went back and forth, back and forth. I gave an example
of the opportunism of international relations: Some years ago
the United States had backed Ethiopia; the Soviet Union,
Somalia. Then Ethiopia switched sides, and the superpowers'
clients were reversed, with Somalia - America's new "friend" -
now using Soviet-made weapons to invade Ethiopia. Gasps of
disbelief.

The youngsters were not just performing; they were jumping
into the argument with hostile questions, declaratory
statements, efforts to score debating points rather than to
exchange information. The watchdog encouraged them, trying to
exhort them to most extreme, hateful, anti-American views. But
they were clearly put off-balance somewhat by my readiness to
criticize American as well as Soviet behavior; I did not seem
to fit the standard mold of propagandist. And slowly, slowly
the rancor ebbed, the interest grew, the questions shifted
until they began to seek answers about American life, about
crime, about narcotics, about young people, and American
reactions to the end of the Vietnam war, about the Middle East,
about arms control.

"What are the reasons for the high crime rate and
narcotics addiction?" one boy asked. The watchdog tried to
answer by saying that they were lower-class problems, born of
poverty. I said there was something to that, but it did not
explain the narcotics phenomenon among the comfortable middle
class. The answers were unclear, I maintained, just as the
causes of crime in the Soviet Union were not known
definitively. Well, said the watchdog, we don't have much
crime, and the loyal children agreed. I countered that I had
done a bit of research on that and had found a considerable
juvenile crime problem right here in Moscow. Hah, scoffed the
kids. For example, I went on, I had had quite a lot of stuff
stolen from me, and I began to talk about the three teenagers
who had broken into the moving van in Brest. The watchdog
quickly called on another youngster, who asserted that the
Soviet crime rate was lower than in the United States. Quite
possibly, I replied, but we don't really know, do we? The
Soviet authorities do not release crime statistics. "Oh, you

can find out the figures," said the boy in an enlightening
statement of ignorance about his own society. No, I explained.
I had tried and was told officially by the Ministry of
Internal Affairs that crime statistics were considered a state
secret. The boy looked suprised and the subject was changed.

Debby watched the faces. They were interested, even
fascinated, she said later, though none had betrayed a hint of
accord with me. A group that had to leave early to attend
another session did so reluctantly, she observed. Yet the
overall atmosphere was so hostile that Yuri Demin, a
representative of the youth committee that had organized the
meeting, felt compelled at the end to lecture the youngsters
sternly.

I was a guest, he said, and therefore was entitled to
courtesy and respect, even when they disagreed. Furthermore,
when I asked them questions about problems in the Soviet Union,
they should have answered honestly, he declared. How could
they say there were no problems? Just the other day he had
bought a pen, and it had already broken. There was a problem
with quality, kachestvo - ah, kachestvo, they all repeated,
recognizing the code word hammered out daily by the mass press
in its criticisms of economic shortcomings. Kachestvo, that
was a permitted word, the formula for summarizing society's
problems. Finally Demin scolded them for not being forthright
about their disagreements with their parents. "Everybody has
disagreements with parents," he said.

Editors' Note

1. They are members of Shipler's family.

SOVIET EDUCATIONAL PHILOSOPHY
AND CURRENT PRACTICE

Every society has its own values, culture, and goals that it wishes to impart on its youth. The formal system of education reflects the culture of the society in which it exists. With this in mind, education is looked upon as a means to achieve an end.

In Soviet society, the main purposes of education are to instill within its people loyalty, dedication, and devotion to the cause of creating a Communist world view among its citizens and to prepare workers to support and benefit society. To meet these goals, the schools and the curriculum are organized and structured the same throughout the entire country under the auspices of the Ministry of Education and the Academy of Pedagogical Sciences. The only exception to this is that the fifteen republics have won the right to use their own local languages for instruction and include their local history along with cultural heroes in their respective curricula.

The first article in this section is an excerpt from a longer paper entitled, "Common Practices in Present Soviet Schools," by Robert B. Davis and Thomas A. Romberg. Although it was originally published in 1979 and it includes observations from a trip the authors took to the U.S.S.R. the year before, their comments are still appropriate, accurate, and consistent with the observations made in non-random, exemplary schools by other Americans in more recent visits.

Davis and Romberg provide us with a general overview of what is analogous to American elementary and secondary education in the Soviet Union. They recognize how dedicated to its children the Soviet society is. Soviet attitudes toward children, influenced by Lenin (i.e., children deserve nothing but the best in their upbringing), are reflected in the schools.

Important concepts of Soviet philosophy such as "upbringing" (vospitaniyeh) and the "collective" are explained and discussed. The authors also describe the nature of instruction in the schools as being highly structured, emphasizing the lecture-recitation method and rote memorization (especially in mathematics), and the formality of the classroom setting. Although it may seem contradictory, they do add that the serious academic classroom atmosphere does reflect the general attitudes of warmth, love, support, concern, and care for children.

The Soviet approach to education is sometimes questioned and critcized because all children throughout the entire country for the most part, are exposed to the exact same lessons and curricula. It is questioned how this can be possible because of the teacher shortage and competence level of teachers in rural areas, and the background differences (i.e., strengths and weaknesses) among children of different socio-economic groups (e.g., the "workers" and the "professionals"). These ignored, unexplained differences contradict the Soviet philosophy regarding it as being a classless society. Also, children's individual differences are not recognized in general schools, but special schools for "gifted" children do exist and special interests can be cultivated by giving all children the opportunity to participate in the many after-school "interest circles" (kruzhki) found at Pioneer Palaces and Pioneer Houses throughout the country.

Davis and Romberg relate many of their observations to current educational practices in the United States and they clearly emphasize the advantages of being familiar with educational practices of our Soviet counterparts as opposed to actually comparing and competing. What works in one society would most likely be inappropriate for another society. As a result, comparisons become purely academic but analyzing the process and approach used to confront problems and difficulties is more than pedantic.

The second selection entitled, "Themes in Current Soviet Curriculum Reform," by Thomas S. Popkewitz and B. Robert Tabachnick, highlights Soviet educators' commitment to "upbringing" and moral education as a reflection of the Marxist-Leninist concept of dialectical materialism (i.e., thinking and learning become meaningful within the context of one's labors). They clearly discuss the relationship among culture, philosophy, politics, and education in the Soviet Union.

Popkewitz and Tabachnick discuss the function of psychological and pedagogical research in developing and applying a learning theory consistent with Soviet philosophy. Studying the human organism (i.e., rationalization) in relation to the environment contributes to the theory and the implications for developing curricula based upon it.

It is important to note that curriculum reform in the Soviet Union is unlike that in the United States. Where in the United States many different syllabi, curriculum guides, textbooks, and project manuals are available from which teachers and administrators may pick and choose, all teachers

298

in the Soviet Union use the same texts for teaching specific subjects. "New" curricula, based upon scientific principles consistent with a Communist world view, are introduced slowly and gradually in the U.S.S.R., only after careful experimentation, analysis of materials, and supervised implementation are they adopted. In the U.S., less quality control exists and the proliferation of innovative, untested ideas abounds.

The authors identify some problems that Soviet educators have. Although teachers boast about the lack of deviant behavior in the schools, there is an increase in juvenile delinquency and alcoholism in the society. Attempting to unify academic teaching and upbringing continues to be a challenge for Soviet educators. Although "lip service" is given to the ideals of Communism, in practice, people are becoming more materialistic and enjoying the fulfillment of individual desires to the detriment of the collective.

The third article is by Delbert H. Long entitled, "Soviet Education and the Development of Communist Ethics." According to Long, the most important task of Soviet education is not the turning out of scientists or engineers, but the moral task of instilling Communist ethics in Soviet youngsters. The role of education then, is to convince the people that the leaders of the Communist Party have the right to control all property, all institutions, all forms of mass media - in short, to control what people think and do. The Communist Party wants to develop the "New Soviet Man" who will be cooperative, selfless and therefore, allow for the building of Communism.

The czars of pre-revolutionary Russia depended upon a system of education to inculcate values and loyalty among the common folk to create a "New Russian Man." Today, creating a "New Soviet Man" requires values that encompass the indoctrination of a Communist world view.

According to Long, the Soviet Union, like many societies, hopes to develop an individual who is honest, truthful, and helpful to others and that he or she must work hard in school to develop intellectual, aesthetic, and physical abilities - that is, to develop a "comprehensive, harmonious personality." In addition, the virtues regarded as the most integral to the development of Communist ethics are the following: Love of Labor, Patriotism, Atheism, and Collectivism.

Furthermore, the Communist Party believes that a model citizen must not only have correct beliefs but must "act on them." The Party therefore relies heavily on the schools, the Pioneers, and the Komsomol not only to teach basic Marxist-Leninist thought but also to provide them with opportunities to put this knowledge into action.

Professor Long, however, points out that there has been a disillusionment among the Soviet people. Teachers are severely limited in molding the "New Soviet Man" by the significant gap between ideology and everyday life in the Soviet Union. Students are aware of the lack of agricultural and consumer goods, they are cognizant of the fact that Party officials have many more material priveleges than other citizens, they see that their parents have only one candidate to vote for, and that bribery and connections are often required to get a better apartment, tickets to the Bolshoi, or a table at a good restaurant.

Long believes that the Soviet leaders have been pragmatic in the past and must be in the future if they are going to stem this widespread disillusionment which has already begun to breed cynicism. Professor Long concludes that this phenomenon may induce Soviet leaders to make significant adjustments in their upbringing process and even in their ideology.

The last selection, "School Reform in the USSR," by Fedor Breus, has been included to provide the reader with the up-to-date revisions and reforms being implemented in the Soviet schools beginning in 1985. The reforms are not viewed solely from a didactic approach but more from a global approach. In attempts to bring the schools into closer compliance with the ideological, social, economical, and political processes, plans for revision were initiated.

Impetus for the reforms was given by the fact that the Soviet work force needs more technical and skilled employees capable of contributing to the improvement and further development of the Soviet economy and social system. As a result, more vocational training has been incorporated in the system. Although this might bring feelings of deja vù with respect to Khrushchev´s influence on education during the 1950s, Soviet educators insist that children will not be working in the fields or factories to satisfy vocational requirements as was the case during the Khrushchev years.

It has been purported by representatives of the Soviet teachers´ trade union that a concerted effort was made to involve many facets of society in the design of the new reforms. Parents, teachers, school administrators on local and national levels, as well as university professors and other citizens, have had input in the planning of the reforms.

It should also be noted that unlike attitudes toward teachers in other societies (e.g., United States), Soviet teachers are held in high esteem because it is recognized that they have such influence over society's most important "commodity" - its impressionable children! Provisions for retraining teachers and updating teaching methods have been included in the reforms.

It is clearly stated in a quotation from Yuri Andropov that the goals of Soviet education have not changed - that is, to instill within its citizens a Communist world view and prepare qualified, committed workers.

By reading the articles in this section, it is hoped that the reader will gain insight into the relationship between Soviet philosophy and teaching ideology reflected by current practices and trends in the schools. In particular, studying concepts such as "upbringing" and the "collective," and the prescribed vehicles used to achieve the goals of society - the schools and youth organizations - exemplify how Soviet ideology, dictates school and after-school practices.

Despite the progress that has been made, it should be kept in mind that the goals of the Soviet system of education have not been realized. The evidence to support this statement include the fact that after over sixty-seven years since the Great Revolution, the Soviet society has not been homogenized (i.e., different nationalities in the 15 republics still demonstrate loyalty, devotion, and commitment to their ethnic origins), and, religion is still "alive" and flourishing among the people (especially in rural areas), although many "Communists" might not admit to practicing their religion for obvious reasons. Also, the quality of workmanship has been criticized and individuality and materialism have somewhat interfered with developing positive attitudes toward the "collective" and other socialist concerns.

Finally, there is a great need to develop and encourage worker initiative and imagination to meet the demands of the scientific-technical revolution. However, the methods of teaching, heavily ladened with collectivist philosophy and rote memorization impede the development of individual critical thinking. Commitment to the development of critical thinking and encouraging innovation might jeopardize the Party's control. This might lead to an open challenge of the basic ideological principles which govern the Party. How this will be resolved in the course of the next decade will be interesting to observe.

COMMON PRACTICES IN PRESENT SOVIET SCHOOLS

Robert B. Davis and Thomas A. Romberg(1)

Some General Remarks

...both of us have had opportunities, as official U.S.
delegates and guests of the Soviet government, to visit schools
in several cities in the U.S.S.R. Considering the size of the
U.S.S.R., the diversity of languages (2) and cultures which it
includes (e.g. Eskimoes), the range of life styles (from
peasants to nuclear physicists, from sparsely populated rural
areas to Moscow and Leningrad, from the Baltic to the Arctic),
and the range of cultures (northern European, southern
European, Asian, and so forth), we suspect that at best we have
seen very, very little of schooling in the U.S.S.R. There is
the further problem that we have seen a non-random sample of
Soviet schools. Yet both of us independently arrived at
similar conclusions, which have subsequently been compared with
those of Bronfenbrenner (3) and of Smith (4) and found to be
substantially similar. Hence, we have some confidence that our
perceptions correspond to at least a piece of the reality of
Soviet schools.

1. The first thing that strikes you, the moment you enter
a Soviet school, is the orderliness. Children are polite to
adults, polite to one another, and attentive during lectures.
For U.S. visitors, this is a surprising novelty.

2. To the preceding remark another must be added
immediately: a visitor can see no evidence of blatant force or
compulsion. Architecturally, schools are reasonably open and
inviting. There are no police in sight. Windows are not
barred, there is no great prevalence of locked doors, keys, and
so forth. Clearly, there is adult control - a world of
children would be far less orderly - but the controls are
subtle, even warm and loving.

3. That brings us to a third point, on which we rely
primarily on the reports of Urie Bronfenbrenner, Hedrick Smith,
and Harold Hodgkinson: the Russians give very high priority,
and a deep, warm affection, to children. The Soviets provide

Excerpts from: "Common Practices in Present Soviet Schools," by
Robert B. Davis and Thomas A. Romberg, in An Analysis of
Mathematics Education in the Union of Soviet Socialist Republics,
ERIC Clearinghouse for Science, Mathematics, and Environmental
Education, The Ohio State University, December 1979. Used by
permission.

food, clothing, and medical care lavishly to children - far
more lavishly than to adults. Children who don´t even like
caviar may get some, at the expense of adults who crave it (and
it is typically in short supply). The Soviets claim that every
school has its own full-time physician, despite evidence of
inadequate medical care for adults. Grandmothers wait outside
schools to walk home with their grandchildren. When the movie
The Russians Are Coming portrays Soviet sailors abandoning
other activities to rescue a child who is in danger, the film
is true to a deep trait in Russian character. Many generally
similar incidents have been reported. This looks very strange
to the eyes of an American visitor.

Workers, astronauts, and top-level scientists all find
time to work with young people: the astronaut [the late] Yuri
Gagarin [sponsored] a club in the Moscow Pioneer Palace: A.N.
Kolmogoroff, one of the greatest mathematicians of the
twentieth century, sponsors a high school and teaches in it
three times a week. (The tradition is not new: Leo Tolstoy
created and operated a school for peasant children.)

Responsibility for young children is enthusiastically
accepted even by teenagers; there are many reports of teenagers
spontaneously (and affectionately) showing care and concern for
children, strangers to them, whom they encounter on the street.

4. One of the most striking characteristics of Soviet
schools, and of Soviet life in general, is the collective. A
student is part of a group of students, and every student in
the group has responsibility for every other student in the
group. If a student is not learning satisfactorily, the group
- called the "collective" - must deal with the problem.
Similarly, if a student is not doing his or her homework, or is
being tardy, the group takes action.

Nor is the collective limited to students in school. Even
the American visitor, traveling for two weeks with a group of
Soviet and American educators, finds that he or she is a member
of a collective. In fact, it can be a surprising supportive
and reassuring environment - one is never alone, never faces
alone the problems of currency or transportation or housing.
The welfare of every member of the group is the business of -
indeed, the responsibilty of - every member of the group.

5. Hedrick Smith reports on "parents night" in a Soviet
school. In the U.S., parents night is typically an occasion
for teachers to report to parents, to be questioned by parents,
not infrequently to be accosted by parental complaints,
requests, and demands. One might give the capsule description:
parents sit in judgment on teachers.

Parents night in the U.S.S.R. is quite the opposite. The voice of authority is the teacher's. If Ivan has not been doing his homework, this deficiency will be publicly proclaimed, and Ivan's parents will be publicly admonished and told that they must correct the problem.(5) There are even reports of authorities restricting the vacations awarded to parents of children who are doing poorly in school.(6)

6. The general atmosphere in schools is regularly reported as warm, caring, even loving.

7. If a great deal is given to children, that does NOT include individual choice. The same is true for visiting U.S. guests: the collective provides good meals and excellent entertainment, but if this evening's schedule calls for going to the circus, Russians will not be prepared for an individual member of the collective to express a preference for going to the ballet. That sort of thing simply isn't done.

8. In regard to the general appearance of Soviet schools that we visited, physically the rooms were clean, well-lit, well-equipped, and attractively decorated. The walls displayed a profusion of social consciousness statements ("A Pioneer does his homework carefully." "A Pioneer obeys his parents."). Classrooms had paired rows of desks firmly fixed to the floor. Students were dressed in uniforms, raised their hands to be called on, and stood up to recite. However, students did talk quietly to their deskmates, with whom they share answers and discuss the work. [Indeed, Soviet students spend more time copying answers from other students, or from the teacher's work, than an American visitor is prepared to accept. This copying is NOT cheating: it is an official (and very common) form of "helping."]

9. As to the role of Soviet teachers, beginning with the fourth grade, mathematics is always taught by a specialist teacher who teaches nothing but mathematics. This applies to every grade level, from grade four upward.

Furthermore, it is always taught in the same way in every class throughout the country. Teachers follow a prescribed didactic sequence involving first a lecture, then questions. Students follow in somewhat rote fashion, upon the prodding of teachers. In the Soviet instructional system, the teacher is viewed as a conduit. Teachers are NOT supposed to adapt or change materials to meet the needs of their students. Teachers are not seen as professional decision-makers responsible for planning the curriculum.

The job of a school teacher in the U.S.S.R. is to carry

out a well-designed, carefully elaborated program of instruction. Indeed, inspectors check on teachers to see that they are teaching the syllabus as intended. If a teacher wants to adapt a program of instruction, it is expected that he or she will get permission and an inspector will in turn check to see that there is a rationale for making the adaptation, and that the results of the adaptation are appropriate. It is assumed that teachers treat all students equally.

In summary, teaching in a Soviet classroom is more formal and institutionally structured than in U.S. classrooms. The teacher´s role is functionally prescribed. Nonetheless - perhaps surprising - the school atmosphere is markedly one that is caring and supportive.

10. The organization of the schools differs from that in the U.S. The education of the young is defined differently in the U.S.S.R., as we shall see in later sections. But it would be fair to say that, to begin with, it is split into two parts: schools and Pioneer Palaces.

From morning through early afternoon each child attends a school. In late afternoon, nearly all children attend a quite different institution, known as a Pioneer Palace. The Pioneer Palace - possibly one of the most impressive structures in town - is something like a combination, in a single institution and a single building, of what in the U.S. would be parceled out to many different institutions: the YMCA/YWCA, museums, zoos, Boy Scouts and Girl Scouts, piano lessons, music clubs, student orchestras, computer clubs, ballet lessons, and so forth.

In a Pioneer Palace you may find:

a. a "Friendship Club," composed of children who are learning English, and who correspond with children in school in various English-speaking countries around the world, read books (in English) from the U.S., etc.
b. ballet classes (Russia is, after all, Russia)
c. a computer club, where students make and use computers
d. a "future astronauts" club, which has flight simulators and other equipment
e. a radio club, where students make radios
f. a zoo, where students care for the animals
g. a "future farmers" club, where students learn about agriculture
h. classes in painting, ceramics, and sculpture
i. cooking classes
j. classes in dressmaking
k. classes in interior decoration
l. science clubs
m. swimming instruction

n. classes in how to set a table, how to entertain, "good manners," etc.
o. a model railroad club
p. an aquarium cared for by students
q. a drama club
and special interest clubs of other types.

The personnel at a Pioneer Palace have quite different educational backgrounds from those in schools. They may be chemists, working part time (perhaps as volunteers) at the Pioneer Palace. Some actually are professional astronauts.

One immediate consequence of the dual system is important for U.S. educators: because the "activity" and "special interest" classes are in the Pioneer Palace, they are not in schools. The school is a formal, academic place. The familiar U.S. problem of seeing demanding courses in Euclidean geometry or English losing out in the competition with more "exciting" (and less demanding) courses in film-making, shop, the lyrics of rock music, or television viewing cannot occur in Soviet schools. These "activity" or "special interest" courses are not part of the school at all. They happen at a different time and in a different place. The school deals with the serious academic subjects.

Soviet Schools and Curricula

Deferring, for the moment, any further discussion of Pioneer Palaces, we turn exclusively to the question of Soviet schools, which children typically attend for the morning and the earlier part of the afternoon. Descriptions of the Soviet system vary somewhat (as do descriptions of the U.S. system), but the general pattern seems to be as follows.

General Pattern
1. For the youngest children - below age 7 - a new system of early childhood education has recently been devised , and is now in the process of being implemented. These schools are an impressive innovation, accepting (if parents request) even very young infants, and placing equal emphasis on academic learning, "up-bringing" (an interesting Soviet feature which we discuss below), physical care, and social development.

2. For children from age 7 to age 15 there is a single kind of school, sometimes called the "eight-year school." This may, in fact, be a separate school, or may be part of a so-called "ten-year school," enrolling students from age 7

through 17.(7)*

3. The first three years of the "eight-year school" (or
of the "ten-year school") may be separated, constituting a
primary school(7), although just how distinct these primary
schools are (or, conversely, how completely integrated into the
eight- or ten-year school) is a matter on which various reports
do not agree. The distinction may or may not be important -
within the U.S., for example, there are isolated cases where
all fourth grades meet in a separate building, cases where
grades 1-3 meet in one building, and grades 4-6 meet in a
separate building, cases where fifth grades meet in a separate
building, and so on. These special arrangements are usually
either the result of attempts to make effective use of existing
buildings of varying sizes, or are caused by constraints in
school bus schedules, or represent attempts at improving racial
integration. Perhaps they do not alter the broad pattern of
U.S. schools, but considering them can greatly - and perhaps
disproportionately - complicate the task of describing U.S.
schools. Presumably there are similar variations among Soviet
schools.

4. Thus the eight- or ten-year school can be thought of,
at least roughly, as a Soviet equivalent of grades 1 through 12
in the United States. What is especially striking to U.S.
observers is the absence of "tracking" or "homogenized classes"
in the usual eight- or ten-year schools. The Soviets believe
strongly in the goal of giving all citizens the same education
- at least in this basic sense - and are very proud of their
success in achieving this. To American eyes this is very
strange indeed, perhaps even incredible. Within the scope of
these eight- or ten-year schools there is apparently no
division into a "college preparatory" track, a "business" or
"retail" track, a "vocational" or "shop" track, or other
tracks. There is just one single version of education, the
same for everybody.

Well, not quite everybody, as we shall presently see. The
Soviets have some remarkable arrangements for a small number of
gifted students, and provide some other forms of variation.
But for most students, from the time they are 7 until they are
15 or so, there is a single basic educational program, exactly
the same for everybody.

5. Attached to the top end of the eight-year school
(thereby transforming it to a "ten-year school"), or perhaps

---

*Editors' Note: With the implementation of new school reforms
during 1985, children begin their formal education at the age
of 6 and are required to complete 11 years of school.

existing separately, one finds at least four kinds of schools:
the "secondary general polytechnical school" for ages 15 to 17,
the "secondary specialized schools" for ages 15 to 19, the
"evening shift" schools and the "correspondence schools" for
ages 15 to 18, and the "vocational-technical schools".(8)   It
is at this point that the major alternatives in Soviet education
- analogous to "tracking" in the U.S. - make their appearance.
These alternatives correspond roughly to U.S. alternatives
provided by "vocational" tracks, by "commercial" tracks, by
"college preparatory" tracks, and by community colleges,
although we shall not try to match the possible route of a
Soviet student through the various schools with corresponding
routes of U.S. students along the variety of paths that are
possible here. Our present data are not good enough to justify
such an attempt at making correspondences.

   6. Soviet schools meet six days a week, Monday through
Saturday. The school year lasts from 35 weeks to 38 weeks,
depending upon grade level.

   7. According to Shabanowitz(7) a student who receives
unsatisfactory grades in three or more subjects must repeat
that year (in U.S. language, the student would be "kept back"
or "not promoted").

   8. Shabanowitz(9) also reports that any Soviet citizen
who completes (at least) grade 10 is eligible for admission to
higher education. There are, however, competitive examinations
for admission to higher education programs.

   9. The basic eight-year school is reported as offering
the following subjects: Russian language, world literature,
world history, social sciences, natural history, geography,
biology, physics, astronomy, drawing, chemistry, English, other
foreign languages, physical culture, labor training - and, of
course, mathematics. This is reported as the universal
curriculum for all Soviet students from age 7 to 15.

   (One has the very strong sense that something here is
being mistranslated, or otherwise misunderstood; a persistent
theme in U.S. attempts to describe and understand Soviet
educational practice - and even more so in the case of research
and educational theory - is the need for clarification and
specificity. There is no shortage of reasons for doubting the
completeness and correctness of our present descriptions.
Getting clear and accurate descriptions could be a strong first
step toward more effective communication. Certainly, a school
program as heavily academic as the one just described, required
for every student, would not be considered a realistic
possibility in the United States at the present time. How,

then, can it succeed in the Soviet Union? There is much here
that requires further clarification.)

10. The present situation can, to some extent, be
clarified by considering how Russian and Soviet education has
evolved. The history of Russian schooling can be seen as the
story of trying to accomplish four main goals:

a. taking the diverse collection of schools of the Russian
past - ranging from the Smolny Institute "for young ladies of
noble birth," founded in 1764, and the Moscow School of
Mathematical and Navigational Sciences, founded by Peter the
Great in 1701 (which, at that time, was one of the leading
mathematical schools in the world), to one-year village schools
that taught some reading, some writing, and the four operations
of addition, subtraction, multiplication, and division - and
from such beginnings creating a unified nation-wide system of
schools that would provide identical educational opportunities
to every child in the U.S.S.R.;
b. within the framework of a deep and publicly declared
belief in the equality of all humans, and in the desirability
of an egalitarian society, somehow providing for individual
differences in people, and for the national economic need for a
diversified work force;
c. relating education to the practical world of work,
including the provision of "labor experiences" for all
students;
d. using systematic study ("educational research") as a
tool to improve the operation of the educational system.

A great deal of what has happened can be seen in relation
to these four themes. In particular, there has been a history
of efforts to get all children to work in some industry or
productive labor, countered by an opposing pressure to keep
students at work learning trigonometry and calculus and English
instead of "running off to the countryside to help bring in the
crops." The more-work-vs.-more-study pendulum has already had
several swings (cf., e.g., 10, 11, 12). Prominent Soviet
professional mathematicians have argued the need to modernize
the mathematical content taught in schools, which is perhaps
one aspect of the general problem of relating school to the
outside-of-school world of work - in this case, to professional
work in mathematics, science, and engineering. In most cases,
however, "labor education" probably refers more to work in
factories and on farms than it does to sophisticated
professions.

11. "Kindergarten" in the U.S.S.R. is sometimes taken to
mean a school that is attended for as long as four years, from
age three until age seven. The actual patterns for attendance

310

seem to vary considerably; for example, Taruntaeva(13) says: "If the children previously attended nursery school, and directly entered the second of the four kindergarten years from their first year, mathematics activities can begin...immediately after September." The interesting word here, of course, is "If."

Teacher Education in the U.S.S.R.

Recall that the ten-year school is not necessarily divided into "elementary" and "secondary." Recall also that all mathematics, after grade 3, is taught by a mathematics specialist who teaches nothing but mathematics!

In general, teachers in the ten-year school have themselves finished the ten-year school, at about age 17. They have then received three years of teacher education at pedagogical institutes. They have almost certainly NOT attended a university. As a result, at what would correspond to U.S. elementary school levels the Soviet child is studying with a teacher who knows substantially more mathematics than his or her U.S. counterpart does, but at the higher grades this may not be true.

The situation is quite different in the various "special" schools... Vogeli(14) reports:

Like the school curriculum it is designed to serve, the program for training teachers of [high school] computer programming is both intensive and of high mathematical quality. Its duration is five years, in contrast to four years for programs without dual specialization ["dual specialization" refers to high school programs that provide simultaneous specialization in mathematics and in computer science]. Teachers for secondary schools with specialization in computer programming [and also mathematics] receive a total 4,388 hours of classroom and laboratory instruction. In contrast, graduates of four-year American colleges or universities receive about 2,000 hours of classroom instruction and laboratory work. Of the 4,388-hour Soviet total, 2,730 hours [or 62 percent of the total college program] are in mathematics, and 450 hours are in physics and electronics [so that physics, mathematics, and electronics together represent 72 percent of their entire "college" education! This is 5 times as much instruction in mathematics and physics as comparable U.S. teachers receive.].

Educational Television in the U.S.S.R.

American visitors in their hotel rooms, seeking

311

entertainment, may find that the television set will bring them mainly the same rote lecture on the hyperbolic sine that they could observe in living color in various school classrooms. We do not have statistics on how much Soviet TV broadcasting is devoted to such lectures; by our very small sample technique, we consider that it might be quite a sizeable proportion.

Student Response
Given the warm and caring school, the formal, academic curriculum, the rote instruction, the cooperation of the collective, and the pressure to take one's work seriously, how do Soviet youngsters respond? One observer reports:

In spite of many reservations I have about the lack of variability of instruction and the lack of attention to individual differences, it was apparent that the students were engaged during instruction. I did a random time sampling in one 50-minute mathematics class. I estimated that for 37 of the 50 minutes of instruction, students were actively engaged in learning. This is considerably higher than any math classes I have observed in [the U.S.]... In particular, there was much less wait-time and transition-time than I have found in American classes. This is partly due to the pedagogical structure: i.e., [mainly] lecture-recitation... Also, there is very little seat work or work with manipulatives.(15)

Equipment in Soviet Schools
There are essentially no computers in Soviet schools, nor hand-held calculators. But the schools we visited were remarkably well equipped with other materials. In a social studies class one would find videotape recorders being used to present material via TV monitors. A special 16mm projector, designed by educators, is said to be in every school in the U.S.S.R. We did NOT, however, observe any Soviet equivalents for Cuisenaire rods, geoboards, or Dienes MAB blocks, which play an important role in many U.S. schools.

Vospitaniyeh
There seems to be no English equivalent of this word. It means "moral education," "the inculcation of good work habits," "teaching good citizenship," "the development of a sense of responsibility." This is VERY prominent in educational thought in the U.S.S.R. U.S. public schools have, today, no equivalent, although in the McGuffy readers they do provide equivalents, however.

312

"How To Be A Parent"

Soviet educational philosophy advocates leaving NOTHING to chance. This includes the question of how parents should behave. There are many books on "how to be a parent," and these are widely read and much discussed. There is a single official Soviet theory on bringing up children - very, very different from the myriad competing theories in the U.S. In the U.S.S.R., deviant theories are denounced, forcefully.

Adult Attention to Children

Soviet and U.S. practice diverge dramatically on the matter of supervision of children. By building large schools, staffed by few adults, the U.S. in effect creates teenage ghettoes. The abundance of rock music and other aspects of teenage culture has created a teenage world where adults are uncomprehending strangers. (Ask a teenager to explain the background music in the movie Coming Home, and compare what they say with your own spontaneous perceptions!)

Russians think children should be brought up closely by adults, supervised by adults, watched over carefully AND CLOSELY by adults. U.S. families in Moscow are always finding themselves accused of neglecting their children. As one example, Soviet grandmothers wait outside schools to walk home with their grandchildren. The U.S. system of having a group of children walk together under a peer leader seems to the Soviets to be a shameful neglect of adult supervisory responsibilities. And letting children walk home from school by themselves (!) - as is done in Urbana, Illinois, in what is probably the typical U.S. pattern would be entirely unthinkable. Scandalous child-neglect!

Caste Systems and Access to Schools

Hedrick Smith reports that the separation in the U.S.S.R. between intellectuals and blue-collar workers is absolute and is hereditary. Children of blue-collar workers do NOT play with the children of white-collar workers. And they know, absolutely, what they'll be when they grow up.

From an observer report is this comment:

In spite of the rhetoric about a classless society, there is very strong evidence of cultural and social class differences. The Estonians made a point of describing the unique Estonian aspects of their program. Their educational system is not identical to that of Moscow. The Soviets also admitted there were problems in rural areas in contrast to city education. And finally, in the English-speaking school we visited in Leningrad, we were told that children of all

313

segments of society had the opportunity to
attend such a school... However, we met and
talked only with children whose parents were in
professional positions.(16)

Control of the Culture

Soviet theory and practice value, and aim for, a high
degree of control of the culture. This is generally well-known
in relation to plays, movies, operas, etc., which present
approved views of approved topics handled in an approved way.
Similar is the case of poetry (which is very important in
Russia). Painting is also similar. The Soviets heavily
subsidize Prokofieff, Mozart, and Beethoven, as well as Russian
folk music, but rock is anathema. So are some western dress
styles. Television presents what is good for Soviet culture
and Soviet society, and NOTHING else.

The extent of this was brought home to us when we met with
members of a committee that approves toys. When a toy is
proposed, this committee studies it carefully. Until and
unless the committee concludes that the toy will teach children
desirable behaviors or values or expectations, and will NOT
teach undesirable ones, it will not approve the toy. And
without the approval of this committee, that toy cannot be
manufactured.

Needs of the Soviet Economy

Analyses seem to indicate that the Soviet economy suffers
from a shortage of skilled workers at nearly every level.
European firms, such as Fiat, have difficulty finding workers
with adequate measurement skills and skill in shop mathematics.
We have heard laments over the Soviet shortage of computer
experts. This seems to represent a marked difference from the
situation in the United States - and it is surprising, given
the goals of Soviet education and the emphasis which seems to
be placed on computer science.

[Concluding Remarks]

Many observers have commented on the contrast between
Soviet and U.S. demographics, in music, athletics, science,
mathematics, and other fields. At the highest levels of
excellence, on a world-wide basis of comparison, one finds
Sergei Prokofieff one of the very greatest composers of the
twentieth century (and probably of all time); David Oistrakh,
one of the greatest violinists of all time; Rostropovitch, one
of the greatest cellists of all time; and so on. The Moscow
Symphony is one of the world's greatest. Soviet ballet is
unexcelled, possibly unequaled. It is the same in many fields
of endeavor, including (emphatically!) mathematics.

But one is talking about a small quality elite. The U.S. has not merely the N.Y. Philharmonic, but also the Boston Symphony, the Philadelphia Symphony, the Pittsburgh Symphony, the Chicago Symphony, the Cleveland Symphony, the Los Angeles Philharmonic, the St. Louis Symphony, and so on, for a VERY long list.

In athletic terms, the Soviet first team is fully a match for anyone, but they tend to lack depth on the bench and in the bull-pen.

There is little to be gained, and much to be lost, by comparing national systems in an "our-system-can-beat-your-system" frame of mind. The important gains are to be had only if each nation tries to learn from the other. This is not unreasonable - no country has an educational system that satisfies all the national needs, and all the personal needs of individual citizens. In that sense, every nation should be seeking improvement. One road toward that improvement may be the careful study of what other nations do, in the hope of learning from them.

Notes

1. We wish to acknowledge the valuable assistance of Bruce Vogeli and Harold Hodgkinson in putting together this view of Russian schools.
2. For example, it is worth recalling that Russian is the principal language of less than 50 percent of the population of the U.S.S.R.
3. Bronfenbrenner, Urie. Two Worlds of Childhood: U.S. and U.S.S.R. NY: Basic Books, 1970. (Revised edition, Pocket Books, 1973.)
4. Smith, Hedrick. The Russians. NY: Ballantine Books, 1977.
5. Here again we see the collective in operation. "Home assignments" - work that a child should do at home - is, in effect, a responsibility of the "home collective." The family is responsible for making sure that Ivan gets the work done, and assists him with it. If the child does not get it done, it is not his fault alone: it is the whole family's fault.
6. Parents are expected to assist the school not only in the matter of home assignments, but in other things as well. We have visited schools and found parents making bookshelves, flooding a playground to make an ice rink, etc. Parents are expected to assist in the operation of the school.
7. Shabanowitz, Harry. Educational Reform and Mathematics in the Soviet Union. In F.J. Swetz (Ed.), Socialist Mathematics Education. Southampton, PA: Burgundy Press, 1978, p. 25.
8. Ibid., pp. 24-25.
9. Ibid., p. 26.

10. Ibid., pp. 23-95.
11. Vogeli, Bruce R. Soviet Secondary Schools for the Mathematically Talented. Washington, DC: National Council of Teachers of Mathematics, 1968.
12. Vogeli, Bruce R. Mathematics Education in Russia and the Soviet Union. Soviet Education, 8(8-9-10), June-July-August, 1971.
13. Taruntaeva, T. Mathematics in Kindergarten. Doshkol´noe Vospitanie, No. 4, 1970. Soviet Education, 8(8-9-10), June-July-August, 1971.
14. Vogeli, 1968, pp. 39-40.
15. Romberg, Thomas A. Impressions of Soviet Research in Mathematical Education, March 1979, p. 8. (Mimeographed)
16. Ibid., p. 10.

THEMES IN CURRENT SOVIET CURRICULUM REFORM

Thomas S. Popkewitz and B. Robert Tabachnick

Soviet educators have historically had two purposes: to instill in students a communist world view and to train them in specific skills necessary to the economy.

Prior to 1966, Soviet educational practices were based on the belief that children should be taught habits and skills through formal rote learning.(1) Criticism of this approach to schooling, summarized in the 23rd Communist Party resolution, argued that the scientific-technological revolution required a new structure for the content and methods of teaching school subjects. The resulting curriculum and teaching revisions called for a reconstruction of the formal education of 50 million students with over 150 different languages and dialects in 15 constituent Soviet Republics. In addition, universal schooling was to be increased from 8 to 10 years. These were the first major changes in Soviet education in the last 40 years.

The reform effort was directed by the Ministry of Education and Academy of Pedagogical Sciences. Each of the Academy´s 13 institutes has a particular mission, such as Curriculum and Teaching Methods, School Equipment and Technical Means of Education, and General and Pedagogical Psychology. Much of the curriculum in language, politics, science, and mathematics is designed and developed at the Academy and implemented nationwide through the Ministry of Education.(2)

Soviet curriculum reform was intended to increase the amount of theoretical and conceptual learning in Soviet schools and integrate the factual knowledge of the traditional school curriculum with theoretical knowledge. From debates similar to those among curriculum reformers in the 1960s in the United States, Soviet scholars redesigned mathematics and science curricula, producing new syllabi and a hundred new textbooks.

Analyses of school enrollment patterns, courses of study,

From: "Themes in Current Soviet Curriculum Reform," by Thomas S. Popkewitz and B. Robert Tabachnick, in Educational Leadership (March 1982): 420-424. Reprinted with permission of the Association for Supervision and Curriculum Development and T.S. Popkewitz and B.R. Tabachnick. Copyright © March 1982 by the Association for Supervision and Curriculum Development.

and textbooks in Soviet mathematics and science point to a
major restructuring and expansion of the scope and content of
these curricula.(3) Mathematics education, for example, was
revised to emphasize theoretical foundations and logical rigor
as well as applications. The result, according to Izaak
Wirszup, a mathematician at the University of Chicago, is that
"in only ten years the Soviet compulsory mathematics program
for all students covers an equivalent of at least 13 years of
American schooling in arithmetic, algebra, and calculus, and
does so much more thoroughly and effectively."(4) Wirszup
concludes that the Soviet reform efforts have far outstripped
those of the U.S. in the quality of scientific and mathematics
education at the elementary and secondary levels.

A second strand of reform movement introduced principles
of cognitive growth and learning. The experiments of L.V.
Zankov, for example, sought to identify principles of
instruction that would enable children at each level of school
to learn, as rapidly as possible, the highest level of
difficulty in theoretical knowledge.(5) Zankov´s work, drawn
from the ideas of Lev Vygotsky, the eminent Soviet psychologist
of the 20s and 30s, was premised on the belief that teaching
precedes development, that the new pedagogy should stress the
emotional involvement of the learner in mastering cognitive
tasks, and that teaching should be directed toward stimulating
the broad interests of the child. Zankov´s experiments led to
a revamping of primary education, which reduced the number of
years from four to three and emphasized the principles of
overall development.

Currently, researchers at the various institutes are
searching out ways to create social contexts of learning that
emphasize the harmonious view of develoment and provide for an
efficient use of school resources such as time, people, and
materials.(6) Their research on teaching and learning,
according to American observers, involves, innovative "natural"
or "formative" experiments that rely principally on observation
and participation in regular classroom settings.(7)

Efforts to develop and implement reforms in the Soviet
schools, however, have met resistance. For example, different
levels of achievement are found in urban and rural schools,
suggesting differences in the implementation of the reforms.
American researchers point out some of these problems, as well
as the fact that Soviet ideological and political organization
makes problematic the wholesale adoption of procedures and
goals in an American context.

The remainder of this paper will give attention to three
general themes that underlie the reorganization of curriculum

318

and teaching in Soviet schools.

The Relationship of Pedagogical Research and Philosophy
The Soviets consciously attempt to develop an integrative approach to pedagogy that is consistent with dialectical materialism.(8) Briefly, dialectical materialism defines thought, reasoning, and learning as an activity of social beings transforming nature and self through the process of labor.(9) Thinking is embedded in time and space, a part of the way in which individuals engage in actions to shape the world around them. This process is dialectical because the movement of thought and practice is seen as interrelated and involving both internal and external contradictions that produce change. The perspective can be contrasted with much American pedagogical research in which the problem is to identify the traits, abilities, or stages of development that occur within the individual, defining the ideas, categories, and mental processes as separate and distinct from the social and historical milieu in which thought and reason develop. Soviet psychology involves continual reinterpretations of consciousness and personality in an effort to bring psychological theories into line with social and philosophical debates in the larger society.

Many Americans are not aware of the linkages of philosophy to educational science in the Soviet Union. Rather than extraneous, the philosophical assumptions of dialectical materialism are central to understanding scientific work and the system of explanation that the Soviets seek to develop.(10) In reviewing Vygotsky´s work, Stephen Toulmin, an American philosopher of science, argues that there is a theoretical power inherent in the attempt to understand how social activities become internalized in the shaping of consciousness.(11) Vygotsky sought to apply the philosophical position of Marx, Engels, and Lenin to the development of a systematic psychological theory. His theory focused on how developmental changes in behavior and consciousness are rooted in society and culture and the origin and course of this development. Vygotsky´s work, Toulmin continues, has given Soviet psychology a level of interdisciplinary collaboration and intellectual integration that has not been achieved in the West.

Current Soviet educational psychology seeks to extend and integrate Vygotsky´s research in detailing individual students´ thought processes and relating this psychological research to curriculum development. The work of the Institute of General and Pedagogical Psychology under the direction of V.V. Davydov, has developed innovative curriculum approaches in mathematics, Russian language, and physics that draw on the theoretical foundations provided by Vygotsky. Menchinskaia, a leading

Soviet psychologist of learning, traces the concept of motive
to the early reaction of Soviet psychology to the idealistic
position that saw consciousness only in relation to
intellectual development.(12) Consciousness and motive, she
asserts, need to be considered within social-historical and
contextual cues.

Upbringing as a Central Focus

Soviet educators look to Western beliefs about the
separation of school from politics as either naive or as a
denial of culture, tradition, and morality. They believe the
school is an artificially created institution to transmit
culture, and culture in the Soviet Union is socialism based on
Marxism-Leninism and built on dialectical materialism. The
prime task of the school is the formation and maintenance of the
socialist outlook.

"Upbringing" gives focus to moral/political tasks of
education.(13) When Soviet educators talk about all-around
development of the individual, they mean the integration of a
moral basis of action with intellectual abilities. Development
of the intellect devoid of larger moral vision and purpose is
considered miseducation. One further needs to understand that
development of the individual does not refer to notions of
individualism found in the United States. The Soviets
emphasize the individual´s acceptance of social goals and
participation in creatively furthering those goals within a
collective. From this perspective, the teaching of ideology
and propaganda are viewed as a necessity of upbringing. The
teacher is first of all an upbringer.

Classroom and extracurricular activities instill in Soviet
youth proper attitudes, activities, and relationships. The
optimism by which these tasks are organized arises historically
and philosophically. The Soviets believe that following their
revolution, the consciousness of the masses was reshaped to the
appropriate moral attitude and world view of socialism. Their
faith is given theoretic potency through the outlook of
dialectical materialism in which all gaps between knowledge and
behavior are viewed as subjectively formed and remediable
through intervention.

While Soviet teaching distinguishes upbringing and
teaching specific subject matter, teaching methods emphasize
socialistic values. Teachers´ manuals, for example, stress the
importance of collective values in class interaction. The
class or subgroups in the class are organized to help
individuals work together to achieve some pedagogical goal such
as a solution to a mathematical problem. Or, as in one school
we visited in Leningrad, children were asked to respond to the
school´s shortage of paper by collecting newspapers and using

money to buy school supplies.

In the laboratory school of the Institute of General and Pedagogical Psychology, V.V. Rybstov has conducted experiments that use children's collectives to further the acquisition and application of physics. In these experiments and resulting curriculum applications, the structure of physics is interrelated with social/psychological structures in the classroom. In each of these instances, the organization of collectives reflects a belief that children should feel an obligation to the larger purposes of the group and work in concert to achieve those purposes. Children are to learn with their peers and from their peers, expressing their own views and cooperating.

The subject matter of Soviet curriculum also focuses on problems of upbringing. Art, history, and political studies teach dialectical materialism. Mathematical examples, children's reading texts, or science problems extol the virtues and values of socialist societies. Science, in particular, fosters atheism; music and physical education teach collective behaviors.

The role of upbringing extends into extracurricular activities organized through the Ministry of Education. Every school has youth groups that contribute to the moral development of children. These groups are the Octobrists, ages 7-10; Pioneers, ages 10-15, and the Komsomol, students over 15. In schools, these groups are organized within classes to work toward social and school goals. A Pioneer detachment, for example, may help younger children study or organize games for them. Or, a Pioneer group may study a public document, such as "The Moral Code of the Builder of Communism," including discussions of the precept, one "must study hard to serve the Motherland." Youth groups also meet after school in places such as the Pioneer Palaces. Here, they participate in club-like activities - sports, cosmonautics, ballet, or music. Although every child does not belong to these groups, many do because it is the only place that such activities occur. From a pedagogical perspective, even ballet is taught to develop collective rather than individualistic attitudes and behavior.

One cannot talk about the idea of upbringing without focusing on Anton Makarenko.(14) A Soviet educator in the 1920s, Makarenko organized schools for juvenile delinquents. He saw a way to seek new reforms of social relations that were based on group solidarity. His reflections on the processes of developing the collective, the elements of competition, moral conditioning, and discipline still underlie Soviet pedagogical practices. One might compare Makarenko with John Dewey, whose ideas were popular in the Soviet Union in the 1920s. For

Dewey, discipline was related to interests; highly interested students disciplined themselves to learn. For Makarenko, discipline was an outcome of learning.

As we look at current practices in upbringing, certain issues emerge. First is the continual search to improve the unity between academic teaching and upbringing. This is a major goal of pedagogical institutes during the next five-year plan. Second is a concern that the idealism and utopian visions of the revolution have become more rhetoric than practice. This is apparent in daily life in the Soviet Union. In most cases, Soviet citizens are loyal and patriotic; individualistic tendencies are sublimated to the group. People are honest and the streets are safe, but there is a rise in juvenile delinquency and in alcoholism. Further, in talking to people, it appears that the learning of Marxism-Leninism is often rote and only superficially integrated into consciousness.

Developing Curriculum for Soviet Schools

Curriculum development in the USSR is based on an inexhaustible optimism. Teachers, administrators, and professional curriculum developers in the Academy of Pedagogical Sciences are confident that for every teaching problem, they can invent a teaching solution. Parents are reassured by the aura of self-confidence that surrounds schooling.(15)

The self-confidence of educators is supported by a theory of curriculum development that assumes the existence of law-like principles of teaching, of learning, and of facts-concepts-generalizations that structure various disciplines or bodies of knowledge. The Soviets search for principles that guide learning, and on which knowledge in a subject depends, and for ways to integrate these principles with those governing successful teaching. The result is a curriculum "based on scientific principles."(16) Such scientific principles must, however, be consistent with a socialist world view, not independent of it. Thus, curriculum development often begins with research that discovers something lacking; for instance, students do not place high value on manual labor; the achievement of students in rural areas is below that of students in urban areas; or with a question such as what principles of physics must students know in order to understand the suject?

Following recognition of a problem, the writings of socialist-political theorists are analyzed to establish the correct ideological orientation. (Sometimes statements of goals such as those made by Party leaders at the National Party Congress become the first step in the process.) Then professional curriculum developers, usually attached to national institutes associated with the Academy of Pedagogical Sciences, propose solutions and test them in schools. If the results meet their expectations, the new curriculum is implemented widely as national policy.

Recently, this process led to the reorganization of the early years of schooling. Soviet scholars demonstrated children's ability to learn to generalize facts into concepts and concepts into principles of knowledge. Such teaching for generalization is efficient since more can be taught when pupils generalize knowledge than when they are taught endless facts. A second line of research established the usefulness of presenting concrete referents for abstract ideas. This led to a quicker grasp of abstractions and decreased the need for reteaching. Finally, when children's understanding was carefully developed through teaching that linked abstractions to concrete examples, pupils were able to deal with abstract ideas at an earlier age. This research led to the compression of the first four years of schooling into three years, while achievement remained the same or increased slightly.

Another example of this methodical approach to curriculum development is found in polytechnical education, which attempts to create an expression of the ideal curriculum from a Soviet point of view. Such a curriculum combines and balances ideas, attitudes, and actions on the part of students that lead to socially productive work. The "harmonious development of the individual" is expected to flow from such a curriculum in which feelings and ideas, intellect and personality characteristics are encouraged to be closely interactive.

Many studies in child development and schooling demonstrate that such a mutual dependence exists, that it is possible to affect intellectual achievement by changing attitudes and feelings, that it is possible to produce correct attitudes by leading pupils to succeed in achieving intellectual goals of schooling. As P.R. Atutov, one of its developers describes it, "polytechnical education is not only directed toward learning about the surrounding world but toward transforming one's surroundings..."(18)

Polytechnical education has its roots in Marxist theory. Marx posited that the mediating element between consciousness and the objective world is human labor. Current Soviet pedagogical theory uses that idea as a way of legitimating modern economic production. The aim of polytechnical education is to have students learn both general scientific knowledge and practical techniques that are used in a highly developed industrial technology. Students encounter many examples of ways basic science has influenced technological development.

Students read, discuss, study, and write about understanding; but an essential component of this form of education is the development of understanding through work. This may be through extracurricular activities or labor in factories, on farms, or in other economic enterprises related to the technology being studied.

Polytechnical education is integrated but it is also conservative. Students are encouraged to accept the production processes that exist in the Soviet Union, including methods of planning, ways of implementing plans, and the evaluation of outcomes. Ideas and actions in this curriculum encourage commitment to existing practices rather than critical analysis of the social relations produced.

Conclusions

This discussion of Soviet pedagogy may paint a portrait that seems rosy and overly optimistic and rational. Soviet schools, like our own, are extremely complex and dynamic, filled with contradictions, ambiguities as well as unanticipated outcomes.

The Soviet concern with all-around development, the careful attention to theory, the consideration of social-philosophical assumptions that underlie practice are important to understanding the particular programs and procedures found in the everyday activities of curriculum planning. While the American curriculum community may view with skepticism some of the values and assumptions that underlie these themes, the Soviet approaches point to the profound and complex social, political, and philosophical underpinnings of all endeavors to create and maintain schools.

Notes

1. Changes in Soviet life are tied to Communist Party policy. The Party is charged with the regulation and development of social life and production of intellectual work. Public debate occurs only in relation to how to best serve that policy.
2. The center-to-periphery model, however, is complex. Each of the 15 constituted republics has research institutes and research is conducted in teacher training institutes that are separate from the academy. (For a discussion of this complexity see T. Popkewitz and B. Tabachnick, "Soviet and American Pedagogical Research: Differences and Similarities in the Two Countries," in Studying Teaching and Learning: Trends in Soviet and American Research, B. Tabachnick, T. Popkewitz, and B. Szekely, eds. (New York: Praeger, 1981), pp. 3-38.
3. See, for example R. Davis, and others, An Analysis of Mathematics Education in the Union of Soviet Socialist

Republics. Clearinghouse for Science, Mathematics, and Environmental Education. Athens: Ohio State University, 1979; and M. Klenetsky and C. White, "Meeting the Soviet Challenge in Education," Fusion (October 1980): 67-78; T. Popkewtiz and B. Tabachnick, "Soviet and American Pedagogical Research: Differences and Similarities in the Two Countries," in Studying Teaching and Learning, pp. 3-38.
    4. See I. Wirszup, "The Soviet Challenge," Educational Leadership, 38, 5 (February 1981): 358.
    5. L.V. Zankov and others, Teaching and Development: A Soviet Investigation, B. Szekely, ed. (White Plains, NY: M.E. Sharpe, 1977).
    6. This is discussed in Popkewitz and Tabachnick," Soviet and American Pedagogical Research.
    7. For discussion of the Soviet idea of experiment, see Davis and others.
    8. R. Bauer, The New Man in Soviet Psychology (Cambridge: Harvard University, 1952).
    9. The issue of the origins and development of thought became a preoccupation of Soviet philosophy following the revolution and continues today as a major dimension of Soviet psychology and philosophy. See Ilenkov, Dialectical Logic (Moscow: Progress Press, 1977).
    10. L. Graham, Science and Philosophy in the Soviet Union (New York: Vintage, 1974).
    11. S. Toulmin, "The Mozart of Psychology," New York Review of Books 25, 14 (September 28, 1978): 51-57.
    12. N.A. Menchinskaia, "Some Aspects of the Development of the Soviet Psychology of Learning," Studying Teaching and Learning: Recent Trends in Soviet and American Research.
    13. See, for example, J. Dunston, "Soviet Moral Education in Theory and Practice," Journal of Moral Education 10 (3): 192-202; K. Weaver, Russia's Future, The Communist Education of Soviet Youth (New York: Praeger, 1981).
    14. A.S. Makarenko, The Road to Life (Moscow: Progress Press, 1951).
    15. See, for example, discussion in B. Szekely, "Introduction: Soviet Educational Research and the Soviet Seminar Contribution," in Studying Teaching and Learning.
    16. See, for example, V.V. Kraevskii, Relation of Pedagogical Science and Pedagogical Practice (Moscow: Knowledge, 1977). (In Russian.)
    17. In a few cases, republics of the USSR will insist on curricular components that are relevant to local culture characteristics and, in matters of use of local languages in instruction and teaching about local history and cultural heroes, they have won the right to deviate from the national curriculum.
    18. P.R. Atutov, "The Polytechnical Principle in Teaching Basic Science" in Studying Teaching and Learning, pp. 238-241.

SOVIET EDUCATION AND THE DEVELOPMENT OF COMMUNIST ETHICS

Delbert H. Long

Turning out scientists and engineers is not the most important function of education in the Soviet Union. The ultimate goal of education in the USSR is not academic but moral. Vladimir Ilyich Lenin, founder of the Soviet state, was clear and succinct on this point. "The entire purpose of training, educating, and teaching the youth today," he said in 1920, "should be to imbue them with communist ethics."

This has not been an esay task. The role of education in Russia is to convince the people that the leaders of the Communist Party have the right to control all property, all institutions, all forms of mass media - in short, to control what people think and do. A properly educated Soviet citizen will happily concede these rights to Party leaders. The challenge of producing good Soviet citizens - people with communist ethics - has become so critically important in recent years that the late Yuri Andropov, then Soviet premier, and [the late] Kostantin Chernenko, then a member of the powerful Politburo, both [spoke at] length on the subject at the June 1983 plenary session of the central committee of the Communist Party.(1)

A subject of such importance to Soviet leaders merits our attention. In this article I will discuss two questions:(2) what are communist ethics? how are they to be instilled in Soviet youth? The process involved, called vospitania, has no exact equivalent in English. Although vospitania is generally defined as "upbringing," the term is closer in meaning to the English expression, "character education." In the Soviet Union vospitania is a planned process involving the cooperative efforts of the home, the community, and the school, guided by the Communist Party, that is charged with the task of coordinating the efforts of the family and the community in the moral upbringing of children. Vospitania is an important part of the Soviet preschool, primary school, and secondary school, but I will restrict my comments to the secondary school (grades 4 through 10), because Soviet educators have given increased attention to this level in recent years.

From: "Soviet Education and the Development of Communist Ethics," by Delbert H. Long, in Phi Delta Kappan (March 1984): 469-472. Reprinted with permission. Copyright © March 1984 by Phi Delta Kappa.

´The New Soviet Man´
     Soviet leaders insist that what is moral is that which
furthers the cause of building a communist society. In a
speech to the 17th Congress of the Leninist Young Communist
League (Komsomol), the late Soviet leader Leonid Brezhnev said,
"Comrades, one of the most important tasks in the Komsomol´s
work is raising young people in the spirit of the new communist
morality, based, as Vladimir Ilyich [Lenin] used to say, ´on
the struggle for the consolidation and completion of
communism.´"

     Who determines what furthers or hinders this cause?
Soviet citizens are told that the Party has this right because
its members understand the truths of Marxism-Leninism and how
these truths may be used as a practical guide in building a
society consistent with communist ethics. This understanding
is presumably gained through years of training and practical
experience in Party affairs. A moral Soviet citizen, then,
should think and act in accordance with the dictates of the
Party. To think and act in this manner is to possess, in the
hierarchy of communist virtues, the highest virtue. A person
who possesses this virtue is commonly referred to, in Party
parlance, as "the new Soviet man" - one who has developed a
communist world view and acts in accordance with this world
view.

     To achieve a communist world view, a Soviet youth must
develop some virtues that are common to good citizens in most
societies. For example, he or she must be honest, truthful,
and helpful to others; and he or she must work hard in school
to develop intellectual, aesthetic, and physical abilities -
that is, to develop a "comprehensive, harmonious personality."
Although these important virtues receive considerable attention
in Soviet schools, the virtues regarded as most integral to the
development of communist ethics are the following.

     - Love of labor - To overcome economic backwardness of their
country, Soviet authorities have placed great emphasis on
inculcating in people a love of labor. A true lover of labor
is one who works not for personal benefit but for the benefit
of society. To do this, one must develop "labor discipline,"
which means, when stripped of Party jargon, the moral
commitment to do willingly whatever task the Party dictates,
regardless of how difficult or unpleasant it may be.

     - Patriotism - A Soviet patriot is an internationalist who
loves the military and the motherland and hates capitalists.
Capitalists are to be hated not only because of their
exploitation of the worker and their imperialistic designs but
also because of their propaganda efforts "to exert a

demoralizing influence on the minds of the Soviet people."

- Atheism - A good communist must be an atheist. Religious
faith is contrary to the materialistic doctrines of Marxism,
and communists claim that churches have always supported the
elite classes that gain and sustain their power and wealth
through the exploitation of the worker. To be an atheist,
however, is not enough. The good communist must be a militant
atheist - not only renouncing all religious beliefs but
striving to convince others to do the same.

- Collectivism - A collectivist is one who recognizes that
to develop a communistic world view is to develop a collective
world view. Such a view is the "enemy of individualism." In
the Soviet Union an "individualist" is one who selfishly works
only for personal benefit; a collectivist works to improve
society rather than to improve his or her own well-being.

Let me point out that having a correct attitude toward
work, patriotism, atheism, and collectivism does not in itself
make a model Soviet citizen. A model citizen must not only
have correct beliefs but must act on them, and it is here that
the school plays an important role. The Communist Party relies
heavily on the school not only to teach students basic
Leninist-Marxist thought but also to provide them with
opportunities to put this knowledge into action.

Developing Communist Character

The Soviet secondary school teacher is expected not only
to know his or her subject well and to teach it effectively but
to be "society´s agent in the upbringing of...children, and the
Party´s trusted support in agitation and propaganda and in all
ideological activities."(3) In the following description, I
will show how the teacher assumes this responsibility and
describe the upbringing process in the secondary schools.

In the classroom and in work with the Pioneer and Komsomol
youth organizations, the primary upbringing tool used by the
Soviet teacher is the collective. From the first day of school
a child becomes a member of various collectives. A group of
eight or 10 students makes up the basic collective, which is
called a "link" (zveno). The entire class forms a larger
collective called a "detachment" (otriad), and the whole school
is a still larger collective called a "brigade" (drushina).
The Soviet child is also a member of various extracurricular
collectives sponsored by the youth organizations.

A collective differs from a group such as a football team
in that a collective must have the same ultimate goal as the
larger society, which is to develop citizens who possess the
virtues described above. To be such a citizen one must first

learn to subordinate individual needs to the needs of the group. A child learns to do this - and develops other desirable character traits as well - through participation in collectives. Pedagogically, the great value of a collective is that it is designed to motivate members to bring pressure on one another to do the right thing.

A collective does not develop spontaneously, however, nor does it come to maturity in a short period of time. There are several stages to its development.(4) In the first stage, only the teacher makes demands on the students.

In the second stage, students begin to exert educational influence on one another. In general, individuals expect more of others than of themselves. However, a few students, called "activists," expect more of themselves than of others and thus provide good examples for their classmates. With the assistance of a few activists, the teacher is no longer forced to do upbringing work alone.

In the next stage of development, most members of the collective exert an educational influence on the individual. At this stage, students understand that "subordination of the minority to the majority is one of the democratic principles of Soviet society." Following the lead of the activists and the teacher, most children now "articulate the public opinion of the collective." At this stage, a student who does not wear a Pioneer scarf at a parade is chastised by most of his or her classmates. The collective no longer needs the help of the teacher in evaluating the conduct of its members. Furthermore, each student usually understands the necessity of the demands imposed by the collective, and, as a result, the conflict between the individual and the collective continues to diminish.

In the final stage of the development of the collective,

the entire collective exerts an educational influence on the individual. The collective is an ideological, intellectual, emotional, and organizational community. Each individual is capable of acting properly when left alone with his conscience, when no other comrades are near, when no one condemns him, and when no one demands that he correct his behavior. The individual´s demands on himself are higher than his demands on others.(5)

Soviet educators point out that the development of the collective to this final stage depends on the knowledge, skill, and tact of the teacher working with the collective. The teacher must guide the development of the collective but must not impose his or her will on it, except in the initial stages. Students must be given responsibility, but neither too little nor more than they can handle. The teacher must make sure that the collective has worthwhile tasks to promote the development of character but must allow the members of the collective to set the tasks themselves (though the teacher may provide tactful suggestions). The teacher must place demands on members of the student collective because students cannot grow morally if they are not constantly responding to increasingly difficult tasks. The teacher must be acutely aware of what each member of the collective, and the collective as a whole, is capable of doing at a particular stage of development.(6) In short, the Soviet teacher must know intimately the abilities, interests, and problems of the students, in order to draw out the best they have to offer to further the goals of the collective.

Youth Organizations
    The Soviet teacher is expected to share knowledge of his or her students with the leaders of the Pioneer and Komsomol youth organizations, as well as to raise the pedagogical consciousness of these leaders and to assist them in carrying out the functions of their organizations. These two organizations are strong political arms of the Communist Party. Nearly all students between the ages of 10 and 15 are members of the Pioneers. The Komsomol is more selective; its members are between 15 and 28 years old. Both organizations are charged with opportunities to put into practice the basic principles of communist morality. As with the school, the basic tool for fulfilling this charge is the collective. Pioneer and Komsomol collectives are often indistinguishable from school collectives; that is, the members of a Pioneer or Komsomol collective are often also members of the same class or school collective.

    The teacher most responsible for working with the Pioneer and Komsomol organizations is the "grade leader" (klassnui rukovoditel), a regular teacher who has upbringing responsibilities for all clases in a particular grade. The grade leader is expected to help Pioneer and Komsomol activists find interesting and socially useful work for the members of their units and to assist them in organizing and evaluating their activities. For example, to develop in Pioneers a love of labor, the grade leader will assist activists in planning such socially useful activities as growing plants, caring for animals, participating in the construction of shops and stadiums, helping collective farmers harvest crops, landscaping cities and highways, caring for parks and gardens, tutoring young children, assisting elderly people in hospitals, and participating (along with adults) in public work days.

Moral Development in Schools

Soviet teachers also play an upbringing role in the actual process of teaching their classes. Teachers are held responsible for teaching students correct answers to such questions as, Is religion inimical to the welfare of workers? Are historical forces such that inevitably capitalism will perish and communism triumph throughout the world? The new Soviet term for such teaching is "educative teaching." The goal of this kind of teaching is to develop in students the ability "to evaluate information from the standpoint of the objectives and tasks of the construction of a communist society."

Soviet educators emphasize that if proper attitudes are to be developed, the teacher must give students something more than correct answers. The teacher is expected to arouse in students a highly emotional, passionate conviction about the correctness of any one answer. It is not enough, for example, to teach students that communists are good and capitalists are bad. The teacher must use the powers of persuasion and moral conviction to instill in students a hatred for capitalists and a love for communists. Students must also be taught how to defend their communist beliefs, because students lacking this ability are subject to the "pernicious influences" of capitalist propaganda.

How might teachers of various disciplines develop appropriate attitudes in their students? Physics and chemistry teachers discuss the various forms of matter, its movements, and the impossibility of its existence outside time and space. Such scientific evidence is supposed to provide a basis for the formation of materialistic/atheistic views. Teachers of botany, zoology, anatomy, human physiology, and general biology are expected to enrich students with "new ideas regarding the material foundations of the development of the natural world, [thus] providing a basis for destroying religious views."

In history, students learn that communism will inevitably replace capitalism and that it is the worker, in the continuing class struggle with capitalists, who is the real creator of history. Most important, students learn in history that only the Communist Party is capable of guiding people in their quest for a better life. In literature, as well as in history, students learn how the church and the clergy have suppressed humankind and how communist heroes have dedicated their lives to the betterment of humankind.

Moral Development in the Family

The constitiution of the USSR requires parents to "devote themselves to the upbringing of their children" and to raise them as "worthy members of the socialist society." In the eyes of Soviet authorities, however, the family is often suspect. Too many parents lack proper ideological convictions, it seems, with the result that they gamble and drink too much and ignore their children. And many parents teach their children religion. In such cases, the school is expected to intervene actively in family education, "especially when children are the victims of religious fanaticism." A blatant example of such intervention in the Soviet Republic of Lithuania is reported in the Samizdat Bulletin, an underground publication distributed by Soviet dissidents.

    In October 1978, teacher Markiene of the First Middle School kept student Santa Bucyte after school. She scolded the girl for attending church and ordered her to bring her mother to school the next day.
    When she arrived at school, the girl´s mother asked the teacher what had happened - perhaps the girl had become a poor student? "No, your daughter is a very good student." "Then perhaps her behavior is bad?" the mother inquired. "No, her behavior is also good. Your daughter attends church!" "And is that a crime?" the mother exclaimed in astonishment. "She wants to go and I don´t forbid her because I also attend churh." The angry teacher retorted: "I don´t want to lose my job because of your daughter.

Disillusionment
    The Soviet people are increasingly disillusioned with Communist Party rhetoric about the new Soviet man.(7) Soviet leaders frankly acknowledge that the Party faces many problems in molding the new Soviet man. Among them are those noted by Chernenko in his keynote address at the recent plenary session of the Party´s central committee. "A most energetic struggle against drunkenness, hooliganism, parasitism, speculation, theft of socialist property, bribe-taking, and money-grubbing," he said, "is part and parcel of forming the new man´s character."(8) Later in the same speech he called for an intensive campaign against religious believers. At this plenary session, Andropov directed Party workers to make the improvement of ideological, upbringing, and propaganda work a priority and to use Soviet schools and other educational institutions to educate people "not merely as vessels containing a certain amount of knowledge but above all as citizens of a socialist society and active builders of communism, with the ideological principles, morals, and interests and the high standards in work and behavior that characterize such people."(9)

The effectiveness of teachers as molders of the new Soviet man will be severely limited by a phenomenon that teachers can do nothing about, i.e., the significant gap between communist ideology and everyday life in the Soviet Union. For example, the more mature young people in the USSR are aware of the frequent scarcity of agricultural produce and the constant scarcity of various consumer goods; they know that such scarcity has spawned a thriving black market. They observe the sharply defined class system in their country, the existence of special priveleges for the upper classes, and the restrictions on speech, religion, movement, and voting rights. They understand that their parents can vote for only one candidate for each office and that they are circumspect when talking on the telephone or writing letters because they assume that phones may be tapped and letters opened. Youngsters know of special stores where the elite may buy consumer goods far superior to those available to the average Soviet citizen. They observe that bribery is often required if their parents want a better apartment, a ticket to the Bolshoi, or a table at a good restaurant. And they are aware that going to church or communicating with foreigners from capitalist countries may be a serious handicap to advancement in their future professions.

Soviet youngsters know these facts of life, yet they have been taught by their teachers - and by all other forms of Soviet propaganda - that the USSR is a classless society and that Soviet citizens are more moral and have a higher standard of living and more freedom of speech, religion, movement, and voting rights than people in any noncommunist country. When Soviet boys and girls observe the disparity between Party ideology and their daily lives, it is understandable that they should experience some degree of disillusionment with Party ideology and with those who propagate it.

Communist ideology and Soviet political practice have been guided historically by pragmatic considerations. Pragmatic concessions in the past suggest that the Party remains capable of making necessary adjustments in its upbringing process. And even Soviet leaders acknowledge that adjustments must be made. But will the Party be sufficiently flexible to make its ideology more consistent with the world experienced daily by young people and adults? A lack of flexibility may heighten the existing disillusionment of many Soviet people with communist rhetoric about the new Soviet man. Disillusionment has already begun to breed cynicism, which may eventually force Soviet leaders to make significant adjustments in their upbringing process and even in their ideology.

Notes

1. Yuri V. Andropov, "Speech to Central Committee," Current Digest of the Soviet Press, 20 July 1983, pp. 1-8; and Konstantin U. Chernenko, "Urgent Questions of the Party's Ideological and Mass-Political Work," Current Digest of the Soviet Press, 13 July 1983, pp. 1-10, 24.
2. In preparing this article I relied on Soviet pedagogical journals and books in Russian and on two English-language publications that translate materials from Soviet sources, Current Digest of the Soviet Press and Soviet Education. But I have made reference only to selected sources in English.
3. Chernenko, p. 8.
4. The description of these stages follows closely that given in Ivan T. Ogorodnikov, ed., "School Pedagogy (Part II)," in Soviet Education, September/October 1980, pp. 47-50.
5. Ibid., p. 49.
6. For a comprehensive list of the character traits that a model Soviet student should have at different stages of growth and for suggested activities that teachers might use to develop these traits, see I.S. Mar'enko, ed., "A Model Curriculum for the Social Upbringing of School Pupils," Soviet Education, April/May 1983.
7. John Bushnell, "The New Soviet Man Turns Pessimist," in Stephen F. Cohen, et al., eds., The Soviet Union Since Stalin (Bloomington: Indiana University Press, 1980), pp. 179-199; and George Feifer, "Russian Disorders," Harper's, February 1981, pp. 41-55.
8. Chernenko, p. 5.
9. Andropov, p. 6.

SCHOOL REFORM IN THE USSR

Fedor Breus

A widespread discussion is beginning in the Soviet Union
on problems of improving education. Being examined is the
Central Committee of the Communist Party of the Soviet Union's
draft, published on January 4 [1984], on "The Main Guidelines
for a Reform of the General-Education and Vocational Schools."

The publication of such an important document did not come
as a surprise to the public. The pressing problems of public
education had been discussed for a long time in every family,
among teachers and university instructors and in the production
collectives of enterprises and offices. What and how should
the children be taught? What should they be oriented to in
choosing their profession? How do we help them find their
calling in life?

The party's Central Committee listened attentively to the
conflicting opinions and proposals coming from everywhere,
analyzed and drew its own conclusions.

The draft proposes changing the very structure of
education. The secondary general-education school now is to
become an eleven-year school instead of a ten-year school. Its
stages will be: elementary school - the first to fourth
grades; intermediate schools - the fifth to ninth grades. Then
come secondary general-education and vocational schools: the
tenth to eleventh grades of general-education school; secondary
vocational-technical schools; and specialized secondary
educational establishments. Thus, nine years of study became
the foundation for obtaining a general secondary or vocational
education in different fields.

According to the draft, the reorganization of schools
should help us to perform both the pressing tasks of the USSR's
current social and economic development and to meet the
strategic goals of the society's and state's development. At
the present stage, says the draft, the interests of the rapid
and harmonious development of the economy and culture, of the
improvement of social relations and the political
superstructure, of man himself as the main productive force and
the highest value of society, require a new and broader
approach to education and the upbringing of coming generations.

From: "School Reform in the USSR," by Fedor Breus, Novosti
Press Agency, Moscow, February 1984.

A long-term perspective can be seen from the programmatic positions of the party. "The party strives to ensure," Yuri Andropov stressed at the June 1983 Plenum of the CPSU Central Committee, "that our people are being educated not simply to amass a sum total of certain knowledge, but, first of all, to be citizens of a socialist society, active builders of communism, with deep-rooted ideological principles, morality and interests and high overall standards of work and behavior."

The Soviet state invests great sums in the education and the upbringing of its younger citizens. With each five-year period and even every year, more and more is being allocated from the State Budget for children's establishments and schools. The State Budget of the USSR, approved by a session of the Supreme Soviet for 1984, appropriated 33.1 billion rubles (41.7 billion U.S. dollars according to the January rate of exchange) for the development and expansion of the network of all kinds of educational institutions and the strengthening of their material and technical facilities. In 1984, the network of pre-school establishments, especially in rural areas, and the network of general-education schools will again be expanded. The number of pupils will exceed 40 million, with 13 million children attending extended-day schools and groups.

A large section in the draft is devoted to the teacher, a trusted and valued member of society, to whom, as the draft says, society entrusts its most dear and most valuable asset - children - its hope, its future. It is intended to raise the quality of training for teachers, to improve their advanced training and refresher courses and to increase their salaries. The beginning of the school year - September 1 - is proposed to be proclaimed a national holiday - the Day of Knowledge.

The reform will bring about changes also in the practice of accepting secondary school graduates in higher educational establishments. New admission rules are being considered, guaranteeing equal conditions for enrollment at higher educational establishments for graduates of general-education and vocational schools, and the terms of competition are being clearly specified.

The improvement of public education is one of the key questions of the larger policy pursuing humane and noble aims. The public so far has shown great interest in the draft.

CURRICULAR EMPHASES IN SOVIET SCHOOLS

How are the Soviet educational goals of creating a New Soviet Man with a Communist world view, and preparing qualified, skilled workers achieved? The content of curricula and the methods of teaching can be thought of as vehicles for accomplishing the goals of education in any formal system. How values and goals of a society are inculcated and what basic skills are needed to function address the curriculum issue.

The teaching of science, mathematics, and physical education (as well as Russian language and literature in some grades), occupy the greatest proportion of instructional time in Soviet schools beginning in the fourth grade. In addition, even before children enter any formal educational institutions, vocational education begins at the "mother's knee" (or the "babushka's knee") and the créches (i.e., the day nurseries). Values of work are inculcated throughout all facets of the society and have a very prominent place throughout the entire curriculum which attempts to emphasize practical applications as opposed to the "bourgeois" attitudes of education for the sake of education. The articles in this section highlight science, mathematics, physical and vocational education so that the reader can examine and appreciate the emphasis these subjects receive in the curriculum and the outcomes.

The first article, "Science and Computers in Soviet Society," is by Loren R. Graham. Although the intent of the author was not to analyze the science curriculum per se, the results of a study of Soviet emigres' experiences and impressions of the philosophy, value, and methods of science education in the Soviet Union as compared with those of the United States are discussed.

Graham reports that the Soviet émigrés identified strengths of Soviet science as including a strong foundation in elementary and secondary education, the Soviet government's commitment to long-range planning and funding of research, and, in general, Soviet society's positive attitudes toward the study of science. All of these are contrasted with the conditions of science and science education in the United States.

It is important for the reader to keep in mind that although Soviet children begin their formal study of science at a very young age, the methods of teaching them stress rote memorization. Children are not encouraged to think for themselves. Whenever experiments and demonstrations are

performed, they are usually executed by the teachers and
children are passive observers. In addition, many schools do
not have the facilities to conduct science experiments.
Despite the claims that the curriculum which is uniform and
compulsory throughout the entire country, attempts to emphasize
practical applications, the Soviet émigrés indicated that
Soviet scientists are less innovative and less productive than
their American counterparts.

Furthermore, deficiencies in and idiosyncracies of the
social system have caused difficulties for the development of
high-technology. One problem is the Party´s obsession with the
control of information. The proliferation of microcomputers
would threaten this control. Graham identifies the Soviet
Union as being "the most secretive industrialized power in the
world."

Recent visits to the Soviet Union and interviews with
representatives of the Scientific and Educational Workers´
Trade Union indicated that although Soviets believe knowledge
about computers might be beneficial and important, they have
not yet found a place for them in the classroom. Some
university professors indicated that the methods of applying
the computer for instruction are being studied. They want to
examine carefully the implications of using such technology in
the classroom. While this may very well be true based upon the
careful planning and experimentation typical of Soviet
curriculum reforms, it is more probable that concern over
access to information, the shortage of raw material (i.e.,
silicon), and the lack of production and innovation are the
more immediate causes for such delays in bringing computers to
the children.

The high probability of a shortage of the necessary raw
materials such as silicon needed to produce integrated circuits
(key components in microcomputer technology) and/or lacking
scientific initiative, innovation, and production, is indicated
in recent Soviet desires to obtain Western technology to supply
schools with personal computers (see "Computer Imports Sought
by Soviet," by David E. Sanger, in The New York Times, February
8, 1985, p. Al).

It is evident that general Party attitudes with respect to
the economic system - discouraging "originality in industrial
products and processes" - are reflected throughout the school
system. That is, the science curriculum and methods of
teaching meet the goals and needs of the society, as directed
by the Party. Many Western educators question whether or not
Soviet society is benefitting as a result of these attitudes
of control and restriction.

The second article is "The Development of Current Trends in Mathematics Education in Soviet Schools," by Frances R. Curcio. In this article, the historical development of mathematics education is traced. Mathematics, a subject of prominence in the curriculum, has been of interest and concern since pre-Revolutionary Russia.

Unlike the philosophy of Soviet education, not all children were educated equally during czarist regimes. The October Revolution attempted to change all of this. However, as discussed in the article, the content of the mathematics curriculum currently mandated has proven too difficult for the majority of students and its egalitarian purpose has been challenged by Soviet mathematics educators, critical of the curriculum.

Curcio traces the development of mathematics education from the Unified Labor School, which is recognized for some of its progressive qualities, only to be replaced by the strict, regimented discipline of the pedagogical methods of Anton Makarenko, to the present proposed reforms. The significant changes made in the mathematics curriculum are noted.

During decades following the October Revolution, under the leadership of Stalin, Khrushchev, and Brezhnev, Makarenko´s pedagogical influence was prevalent. The study of mathematics was subjected to a few changes, the most significant since the Unified Labor School curriculum were in recent years.

During Joseph Stalin´s reign and his introduction of the Five-Year Plans, the curriculum was an academically oriented curriculum which emphasized mathematics with respect to preparing citizens for industrial labor. The application of mathematics received maximum attention. Methods of teaching and learning mathematics were by rote memorization - not much different from instruction during pre-Revolutionary times.

Nikita Khrushchev´s educational plan was to move the process of education into the world of work. His polytechnic program combined learning and labor. Children spent a major portion of their time in the fields and factories. Due to the decline of the general study of mathematics, special schools were established for the mathematically talented.

Leonid Brezhnev eliminated many of the educational policies implemented by Khrushchev (who lost favor with the Party). In particular, children were returned to their "rightful" place - the classroom. Interest in mathematics education was revived and restored when Brezhnev appointed a commission to upgrade the mathematics curriculum. The new curriculum that was proposed and then implemented had its disciples and its critics. In attempts to upgrade the mathematics curriculum, Soviet mathematicians and educators to a certain extent, overestimated the ability of children to learn abstract, technical, sophisticated mathematical terminology (experiencing some of the same repercussions of the "New Math" movement in the United States). Less application of mathematics was included in the new curriculum.

During Brezhnev's later years, being influenced by some of the critics of the mathematics curriculum, he urged another reform. Proposals of the new reform include the elimination of the technical terminology criticized by the reformers, and the addition of more application problems. An outline of the proposed curriculum is included in an appendix.

Curcio adds that new methods of teaching, being influenced by contemporary psychologists such as L.V. Zankov, are also having some influence - less emphasis on rote memorization and more stress on meaning and understanding. However, at this time, it is not common to find the cultivation of independent, critical, creative thinking in any part of the Soviet curriculum - why should the study of mathematics be any different?

The third article is entitled, "Physical Education in USSR Schools," by Victor Zilberman. Why does physical education deserve such a prominent place in Soviet education? Zilberman tells us that physical education contributes to moral development by instilling within youngsters the value of comraderie, collectivism, and discipline, among others. It is believed that through physical training, in addition to academic "training," the Marxist-Leninist objective of all-round development for labor and defense can be achieved.

It is interesting to note that although Marx was not an avid practitioner of physical education (his "sport" was chess), Lenin made the pursuit of physical fitness part of his lifestyle. Whether by word or by deed, both saw the value of developing a sound mind in a sound body.

Unlike the emphasis on play, fun, and recreation typical of American physical education classes, Zilberman describes the Soviet program as being rather formal, stressing skill development and perfection. Similar to other curricula, the physical education curriculum is uniform throughout the Soviet Union.

The Soviet society can boast about organized sports programs for citizens spanning the ages of 10 to 60. Physical education is not limited to the school curriculum. Children can participate in interest circles and clubs affiliated with

Pioneer Houses and Pioneer Camps. Special boarding schools and sports institutions for the athletically inclined have been established to offer training for Soviet and international competitions.

Zilberman identifies some of the problems in trying to bring physical education to all children throughout the USSR; teacher shortages and lack of adequate facilities and equipment are among a few of these. Soviet educators are faced with the challenge to remedy these problems.

The unity of ideological and scientific principles is reflected in the Soviet physical education curriculum. In short, the content and methods of teaching physical education contribute both to developing a Communist world view as well as preparing citizens physically and psychologically for the world of work.

The last article is "Vocational Education in the USSR," by Felicity O´Dell. The author indicates that the three basic goals of Soviet vocational, polytechnical education, that is, moral training, skill training, and vocational guidance, reflect the Communist ideology and attempt to meet the demands of economic needs.

The inculcation of moral values with respect to work begins at a very early age. Every citizen is expected to be a "Builder of Communism." Marxist principles are the foundation for instilling within children positive attitudes toward work (i.e., a love of work, a commitment to quality), and respect for all types of work.

Soviet leaders have recognized that the contemporary worker, faced with the technological revolution, must be flexible and capable of adapting to change. In general, there is a shortage of skilled workers. In particular, improvements in labor training are trying to overcome the shortage of creative and innovative workers.

O´Dell discusses the features of vocational education at different levels: pre-school upbringing, secondary schools, out-of-school education, technical trade schools, secondary specialized colleges and higher education. Contrary to the rote learning methods used throughout the general school curriculum, the hands-on, learning-by-doing approach is employed at all levels. Some programs purport to include more problem-solving and employ programmed learning. In addition, working as a cooperative member of a team and the value of the collective are emphasized.

Pioneer Palaces and Pioneer Camps also provide children

with opportunities to become familiar with the world of work at no charge to parents. O´Dell states that the activities in which children are involved usually have a "vocational bias and their activity is guided by trained adults." Special schools, offering after-school instruction in music, art, and dance exist for children who want to pursue careers in these professions. Unlike the free attendance at the Pioneer Palaces and Camps, parents pay a small fee for the instruction.

Despite the fact that over 85% of women of working age are in the Soviet workforce, sex-role stereotyping continues to be prevalent. Boys are channeled into woodworking and metal shops and girls are enrolled in sewing and cooking classes. This does not prepare the majority of women who are assigned to factory work. O´Dell describes other patterns of male and female vocational preparation.

Since it has become more desirable for young people to live in urban centers, the availability of competent workers and professionals in rural areas has suffered. In attempts to curtail the exodus to the cities, current practices make it difficult for citizens to move from villages and farms to urban centers.

O´Dell describes the first level of professional training in technical-trade schools, secondary technical-trade schools, and technical schools. These institutions provide specific training for employment. At least eight years of general education are required for some of the courses; others require ten years. Some programs allow citizens to attend evening classes so that they can maintain their daytime jobs. Students completing programs are guaranteed employment and they are expected to stay in their assigned job for at least three years. Students who excel are exempt from the three-year assignment rule and may pursue higher education or enroll in evening courses. It is important for the reader to keep in mind that O´Dell does not mention that students do evade the requirements of the system by resorting to other means such as bribery, favors, etc.

Vocational preparation permeates all facets of higher education. Unlike the approaches used in the earlier grades, methods of teaching have emphasized independent, creative thinking in terms of practical applications in the advanced levels. To a Western educator, this may seem to be a contradiction of terms; that is, independent, creative thinking should not have to be confined to immediate practical applications. The benefits of cultivating inventiveness and creativity might not be reaped for many years. In any case, regardless of the methods employed, many citizens aspire to higher education as a means for social mobility.

Finally, O'Dell describes some of the problems facing vocational education in the Soviet Union. Among these are the many and varied alternatives to obtain training for employment resulting in the questionable quality of the finished product, the lack of prestige of vocational courses attributed by society in general, the methods of teaching and the content of vocational courses, the strained relationship among schools, training schools, colleges, factories, etc., and the questionable success of the labor training process.

At the present, Soviet society is faced with scarce labor resources, a quality of work not worthy of the Communist work ethic, a new generation concerned with materialism, and a low level of attractiveness of certain "menial" jobs. It is reported that there is an increasing number of workers and students who are victims of alcoholism resulting in undisciplined and irresponsible behavior. Solutions to some of these problems are proposed by upgrading pre-vocational education to emphasize the development of positive attitudes toward employment, discipline, standardized training, and more career guidance at younger ages.

The four selections in this section focus on science, mathematics, physical, and vocational education. These were chosen so that the reader could compare Soviet ideology, the content of the curriculum, and methods of teaching.

Although some instances of developing independent, creative thinking are reported, it can be observed that the methods of achieving the goals of the Soviet educational system rely heavily on rote memorization, strict regimentation and discipline. Many Soviet educators, not yet influenced by the work of Zankov and others, still believe that imitation is the best way (and in some cases the only way) for children to learn.

Some Soviet educators have recognized that the rote approach has created a limitation of their system and it has resulted in a shortage of creative, innovative personnel. In attempting to meet the challenge of this weakness and break out of the mechanical teaching methods, they are wary of threatening bureaucratic security.

Although the Party's intent to provide equal educational opportunity for all is commendable, as the authors in this section point out, it has not been achieved. Also, neither the goal of preparing competent workers nor that of creating the New Soviet Man with a Communist world view has been realized.

As much as each educational system has its strengths and

weaknesses, no educational system is perfect. Soviet leaders
and educators are to be commended for inculcating within their
citizens a genuine respect and love of learning. Soviet people
are known to be avid readers, and many adults continue their
education through correspondence and evening courses.

How each society deals with evaluating its progress and
achievement of its goals is subject for continued study. It
appears as though the creation of a New Soviet Man with a
Communist world view and the preparation of qualified,
competent workers continue to be goals of the Soviet
educational system. The goals are as imperative to the Soviet
leadership today as they were sixty years ago.

SCIENCE AND COMPUTERS IN SOVIET SOCIETY

Loren R. Graham

The Soviet Union possesses the largest scientific establishment in the world. In the fields of natural science and engineering, it has about a third more researchers with a Ph.D. degree or its equivalent than the United States. Furthermore, the Soviet Union has for decades devoted a larger share of its GNP to research and development than has the United States.

Of course, numbers do not tell everything. The Soviet Union's quantitative achievement in building the world's largest research establishment has not been matched by equivalent qualitative gains. As Thane Gustafson has observed, "by any measure - whether Nobel prizes, frequency of citation by fellow specialists, origin of major breakthroughs, or simply quantity of publications - U.S. scientists lead their Soviet colleagues in most disciplines, and in many there is simply no competition."(1)

One of the striking characteristics of Soviet science and technoloy is its qualitative heterogeneity. In some fields, Soviet researchers are among the best in the world; in others, they are mediocre. The disparity in quality in different fields is remarkable, especially when viewed against the background of Soviet efforts to be the leader in many, if not all, fields. To anyone interested in how science develops, its history, and its social foundations, the unusual pattern of strengths and weaknesses in the Soviet Union is a genuine challenge, a set of important questions demanding answers.

By the early 1980s a number of important studies of Soviet science and technology had been published in the West. These studies concentrated on the issue of political intrusion in Soviet science, the relationship of science to Marxist ideology, military technology, Soviet science policy, and the growth of the Soviet scientific establishment. The Social Context of Soviet Science, published in 1980, interpreted the features of Soviet science from the standpoint of Soviet politics and culture.(2) Other valuable studies of Soviet research came out of the exchanges and bilateral agreements that flourished in the 1970s, particularly the Kaysen report of

From: "Science and Computers in Soviet Society," by Loren R. Graham, in The Soviet Union in the 1980s, 1984, The Academy of Political Science. Used by permission.

the National Academy of Sciences.(3)   This report was based on
questionnaires submitted to hundreds of American scientists who
had worked closely with Soviet scientists.   It contains a great
deal of valuable information on the strengths and weaknesses of
fundamental research in the Soviet Union, and it has the
advantage of being based both on quantified empirical data and
on qualitative assessments made by leading American scientists.

   None of these studies included reports from Soviet
scientists themselves.   The Kaysen committee had attempted in
the late 1970s to involve Soviet scientists in its study of the
exchanges, but the Soviet Academy of Sciences refused to permit
its researchers to participate.   In the 1970s, however, large
numbers of Soviet scientists and engineers emigrated to the
West and provided an opportunity for studies of Soviet research
based on information given by recent native participants.   At
Harvard and MIT two projects of this type have recently been
completed: one, financed by the National Council for Soviet
and East European Studies, was based on interviews with several
hundred émigré scientists and engineers.   The other was the
Eyewitness Seminar series.(4)   This essay will present an
overview of some of the findings from these projects, relying
primarily on the series of Eyewitness Seminars.

   The goal of these studies was to define the strengths and
weaknesses of Soviet science and technology and to explain them
in terms of the intellectual, political, and social
characteristics of the Soviet Union.   Among the strengths of
Soviet science and technology that emerged were the following:
a strong elementary and high school educational system,
continuity in research efforts, a tradition of excellence in
some areas of fundamental research, a high esteem for science
in Soviet society, and a system of research priorities that
permit the government to accomplish many of its goals.   Among
the weaknesses of Soviet science and technology were the
following: a lack of innovation, limited contact between
research and industry, political and ethnic discrimination,
poor supply and distribution, and inadequate communication -
both among Soviet scientists and between Soviet and foreign
scientists.

Strengths of Soviet Science

   Almost all of the émigrés who were interviewed had a higher
opinion of Soviet elementary education than they do of American
education; some of them also believed that Soviet university
education is superior to American education, especially in
mathematics and physics.   While the United States has gradually
declined in science education, the Soviet Union has continued
to build an impressive system.   Soviet high school students are
given much more work in mathematics and science than American

students. Several years ago only a few more than 100,000
American high school students were taking calculus each year,
while 5 million Soviet students did so. Perhaps these
statistics have changed somewhat, since the United States has
tried to improve its system of mathematics and science
education, but a severe shortage of qualified high school
mathematics teachers has hampered real improvement.

On this topic, there was considerable agreement between
the émigrés and Professor Izaak Wirszup of the University of
Chicago, who has maintained that "the disparity between the
level of training in science and mathematics of an average
Soviet skilled worker or military recruit and that of a
non-college-bound American high school graduate...is so great
that comparisons are meaningless."(5)

By concentrating on curricula rather than on results,
Wirszup has probably exaggerated the difference in the quality
of Soviet and American science education. The impressive and
rigorous Soviet science and mathematics curricula do not always
succeed on the local level, especially in schools that are far
from the major cities. In provincial schools, Soviet education
is plagued with problems similar to those of American
education: poorly trained teachers, apathetic students, and
inadequate resources. Furthermore, part of the deficiencies of
American high schools are compensated for in the better
universities. Vladimir Kresin, an émigré physicist now working
at the Lawrence Laboratory in Berkeley, agreed that Soviet
elementary and high school education is superior to American
education on the same levels, but he disagreed with some of the
other émigrés by maintaining that "on the university
level...the American system makes a giant leap forward leaving
the Soviet system behind."(6) Even if this correction takes
place in the best American universities, such as Berkeley, it
would not affect the conclusion that one of the strengths of
the Soviet Union in science and technology is its educational
system on the elementary and secondary levels.

The Soviet system supports specific lines of research over
very long periods of time. American researchers have to
contend with much greater oscillations of funding from year to
year. The NASA budget, for example, increases and decreases in
step with national and congressional moods. The same is true
for many other areas of American research. The United States
lurches from one research fad to another, from "Wars on Cancer"
to "Campaigns Against Aging" to "Synthetic Fuels."
Furthermore, the system of contracts and grants prevalent in
American research, while possessing many strengths, is also
time consuming. Several of the émigrés were critical of the
American grant system, which they consider somewhat chaotic and
inefficient. In the Soviet Union the budgets for most lines of

research are rather constant. Few areas of research are
dramatically cut, and institutions are almost never eliminated.
While this degree of continuity of research strategy leads to
conservatism and may inhibit innovation, it also has certain
real advantages; Soviet researchers in leading institutions
feel free to embark on long-term projects without fear that
their budgets will be eliminated before they can complete their
work. For example, continuity of research effort significantly
helped the Soviet Union in magnethydrodynamics, an area where
the United States discontinued an important line of research
only to have to do catch-up work later when it appeared that
the Soviet decision to continue had proved correct.

The strength of Soviet mathematics and physics is a
tradition that began before the Russian Revolution. Moscow
today probably contains more outstanding mathematicians than
any other city in the world. The more abstract and
mathematical an area of science is, the more likely the Soviet
Union is to be a leader in that area. Indeed, Western
specialists on Soviet science and technology often speak of
"The Blackboard Rule" - meaning that Soviet science is likely
to be strong in any area where the main tools of research are a
blackboard and chalk and weak in areas requiring material
support, sophisticated instrumentation, or close contact with
industry. There are exceptions to "The Blackboard Rule," to be
sure, but it is often strikingly accurate.

Science as a field of study and scientists as members of a
profession are held in high esteem in the Soviet Union. In the
United States and other Western countries one often hears of
revolts against science, or even of antiscience movements.
Such social attitudes are rare in the Soviet Union. Full
members of the Academy of Sciences are the most prestigious
members of Soviet society, enjoying far more admiration than
the top leaders of the Communist party or the government.
Soviet television and the Soviet press are filled with features
on the lives of the leading scientists. Americans, however,
are skeptical of scientists and engineers described as culture
heroes, pure in motive and action.

Soviet science also benefits from political leaders´ and
science administrators´ ability to select a few high-priority
areas of research and to support them with vast quantities of
funds and personnel. The centralized planning system in the
Soviet Union does not work well in running an entire economy -
especially the consumer economy - but it does operate rather
well in choosing a few selected issues for special emphasis,
both military and nonmilitary - including scientific research.
At the present time the Soviet Union places great emphasis on
biotechnology. There are already signs of significant
improvement in research and development in these areas,

accompanied by difficulties in moving beyond the research to
industrial applications. This pattern of strengths and
weaknesses is a common one.

Weaknesses in Soviet Science and Technology

As mentioned earlier, former Soviet scientists and
engineers now working in the United States often reported that
they received a more rigorous education in mathematics and
science in the Soviet Union than their American colleagues
received in the United States. They did not feel, however,
that Soviet advanced research in their particular area was
superior to that in the United States. Soviet engineers
sometimes maintained that although they know much more
mathematics than their American coworkers, they had great
difficulty keeping up with them in terms of productivity and
innovation. In other words, the émigrés believed that Soviet
scientists and engineers are better educated than American ones
but much less productive and innovative.

A number of émigrés often explained that the most exciting
aspect of American research and development is the sense of
which topics are "hot" and which are not. Among Soviet
researchers, this ability to choose independently which issues
are crucial seems to be less developed; Soviet researchers seem
to feel that the important products of research are papers and
publications. Little thought is given to their relative
importance or possible industrial applications. American
research is more competitive, more selectively directed toward
breakthroughs, and more concerned with developing products that
can be commercially utilized. Soviet research is directed
toward the building of individual or institutional reputations
by producing publications. Once the publication has appeared,
the Soviet researcher often loses interest in the topic. To
American researchers, publication is frequently viewed as a
step toward developing something more concrete, either a
commercial application or the next step in the research
process. Indeed, Soviet researchers seem to value publication
more highly than American researchers - an observation that may
amuse Americans familiar with the "publish or perish" syndrome.
The difference is that in the United States publication is not
the final or only goal. The functional importance of
publication to Americans is undermined by other means of
communicating research results, such as preprints and telephone
calls among the small circle of leaders in any given area of
research.

Another obstacle to innovation in the Soviet Union is the
economic system, which discourages originality in industrial
products and processes, Traditionally, Soviet industrial
planners are rewarded for increasing quantitative output, not

for qualitative improvements. Despite enormous efforts to
change this emphasis over the past thirty years, progress has
been very slow. There is no "market pull" for the introduction
of innovation in the Soviet Union, only "bureaucratic push."
And even the bureaucracy is often afraid of innovation, because
it undermines careers and leads to unsettling changes.

Since most of the émigré scientists were Jewish, it is not
surprising that many of them reported on anti-Semitism in the
Soviet Union. A sobering conclusion must be drawn from their
reports, however, is not only that anti-Semitism exists in
Soviet academic life but also that it is growing in
significance and has now affected the quality of scientific
research in a number of fields.

Most entrance examinations to Soviet universities are
oral, and it is at this stage that Jews or politically suspect
students are often eliminated. Jews are given much more
difficult questions than non-Jewish students. One of the
émigrés was denied admission to Moscow University because he
could not describe how the Dalai Lama in Tibet is selected.
The question was obviously designed to eliminate him, despite
his excellent record in mathematics and science.

Since the early 1970s Jewish mathematicians have been
virtually eliminated as authors in several of the leading
mathematics journals in the Soviet Union. The quality of the
strongest areas of Soviet science - mathematics and physics -
is being damaged by the growth of anti-Semitism. Although the
depth of talent in these fields is so great that the damaging
effects can probably be tolerated by the Soviet authorities,
the injury that has been done to Soviet intellectual life is
visible.

Yet another weakness of Soviet science is the poor supply
and distribution system. The Soviet émigrés reported that
supply and distribution problems are some of the most
significant drawbacks in Soviet science and technology.
Shortages of materials extend, at different times, from
sophisticated equipment to the most simple reagents - even to
nuts, bolts, and paper. Obtaining supplies for research is a
never-ending task in the Soviet Union, involving an enormous
waste of time and effort. It is not unusual for a laboratory
to halt its work for several weeks while searching for rather
trival supplies. And in areas like astronomy, important
results are sometimes lost forever because the right kind of
photographic plate was unavailable at the required moment.

Finally, Soviet science is isolated from the West and
compartmentalized at home. As a result, Soviet researchers
suffer from communication lags, learning what is going on in

352

their fields only after researchers in other countries have
utilized the latest findings to further their own research.
Western journals are received late in the Soviet Union, and
they often go first to senior scientists. The more creative
junior scientists have difficulty obtaining them early enough
for the information to be useful. Furthermore, scientific
journals are censored along with all other publications.

Even within the Soviet Union communication lines are weak.
Although abstract and indexing services are highly developed,
these services are not computerized to the degree that they
have been in the West. Furthermore, new fields and
interdisciplinary efforts do not receive attention before it is
too late. Western scientists visiting the Soviet Union often
find that a Soviet scientist working on a given problem in one
institution does not know of the existence of another Soviet
scientist working on the same problem in another institute in
the same city. The foreigners often bring the two researchers
together.

Receptivity to Technological Change

Western analyses of Soviet science and technology usually
concentrate on hardware and technology rather than on the
receptivity of Soviet society to technological change. Yet the
rapidity with which a society absorbs a new technology is a
crucial factor in determining the rate at which that technology
will develop. The development of computers in the Soviet Union
illustrates the importance of this absorptive capacity.

During the early phase of computer development, the major
emphasis was on large mainframe computers, which were, by
necessity, institutionally controlled and best adapted to
centralized functions. These computers were attractive in
terms of Soviet ideology, centralized planning, and traditional
Soviet tendencies toward "gigantomania." Recently, however,
microcomputers and personal computers have been developed with
so much power that they are beginning to rival in capacity
their larger ancestors. Today one can buy in almost any
computer store in the United States an Apple Computer or an IBM
PC with internal memory capacities up to 640 kilobytes, or even
higher, which only a decade ago would have been a respectable
memory for a large mainframe computer. Furthermore, the
versatility of these small desk-top computers can be vastly
increased by connecting them to larger mainframe computers. As
a result, it is becoming increasingly clear that the most
efficient use of computers for a great range of applications is
based on decentralized systems in which, at the local level,
microcomputers can be used either alone (for simpler tasks) or
in connection with a larger coherent system (for assignments
demanding greater capacity or access to centralized data

banks).

The Soviet social and political system is having
difficulty adapting to the new trend toward personal computers
controlled by private individuals. Every microcomputer or word
processor connected to a printer is a potential printing press.
In the Soviet Union, private possession of printing presses
and even photocopy machines is prohibited; yet a microcomputer
can print the desired number of copies. Anyone who remembers
how Soviet dissidents of the 1960s spent days typing samizdat
documents on typewriters stuffed with five or six carbon copies
will understand the significance of the new technology. In
Poland, some members of the scientific intelligentsia who
support the Solidarity movement have turned out political
documents on computers in government offices. These computers,
however, used old-fashioned tapes instead of disks, were
centrally controlled, and were not located in private homes.
The authorities cannot permit Soviet citizens to acquire
personal computers or word processors without risking the
repetition of such events on a much broader scale.

Of course, the Soviet leaders have several possible
solutions to this challenge: all computers, like all
photocopiers, could be housed in institutions and controlled by
institutional officials. Or, if microcomputers were permitted
in homes or under decentralized control, they would not be
accompanied by printers; printing would take place in a central
institutional office where it could be both printed and
censored. Or, finally, all microcomputers could be connected
to central computers that would record all manuscript files as
they are created; if the local computer were unplugged from the
central network, it would not work. Thus, security officials
would have records on everything that Soviet citizens did with
computers. Big Brother would triumph after all.

Soviet authorities certainly have the power and the
technical capabilities to try to enforce such rules, and in
fact they are doing so already, by requiring all computers to
be institutionally housed and controlled. But the Soviet
authorities will pay a high price for these regulations by
severely limiting the rate of the growth of the computer
culture, by hampering the spread of computer literacy among
young people, by losing the advantages of economies of scale
that the mass production of computers is bringing, by failing
to take advantage of the efficiencies in financial transactions
- including personal ones - that computers can bring, and by
watching the West become a true "information society" that they
will be doomed to follow enviously unless they loosen up their
society. Furthermore, they can never be sure that someone will
not circumvent their controls; if American authorities worry

354

about the teenagers in Milwaukee and Seattle who break <u>into</u>
central data banks without authorization, the Soviet
authorities have the opposite worry that an undergraduate in a
Soviet technological institute may break <u>out</u> of the central
computer surveying his activities, because if he succeeds then
by definition he does not leave traces.

A great many factors influence a culture´s receptivity to
new computers, and in all of them the United States seems to
have the edge over the Soviet Union. These factors include:
(1) a tradition that successful technologies should be
privately owned and controlled if it is advantageous to do so;
(2) a tradition of free access to information; (3) a tradition
of creating large amounts of reliable and accurate data about
the economy and about society; (4) a financial system offering
diverse business and consumer services; (5) widespread
education in business and technological skills, including
typing and programming; (6) excellent telephone lines that can
be used for remote access to data bases; (7) close
relationships between sellers and buyers of technology,
including consulting services, maintenance, and spare parts;
and (8) a tradition of entrepreneurship and innovation under
which a person who develops a successful product - whether
hardware or software - can legally make and attempt to sell it.

The Soviet Union has major problems in every one of these
areas. It has a tradition of prohibiting individual control
over communication technologies. The most secretive
industrialized power in the world, it controls information
zealously. Under its financial system, private checking
accounts are almost unheard of and individual credit
arrangements are extremely cumbersome. Its telephone system is
of such low quality that the attempts made so far to establish
modem communication have had to rely either on special lines or
on a "search" system by which only one out of some twenty
possible circuits is deemed good enough for high-speed
communication. The Soviet Union´s educational system does not
emphasize business or "hands-on" technological skills, and
typing is not widely taught in Soviet schools; Soviet
college-level education about computers is strong on the
theoretical or mathematical side but weak on the practical
side. A "hacker culture" does not exist in Soviet
universities. The technical consultation, maintenance, and
spare-parts services that good computer dealers provide in the
West are notoriously poor in the Soviet Union; yet computers
are so complex that without helpful dealers, start-up and
maintenance problems can become insurmountable difficulties.
Finally, business entrepreneurship is prohibited in the Soviet
Union.

The last point needs elaboration. The most vigorous

355

aspect of the computer business in the United States today is
the production of software. Software programming seems to be
an activity similar to a cottage industry, but there are no
legal cottage industries in the Soviet Union. Rather than
allowing a cottage software industry to develop, Soviet
authorities have turned software production over to enormous
institutes and production facilities, where several thousand
researchers work. Yet in the United States even giant
companies like IBM often buy their software from individuals or
small firms. While the popular picture in the United States of
the reclusive genius who descends from his mountaintop twice a
year with a new brillant piece of software may be exaggerated,
it is nonetheless true that enormous organizations have not
produced the most innovative software. The evidence so far
seems to indicate that a wide open, chaotic, competitive
marketplace with a staggering variety of contenders is the best
environment for producing ingenious computer programs. In
Silicon Valley in California about one hundred new
high-technology firms - most of them computer related - have
been established in the last twelve months. The Soviet Union
could not duplicate this environment without contradicting its
most cherished economic principle - the elimination of private
enterprise.

One of the principles known to every computer specialist
is "garbage in, garbage out." That is, the best computer in
the world cannot produce a good product if the information fed
into it is inferior or incomplete. Some economists doubt that
centralized planning of an economy is theoretically possible,
but even those who defend it admit that it must be based on
accurate data. Yet much of the economic, demographic, and
sociological information available in the Soviet Union is
inferior and incomplete. Why have the Soviet authorities
failed to improve the quality of their data? Within limits,
they are trying to do so, but some of the information necessary
for social planning would be embarrassing, even if available.
Infant mortality rates, necessary for health planning, have not
been published in the Soviet Union since 1975, soon after a
sharp increase in this vital death indicator. By Western
standards, the Soviet Union has a measurable unemployment rate
- another fundamental statistic - yet no figures on
unemployment are available. Grain production in the USSR has
been a state secret since 1981. Other economic data are
statistically inferior, at least when compared with those
available for Western countries. Local managers may not even
want the information to be more accurate, since it could reveal
corruption or managerial ineptitude. Rewards exist in the
Soviet system for incomplete or false reporting, just as they
do in the United States (income tax returns, for example), but
in the Soviet Union the tradition of secrecy and the absence of
investigative reporting aid the person trying to cover his

tracks.

This inadequacy of accurate information decreases the
efficiency of the Soviet system while making the application of
computers more difficult. After games and word processing,
probably the most common nonmilitary use of computers in the
United States is financial and business planning, as the
popularity of the "financial spread-sheet" programs indicate.
Computers increase the velocity of local decision making; and
the faster the planner operates, the more important it is that
one's data be accurate and that one have the authority to make
a quick decision. The centralized Soviet system relying on
data of questionable accuracy does not seem well suited for
this new business era.

All the above arguments suggest that the Soviet Union will
have unusual difficulties in adjusting to the computer
revolution. But do these same arguments mean that computers
will undermine or destroy the Soviet system? Not at all. The
Soviet leaders are experienced in maintaining their control,
and they will find ways of containing the implicit threat to
their authority that the new computers pose. Complete computer
systems and access to international telecommunication networks
will not be placed in the hands of individual Soviet citizens.
Institutions will control access to the computers.

Conclusion

With the exception of a few fields, the Soviet Union is
not a leader in science and technology. For decades it has
invested an enormous share of its talent and material resources
in science, but its has not yet won the premier place that its
leadership has sought. Failure to be a winner in science and
technology, however, is not the same as being a loser. In
fact, the Soviet Union has a solid record in science and
technology as a rather good follower. Again and again, people
in the United States have noticed deficiencies in Soviet
research and then have gone on to underestimate seriously the
ability of the Soviet Union to stay close behind the United
States in technical achievements. Being first in technological
competition may not be as important as being able to stay close
behind the leaders in the areas that count. At the end of
World War II, many Americans predicted that it would be ten or
fifteen years before the Soviet Union could produce an atomic
bomb; it produced one within four years. Then it was said that
the Soviets would have difficulty developing the hydrogen bomb,
but they produced it at about the same time as the United
States. Then it was said that they could not produce accurate
intercontinental ballistic missiles, but they soon did. Then
it was said that they could not develop MIRV´ed warheads for
their missiles, but they did, and now the United States is

having trouble living with the results. Then it was said that they could not develop look-down, shoot-down radar, but they now have that, too.

The story of American-Soviet competition in science and technology is not a refrain from the old song "Anything you can do, I can do better," but "Anything you can do, I can do a bit later." This is particularly true in military technology, where the Soviet system of governmentally determined research priorities and centralized control over resources enables the USSR quickly to focus its efforts in any direction it sees its competitors pursuing. This ability should cause the United States to hesitate before opening up new areas of expensive competition in military technology, such as the militarization of space. In military technology the Soviet Union is a very good follower. Being a follower may not be the same as being a leader, but the results are often similar. At any rate, the results are extremely costly for the United States.

The Soviet ability to keep up in civilian technology is much less well developed, which should spur the use of computers in Western economies. In the civilian computer revolution, the Soviet Union will have enormous difficulties keeping pace, and time is on the side of the West. If the United States and its allies can slow the competition in military technology that can so easily destroy us all, and in which the Soviet Union is faring rather well, then the competition in civilian technology that has begun penetrating to the lowest levels of Western societies, and in which the Soviet Union is faring poorly, will give the Western alliance real advantages over its Soviet bloc rivals.

Notes

1. Thane Gustafson, "Why Doesn't Soviet Science Do Better Than It Does?" in The Social Context of Soviet Science, Linda L. Lubrano and Susan Gross Solomon, eds. (Boulder: Westview Press, 1980), p. 31.
2. Linda L. Lubrano and Susan Gross Solomon, eds. The Social Context of Soviet Science (Boulder: Westview Press, 1980).
3. National Academy of Sciences, Review of the U.S.-U.S.S.R. Interacademy Exchanges and Relations (the Kaysen report), Washington, DC, 1977.
4. The Eyewitness Seminars lasted from 1981 to 1984. They were funded by the Ford Foundation and jointly sponsored by the Program on Science, Technology and Society at the Massachusetts Institute of Technology and the Russian Research Center at Harvard University. The cochairmen were Loren R. Graham, professor of the history of science at MIT and Mark Kuchment, research associate, Russian Research Center, Harvard University.

5. Report of Dr. Izaak Wirszup to Drs. D. Aufenkamp and J. Lipson, National Science Foundation, 14 December 1979, p. 13.
6. Vladimir S. Kresin, "The State of Natural Sciences in the U.S.S.R.: A Physicist´s Point of View," Eyewitness Account no. 5, Russian Research Center, Harvard University, p. 24.

THE DEVELOPMENT OF CURRENT TRENDS IN MATHEMATICS EDUCATION IN SOVIET SCHOOLS

Frances R. Curcio

Introduction

The launching of the first man-made satellite, Sputnik, by the Soviets on October 4, 1957, generated the interest and attention of American mathematics educators. This event gave impetus to reforming American mathematics and science education. However, Soviet excellence in the mathematical sciences has not been limited to the second half of the 20th Century. Formal education emphasizing the mathematical sciences has been known to be a tradition, dating back to 18th-Century Russia.

As early as 1701, a special school, the Moscow School of Mathematical and Navigational Sciences, was established by Peter the Great. "The curriculum, unique in Europe at that time, included arithmetic, geometry, trigonometry, astronomy, and navigation."(1) Other Russian schools established to provide a liberal education for well-to-do women as well as men during the 18th Century, taught mathematical topics in arithmetic and geometry.

During the czarist regimes of the 19th Century the very few public schools that existed did teach priveleged children the four arithmetic operations and some geometry, among reading and writing. By 1850, some secondary schools required six to seven-and-a-half hours of mathematics instruction per week.(2)

Russian mathematics textbooks, prepared by A. P. Kiselev in 1888, were used up to the first half of the 20th Century "practically unchanged."(3) Unlike texts in other subjects, this is due to the "apolitical" nature of the content of mathematics.

The schools that were established in Imperial Russia were influenced by the strict regimentation and discipline found in the German-French tradition, monitored by the absolute monarch. However, education in Russia was not universal; that is, not all children were admitted into the schools. It is recorded that in 1887, the Minister of Education ordered that "`children of coachmen, lackeys, cooks, washerwomen, small herdsmen, and their kind,`" be excluded from the secondary schools.(4) A firm foundation in mathematics was available, therefore, only to a select few. This practice was not unique to Russia; it was typical of many 18th- and 19th-Century European societies.

Education in the New Soviet Society

Education after the October Revolution attempted to provide equal education for all, not only for the select few. Attitudes toward children and what they could do are reflected in the curriculum which dictated that all children be exposed to the exact same curriculum, taught the exact same way throughout the country. However, it was recognized at this time that the rigorous curriculum including analytic geometry and introductory calculus in the eighth and ninth grades was too difficult for the general school population "and a less demanding syllabus - known as the minimal syllabus - was employed by most schools."(5)

The Unified Labor School, established after the October Revolution, attempted to provide equal education for all and followed the dialectical philosophy of Karl Marx (i.e., direct interaction with the environment contributes to the development of higher-order mental processes). "The mathematics syllabus of the Unified Labor School, published in 1921, included many innovations. The study of arithmetic was compressed into four years, and plane and solid geometry were partially integrated. The function concept was emphasized as a major unifying theme."(6) The curriculum, quite novel and progressive for its time, resembled some of the features of the "New Math" programs in the United States in the late 1950s through the 1960s.(7) Where American curriculum continues to devote the first eight years of formal education to the study of arithmetic, the Soviet attempt to consolidate and compress the study of arithmetic to the first four grades and integrate different mathematical topics, is commendable.

According to Fred Hechinger,(8) the general methods of teaching in the Soviet Union between 1920 and 1928 were similar to those of progressive education in the United States - "learning by doing," "teaching the whole child," and "informality." This rather "open" approach to education was replaced with the ideas of Anton Makarenko, whose methods dominated Soviet pedagogy for four decades following the October Revolution.(9) Makarenko, who worked with abandoned, delinquent, disadvantaged adolescents, devised methods which included training for the collective, strict discipline, formality, rote learning, and social responsibility.(10) The methods were successful because they reflected the philosophy of the new Soviet society in its attempt to create a "New Soviet Man." Although many of Makarenko's ideas might not be considered to be progressive, two concepts of progressive education which can be found in his approach are "learning by doing," originally attributed to Lenin's idea of polytechnic education, and, "freedom of choice in the classroom."(11) With the exception of the latter, Makarenko's ideas are still influencing the methods of teaching used in Soviet education today.

Mathematics Education During Stalin's Reign

During the early days of the new Soviet society, the purpose of formal education was two-fold: to develop the "New Soviet Man," and to impart knowledge as a means to modernize society. It was expected that imparting the Communist ethic using Makarenko's methods would accomplish the first goal, but what was needed to accomplish the modernization of society was advanced scientific and technical education. The schools that existed were doing an inadequate job.

By the end of the 1920s, the lack of theoretical knowledge in mathematics and the other academic disciplines displayed by graduates of the Unified Labor School, who were not equipped with the basic reading and mathematical computational skills necessary for employment in the burgeoning industrial labor force for Stalin's first five-year plans, became a national issue.(12)

Joseph Stalin's mark on education during the 1930s and 1940s reflected the need for "rapid industrialization" demanding the type of schools "which would train, at maximum speed, the human cogs in the machinery of new progress."(13) The curriculum was rigid, inflexible, and had to be followed strictly. The mathematics curriculum was not much different from that in the schools under the czars, but what was emphasized, more than ever, was the practical aspects of the study of mathematics - its applications. The method of teaching and learning mathematics was rote memorization.

In efforts to meet the needs of industry, beginning in 1940, males between the ages of fourteen to seventeen were drafted to spend between six months to two years (depending on skills to be learned) in vocational training. Upon completion of their training, they were placed in a four-year occupational assignment. Young women between the ages of sixteen and eighteen were also drafted and placed in jobs. The schools that trained these youths were called Labor Reserve Schools.(14)

Khrushchev's Influence on Mathematics Education

Although Khrushchev eased many of the sanctions imposed by Stalin and he took a personal interest in the school system, the quality of formal, academic education for the general population suffered during his reign.(15) In particular, the mathematics program was severely diluted(16) when the manual training requirement was introduced in 1958-1959. Children in the primary grades were taken out of their classrooms and assigned to work-related activities as part of the school curriculum.

The Khrushchev years were characterized by what was called polytechnic labor training, that is, vocational training. Although the concept of polytechnical training is attributed to Lenin, Khrushchev's interpretation of this idea was different from Lenin's intent. Lenin's idea of polytechnical education "had a strong ideological base: the role of the worker was to be truly exalted and dominant, both in economic matters and in intellectual and cultural spheres;" whereas Khrushchev's use of the concept was "much less ideological."(17)

The few hours per week devoted to mathematics instruction stressed concrete mathematical concepts and those related to practical applications. The move away from abstract, theoretical mathematics created a problem in society similar to that encountered during Stalin's first five-year plan.

Because the diluted elementary and secondary mathematics curricula were not sophisticated enough to prepare mathematics specialists needed by society, special schools with an enriched mathematics curriculum were established for the gifted and talented. There were secondary day schools and boarding schools that specialized in computer programming and mathematics and physics, respectively. The part-time schools that were established offered "supplementary instruction in mathematics only."(18) Although the Khrushchev reforms are criticized for jeopardizing the quality of Soviet education, the establishment of these schools was a positive contribution to the cultivation of mathematical talent as well as to the goal of modernization.

Being impressed with Soviet scientific accomplishments and attempting to "catch up," Americans tried to revamp their own mathematics curriculum. Simultaneously in 1958, one year after the success of Sputnik, the above-mentioned Khrushchev reforms, along with their shortcomings, were implemented.

Brezhnev's Influence on the Mathematics Curriculum

Dissatisfaction with Khrushchev's educational reforms became evident with Brezhnev's ascent to power in 1964. Khrushchev's mandatory vocational training was eliminated.(19) In 1966, a commission was appointed, headed by A. N. Kolmogorov(20) to upgrade the mathematics curriculum.

The Kolmogorov curriculum increased the time allotted to the study of mathematics in grades 1 through 8 to six hours per week, and in secondary school to five hours per week.(21) Although American mathematics educators such as Davis,(22) Romberg,(23) and Wirszup(24) identified the Kolmogorov curriculum as being innovative, modern, well-integrated, and highly sophisticated, Soviet critics complained that the use of set theory was too abstract and meaningless, and the extensive use of abstract terminology in modern texts was more confusing than informative.(25) In addition, the curriculum has proven to be too sophisticated for all students.(26) Some of these problems noted by the Soviet critics were similar to those encountered with the "New Math" which led to the back-to-basics movement in the United States.(29)

Education during the Brezhnev years included more sophisticated curricula emphasizing theoretical natural and physical sciences over mathematical applications. Unable to strike a balance between theoretical and applied mathematics, it seems as though Soviet schools have been producing students unable to apply their knowledge.(28) Some strong criticism from mathematicians such as Pontriagin,(29) and, Moiseeva, Tichonov, and Vladimirov,(30) gave impetus to the organization of a new reform. In 1977, the Central Committee of the Communist Party passed a resolution to revise the 1966-1977 curriculum.(31) Since the Kolmogorov curriculum took approximately ten years for implementation,(32) it is expected that any new reforms in the mathematics curriculum might not be completed until 1987 - at least.(33)

<u>Proposed Changes in the Mathematics Curriculum</u>
    In response to the limitations identified by critics of the Kolmogorov curriculum, the draft of a proposed new mathematics curriculum(34) is presented in Appendix 1. It should be noted that in comparison with the Kolmogorov curriculum,(35) set theory is not used as a unifying concept in the draft. In fact, the study of set theory in and of itself has been eliminated along with unnecessarily complicated terminology. This is similar to revisions of mathematics curricula in response to the back-to-basics movement in the United States during the 1970s.

    Geometric constructions, originally found in the grade 5 course of study is to be replaced with the study of polygons and symmetrical figures, and perimeter and area. Elementary constructions, employing the use of a ruler, compass, and protractor is presented with topics of geometric shapes. The study of complex numbers, not found in the Kolmogorov curriculum, has been added in grade 10 according to the draft.

    Unlike the Kolmogorov curriculum, common fractions are presented before decimal fractions in the draft. One reason given is that it is easier to understand the comparison of fractions using geometric illustrations than to present comparison of rational numbers represented in decimal form.(36) Although the advent of computers and the hand-held calculator might suggest that we do otherwise (i.e., present decimals before common fractions), Soviet schools have not been affected by any new technology. In any case, concrete representation of fractions and decimals can be made using geometric illustrations as mentioned, and using money, respectively. The method of presentation, not the order of the content, is what is crucial.

Although algebra and geometry are taught "simultaneously" in grades 6-10, there is no indication that the approach taken is an integrative one. After reviewing some of the required textbooks, I observed that the content of each subject is kept separate unless a geometric representation can be helpful to visualize an algebraic concept.

The draft includes suggestions for presenting "problems with practical content, especially in the study of percentages, scale, and the construction of diagrams."(37) Relating mathematics to real-life situations makes the learning meaningful. All teachers of mathematics can benefit from this valuable suggestion.

The idea of compressing and consolidating arithmetic to the first four grades and introducing algebra and geometry in the middle grades is commendable. The proposed curriculum appears to be well-developed. It will be interesting to see how much of this proposed curriculum becomes the official mathematics curriculum in Soviet schools.

Soviet Mathematics Education Today
Since Stalin, not much has changed in the attitudes toward rote methods of teaching mathematics. In recent visits in 1984 and 1985, I observed classroom presentations which stressed rote methods. My observations are consistent with the observations of other mathematics educators who observed Soviet classes in session.(38)

After observing a mathematics class emphasizing rote memorization, Davis and Romberg questioned Soviet teachers about the method used. The response was "isn't this the way that everybody teaches mathematics? Isn't it the ONLY way to teach mathematics? Mathematical facts are facts, and if you want someone to know a fact, you tell him!"(39)

Being familiar with the Soviet Studies in the Psychology of Learning and Teaching Mathematics(40) and how carefullly curriculum is developed in the Soviet Union,(41) it is quite surprising to observe the diversity between learning and teaching research methods and actual classroom teaching methods (i.e., the qualitative, one-to-one, probing, discovery-type research approach is the antithesis of the rigid, rote,

366

collective approach used in the classroom). This was also expressed by Davis and Romberg.(42)

L. V. Zankov, a contemporary leader in Soviet learning theory, influenced by the philosophy and work of John Dewey, has refuted the rote-learning approach common in Soviet schools.(43) In addition, the Editors of Kommunist cite another Soviet educator, V. A. Sukhomlinskii, who agrees with Zankov. He stated that "`Not one concept, judgment, conclusion, or law should be memorized without understanding. In childhood, this causes so much damage, and in adulthood, it is a menace.´"(44) Perhaps the new reforms, currently under consideration, will reflect the concerns of these educators. However, since independent, creative thinking is not generally encouraged in Soviet schools,(45) it will be interesting to see whether any compromises are made in teaching methods.

According to Delbert Long,(46) the primary goal of education in the USSR is not to create scientists, mathematicians, or engineers, but rather, to create moral, loyal citizens dedicated to the cause of communism. So messages with political overtones are found even in the elementary story problems presented to children in their mathematics classes:
    The first cosmonaut was a citizen of the Soviet Union, Communist Yuri Gargarin. He made a flight around the earth in 108 minutes. How many hours and how many minutes did the first flight around the earth last?
    A sovkhoz [state farm] pledged itself to give the state 3,350 tons of cotton. But it gave 4,200 tons, then added another 1/10 of this quantity. By how many tons did the sovkhov overfulfill its obligation?(47)

It is obvious how values and virtues are inculcated and indoctrinated even in the mathematics class.

Mathematics is taught by specialists (i.e., not in the self-contained classroom), beginning in the fourth grade. After a foundation in reading, writing and Russian in grades 1 to 3, emphasis is placed on science and mathematics as early as fourth grade. "By seventh grade, the dominance of mathematics and physical science over the humanities and social sciences is firmly established."(48) Some Soviet educators believe that the emphasis on science and mathematics does not contribute to raising people with feelings and concern for others like the study of the humanities can.(49) However, Markushevich believes that

    Mathematics is capable of educating in its own way
    what is human in man... The study of mathematics and
    natural science can educate...man´s feelings and

367

willingness for service...we fulfill our debt to the
young generation only when we are able to instill in
the children in our lessons the idea that science is an
endless search for the sake of the best possible future
of mankind, requiring immense persistence, heroic work,
and energy, and when we bring to them that boundless
courage, love for people, and sacrifice which are hidden
behind the terse symbolism of scientific laws, formulas,
and theorems.(50)

Concluding Remarks

Every society has values and needs that are reflected in
its formal system of education. The Soviet society is rich in
history, culture and heritage. The emphasis on mathematics
education, for the most part, has been a tradition. By
exploring the content and methods of general education in the
Soviet Union, and mathematics teaching in particular, we can
achieve a better appreciation and understanding of the
accomplishments and problems of our Soviet counterparts.

Notes

1. Vogeli, Bruce. Mathematics education in Russia and the
Soviet Union. Soviet Education XIII (8-9-10), June-July-August
1971, p. 5.
2. Vogeli, 1971.
3. Hechinger, Fred. The big red schoolhouse. Gloucester, MA:
Peter Smith, 1968, p. 130.
4. Ibid., p. 50.
5. Vogeli, 1971, p. 5.
6. Ibid., p. 6.
7. Davis, Robert B. A more detailed look at Soviet
mathematics curricula. In R.B. Davis, T.A. Romberg, S.
Rachlin, & M.G. Kantowski (Eds.), An analysis of mathematics
education in the Union of Soviet Socialist Republics. Columbus,
OH: ERIC Clearinghouse for Science, Mathematics and
Environmental Education, December 1979.
8. Hechinger, 1968.
9. Jacoby, Susan. Inside Soviet schools. NY: Hill & Wang,
1974.
10. Makarenko, Anton. Road to life. Moscow: Progress
Publishers, 1951.
11. Matthews, Mervyn. Education in the Soviet Union: Policies
and institutions since Stalin. London: Allen & Unwin, 1982, p.
5.
12. Vogeli, 1971, p. 6.
13. Hechinger, 1968, p. 43.
14. Hechinger, 1968.
15. Jacoby, 1974, pp. 19, 100.
16. Vogeli, Bruce. Soviet secondary schools for the
mathematically talented. Washington, DC: National Council of

Teachers of Mathematics, 1968, p. 67.
17. Hechinger, 1968, p. 147.
18. Vogeli, 1968.
19. Jacoby, 1974, p. 13.
20. Davis, 1979, p. 41; Maslova, G.G. & Markushevitz, A.I.
[Mathematics in the schools of the U.S.S.R.] (trans. Bruce
Ramon Vogeli). The Mathematics Teacher, 62, March 1969, p. 231;
Vogeli, 1971, p. 1.
21. Maslova & Markushevitz, 1969.
22. Davis, 1979.
23. Romberg, Thomas A. One view of Soviet research in
mathematical education. In Davis et al. (Eds.), An analysis of
mathematics education in the Union of Soviet Socialist
Republics.
24. Wirsup, Izaak. The Soviet challenge. Educational
Leadership, 38, 1981, pp. 358-360.]
25. Pontriagin, L. Mathematics and the quality of its
instruction. Soviet Education XXV (4-5), February-March
1983,pp. 12-30.
26. Markushevich, A.I. Certain problems of teaching
mathematics in the school. Soviet Education XIII (8-9-10),
June-July-August 1971, p. 22; Maslova & Markushevitz, 1969, p.
234; Pontriagin, 1983, p. 26.
27. Romberg, 1979, p. 107.
28. Hechinger, 1968, pp. 132-133; Sanger, David E. Computer
imports sought by Soviet. The New York Times, February 8, 1985,
pp. Al, D3.
29. Pontriagin, 1983.
30. Keitel, Christine. Mathematics education and educational
research in the USA and USSR: Two comparisons compared. Journal
of Curriculum Studies, 14(2), 1982, pp. 109-126.
31. Ibid., p. 111.
32. Davis, 1979, p. 41.
33. Zaslavsky, Claudia. Are the Russians ahead in math ed? New
York State Mathematics Teachers' Journal, 34(2), 1984, pp.
89-92.
34. Vladimirov, V.S., Pontriagin, L.S., & Tikhonov, A.N.
Mathematics in the schools. Soviet Education XXV (4-5),
February-March 1983, pp. 37-69.
35. Maslova & Markushevitz, 1969.
36. Vladimirov, Pontriagin, & Tikhonov, 1983.
37. Ibid., 59.
38. Romberg, 1979; Zaslavsky, 1984.
39. Davis, R.B. & Romberg, T.A. Common practices in present
Soviet schools. In R.B. Davis et al., An analysis of
mathematics education in the Union of Soviet Socialist
Republics, p. 18.
40. Kilpatrick, Jeremy & Wirsup, Izaak, (Eds.). Soviet studies
in the psychology of learning and teaching mathematics, Vols.
I-XIV. Chicago: University of Chicago, 1969.
41. Keitel, 1982, p. 124.

42. Davis & Romberg, 1979.
43. Zankov, L.V. et al. Teaching and development. White Plains, NY: M.E. Sharpe, 1977.
44. Editors of Kommunist. In Soviet Education XXV (4-5), February-March 1983, pp. 30-36.
45. Curcio, Frances R. Soviet education: An American professor's perspective. Terrier - St. Francis College Alumni Magazine, 49(2), Winter 1985, pp. 4-5, 10; Jacoby, 1974, pp. 193, 197.
46. Long, Delbert H. Soviet education and the development of Communist ethics. In this text, pp. 327-335.
47. Shipler, David K. The willing suspension of disbelief. In this text, pp. 273-274.
48. Jacoby, 1974, p. 103.
49. Curcio, Frances R. Growing up Communist. Staten Island Advance, October 7, 1984, p. A29; Zaslavsky, 1984.
50. Markushevich, 1971, p. 24.

Appendix 1

Draft of the New Mathematics Curriculum[a]

Arithmetic, Algebra, and Geometry

Grade 4 (6 hours per week)[b]

		Total Hours
1.	Natural numbers and zero	60
2.	Simple geometric figures	10
3.	Fractions	112
4.	Measurement of geometric figures	20

Grade 5 (6 hours per week)

5.	Decimals	76
6.	Polygons and symmetry figures	24
7.	Rational numbers	64
8.	Elementary algebraic concepts	26
9.	Perimeter and area	10

Algebra

Grade 6 (6 hours per week)

1.	Algebraic expressions	50
2.	Linear equations	22
3.	Algebraic fractions	40
4.	Systems of two linear equations	20

Grade 7 (3 hours per week)

5.	Inequalities	16
6.	Approximate calculations	12
7.	Square roots	20
8.	Quadratic equations and inequalities	46

Geometry

Grade 6 (2 hours per week)

		Total Hours
1.	Plane geometric figures	25
2.	Triangles	25
3.	Right angle, Right triangles	12

Grade 7 (3 hours per week)

4.	Axial and central symmetry	14
5.	Parallel lines	12
6.	Quadrangles	15
7.	Equality of figures, Area of polygons	26
8.	Similar triangles, Pythagorean theorem	14
9.	A circle	14

Appendix 1 (Continued)

Algebra

Grade 8 (3 hours per week during first half of the year, 4 hours per week during the second half of the year)

	Total Hours
9. Arithmetic and geometric progressions	30
10. Rational exponents	42
11. Decimal logarithms	12
12. Elements in computer mathematics and programming	12

Algebra and Analysis

Grade 9 (3 hours per week)

	Total Hours
1. Real numbers	8
2. Elementary functions	32
3. Trigonometric functions	55

Grade 10 (3 hours per week)

	Total Hours
4. Derivatives	46
5. Complex numbers	20
6. Combinatorics and probability	15

Geometry

Grade 8 (3 hours per week during the first half of the year, 2 hours per week during the second half of the year)

	Total Hours
10. Vectors	20
11. Coordinates on a plane	14
12. Trigonometric functions, Metric correlations in a triangle	18
13. Similar figures	12
14. Regular polygons	14

Grade 9 (2 hours per week)

	Total Hours
1. Axioms of solid geometry	18
2. Vectors in space	16
3. Perpendicularity of straight lines and planes	16
4. Polyhedrons	12

Grade 10 (2 hours per week)

	Total Hours
5. Coordinates in space	20
6. Volumes of polyhedrons	12
7. Figures generated by revolution	18

---

[a] From V.S. Vladimirov, L.S. Pontriagin, & A.N. Tikhonov, Mathematics in the school. *Soviet Education* XXV (4-5), February-March 1983, pp. 37-69.

[b] Hours allotted for formal review have been omitted from this listing.

372

PHYSICAL EDUCATION IN USSR SCHOOLS

Victor Zilberman

The Soviet government places great importance on the
physical education program in the general schools, believing
that through physical education and sport, students develop
character, comradeship, collectivism, discipline and many other
desirable qualities. School age is looked upon as the prime
time to teach love of and need for physical activity and sport
that will last a lifetime.

Physical education and sport have gone through tremendous
changes over 65 years of Soviet political existence. Following
the 1917 Revolution the Soviet government began to create a new
educational system extremely different from that of Czarist
Russia. "The new Soviet government," J.J. Tomiak observes,
"quickly began to introduce a series of fundamental education
reforms...making education compulsory, constructing new
educational system, literature, pedagogics. The whole system
of schools from kindergarten to university was declared to
constitute one school, one unbroken ladder...the basic link was
to be a universal, free, secular and undifferentiated
school."(1)

In contrast to the educational systems of most western
countries, the Soviet system is very centralized. This is
required due to the Soviet Union's large territory and
population, the government's goals and objectives in education,
and the multinational character of the U.S.S.R. (over 100
nationalities). With some exceptions dictated by the
recognition of the minority languages, all Soviet children of a
given age should be studying the same lesson on the same day.
Because of the government's control of the curriculum, it is
able to influence the education of all nationalities by
prescribing that the Russian language, culture, and Communist
ideology be taught in school.

Responsibility for general schools rests with the U.S.S.R.
Ministry of Education which controls school curriculum.
Decisions affecting physical education in the general schools

From: "physical Education in USSR Schools," by Victor Zilberman, in
Journal of Physical Education, Recreation and Dance, August 1984.
Reprinted by permission of the American Alliance for Health,
Physical Education, Recreation and Dance, 1900 Association Drive,
Reston, VA 22091.

are made by the ministry in conjunction with the U.S.S.R. Committee on Physical Culture and Sport and the All-Union Physical Culture Research Institute. Instructions are passed from the U.S.S.R. Ministry of Education to the Ministries of Education in the republics, from them to regional, city, and district educational departments, for implementation by school directors and teachers. Grant has noted that "by the time it comes to the teacher, the area of personal discretion, though greater than it used to be, is very small...not only basic policy, but the content of the curriculum, schemes of work, textbooks, and the like are prescribed for the teacher in considerable detail."(2)

Ideological Basic of Physical Education

Ideology is a very important part of education, literature, sports, arts and other aspects of Soviet life. The Soviet government considers the upbringing of the young generation, the future builders of the Communist society, to be the principal task of the schools and other social institutions. "Education is viewed by the Communist Party," Folsom writes, "as an instrument for the formation of a Communist society."(3) This direction is carried on through the school system many different ways: through subjects taught, through the Communist youth organizations, through school celebrations, sports and other means. Through such school activities an attempt is made to produce "politically trained, disciplined builders of Communism, patriots and internationalists."(4) In the U.S.S.R. the physical, ethical, aesthetic, and cognitive aspects of education are supposed to complement each other in achieving a common goal, expressed in terms of raising a worthy citizen of a Communist society. From early childhood, education seeks harmoniously to develop mind and body. For this reason, the program of the Communist Party encourages all forms of mass sport and physical training.(5)

Teaching and learning in Soviet schools inculcates responsibility to the collective. This feature of Soviet education has its origin in the work of Makarenko who experimented with collectivistic methods of raising children and adolescents during the early 1920s. In his view, the purpose of the collective in Soviet education is to develop such qualities as discipline, comradeship, respect for elders and teachers, and patriotism. This is considered essential to the upbringing of a builder of Communism - a long and complex process. Makarenko believed that children are more easily influenced and disciplined through peer pressure. For example, if a student is not spending enough time to do well in his or her studies, according to Makarenko, remediation is more likely if the collective (classmates) talk, encourage study, offer help, and try to show that poor grades reflect on the class as a whole.

Responsibility for monitoring behavior is placed on
students under the teacher's guidance as well as on the youth
communist organizations. A friendly, purposeful collective is
thought to provide a positive environment where the best
qualities of an individual should develop. Soviet pedagogy
stresses that the collective is a minisociety which helps to
inform the individual's response to the surrounding world. It
is a model of adult society relations - an environment where
the individual learns and experiences relations between self
and society. A.S. Makarenko used sport terminology in
describing the collective. He pointed out that Communist
resoluteness, spirit, and purposefulness cannot be fostered
without exercise in appropriate behavior. And the collective,
he added, is the gymnasium for this type of gymnastics.(6)

Soviet Sport Rating Systems
        Much of the Soviet Union's accomplishments in physical
education and sport should be attributed to the All-Union Sport
Classification Edinaya Vsesoyuznaya Sportivnaya Clasifkatsya
and GTO Gotov k trudu i oborone, or Ready for Labor and
Defense, which facilitate mastery in sport and mass
participation in the sport movement. The All-Union Sport
Classification is a system of norms and requirements according
to which athletes are awarded ranks, titles, and categories of
proficiency in different sports. It covers 56 sports and is
updated every four years after the Olympic Games. The 1977-80
Classification includes (1) Juniors (Third, Second and First
levels) and Seniors (Third, Second, First, Candidate for Master
of Sport, Master of Sport in the U.S.S.R. International Class,
Grand Master in Chess and Checkers, and Merited Master of
Sport).

        The GTO system was designed to encourage sport in everyday
life of the Soviet people, to enhance military preparedness, to
teach civil defense and to improve personal hygiene. GTO
programs span the ages of 10 to 60 and are organized into five
stages (categories). First Smelye i Lovkie (The Daring and
Agile) for boys and girls 10 to 13 years old; Second,
Sportivnaya Smena (Sporting Reserve) for boys and girls 14 to
15 years old; Third, Sila i Muzjestvo (Strength and Courage)
for boys and girls 16 to 18 years old; Fourth, Fizicheskoe
Sovershenstvo (Physical Perfection) for men 19 to 39 and women
19 to 34; and Fifth, Bodrosti i Zdorovye (Vigor and Health) for
men 40 to 60, and women 35-55.

        The GTO system is considered a fitness program that helps
people improve their physical abilities and health. The GTO
test consists of two parts; the requirements of both must be
satisfied in order to obtain the GTO badge for a particular age
group. The first, which is most difficult and important,

involves a physical test with a point system using various sports and exercises (for example, running, long or high jump, swimming, skiing, rope climbing, and others). The physical or practical part of the GTO could be compared to a decathalon; the only difference is that the participant can choose any sport or exercise included in the GTO requirements. The second part is academic, and the participants are examined on personal hygiene, civil defense, and on the organization of the Soviet physical education and sport systems. Depending on the points accumulated in the academic and practical tests, badges are awarded.

The goals of the GTO and the All-Union Sport Classification are similar, both encouraging people to participate in physical activities, recreation and sports. The two rating systems differ in their specific objectives. The GTO was introduced to increase mass involvement in sport, to provide basic requirements for physical education in the school systems and physical education programs for the military and for rural and urban collectives. The main objective of the All-Union Sport Classification, on the other hand, is to raise the proficiency of Soviet athletes to the level of winning major Soviet and international sport competitions.

Physical Education in the Schools
The U.S.S.R. Ministry of Education is primarily responsible for planning and organizing physical education programs for students in general schools. Assisting the Ministry are the U.S.S.R. Committee on Physical Culture and Sport, the All-Union Physical Culture Research Institute, the U.S.S.R. Ministry of Health, and the Central Committee of Komsomol (Youth Communist Organization). The programs designed by these organizations seek to improve students´ health by developing motor skills useful in their daily lives, to encourage fitness and participation in sport, to raise the level of sport achievements, to instill moral and aesthetic values consistent with Communist ideology, and to prepare students over 10 years of age to pass the GTO tests.(7)

From grade one onward, students are divided into three groups for physical education according to their health and physical abilities.

- The basic group - all healthy students who exhibit normal or above normal development;
- The preparatory group - pupils who are in poor physical condition, overweight, or physically underdeveloped;
- The special group - students with physical or mental disabilities.

This article deals with physical education programs

oriented to the needs of children without physical deficiencies.

Physical education is provided in various ways by the schools: regular classes included in the general education curriculum, recreational activities during school hours, after-school recreational activities conducted within the school´s general education program, and athletic competitions and special events supervised by the school, in which participation is voluntary. Physical education lessons are based on the requirements of the Curriculum of Physical Education for each school grade. The curriculum includes compulsory and, in later grades, elective physical education subjects depending on the qualifications of the teachers, the school´s geographical location, the availability of suitable facilities and equipment, and so on. No elective subjects are offered in grades one to four, whereas in the higher grades electives comprise about 10% of physical education classes.(8)

Table 1 shows the percentage of time devoted by schools to various activities according to the age of the students. Here gymnastics refers to general exercises used in many sports for warm-up, conditioning, and other purposes. Games include basketball, volleyball, soccer, and low organized games. Sports denotes such activities as track and field, gymnastics, skiing, and swimming.

In allocating time for different activities within the curriculum, physiological and psychological differences among children of different ages are taken into consideration. For example, the table shows that during physical education classes

Table 1

Percentages of Total Time Devoted to Physical Education Activities in the General Schools(7)

Age	Gymnastics	Games	Sports	Hiking	Total %
8- 9	40%	50%	5%	5%	100%
10-11	40	40	10	10	100
12-13	30	35	20	15	100
14-15	30	25	25	20	100
16-17	20	25	35	20	100

for children between 8-9 years of age (grades two and three), half of the instructional time is spent on games. Children of that age have difficulties concentrating on physical activities requiring sustained performance; therefore, learning motor skills is often undertaken in the context of games. Games (50%) and gymnastics (40%) account for most of the time allocated for physical education at this age, but decrease in importance as the children get older. In the final grades of school the teacher can concentrate more on teaching various sports. Nevertheless, games remain an important part of the physical education program. Even at the 16-17 age level, games are still scheduled for 25% of the physical education curriculum in the general schools.

Considering that children spend up to 10 years in general schools, it is understandable that their exposure to physical education is felt to affect their future involvement in sport. Physical education classes are compulsory from grades one through ten, with two 45 minute periods of instruction per week under the supervision of a teacher. Following language and mathematics, physical education requires the next highest number of hours in the curriculum over the 10 year period, an indication of its importance.

Many schools begin their day with eight to twelve gymnastic exercises for about 10 minutes. These are usually conducted in the school yard, auditorium, or school corridors, depending on weather conditions. Such exercises are also urged during breaks between other activities to help reduce fatigue and to refresh the students by giving them a change in routine. Recess is usually spent playing games or in activities using sports equipment set up in the schoolyard. Students participate voluntarily in these activities. The games and exercises are simple like soccer or basketball, and students are well acquainted with them.

The syllabus and class guides prescribed for physical education programs include suggestions for teachers. Teachers are advised to pay close attention to the body construction of the children. They are shown how to prevent injuries and given necessary first aid information. Beginning with grade four physical education classes, children are prepared for the GTO and participate in trial competitions. This is not the sole purpose of physical education classes, but preparation for GTO orients the physical education program, and teachers are expected to prepare a certain percentage of students to become GTO badge holders.

Hygienic and medical aspects of physical education and sport are uniform, and are controlled throughout the U.S.S.R. (For example, most sport facilities are kept very clean, and no one is allowed to partake in physical education and sport without a doctor's written consent.) Physical education teachers are totally responsible for the health and safety of the students in their classes. The teacher is expected to conduct proper warm-ups at the beginning of class, provide the students with adequate exercises according to their age and abilities, and to provide spotting and safety in the use of different sport equipment.

The republic Ministries of Education regularly inspect the physical education programs of the general schools. These inspections are of great importance. Each Ministry of Education maintains a staff of inspectors who visit schools in their assigned areas to ensure that approved teaching standards are being followed. Inspectors sporadically attend examinations and lessons, analyze the staff's teaching methods and techniques, class discipline, and so on. Inspectors monitor compliance with the prescribed curricula.(8) By keeping a watchful eye on teachers, universal standards are maintained and the Ministry is informed of problems at the school level and of the need for specific changes in curricula and teaching techniques to maintain a high teaching standard. Teachers are also periodically assessed by the school director. A very popular Russian proverb Doveray no Proveray - Trust but Verify - is applied in education as well as in many aspects of Soviet life. Verification of the implementation of the Ministry's approach, philosophy, and directives provides the Soviet school system with unified educational standards, continuity, and quality of physical education instruction and training.

The lack of adequate sport facilities and professionally qualified teachers, especially in the rural areas, is a major source of concern to Soviet educators. While the number of school sports facilities is impresive, according to the central newspaper Sovetskiy Sport, many physical education teachers from backward areas of the U.S.S.R. have complained about the poor facilities and sport equipment. The deficit of sports facilities and equipment in rural schools is reported to be growing larger every year.(9) Soviet Deputy Minister of Education, M.I. Kondakov stated that in 1968, 50% of the schools did not have the appropriate sport equipment to conduct compulsory physical education lessons, and 40% of the physical education instructors were unqualified. Of the 85,000 primary schools (grades one to four), 80,000 were understaffed and underequipped for physical education.(8)

Competition
Athletic competitions constitute an important part of the physical education program and are used to improve the health and fitness of the students, to develop such qualities as

379

friendship, collectivism, determination, and class and school
spirit, to name a few. Competitions are organized on various
levels. There are interschool competitions from which the best
athletes are selected for the district competitions. From the
district competitions the best athletes and teams are selected
to participate in the city championships. Then there are the
regional, republic, and national championships. In contrast to
North America, dual meets are less popular. The format used
most frequently is a multiteam tournament, and the students are
divided into four age groups (11-12, 13-14, 15-16, and 17-18)
for interschool competitions. Usually, students compete in up
to 14 sports: basketball, volleyball, water polo, cycling,
gymnastics, track and field, swimming, diving, table tennis,
lawn tennis, soccer, shooting, canoeing, and chess. The sports
and events vary for each age group; Research Institutes of
Physical Culture establish guidelines for these competitions.
For example, the 13-14 age group run the 400 meters, but are
not allowed to compete in the 800 meter race.(10) To
participate, students must have a physician's permission; the
competition site and sports equipment are inspected to prevent
any harm or injury to the children.

The highest level of competition for the general school
students occurs at the U.S.S.R. School Games which the press
refers to as a "holiday of children's sport and a festival of
friendship." U.S.S.R. School Games finals are preceded by
city, district, regional, and republic tournaments in which
millions of school children compete.(11) During these
competitions many boys and girls receive GTO badges and qualify
for sports ratings. The best stadia, gymnasia, and swimming
pools are put at their disposal. The 1964 Olympic high jump
champion, Valerie Brumel and Vladimir Iashenko, world record
holder in the high jump, were discovered at school
competitions, along with many other top Soviet athletes. These
competitions are also used to judge the quality of work of the
physical education teachers and coaches. Additionally, these
competitions indicate the development of sport in republics,
cities, districts and schools at the junior and pre-junior
levels.

Special Schools for Sports
Students who have exhibited a desire and talent for a
sport may attend special sports institutions. There are sport
boarding schools where children continue their general
education and perfect their mastery of a particular sport under
the guidance of well-qualified coaches. To be accepted by such
a boarding school, a young athlete must achieve at least first
ranking in his/her chosen sport according to the criteria
employed in the All-Union Sport Classification. Applicants are
rigorously screened for admission. Room and board, as well as

coaching fees and travel expenses to competitions, are paid for by the state. Students study and practice their sport six days a week.

There are also nonresidential children's sports schools which students who wish to improve their mastery of a particular sport may attend afternoons or evenings. The local boards of education and sport societies usually operate such schools free of charge. The children are coached by professionally qualified instructors who work as coaches on a full time basis. In 1974 there were more than 4,600 children's sport schools in the U.S.S.R., with over 1.6 million children aged 9 to 14 years attending.(5)

The organization of sport in the U.S.S.R. at the school age, as well as in later years, is in contrast to the organization of sport in North America. In the U.S.S.R. the centers for identifying and cultivating athletic talent are in the clubs and sport schools, where the best facilities and equipment are offered, and where coaching is given by the best qualified personnel. Such schools devote their full efforts to producing top athletes and account in large part for the U.S.S.R.'s success in international competitions.

Conclusion

The ideological purpose of physical education, according to Lenin, was to develop the New Socialist Man. His views on physical culture were adopted by the leading Soviet educators, Krupskaya and Makarenko among others. During the early years of the Soviet state, mass participation in the sport movement was emphasized over international athletic competitions. However, a major change in the Soviet sport movement occurred after the 1952 Olympic Games in Helsinki, when the U.S.A. and U.S.S.R. competed for medals and team standings. While the Soviet Union could not favorably compete with western countries in agriculture, industry, science, or standard of living, it recognized the opportunity for domination in sports and the advantage of associating international sport success with the Soviet political system.

The general school plays an important role in the development and implementation of sport among Soviet youth. The primary objective of physical education in Soviet schools is well-rounded physical development and enhancement of love for sport for a lifetime. In contrast to North America, the development of mastery and proficiency in sport in the U.S.S.R. is delegated to the clubs, sport schools, and societies where coaching expertise, the best facilities, and sport equipment are concentrated. Soviet physical education contrasts with western countries in its centralization and uniformity. The physical education curricula of the general schools is

381

determined by the U.S.S.R. Ministry of Education and is, in
most respects, uniform throughout the various republics.
Physical education occupies a central place in the school
curricula. The time devoted to it equals that assigned to such
academic subjects as mathematics and language. Physical
education programs in Soviet schools seek to develop fitness,
improve personal hygiene and, more significantly, to instill a
love of sport that will continue throughout the student's
lifetime.

References

1. Tomiak, J.J. The Soviet Union. Great Britian: David and
Charles (Publishers) Limited, 1972.
2. Grant, Nigel. Soviet education (3rd ed.). Baltimore:
Penguin Books, 1972.
3. Folsom, M.B. Education in the U.S.S.R. U.S. Department of
Health, Education and Welfare, Office of Education.
Washington: U.S. Government Printing Office, 1957.
4. Pravda. Moscow: August 22, 1969.
5. Sovetskiy Sport. Soviet Sport, Questions and Answers.
Moscow: Novosti Press Agency Publishing House, 1974.
6. Krasovitskiy, M.U. Formirovanie nravstennih otnosheniy v
uchenicheskom kollective, Fizichesakaya kul´tura v shkole, n.
111. Moscow: Pedagogika, 1978.
7. Kukushkin, G.I. Sovetskaya sistema fizicheskogo
vospitaniya. Moscow: Fizkul´tura i sport, 1975.
8. Schneidman, N.N. The Soviet road to Olympus. Toronto: The
Ontario Institute for Studies in Education, 1978.
9. Riordan, James. Sport and physical education in the Soviet
Union. An Outline, 1975. Society for Cultural Relations with
the U.S.S.R. University of Bradford, 1975.
10. Sovietskiy sport. Moscow: May 11, 1979; May 14, 1979.
11. Howell, M.L. and Van Vliet, M.L. Physical education and
recreation in Europe. Ottawa: Fitness and Amateur Sport
Directorate, Department of National Health and Welfare, Canada,
1965.
12. Shtukalo, F. "School games: A test of maturity," Sport in
the U.S.S.R. no. 9. Moscow: Physical Culture and Sport
Publishing House, 1976.

VOCATIONAL EDUCATION IN THE USSR

Felicity O´Dell

Vocational education in a broad sense is the theme of this [article]. All the main aspects of Soviet education that are directly aimed at teaching people to work will be examined. Labour training for school-leavers is one important area but it does not stand alone in that education for work is fundamental to the whole of the Soviet education system from creche onwards.

The topic falls into three areas each of which will be examined in turn: (1) The place and purpose of Soviet vocational education; (2) Labour training at the different stages of the contemporary education process; (3) Problems and trends in the vocational schools and colleges. Concern throughout is with the contemporary situation and the ways in which it is likely to develop in the eighties.

The Place and Purpose of Soviet Vocational Education

Soviet education is explicitly vocational. It declares its main purpose to be the development of people capable of being "Builders of Communism." What does this lofty title mean in practice? It refers to a range of moral values and practical skills which will enable Soviet citizens to bring their country to the desired level. Many of these values and skills are closely associated with labour training in that communism is seen as being attainable only through the establishment of a strong industrial state.

The reasons for the significance of vocational education in the USSR are both ideological and economic. Love of work occupies an important position in the Soviet moral code. It is through his attitude towards work that a man can ultimately be judged.[1] The good citizen loves his own work and aspires to do it to the best of his ability; he also respects the labour of others. The extent to which a person possesses these qualities is the yardstick whereby we can measure his worth. It is also through work that the individual is expected to find his purpose in living and his happiness. Because of this fundamental position of the virtue of love of work Marcuse has termed Soviet morality a work-moral.[2] From another point of view too, love of work is ideologically important; it is a

From: "Vocational Education in the USSR," by Felicity O'Dell, in Soviet Education in the 1980s, edited by J.J. Tomiak and reprinted by permission of St. Martin's Press, Inc.

quality which is both desired by the Soviet authorities and easily legitimated by reference to Marx and Lenin. It is much less easy to justify the other basic Soviet virtue of patriotism through quotations from the Marxist classics.(3)

Economically, the need for vocational education is clear. After taking power the Bolshevik Party was faced with an economy in ruins and a depleted and largely unskilled work force. To achieve their aim of rapid industrial growth they had to train people in the skills necessary to develop the economy and to instil in them the commitment to the cause that would make them willing to labour unstintingly in the name of communism.

The ideological and economic imperatives for the development of vocational education are no less significant now than they were in the twenties. In addition, there are certain aspects of the contemporary Soviet economic position which are causing concern and are affecting the current nature of labour training. There is still as strong a need as ever to develop disciplined, committed workers who are prepared to do humble jobs and to devote themselves to the building of communism. Other factors, however, are new.

Certain of these are due to the nature of the technological revolution. This is leading in many cases to quick changes in the precise character of the jobs which many workers are required to carry out.(4) In other words, the economy now needs workers who are flexible enough to be able to change their specialisms as changing circumstances necessitate. Their initial labour training needs to give them the basic technical knowledge and skills which will stand them in good stead however technology develops. In addition, workers at all levels need to be creative if the economy is to benefit from the technological revolution to the full. Lack of an innovative, imaginative approach to work is one weak area of Soviet workers´ attitudes which is causing planners concern and which they are currently trying to remedy through an improved labour training programme.

Another fundamental problem of the contemporary situation is the fact that labour is now quite a scarce resource. There are more jobs than there are people. As a result, labour turnover is high as people move from factory to factory trying to find the position which suits them best. Among a certain group of workers there is little fear of being punished for infringement of labour discipline - they know that if they lose their job they will find another without any difficulty. Excessive labour turnover is felt to be harmful to the economy and legislation has been introduced restricting the right to change jobs twice in any one year without reduction of certain

384

pension rights. Vocational training is also expected to play
its part in reducing turnover by improving vocational guidance
and by strengthening moral education to increase young people's
feelings, of responsibility and disipline, towards their
work.(5)

The fact that labour is no longer plentiful means that
productivity can be increased only through a better work
discipline and a higher standard of working.(6) Recent party
pronouncements on work tend to emphasise quality and
efficiency. A greater concern with these virtues is seen as
essential for the improvement of the Soviet economy if it is to
be able to satisfy its own requirements and to compete in world
markets. The Soviet agencies of labour training are
accordingly increasingly concerned with developing efficient
work habits and attitudes of always striving to do one's best.

Two areas of activity have particularly suffered from
their low prestige in the Soviet Union and attempts are
currently being made to improve their position. These areas
are the service sphere and agriculture. Young people have
shown a reluctance to go into these fields and so there has
been a heightened concern, on the one hand, with raising their
status and, on the other, to promote more effectively the tenet
fundamental to Marxist morality that all work is valuable no
matter how humble it may seem.

The above problems relating to the technological
revolution, scarce labour resources, quality of work and a low
level of attractiveness for certain jobs are those which are
currently giving rise to most debates among those involved in
vocational education in the USSR and in looking at the
contemporary labour training process it will be seen how
attempts are being made to solve these problems.

Vocational education in the Soviet Union is seen as having
three basic facets. At different levels of the education
process these facets have differing degrees of importance.
They are:

1. Moral education in the desired attitudes towards work;
2. Training in practical work skills and habits;
3. Vocational guidance.

The moral education element means giving young people
certain attitudes towards work. They are to be trained to see
in it their main path to individual fulfillment. They are to
see it as a way of contributing to their motherland, which
should be for them both a duty and a joy. They are to respect
all kinds of work regardless of the level of qualification
necessary to carry out the job in question. On the other hand,

they must also be encouraged to study to the full extent of
their abilities so that they can give "more" to the motherland.
The paradoxes inherent in some of these elements of the Soviet
work ethic have been discussed elsewhere.(7) The moral
education facet of the labour training process is important at
all stages of the education system.

Training in practical skills also begins with the youngest
pupils but becomes more precise as the children grow older,
achieving its greatest significance perhaps in the post-school
stages of vocational education. This facet of labour training
does not consist merely of teaching youngsters how to use their
hands and how to manage different tools and materials. It is
also a matter of training people in certain work habits basic
to the whole organisation of Soviet society in general and that
of work-places in particular. This means learning to work as
part of a collective, subordinating oneself to the requirements
of the leaders of the collective and acting first and foremost
in accordance with the needs of the group. Discipline is
another work habit important to the Soviet structure of work.
It is necessary to discipline oneself in order to fit in with
the demands of the collective and of the plan. The plan is a
feature of Soviet life dominating work in all spheres. From
the earliest age, schoolchildren have to learn to regulate
their activity according to a plan imposed from above.
Socialist competition is another characteristic of the
structure of work in the Soviet Union and this also is a
feature of labour training at all levels. Many of these work
habits are learnt simply through the overall structure of the
activities of the school or college in that these, with their
pupil and staff soviets, their plans and competitions and their
collective discipline, are but a parallel of Soviet work life
in general.

Vocational guidance is the third facet of labour training
and this is mainly limited to work in the later years of the
secondary school. It is an area to which greater attention is
recently been paid.(8) The aim is to guide pupils into those
occupations where the economy has a need of workers.

How are these aspects of labour training put into practice
at the different stages of the education process?

Labour Training at the Different Stages of the Contemporary Education Process

At present, the Soviet child has a compulsory ten years of
education. After eight years, at 15, he can choose whether to
stay at secondary school or to enter a vocational school and
combine the last years of general schooling with trade
training.

Soviet educationalists divide their education system into six areas - pre-school upbringing, secondary schools, out-of-school education, technical trade schools, secondary specialised colleges and higher education - and the nature of vocational education in each of these six areas is considered below. The vocational element is clearly most significant in the technical trade schools and secondary specialised colleges which have training for work as their primary function but even pre-school upbringing is expected to make its contribution towards the training of the future Soviet work force.

Pre-school Upbringing. Pre-school upbringing covers training both at home and in an institution. It is naturally harder for the state to control the upbringing of children at home. Nevertheless, with work training as with other aspects of moral upbringing, the state does try to guide parents to teach children the values with which they would be inculcated at pre-school institutions. To do this, the help of all the media is enlisted. Television programmes for parents suggest the need for and ways of teaching youngsters a love of work, and children's programmes demonstrate, for example, modelling skills or show adults doing different jobs stressing the social significance of even the most humble work. Books and magazines for parents and pre-school children carry the same message. Some work-places run courses for parents of young children and labour training is an inevitable component of such a course.

It is easier to organise systematic labour training if the pre-school child is at a kindergarten. There the child will spend a lot of his day playing, walking in the fresh air and resting; but from the youngest group upwards there are expected to be some daily periods of learning activity. For the youngest pupils there will be one such session of 15-20 minutes in the morning and one in the afternoon. The frequency and duration of such activities increase as the children get older. Many of the learning sessions have a direct work training focus, for example, simple handicrafts and work on the kindergarten's plot of land. Children are also taught in such sessions about the jobs of adults, particularly about those doing work characteristic of the local area. Play, too, is expected to be directed to train, where possible, in basic labour attitudes. All pre-school institutions possess a range of construction toys, model tractors and toy washing-machines.(9)

Such toys would be found in most Western kindergartens but a more Soviet flavour becomes evident when one looks at recommendations to Soviet upbringers on how to guide play and learning activities. These guidelines were prepared by an educationalists' conference on the work instruction of children in pre-school institutions.(10) The conference was held in

1978 and its proposals indicate areas where results have not been satisfactory up to now and to which especial attention must be paid in the eighties. Above all, they stress that work activities are to be used to develop feelings of responsibility, duty and love for work. Work attitudes are, thus, given more prominence than actual practical skills. From the earliest age a greater independence is to be promoted. Children are to be helped to reason for themselves how best to do something rather than simply to be shown what to do. They must be trained always to do a task to the best of their ability, to distribute among themselves responsibilities for the work of the collective and to act in a cooperative way, planning their work as a team and giving help to each other where needed. The aim of what is being done is always to be made clear to the children and in such a way that they are inspired to achieve the aim. From the earliest opportunity the Soviet authorities are trying to prepare the well-organised, perfectionist, independently creative and work-loving adults they would like to see in their factories and farms but who, all too frequently, are lacking at present.

<u>Secondary Schools</u>. The training begun in the kindergarten is continued and developed in the secondary school. An important aspect of vocational education here is that many schools have as their patron one local factory or farm. As a result, much of the labour training given at the school is linked to the work of the patron enterprise.

The standard curriculum gives Soviet pupils two lessons in labour training per week for the first eight years of their course followed by four hours in the ninth and tenth years. In addition, they have five full days of practice in the fifth, sixth and seventh years and a month in the ninth year. Children at schools where language of instruction is not Russian have an extra burden in having to study their native language and literature as well as Russian and a Western foreign language and most such schools help to make time for this by reducing labour training lessons from two periods to one in the first seven years. Apart from the amount of time allowed for options other subjects are not affected. Labour training is possibly permitted to be cut in this way because the work done in its sessions is paralleled in so many extra-curricular activities and the work attitudes taught are not the exclusive concern of the labour training classes but are reinforced in all other class subjects.(11)

In the secondary school, attention is paid to all three basic aims of vocational education. The first two are an extension of those of the kindergarten - to socialise in attitudes of enthusiasm and responsibility towards work and to teach practical skills. The third aim, that of vocational

388

guidance, has been increasing in importance over the last
decade and is likely to continue doing so in the eighties. It
is hoped both to guide pupils into jobs where there are acute
labour shortages and to avoid later labour turnover by a more
thoughtful and thorough system of career guidance. A
pedagogics´ textbook for training teachers finds four basic
tasks for vocational education in the school, though the first
two just emphasise slightly different aspects of the
fundamental socialisation goal.(12) Firstly, it points to the
need to educate an interest in and love for different kinds of
work and to foster a desire to work. Secondly, there is the
nurturing of a communist attitude towards work. Thirdly, comes
the equipping of pupils with labour knowledge, skills and
habits and, fourthly, providing pupils with an interest in
different kinds of jobs, helping them to choose a profession
for themselves and to find suitable employment.

What exactly are schoolchildren taught in their labour
lessons? In the three primary years, they cut paper, make
plasticine clay and papier-mache models, look after plants,
arrange and tidy the classroom and do other light school
maintenance tasks. Pupils from the fourth to the eighth
classes usually spend their labour training lessons in the
school workshops. Objects are made from metal, cloth, wood and
other materials and pupils learn to handle simple tools and
machines. During this period, boys and girls often, though not
always, are separated for their labour lessons with the
traditional guiding of boys into metalwork and girls into
sewing. It is at this age also that serious vocational
guidance work begins. Work instructors and class teachers
provide information about the nature of specific jobs. Where
possible, outside speakers are brought in to talk to the
children about their work and workers from the patron
enterprise; parents and instructors from local vocational
schools are made especial use here.(13)

Thus pupils learn most about the kind of work available in
their local area. The emphasis in Soviet vocational guidance
is much more on encouraging people into specialisms for which
there is a local or general need rather than on analysing the
aptitudes of the individual and fitting these to a profession
regardless of whether or not there is work available or social
requirement for people with that profession.

After the eighth class an increasing number of pupils
leave to enter a vocational school. Those who remain at
secondary general school have an even greater element of
vocational guidance in labour lessons. Excursions to local
work-places are organised and discussions with workers
arranged. At this age also pupils often do some of their

practical work in the ninth grade, in real factory conditions, both helping the enterprise to fulfill its plan and themselves to learn about the use of real machines and materials. They are also paid for such labour. The press prints glowing reports of pupils who use their wages to buy their schools equipment or to arrange excursions for groups of pupils. It was estimated in 1978/9 that of all senior pupils doing practical work in real working conditions, 25 percent were involved in work in industry, 39 percent in agriculture, 17 percent in transport and communications, 4 percent in catering and trade and 2 percent in construction.(14)

Apart from work actually in the factory, the building site or the fields or in the school workshops, there has been a growing tendency in the late seventies for pupils to receive much of their labour training in inter-school production combines. These started in Moscow but now exist in many other places.(15) They are frequently housed in schools that are no longer used and they consist of a range of workshops, laboratories, vocational guidance centres and labour museums. Local enterprises each have departments in the combine and send workers to act as instructors there, so that pupils are trained by specialists and in realistic conditions. Pupils from different schools attend the combine and have the advantage of being able to sample a variety of jobs while under one roof. It is likely that the provision of such combines will continue increasing and there will be attempts to improve their facilities. At present, pupils are often felt to spend too short a time per week there and the range of jobs in which the combines offer training is not always wide enough.(16)

As well as the timetabled labour lessons, other school classes have a direct vocational element. Once a week the class teacher has a period with her class and this is supposed to be used regularly to reinforce socialisation in work values. Optional subjects, for which two hours are now allowed in the seventh year, three in the eighth and four in the ninth and tenth, are frequently work-related. Car mechanics and typewriting, for instance, are subjects offered in many schools. Technical drawing is also studied once a week by all pupils in the seventh and eighth classes. All in all, the Soviet secondary school justifies, in the prominence it gives to a range of technical subjects, the description of polytechnical which it frequently applies to itself.

Even in less obviously relevant subjects a work training element is often present both in teaching about practical skills and in socialising the desired work attitudes. This is noticed, for example, even on the very first page of a primary class reading book. This addresses itself to Octobrists, the youth movement for the youngest pupils and it says

Octobrists are the Pioneers of the future.
Octobrists are industrious children who love their
school and respect their school. They respect
older people.
Only those who love to work can be called Octobrists.(17)

   Geography courses emphasise the economic geography of the
countries studied and point out the differences in working
conditions under capitalism and socialism. Practical work is
also an important part of geography classes with much field
work involving the use of map, compass and so on.(18) In the
teaching of all science subjects the applied possibilities of
any topic are always stressed. History lessons look
particularly at workers´ movements over the years in different
parts of the world. Soviet history for fourth formers focusses
on such work-related topics as "the labour victories of Soviet
people after the Great Patriotic War... electrification... the
construction of new plants and factories... on the collective
farm... shock-workers of Communist labour."(19)

   Few English eleven-year-olds would have their history
lessons give such attention to British labour achievements or
parallel aspects of working life here.

   Foreign language classes read texts emphasising the heroic
nature of Soviet work, contrasting it with alienated labour in
the West. English textbooks particularly stress how Lenin
studied and loved English. A typical poem about Lenin follows.
This encourages children to work and study and be inspired by
Lenin and it is intended for use as choral recitation practice
by fourteen-year-old learners. The verses go well to the tune
of "Thy hand, O Lord, has guided Thy flock from age to age" and
the words have a not dissimilar religious feel.

   We stand before a portrait
   Upon the schoolroom wall
   We see the face of Lenin
   So known and loved by all.

   We often bring him flowers
   And twine them round the frame
   We children honour deeply
   His ever-cherished name.

   We promise `we shall study
   To master all you taught´
   And say `we´re always ready
   In lessons, work and sport.´(20)

   The social studies course for final-year pupils has a

391

section devoted exclusively to labour which, it says, will be the main purpose of the private life of each person under communism. The communist man will not only have a deep need for work, he will also need to work according to his full abilities.(21)

In different ways, therefore, all subjects in the Soviet school curriculum now play some part in vocational education. How is the role of the secondary school in labour training likely to develop in the eighties? There are not infrequent press reports of dissatisfaction with what is done at the moment. The odd paradox has been noted, for example, that children spend more time writing in labour lessons than in Russian language classes.(22) Fewer than a quarter of school-leavers and young workers in one survey said that a school teacher or even a parent had been the deciding factor in their choice of future job.(23) There is criticism that labour lessons are dull, irrelevant and waste useful resources.(24) That the socialisation work carried out by the school as a whole is not fully satisfactory is evident from the reiterated demands to improve in this area.

Already new syllabuses for labour training courses have been drawn up and have started being implemented in 1981/2. The overriding aim here seems to be to give pupils skills which will be directly useful to society. Some pupils in the fourth to sixth classes are now following courses dealing with service labour - they learn, among other things, how to prepare sandwiches and coffee, how to use and repair a sewing machine and how to do simple household electrical work.(25) There is a growing tendency to give schoolchildren labour tasks to perform which are in themselves beneficial to the economy. Some educationalists feel that children would be better encouraged to work as postmen or in the service sphere than to do unproductive exercises in school workshops.(26) An extremely effective agricultural brigade of schoolchildren in the Altai region is commended. This brigade has organised a highly mechanised plot of land whose revenue has risen from 16,000 rubles in 1970 to 52,000 in 1973.(27) Both the moral benefits for the schoolchildren involved and the economic benefits for society are to be admired. Greater creativity and independent thought are to be promoted. Praise is given to schools in Azerbaidzhan where pupils are involved in all sides of agricultural work on the schools´ plots of land - planning, book-keeping and evaluation of results as well as practical work on the land.(28) Attention is also drawn to the practice of schools in Buryatia where labour training frequently takes the form of problem-solving activities. Children are sent out to do research into the working habits and histories of people in their area.(29) Other groups of children in Dagestan are studying the effects of pests in forest areas and are trying to find ways of combating them.(30)

To sum up, vocational education in the secondary school in the eighties is likely to develop along the following lines suggested above:

1. The tendency to increase vocational guidance will continue and attempts will be made to improve as well as to increase provisions for fulfilling this aim.
2. There will also be an increase in both the quality and the quantity of inter-school production combines.
3. There will be more emphasis in labour training syllabuses and classes on skills that are most urgently needed by contemporary society.
4. Schoolchildren will be increasingly used to carry out productive tasks useful to the economy.
5. Ways will be investigated of encouraging pupils to think in an independent and creative manner.
6. The struggle will continue to try to educate pupils with a communist attitude towards labour, with a strong sense of responsibility and cooperation and with a desire always to do their best at work. An interdisciplinary approach is likely to be at least as fully used as it is at present.

Out-of-school Education. What the child does out-of-school is also not neglected by Soviet educationalists nor is his spare time considered as purely recreational. It is thought of as being yet another opportunity for education, frequently in relation to work. Out-of-school activity is organised by a large number of institutions - the school, the youth movement, inter-school production combines and so on. The provision of facilities for children's out-of-school entertainment and instruction is already extensive, but is rapidly expanding.

In 1979 there were 4,785 Pioneer or Pupil Palaces or Houses in the USSR, an increase of just over 40 percent over the number existing in 1965.(31) These buildings are clubs organised either by local schools or, more often, the youth movement (the Pioneers). The largest are called Palaces and they are found in the capitals of all the republics and in other important regional towns. In appearance and content they are indeed palatial and the Leningrad Pioneer Palace is even housed in a former palace on the Nevsky Prospect. Their aim is to "develop the creative interests and individual abilities of children."(32) Each House or Palace contains a variety of special interest clubs catering for enthusiasts in, say, chess, physics, aeroplane modelling, drama or sport. The work of the clubs often has a vocational bias and their activity is guided by trained adults.

In addition, in 1979 there were 1,273 Young Technicians'

and 793 Young Naturalists´ Centres, an increase of 220.65 percent and 175.34 percent, respectively, over the 1965 figures. These, as their names suggest, are clubs for children with particular technical, botanical or zoological interests. Equipment and materials are supplied for the technicians to develop their creative skills and the young naturalists are encouraged to study their local flora and fauna. They also help with conservation work in their area and look after and observe small animals and birds.

Another interesting facility available for children in some parts of the Soviet Union and with a clearly potential vocational significance is the Children´s Railway. There were 39 of these in 1979. In 1965 there were 33 showing that there has been a dramatic increase here. Children´s railways are staffed entirely by children who act as drivers, ticket sellers and collectors, planners and maintenance workers and so on.

Summer Pioneer Camps are the most numerous facility provided by the Soviet state for its children. In 1979 there were 57,763 of these, an increase of 138.6 percent over the provision for 1965. Large numbers of children spend at least part of their three-month summer vacation at a camp. The camps are often under the aegis of a particular factory or institution so that a parent will obtain a place for his child through his work-place. Usually, children spend one month there and the average size of a camp is 500 children at any one time. The routine of camp life is very strong and, like Scout and Guide camps, has a distinct military flavour. The very routine helps to train in the work-related virtue of discipline. A variety of clubs operate in the camp, modelling, musical, chess and so on and the children spend time in sporting, hiking and para-military activities. These are often competitive, so that the Pioneer camp in its organisation backs up the work of the school in preparing young people for the kind of social organisation they will later meet in factory or on collective farm.

Music, Art and Dance Schools are another facet of the extracurricular opportunities available to Soviet youngsters. There were 7,364 of these in 1979, an increase of 160.3 percent over 1965. Similarly, there were 6,196 Sports Schools, an increase of 144.41 percent. These figures do not refer to the special schools attended full-time by children with a particular artistic or sporting talent. They offer after-school facilities to those with perhaps less outstanding ability. Music schools, for example, take children from the age of seven. Parents have to pay for the instruction given and their children will be taken only if they pass a hearing and a musical aptitude test. Many of the young people who attend these schools two or three times a week, later enter musical vocational colleges and become professional musicians of some kind.(33) Similarly, children who have attended art, dance or sports schools not infrequently end up in professions using the skills that were developed there.

The overall number of facilities for children to use in their spare time rose by approximately 100 percent between 1965 and 1979. Other opportunities not mentioned above include children's libraries, theatres and clubs organised by the armed forces and by individual factories.

Out-of-school activity is important in two ways as far as vocational education is concerned. Firstly, it gives children an opportunity to develop in a more sophisticated way any particular talents or interests that they may have and which the school programme does not give full scope to. Secondly, it reinforces the work of the school in terms of work values and habits. At the Pioneer Club or the Young Technicians' Centre the child will be encouraged to respect work and to do it as diligently as he can in the same way that he is taught to do so at school. It is likely that the facilities will continue increasing and improving in an attempt to restrict young people's exposure to potentially different, even hostile, attitudes towards work which they might come across at home or on the street.

Technical-trade Schools. This section of Soviet education and that which follows are those which are concerned most exclusively with vocational training. The intention here is to give a brief outline of the structure of these two fields of education and then to return to specific problems and trends in their development after a consideration of the role of higher education in vocational training.

Technical-trade schools(34) cover the lower levels of institutionalised vocational training. The current Soviet trend is to give work training even for an elementary type of job at an institution rather than on-the-job. The institutions at which the first levels of professional training are given are:

1. Technical-trade Schools (PTUs)
2. Secondary Technical-trade Schools (SPTUs)
3. Technical Schools (TUs).

For all such schools there is rarely an entry examination. Pupils are selected on the basis of their general school marks and a test is given only when the specific job to be taught requires it. Thus, for example, a drawing test may be given to those wishing to enter the Leningrad school for china-painters and a language examination to aspiring type-setters. Certain applicants are given preference: orphans, children from children's homes, children of invalids, young people recommended to the school by the enterprise or the collective farm where they are already working, children of workers at the factory or farm to which the school is affiliated and young men just demobbed after their National Service.

Pupils are given some material incentives to attend such schools. Time spent studying there is counted as work experience in future salary calculations. Payment is given for work done in the base enterprise while training. Hostels are provided when the school accepts pupils from other towns and pupils are given free food and work clothing. In agricultural technical-trade schools pupils also receive a grant.

On graduation, all pupils are given work in their specialism and are expected to stay in that job for three years or at least until, if boys, they are called up. Graduates may be exempt from immediate work on production if they gain particularly high marks and would like to continue studying. They may, for example, enter a secondary specialised institution without taking an entrance examination or they can apply for a place on a daytime higher education course. If their aim is to be an "engineer-pedagogue," the lofty name given to teachers of practical subjects in a technical school, then they are allowed precedence in entry to an appropriate higher educational institution.

The above conditions apply to all three types of technical-trade schools but there are also some differences between the training offered by these different institutions.

Technical-trade Schools (PTUs). These schools provide pupils with a basic work training but not with any general education. Often their main role is now not so much to run daytime classes but to give evening and shift courses so that workers can study at times compatible with their work shifts. In this way workers gain a qualification without leaving their jobs. Work-places cooperate in this by permitting study leave. To prepare for and sit for examinations, workers are allowed 30 days off per year during which time they are paid 50 percent of their average salary.

The length and level of courses offered by PTUs vary. PTU no. 19 in Leningrad offers evening courses for technical draughtsmen lasting 20 months and open only to those who have completed a full ten-year general education. PTU no. 71 in Leningrad, on the other hand, provides evening and shift courses of 7 months for railway attendants and these are open to applicants with a minimum of eight years schooling. Some

PTUs, moreover, do not only give initial job training but also run courses enabling experienced workers to raise their qualifications.

Secondary Technical-trade Schools (SPTUs). These are schools which take pupils who have completed eight years at secondary school and provide them not only with work training but also with the final two years of compulsory general education. If he passes his final examination after three years of study and practical work, the pupil receives both a general education certificate and a diploma in, say, lathe-turning, tractor-driving or watch-repairing.

The network of secondary technical-trade schools has grown very rapidly in recent years and the authorities are anxious to persuade eighth class school pupils that SPTUs form a worthy alternative to the final two years at a general secondary school. As has been seen, attending a vocational school offers slight material advantages and pupils are encouraged to feel that they are not abandoning their chances of higher education if they leave the general secondary school after the eighth class. It will be seen later how far the incentives are successful and the encouragements justified.

Technical Schools (TUs). These schools offer full-time courses and are open only to pupils who have completed ten years of secondary schooling.They do not give general education classes. Like pupils at agricultural PTUs and SPTUs, pupils at all technical schools are paid a basic grant. This is usually 30-37 rubles but increases by 15 to 20 percent if excellent marks are achieved in all subjects. Technical schools provide courses preparing pupils to be, for example, house-painters, photographers or waiters with knowledge of a foreign language for Intourist hotels. Particularly successful graduates of these schools are given preferential treatment if they decide to apply for an evening or correspondence course at a higher educational institution. Courses in TUs usually last from a year to eighteen months.

Secondary Specialised Colleges. The technical-trade schools described above are administered by the State Committee on Vocational and Technical Education which is responsible for all aspects of their courses and planning. Secondary specialised colleges,(35) on the other hand, come under the auspices of the Ministry of Higher and Secondary Education. They provide vocational training in the Soviet literature into technicums and colleges but the different name signifies only the type of specialism offered by the institution. Technicums train personnel for industry, agriculture, construction and transport whereas colleges (uchilishcha) mainly train specialists in

397

health, education and culture. Thus, Leningrad has 57
technicums training, for example, ship-builders, veterinary
assistants and computer technicians and 36 colleges preparing
nurses, upbringers for pre-school institutions and cultural
club organisers.

Some of the courses offered at these colleges accept
students who have completed only eight years of school, whereas
others stipulate a full secondary education. Students enrolled
after only eight years' schooling are expected to complete
their secondary education at the college itself or in an
evening school. The length of courses varies with both the
type of specialism and with the educational level of the
student intake. Leningrad's regional medical college trains
nurses and midwives in two years ten months if they have eight
years of schooling and in one year ten months if they have
already completed their secondary education.
Radio-constructors are similarly trained in either three years
ten months or in two years eight months. Some specialisms can
be studied on evening or correspondence courses run by these
colleges. Through evening classes, one can, for example,
become a rubber technologist, a choir leader or a nurse.
Nursing is not available as a correspondence subject but many
technological and cultural professions are.

As well as in the level of their courses, these colleges
differ also from the technical-trade schools in that applicants
are selected on the basis of special entry exams. Those who
have eight years of secondary education and wish to enter a
college to study one of most of the available specialisms must
take a dictation test in Russian and an oral mathemaics exam.
Eighth class school-leavers who apply for a music, art, theatre
or other cultural college, replace the mathematics test with an
oral examination in Russian language and literature. There are
three different sets of examinations for applicants who already
have a full secondary education. Candidates for all types of
college must do a written examination in Russian language and
literature but they also have an oral test in either
mathematics, chemistry or the history of the USSR, depending on
what type of course they wish to follow.

Anyone who has at least eight years of secondary schooling
may apply to do an evening or correspondence course at a
college but there is an age limit of 30 years on applicants to
full-time courses. Certain applicants are given precedence:
those who got excellent marks on leaving secondary or
technical-trade school; those who have at least two years of
work experience in an area related to the specialism applied
for; men who have just been demobbed; people directed to the
college by the factory or farm where they are already working
and orphans.

Many of the students at these colleges receive grants,
particularly if they are doing courses related to agriculture
where there is felt to be an especial need for specialists. In
less urgent fields, they may receive a grant only if they have
already two years of practical experience. All students are
paid for any productive work they may do as part of their
working practice and are given free working clothes.

On graduation, all students are found work in their
specialism and are expected to stay in that job for three
years. Exceptions to this are those students who obtain
excellent marks in all subjects and ten percent of those who
have a combination of excellent and good marks. These top
graduates have the right immediately to enter the day
department of a higher educational institution. Other
graduates have the right to enter directly only the evening or
correspondence departments of higher educational institutions.

More attention will be paid to the nature of the
programmes at technical-trade schools and secondary specialised
colleges and to particular problems of their organisation and
place in modern Soviet society after a brief discussion below
of higher education.

Higher Education. Like other areas of education in the USSR,
Soviet higher education has a strongly vocational flavour.
Courses not only give students theoretical information but also
train them to do specific jobs. Students of English at the
Maurice Thorez Institute of Languages in Moscow, for example,
do not merely study the language in depth, they also choose to
train as either a translator or a teacher. Practical work
forms a major part of the programme on any course.

Entry into higher educational institutes (whose courses
usually last five years) is selective through an entrance
examination. Attempting to be helpful to those who have left
school some time previously, many institutes have now opened
preparatory departments.(36) These were first set up at some
institutes in 1969 to try to iron out social differences in
opportunities and to give those who are already working the
chance to raise their level of qualification to that of higher
education. About one-fifth of all students in their first year
of study at many institutions now come from preparatory
departments.(37) These have not proved quite so satisfactory
as was hoped. Students who have come from preparatory
departments tend to have a lower success rate throughout their
courses than do students who have come straight from
school.(38) Moreover, the departments tend to be exploited by
students who failed to get a place in higher education on first
leaving school and who have worked the statutory two years

before joining a preparatory department.(39)   In other words, these departments are seen as an easy route to higher education rather than being used by workers who after some years of experience on the job wish to give their practical knowledge a stronger educational basis.

There is a lower level of competition for entry to evening or correspondence departments of higher educational institutions than to day departments. Many Soviet students take advantage of these opportunities for part-time study, combining work on production with studying for a degree. In the academic year 1979/80 there were 5,186,000 students in Soviet higher education of whom 653,000 (13 percent) were in evening departments and 1,601,000 (31 percent) were in correspondence departments.(40) It is accepted that the difficulties of combining work and study make a slightly lower standard of degree inevitable for those who are not studying full-time but, nevertheless, such students are felt to be more valuable to the economy in that they give a more rational use of labour resources and also help to spread the skills provided by higher education throughout production.

An interesting type of higher educational institution found in the Soviet Union is a technical institute attached to a large industrial enterprise. These institutes are referred to as zavody-vtuzy.(41) The aim of these is to prepare engineers from among the workers already attached to the patron enterprise. The average period of study is five and a half to six years. Students also tend to receive a grant that is 15 percent higher than that received by other students. The extra material incentive thus given to students at zavody-vtuzy is doubtless due to the important practical role they are felt to play in the economy through attracting those who already have strong practical knowledge of an enterprise into a scheme which will prepare them to be engineers of exactly the profile required by the enterprise in question.

Over the seventies there has been an increasing tendency in higher education, as at lower levels, to try to encourage more independence and creativity on behalf of the taught. This has made itself felt at institutes through students - even at undergraduate level - being encouraged to devise and carry out their own small research projects.(42) This is likely to be a continuing trend as the authorities try to produce a generation of more inventive and innovative engineers and other specialists.

In one area in particular the higher educational institution is blamed for not carrying out its development of students´ work values adequately. This is in fostering any desire of the students to put what they have learnt into

practice on production after graduation. Far more students
aspire to do research or design work than are needed by society
and there is a reluctance to go into work in industry.(43)
Those who are compulsorily sent to work on production after
graduation do so often with a bad grace and change positions at
the earliest opportunity. Such attitudes clearly are not
likely to create a lively productive atmosphere among those
doing engineering level jobs at the factory.

As a result, the once high prestige of engineering as a
profession is declining. Komsomol´skaya Pravda recently wrote
with concern that there is now much less competition for places
at engineering institutes and students of only poor quality are
enrolled. The newspaper points out that this is certainly not
advantageous for society as a whole but it is advantageous to
certain groups. Parents are glad to see their offspring obtain
an education. The young people concerned are only too happy to
get a diploma. The institute staff find life easier if they do
not fail their students - how then can they complain? The
factory director then gets skilled manpower "cost-free" and so
why should he not use it cheaply in place of technicians,
foremen and sometimes even workers while sending the hourly
wage earners off to help at vegetable depots, Pioneer camps or
with the mowing.(44) Reports are also frequently heard of
engineers being sent off to bring in the harvest. It would,
thus, seem that it is not only the higher educational
institution which is to be blamed for not instilling their
students with an enthusiasm for work on production but also the
system is to be blamed for not always using its engineers and
their professional training to the best possible advantage. It
is probable that educational theorists will continue to tell
the institutes to improve their character education work but
the attitudes which are causing concern are unlikely to alter
unless there is a more fundamental change in the organisation
of labour at the factory.

Higher education in the USSR is systematically and
emphatically vocational, building as much practical work into
the courses as is possible and finding different ways of
encouraging those who already have work experience to study for
a degree. Such students bring valued practical knowledge to
their studies and they are also socially useful in that they
demonstrate clearly that social mobility is possbile through
the Soviet system of education. Innovation is possibly easier
to implement at the higher levels of education and certainly
the current stress on more independent, creative work has been
put into practice most quickly here. Work values are, however,
probably harder to influence at this stage of development,
although this is an area that is still causing some concern.
Having outlined some of the main aspects of vocational training
in relation to Soviet higher education let us now turn to

consider some of the main preoccupations in connection with the
vocational schools and colleges.

Problems and Trends in the Vocational Schools and Colleges

There are a number of problems and trends which relate to
the process of labour training as a whole, or to the vocational
schools and colleges in particular, which need further
attention. These can be considered under the following broad
headings:

1. Contingents of students doing different types of
vocational training;
2. The prestige of vocational courses;
3. Teaching and content of vocational courses;
4. Vocational schools´ relationship with other
organisations;
5. Success of labour training process.

Contingents of Students Doing Different Types of Vocational Training.

At the age of fifteen, the Soviet child either stays
at the general school or else leaves to attend a secondary
technical-trade school. Which path do most youngsters choose
to follow?(45) In the 1979/80 academic year there were
approximately 5,500,000 children in the ninth, tenth and
eleventh forms of the general school (the eleventh form exists
in certain republics where the local language poses particular
problems). In comparison there were 3,935,000 students in
PTUs, of whom 2,069,000 were in schools giving a secondary
course as well as trade training. As has already been seen,
some eighth-form leavers go straight to a secondary specialised
college although many of the student body there have a full
secondary education. In the same academic year there were
approximately 4,646,000 students in such colleges of whom 62.6
percent were on daytime courses, 11.2 percent were in evening
departments and 26.2 percent were in correspondence
departments.

If we compare these figures with those of only nine years
previously, the most dramatic change is seen in the area of
secondary technical-trade education. In 1970/1 there were only
approximately 180,000 pupils in the day departments of
secondary PTUs. Over the decade there has thus been an
increase of 1049 percent. The number of such schools has risen
over the same period from 615 to 4026, an increase of 555
percent. These striking changes are simply due to the central
decision to develop this type of education in the early
seventies in order to create a generation of young people more
thoroughly trained for work than those who had started work
imediately after leaving school.

A comparison of the numbers of students in secondary

402

specialised colleges over the same period shows that numbers
here have also risen, though less sharply. The total number of
students in this branch of education has increased by 5.9
percent. There has been a slight decline in the number of
evening students with only a very slight increase in those
doing correspondence courses. The proportion of those doing
daytime courses has risen from 58 to 62 percent. The
sociologist, Filippov, approves this tendency in that the
standard reached by day students is inevitably higher.
Moreover, after graduation it is easier to distribute day
students into those jobs for which there is the greatest need
for them.(46)

The increases noted above in the members of those doing
institutionalised vocational training become even more striking
when it is remembered that the size of the school-leaving
age-group which forms the bulk of the student population has
fallen throughout the seventies. Nevertheless it must not be
felt that there are hardly any young people left going straight
into work after leaving the general school. It has been
estimated that approximately two million school-leavers,
one-third of the total age-group, go straight to a job
receiving there their basic training.(47) This is felt by many
planners to be a problem both for the factories which have to
provide on-the-job training and for the young workers who are
less likely to experience job satisfaction or to get a training
which will stand them in good stead in their future career.(48)
There is still scope, therefore, for the expansion of the
institutionalised vocational training programme and it is
certain that this will continue to develop in the eighties.

Are young people who attend vocational schools or
colleges, as opposed to going either straight to work or to a
higher educational institution, typical of the population as a
whole in terms of sex and social background and are there
republican or urban/rural differences in the patterns of labour
education?

As far as sex is concerned, there are differences in the
vocational education patterns of boys and girls. Women have an
appropriate share of the places in higher education (52
percent) and a rather favourable proportion of those in
secondary specialised colleges (56 percent).(49) They are a
small proportion of the pupils PTUs, however; they do not
provide more than 30 percent of the intake there and in some
republics their share is substantially less. It is not more
than 1 to 3 percent in such schools in rural areas of
Lithuania, Estonia and Tadzhikistan.(50) For those girls who
leave school and go straight to work without any formal
training the standard of on-the-job preparation is felt to be

particularly low. In a study of some machine-tools
enterprises, it was found that despite the fact that the
average level of schooling was slightly higher for girls than
boys; boys made much more rapid progress through the low job
grades, staying only 1.5 years in the first grade, whereas
girls stayed 4.6 years.(51) The Soviet writers commenting on
these figures blamed the factory authorities for undertraining
the female members of the work force and for neglecting the
fact that women are on average more disciplined and responsible
than men. The not untypical pattern emerges that women fare
well in the educational process, particularly at its higher
levels, but when it comes to their job experience they are less
likely to succeed than men are.

A school-leaver´s social background affects the
educational path he is likely to follow also. The higher the
level of the educational institution and the higher its status,
the greater the proportion of the children of the
intelligentsia to be found there.(52) This does not, of
course, mean that there are no children of working or peasant
origins at Moscow University but their share of the student
population does not correspond to their share of the total
Soviet population of the appropriate age. At the lower levels
of vocational education, workers´ children participate fully.
A study of students at secondary specialised institutions in
Nizhni Tagil found that their social background was more or
less equivalent to the distribtion of social classes in the
town as a whole.(53) The vocational school with the lowest
status in the USSR is the agricultural PTU and it is there that
the social group with the lowest prestige, the collective farm
peasantry, is much more extensively represented than
elsewhere.(54)

Geographical factors, as well as those of gender and
social background, help to determine likely educational
patterns. The development of PTUs has taken place in all the
republics where there is an especial demand for qualified
labour. The increase in numbers of PTU graduates over the last
few years has been most marked in Uzbekistan, Georgia,
Azerbaidzhan, Kirgizia, Tadzhikstan, Armenia and Turkmenistan.
The average increase in output in the USSR between 1975 and
1978 was 8.4 percent. The percentages for the above seven
republics were 36, 20, 23, 17, 15, 38 and 50 percent,
respectively.(55) The growth has been slowest in the Baltic
republics where the system was more fully developed prior to
1975, and industry was already better supplied with qualified
workers. Despite the increase noted above, the proportion of
students in PTUs in Central Asia still falls below that of the
Slav republics; in Central Asia only seven to eight percent of
the 16 to 18 age-group were in PTUs in 1978, when it was twice
that proportion in Russia, the Ukraine, Belorussia or

Kazakhstan.(56)

The urban rural distinction is an extremely important one in the Soviet Union. There is a tendency for young people to want to move to the towns, causing a shortage of young labour in rural areas. Specialists are reluctant to return to work in country areas so that skilled workers (including teachers, doctors and so on) are also in regrettably short supply. Vocational schools are being built to train specialists in agriculture both to improve the efficiency of work done on the farms and also to raise the status of those working in agriculture. Building agricultural PTUs has not always reached its planned levels; in 1979, the chairman of the State Committee on Vocational and Technical Education, Bulgakov, insisted that each region must have its own PTU preparing workers for collective and state farms, adding that this aim had been achieved in the Leningrad region and in the Mari ASSR but that many areas were still deficient.(57)

In conclusion, the contingents of students at Soviet vocational schools and colleges are not representative of the population as a whole in terms of gender and social and geographical background. This is causing concern for economic planners mainly with regard to the urban/rural dimension but attempts are also being made to create a more balanced system within the union republics and to provide greater opportunities for people of working origins in the higher levels of the educational process (through the establishment of preparatory departments, for example).

The Prestige of Vocational Education. Many of the points made above relate very closely to the question of the prestige of different types of educational paths. Generally speaking, the type of education which enjoys the highest prestige is that where the student body is primarily urban, from the intelligentsia and in an industrially advanced republic.

The situation has changed in recent years, however, in that the disproportionately high status of the higher educational institution has diminished.(58) In the sixties and early seventies, 80 to 90 percent of school-leavers aspired to higher education and many of these were inevitably destined to disappointment. Through the seventies the prestige of other forms of institutionalised vocational training has risen. In a survey carried out in 1979, among older schoolchildren it was found that 33.5 percent wanted to go straight into higher education whereas 14.9 percent wanted to study in a technicum and 12.9 percent wanted to go to a technical-trade school.(59) There are thus going to be fewer disappointed school-leavers in the next year or two. This does not mean that the aspirations of young people now fully correspond with the plans of the

405

state. Filippov reports that there is a serious lack of
applicants for certain types of technical-trade schools, for
some technical higher institutes and for certain departments of
teacher training colleges.(60) The technical-trade schools
where there is a shortfall of applicants are in particular
those with an agricultural profile, but the attempts to raise
the status of agricultural work have not so far been
successful.

The other professional area with particularly low prestige
in the sixties and early seventies was the service sphere.(61)
Here the position has changed, if not for the reasons sought by
the state. Work in a shop has now become an attractive job and
pupils are happy to attend schools training for such work.(62)
The shortage of certain products in Soviet shops gives those
who work in them a strong bartering position as their access to
scarce goods is so much easier than that of the majority.

To sum up, the higher educational institution is still the
most prestigious form of education in the USSR but many
school-leavers have now become more realistic in their
aspirations. The establishment of a fuller system of
institutionalised vocational training has doubtless facilitated
this in that there are still very few school-leavers who would
like to go straight to work on production.(63) Those who would
once have opted for a university are now content with a
specialised college or even a technical-trade school.

Teaching and Content of Courses. There are a number of
problems concerned with the teaching and content of courses at
vocational schools and colleges. It is frequently pointed out
that, although the secondary PTUs are intended to give a
general education that is as good as that of the ordinary
secondary school, the standard of general education there is
not so high as in the ordinary school.(64) This is partly
because the best pupils stay at school so that they can try the
easiest route to higher education and partly because the better
teachers of academic subjects prefer to stay in the schools
with the better children and the higher status.

What is the training for the teachers of practical
subjects in the technical-trade schools? Usually they are
people with a secondary specialised education, less commonly a
higher one, and who have spent some time working on production.
Training of teaching staff for vocational institutions takes
place mainly in industrial-pedagogical technicums and
occasionally in engineering-pedagogical departments attached to
a number of higher educational institutes. In 1978, the first
special institute devoted to training engineer-pedagogues was
opened. This is located in Sverdlovsk and it aims to give both
an initial training for teachers of practical subjects in

406

vocational schools and colleges and also to provide courses for raising the qualifications of those who are already working in the field. It is planned in the future to open other institutes of this profile.(65) In this way it is hoped to raise both the standard and the status of teaching vocational subjects. In comparison with teachers of other subjects, those involved in labour training have had a relatively low likelihood of having higher education and this has lowered the standing of the profession.

To turn to the content of courses at the vocational school, there is particular concern to give these a broad profile, so that students can transfer their skills to another related specialism without too many problems if changing industrial conditions necessitate this. In this way PTU pupils are taught not only the subjects narrowly related to their own future job, they also learn the fundamentals of mechanics, electronics, technology and the organisation and economics of production.(66) It has been stated by the last Party Congress that improved methods of training in vocational schools are necessary to create a work force that can cope with the demands of technical progress and that will be able to raise labour productivity,(67) two of the particular problems of the contemporary Soviet economic situation referred to at the beginning of this [article]. The programmes being developed to try to help overcome these difficulties include far more problem-solving and programmed learning. In the new courses, pupils at secondary PTUs spend about 60 percent of their 36-hour week on production training and subjects related to their profession.(68) Teachers are urged to link the information given in general education classes to the specific working qualifications aimed at. The priority is not, therefore, to make courses identical to those of the general secondary school.

Although it is protested that educational standards should not be reduced for those children who have left school after the eighth class, it is clearly felt that it is the vocational element that is of prime importance. It would seem unlikely that the academic standards of the secondary PTUs will ever equal those of most general schools. The basic aim of the SPTU is naturally more to train skilled workers than to ensure that its graduates are well-equipped to enter a higher educational institution. There are already more than enough aspirants for higher education leaving the secondary schools. While Soviet educationalists are proud that their system provides relatively easy access to all types of learning for all those who might at any time wish to take advantage of it, they are on the whole more anxious about the quality and efficiency of the future work force.

<u>Vocaticnal Schools´ Relationship with Other Organisations.</u>
Some problems are also arising from the relationships of the
vocational schools and colleges with other organisations.
Their relations with both local schools and factories are far
from simple. The general school, for instance, is often
reluctant to lose its pupils to the SPTU, just as the pupils
are frequently unwilling to go, and so the vocational schools
do not always find it easy to achieve their planned intake
figures.(69) In the Russian republic in 1973, there was a
shortfall of 18.5 percent between the planned intake figure of
715,500 and the realised one of 583,000. In the Ukraine the
shortfall was similar, at 18.6 percent.

   Links with local factories are also problematic. Some
factories have refused to take PTU graduates, saying that they
do not remain long enough in a job.(70) Training pupils so
that they have a flexibility to change jobs easily is perhaps
having some rather undesirable side-effects. It is also felt
by some factories that vocational schools concentrate too much
on theory to the detriment of practical training. Thus
graduates may know quite advanced mathematics but are scarcely
able to hold a hammer.(71) For many factory foremen such a
sense of priorities is faulty and they prefer to have workers
who have learnt their skills on-the-job, regardless of their
level of theoretical knowledge. It would also seem probable
that vocational college graduates are not always welcome on the
shopfloor in that they may arrive at work with feelings of
superiority over the other workers and may criticise the
established order of things.

<u>Success of Labour Training Programme.</u> Some final problems and
trends are highlighted if the question of the overall success
of the labour training programme is examined. It has been seen
how Soviet vocational education has three basic goals - moral
education, skill training and vocational guidance. To what
extent are these goals achieved?

   As far as moral education is concerned, there are clearly
problems. In this area, as in many other fields of life, the
Soviet system invites criticism by setting extremely high goals
for itself. Any failures to attain these goals are sometimes
used by hostile critics who jump at the opportunity to judge
the system on its own terms and denounce the entire system
regardless of any achievements it may have made.

   In the field of moral education the goals are particularly
high. It is impossible to estimate accurately overall levels
of success in inculcating the desired attitudes to work. It is
evident that there are many weak spots. One sociologist, for
example, reports too strong an element of what he terms

"thingism," meaning that young people are too concerned with possessions and not enough with labouring for the good of society or even with working for its own sake.(72) Similarly, an unsatisfactory level of discipline and responsibility towards one's work is regularly bemoaned and alcohol as a factor behind undisciplined, irresponsible behaviour at college or work is often mentioned. Deliquency seems to be disproportionately high among PTU pupils compared with their peers at school or at work.(73) For many of those "PTUshniki" who leave their country home at 16 to go to technical-trade school in the town, the temptations of alcohol and petty crime, offered by those of older pupils sharing their hostel accomodation, are too strong to resist.

One aspect of education in work values seems to have met with a great degree of success, namely that of creating a respect for learning. Although fewer now aspire to higher education, the majority of Soviet young people are eager to continue studying in some way or another. A survey of the value orientations of young people in the agricultural Kirov region, for example, showed that over 80 percent wished to go on studying.(74) For some, of course, the motivation to study is not so much to improve society as to advance their own career, but nevertheless it would seem that a respect for learning and a desire to study are values that have been genuinely assimilated by many young people.

As far as any teaching of practical skills is concerned, there are also successes and weaknesses. Young workers trained at SPTUs proceed through the working grades faster than those who were trained on-the-job.(75) It has also been noted how PTU graduates seem particularly inclined to change their jobs quickly. This shows a certain success in the aim of creating flexible workers but the consequences of this are double-edged for the economy. Movement between jobs is seen as positive only when necessitated by changing economic circumstances.

A major difficulty in the training of skills in a planned system lies in predicting accurately how many specialists of each variety are needed and then in producing the right numbers of each. There are inevitably failures both in prediction and in directing youngsters into the required professions. There have been complaints of too few masons and not enough house painters, for instance. Agriculture has particularly suffered. Between 1965 and 1975 the output of industrial specialists from PTUs trebled, whereas the number of agricultural specialists rose only 1.8 times. There are too few tractor-drivers, for example, and there is an urgent need for skilled farm workers of many other profiles.(76)

Despite the recent expansion of the structure of

vocational guidance work, there are regular calls for improvement here. Indeed, poor work in this area is often blamed for the shortages of workers of certain types noted above. It is deplored that children frequently have a weak understanding of the nature of particular jobs even of those common in their own town.(77) The relatively insignificant role of the school reported by youngsters in influencing them in their choice of job is felt to be unsatisfactory. The systematisation of vocational guidance work through a variety of agencies is called for, but it is admitted that this is a complex problem and no quick answer is likely to be found.(78)

The vociferous concern noted throughout to improve all three aspects of Soviet vocational education shows a lack of official satisfaction with the current state of affairs. Schools and colleges are constantly urged to better their work here. The Utopian heights of the goals presented make success on all fronts improbable. Indeed, the goals aspired to contain contradictions that make success in achieving all the desired aims impossible. An expected norm of respect for institutionalised education is hardly compatible with an equal feeling of respect for unskilled work. Investigations of later job satisfaction have shown that those who failed to enter a higher educational institution were more content with their work than those who obtained a degree.(79) It would seem that the higher one's education the less likely one is to be satisfied with a menial job. One Soviet sociologist has pointed out that it is ridiculous to expect today's educated school-leaver to find his job as a loader noble and has suggested that the solution lies in automating industry as much as possible, ridding it of its tedious jobs and leaving only the more interesting work for people to perform.(80) It would certainly seem that attitudes towards labour are conditioned at least as much by the actual working situation in society as by education. Large numbers of young people are unlikely, for example, to go into agricultural work while the conditions of rural life contrast unfavourably with those in towns, despite attempts at persuasion by their teachers. Consequently, improvements in work orientations will need to stem not merely from school textbooks, teachers' homilies and the other provisions outlined in this paper but also from changes in the organisation and content of work in the factory or on the farm.

Notes

1. L.G. Grinberg et al., Osnovy kommunisticheskoi morali (Moscow, 1980), p. 98.
2. H. Marcuse, Soviet Marxism (Penguin, Harmondsworth, 1971), p. 19.
3. F.A. O'Dell, Socialisation through Children's Literature:

The Soviet Example (Cambridge University Press, 1978), pp. 36-39.
4. S.P. Aksenov et al., (Eds.), Rabochemu klassu - dostoinoe popolnenie (Moscow, 1981), pp. 22-23.
5. Ministerstvo prosveshcheniya SSSR, Rekomendatsii vsesoyuznoi nauchnoprakticheskoi konferentsii 'Aktual'nye sotsial'nye ekonomisticheskie problemy razvitiya narodnogo obrazovaniya' (Moscow, 1979), p. 7,
6. V.P. Tomin, Uroven' obrazovaniya naseleniya SSSR (Moscow, 1981), p. 117.
7. D.S. Lane and F.A. O'Dell, The Soviet Industrial Worker: Social Class, Education and Control (Martin Robertson, London, 1978), pp. 56-64.
8. F.R. Filippov, Sotsiologiya obrazovaniya (Moscow, 1980), p. 111.
9. L.I. Muzhelevskaya and L.V. Russkova (Eds.), Spravochnik po doshkol'nomu vospitaniyu (Moscow, 1980), pp. 377-380.
10. Ibid., pp. 263-265.
11. F.A. O'Dell, Socialisation, pp. 94-95.
12. I.T. Ogorodnikova, Pedagogika shkoly (Moscow, 1978), p. 190.
13. Ibid., 194.
14. Deti v SSSR (Moscow, 1979), p. 29
15. V.A. Zhamin, Sotsial'no-ekonomicheskie problemy obrazovaniya i nauki v razvitom sotsialisticheskom obshchestve (Moscow, 1979), p. 41.
16. A.I. Novikov, 'O proizvoditel'nom trude podrostkov', Sotsiologicheskie issledovaniya, no. 3 (1981), p. 94.
17. Rodnaya rech' (Moscow, 1981) p. 3.
18. Programma vos'miletnei i srednei shkoly: geografiya (Moscow, 1980).
19. Programma vos'miletnei i srednei shkoly: istoriya (Moscow, 1980).
20. L.N. Tokareva et al., (Eds.), Materialy k leninskim urokam na inostrannykh yazykakh (Tashkent, 1977), p. 25.
21. G.Kh. Shakhnazarov et al., Obshchestvovedenie (Moscow, 1980), pp. 310-312.
22. I. Markus', "Teoriya bez praktiki," Uchitel'skaya gazeta, 21 Oct. 1976.
23. V.F. Odintsov, "Nekotorye rezul'taty izucheniya professional'nykh orientatsii molodezhi kirovskoi oblasti," Sotsiologicheskie isseldovaniya, no. 2 (1981), p. 113.
24. G. Bol'shakov, "KPD shkol'nykh masterskikh," Uchitel'skaya gazeta, 26 Mar. 1977.
25. N.K. Fomina, "Primernoe tematicheskoe planirovanie zanyatii po obsluzhivayushchemu trudu v IV-VI klassakh," Shkola i proizvodstvo, no. 8, 1981.
26. Novikov, "O trude," p. 93.
27. Ibid., p. 96.
28. I. Belonin et al.,"Iz opyta trudovoi podgotovki shkol'nikov," Sovetskaya pedagogika, no. 6 (1981), p. 67.

29. Ibid., p. 70.
30. Ibid., p. 74.
31. The figures throughout this section all came from Narodnoe khozyaistvo v 1979 godu (Moscow, 1980), p. 492.
32. M.A. Denisova, Lingvostranovedcheskii slovar´ (Moscow, 1978), p. 105.
33. Ibid., p. 145.
34. The factual information in this section comes from Professional´no-teknicheskie uchebnye zavedeniya Leningrada: spravochnik dlya postupayushchikh (Leningrad, 1980).
35. The factual information in this section comes from Tekhnikumy i uchilishcha Leningradskoi oblasti: spravochnik dlya postypayushchikh (Leningrad, 1980).
36. F.R. Filippov, Sotsial´nye peremeshcheniya v razvitom sotsialisticheskom obshchestve (Moscow, 1979), p. 11.
37. Idem.
38. F.R. Fillippov, Yu. N. Kozyrev and D.I. Zyuzin (Eds.), Obrazovanie i sotsial´naya struktura (Moscow, 1976), p. 65.
39. M.N. Rutevich and F.R. Filippov (Eds.), Vysshaya shkola kak faktor izmeneniya sotsial´noi struktury razvitogo, sotsialisticheskogo obshchestva (Moscow, 1978), p. 20.
40. Narodnoe khozyaist´vo v 1979 godu (Moscow, 1980), p. 492.
41. Denisova, Lingvostraovedcheskii, pp. 108-109.
42. V.T. Lisovskii and V.A. Sukhin, Kompleksnoe isseldovanie problem obucheniya i kommunisticheskogo vospitaniya spetsialistov s vysshim obrazovaniem (Leningrad, 1980), p. 74.
43. Filippov, Sotsiologiya, pp. 126-127.
44. Komsomol´skaya pravda, 3 June 1981, p. 2.
45. Narodnoe khozyaistvo v 1979 godu (Moscow, 1980), pp. 486, 489, 492 for the statistical data in this section.
46. Filippov, Sotsiologiya, p. 120.
47. Tomin, Urovin´, p. 111.
48. Idem.
49. Narodnoe khozyaistvo v 1979 godu (Moscow, 1980), p. 502.
50. Zhamin, Sotsial´no-ekonomicheskie problemy, p. 57.
51. D.N. Karpukhin and A.B. Shteiner ´Zhenskii trud i trud zhenshchin´ EKO, no. 3 (1978), p. 43.
52. Lane and O´Dell, pp. 108-116 discusses this point more fully.
53. Filippov, Sotsiologiya, p. 121.
54. Sbornik prikazov i instruktsii Ministerstva prosveshcheniya RSFSR, no. 2 (Moscow, 1980), p. 3.
55. Tomin, Uroven´, p. 113.
56. Zhamin, Sotsial´no-ekonomicheskie problemy, p. 57.
57. Tomin, Uroven´, p. 114.
58. Filippov, Sotsiologiya, p. 110.
59. E.V. Belkin, "Professional´no-teknicheskoe obrazovanie v zhiznennykh planakh molodezhi, Sotsiologicheskie issledovaniya, no. 2 (1981), p. 107.
60. Filippov, Sotsiologiya, p. 110.
61. V.V. Vodzinskaya, "Orientations to occupations," in M.

412

Yanowitch and W.A. Fisher, Social Stratification and Mobility
in the USSR (International Arts and Sciences Press, NY, 1973),
pp. 169-170.
62. Lisovskii and Sukhin, Kompleksnoe issledovanie, p. 16.
63. Filippov, Sotsiologiya, p. 109.
64. E.K. Vasil'eva et al. (Eds.), Naselenie Leningrada
(Moscow, 1981), pp. 59-60.
65. Filippov, Sotsiologiya, pp. 144-145.
66. Tomin, Uroven', p. 109.
67. Aksenov, Rabochemu klassu, p. 123.
68. Ibid., p. 124.
69. Tomin, Uroven', pp. 113-114.
70. Filippov, Sotsiologiya, p. 118.
71. Personal conversations.
72. V.T. Lisovskii et al., Zhit' dostoino (Moscow, 1979), p.
85 and elsewhere.
73. V.O. Rukavishnikov et al., "Podrostok v shkole i doma,"
Sotsiologicheskie isseldovaniya, no. 2 (1981), p. 122.
74. Odintsov, Nekotorye rezul'taty, p. 113.
75. Filippov, Sotsiologiya, pp. 114-115.
76. Ibid., pp. 116-117.
77. Odintsov, Nekotorye rezul'taty, p. 113.
78. Filippov, Sotsiologiya, pp. 111-112.
79. I.S. Kon, Psikhologiya yunosheskogo vozrasta (Moscow,
1979), p. 154.
80. M. Titma (Ed.), Sotsial'naya i professional'naya
orientatsiya molodezhi v usloviykh razvitogo
sotsialisticheskogo obshchestva v SSSR (Tallin, 1977), p. 75.

Bibliography

Aksenov, S.P. et al., (Eds.), Rabochemu klassu -
    dostoinoe popolnenie (Moscow, 1981)
Belkin, E.V. "Professional'no-teknicheskoe
    obrazovanie v zhizneniykh planakh molodezhi,"
    Sotsiologicheskie issledovaniya, no. 2 (1981)
Belonin, I. et al., "Iz opyta trudovoi podgotovki
    shkol'nikov," Sovetskaya pedagogika no. 6 (1981)
Bol'shakov, G. "KPD shkol'nykh masterskih,"
    Uchitel'skaya gazeta, 26 Mar. 1977.
Denisova, M.A. Lingvostranovedcheskii slovar'
    (Moscow, 1978)
Deti v SSSR (Moscow, 1979)
Filippov, F.R. et al., (Eds.), Obrazovanie i
    sotsial'naya struktura (Moscow, 1976)
_____ Sotsial'naya peremeshcheniya v razvitom
    sotsialisticheskom obshchestve (Moscow, 1979)
_____ Sotsiologiya obrazovaniya (Moscow, 1980)
Fomina, N.K. "Primernoe tematicheskoe planirovanie
    zanyatii po obsluzhivayushchemu trudu v IV-VI
    klassakh," Shkola i proizvdstvo, no. 8 (1981)

Grindberg, L.G. et al., Osnovy kommunistcheskoi morali (Moscow, 1980)

Karpukhin, D.N. and Shteiner, A.B. "Zhenskii trud i trud zhenshchin" (EKO, no. 3, 1978)

Komsomol´skaya pravda

Kon, I.S. Psikholgiya yunosheskogo vozrasta (Moscow, 1979)

Lane, D.S. and O´Dell, F.A. The Soviet Industrial Worker: Social Class, Education and Control (Martin Robertson, London, 1978)

Lisovskii, V.T. et al., Zhit´dosroino (Moscow, 1979) _____, and Sukhin, V.A. Kompleksnoe issledovanie problem obucheniya i kommunisticheskogo vospitaniya spetsialistov s vysshim obrazovaniem (Leningrad, 1980)

Marcuse, H. Soviet Marxism (Penguin, Harmondsworth, 1971)

Markus´, "Teoriya bez praktiki," Uchitel´skaya gazeta, 21 Oct. 1976.

Ministerstvo prosveshcheniya SSSR, Rekomendatsii vsesoyuznoi nauchnoprakticheskoi konferentsii ´Aktual´nye sotsial´nye ekonomisticheskie_ problemy razvitiya narodnogo obrazovaniya´ (Moscow, 1979)

Muzhelevskaya, L.I. and Russkova, L.V. (Eds.), Spravochnik po doshkol´nomu vospitaniyu (Moscow, 1980)

Narodnoe khozyaistvo SSSR v 1979 godu (Moscow, 1980)

Novikov, A.I. "O proizvoditel´nom trude podrosrkov," Sotsiologicheskie issledovaniya, no. 3 (1981)

O´Dell, F.A. Socialisation through Children´s Literature: The Soviet Example (Cambridge University Press, 1978)

Odintsov, V.F. "Nekotorye rezul´taty izucheniya professional´nykh orientatsii molodezhi Kirovskoi oblasti," Sotsiologicheskie issledovaniya, no. 2 (1981)

Ogorodnikova, I.T. Pedagogika shkoly (Moscow, 1978)

Professional´no-tekhnicheskoe obrazovanie

Profesional´no-teknicheskie uchebnye zavedeniya Leningrada: spravochnik dlya postupayushchikh (Leningrad, 1980)

Programma vos´miletnei i srednei shkoly: geografiya (Moscow, 1980)

Programma vos´miletnei i serdei shkoly: istoriya (Moscow, 1980)

Rodnaya rech´ (Moscow, 1981)

Rukavishnikov, V.O. et al., "Podrostok v shkole i doma," Sotsiologicheskie isseldovaniya, no. 2 (1981)

Rutkevich, M.N. and Filippov, F.R. Eds.), Vysshaya shkola kak faktor izmeneniya sotsial´noi struktury razvitogo sotsialisticheskogo

obshchestva (Moscow, 1978)
Sbornik prikazov i instruksii Ministerstva
prosveshvheniya RSFSR (no. 2, Moscow, 1980)
Shakhnazarov, G.K. et al., Obshchestvovedenie
(Moscow, 1980)
Shkola i proizvodstvo
Srednee spetsial´noe obrazovanie
Tekhnikumy i uchilishcha Leningrada i Leningradskoi
oblasti: spravochnik dlya postupayushchikh
(Leningrad, 1980)
Titma, M. (Ed.), Sotsial´naya i professional´naya
orientatsiya molodezhi v usloviyakh razvitogo
sotsialistcheskogo obshchestva v SSSR (Tallin,
1977)
Tokareva, L.N. et al., Materialy k Leninskim urokam
na inostrannykh yazykakh (Tashkent, 1977)
Tomin, V.P. Uroven´ obrazovaniya v SSSR (Moscow, 1981)
Uchitel´skaya gazeta
Vasil´eva, E.K. et al., (Eds.), Naselenie Leningrada
(Moscow, 1981)
Vodzinskaya, V.V. "Orientations to Occupations" in M. Yanowitch &
W.A. Fisher, Social Stratifi-
cation and Mobility in the USSR (NY, 1973)
Zhamin, V.A. Sotsial´no-ekonomicheskie problemy
obrazovanii i nauki v razvitom sotsialisticheskom
obshchestve (Moscow, 1979)

415

Biographical Sketches

Frank Michael Sorrentino

Frank Michael Sorrentino was born and raised in New York City. He received his doctorate from New York University where he specialized in American Political Institutions and Processes and Public Administration.

Dr. Sorrentino is the author of American Government: Power and Politics in America, 1983, and Ideological Warfare: The FBI's Path Toward Power, 1985. In addition he has written many articles for various newspapers and journals and is very active in delivering scholarly papers at various professional conferences in Political Science and Public Administration. He was the politics consultant and tour leader of a Soviet study-tour for teachers in 1985.

Dr. Sorrentino has taught at every level including graduate school, college, high school, and elementary schools. He has taught at many of the institutions of higher learning in the New York Metropolitan area including: St. Francis College, New York University, Long Island University and Kean College of New Jersey.

Frances Rena Curcio

Frances Rena Curcio is currently a member of the faculty at Queens College of the City University of New York, Flushing. She is the former chairman of the Department of Education at St. Francis College, Brooklyn and has been a consultant for the Office of Educational Evaluation for the Board of Education of the City of New York. She has also taught junior and senior high school mathematics in New York City prior to receiving her doctorate in Mathematics Education Supervision and Administration from New York University.

Dr. Curcio is the editor of the New York State Mathematics Teachers' Journal and has written many articles on mathematics and computer education. She is very active in local, state and national organizations of teachers of mathematics where she frequently presents workshops and worksessions for conferences.

During 1985 she conducted a teachers' study-tour of the Soviet Union and has written newspaper and journal articles on Soviet education.